READER'S DIGEST
CRIME CASEBOOK

READER'S DIGEST
CRIME CASEBOOK

PUBLISHED BY THE READER'S DIGEST ASSOCIATION LIMITED

LONDON • NEW YORK • SYDNEY • MONTREAL

READER'S DIGEST CRIME CASEBOOK

Designed and produced for The Reader's Digest Association Limited
by Pardoe Blacker Limited

Text edited by The Reader's Digest Association Limited, London

For Pardoe Blacker Limited:

Designers	Simon Blacker
	Matthew Wilson
Editorial Assistant	Clare Hollyman
Picture Research	Sarah Sole

For The Reader's Digest Association Limited:

Editor-in-Chief	Russell Twisk
Roving Editor	Tim Bouquet
Project Editor	Anne Jenkins
Art Director	Adam Craig

The stories in this volume have previously been published in the
Reader's Digest Magazine and the credits and acknowledgments that
appear on page 384 are hereby made a part of this copyright page.

© The Reader's Digest Association, Inc, 2000
© Reader's Digest (Australia) Pty Limited, 2000
© Reader's Digest (New Zealand) Limited, 2000
© The Reader's Digest Association (Canada) Limited, 2000
© The Reader's Digest Association South Africa (Pty) Ltd, 2000
© Reader's Digest Association Far East Limited, 2000
Philippines Copyright © Reader's Digest Far East Limited, 2000

First edition Copyright © 2000 The Reader's Digest Association Limited
11 Westferry Circus, Canary Wharf, London E14 4HE
www.readersdigest.co.uk

Reprinted 2001

Library of Congress Cataloging in Publication Data has been applied for.

ISBN 0-276-42495-6

Printed in Italy

POLICE DEPARTMENT • CITY OF NEW YOR

IDENTIFICATION
CARD

This is the ONLY type
identification card issued
members of the N. Y. C
Police Force.

It shall serve to ident
the bearer as an accredit
member of the force, wh
and only when present
with an official shield
this department.

Postmaster—Return to
POLICE HEADQUARTER
240 Centre St., N. Y. 1

SIGILLVM CIVITATIS NOVI EBORACI
·1664·

RANK

Ptl.

NAME

Frank P. McDonald

SHIELD NO.

26732

EXPIRES DECEMBER, 1968

TAX REGISTRY N

856984

CONTENTS

FOREWORD

Writing, filming and televising crime fiction has never been more popular than it is today. At Reader's Digest we love crime stories and our millions of readers around the world love them too. But we make one unique demand—we insist they have to be true. Every fact is double-checked, witnesses are interviewed and often reinterviewed, court records and police files examined and from this investigation our writers assemble a mountain of material. Only then does the storytelling begin.

Every writer knows the importance of telling a good story well and we like to think our writers possess all the narrative skills and imagination of the world's great mystery writers. But, unlike masters such as Dick Francis, Patricia Cornwell, Elmore Leonard and Ruth Rendell, our writers have to stick not only to a story line but also to the facts. This dogged pursuit of the truth enables them to capture those small but vital details that shine the spotlight clearly on the characters and bring them to life—real life. Where others settle for headlines we travel that extra mile to bring you the real story.

With over 50 international editions of the magazine, I'm very proud that my fellow Editors-in-Chief have allowed me to raid their files in pursuit of the best stories published during the decade or so that I've been the Editor of the British edition. In the 34 stories in this volume you'll find tales of guns, Mafia hitmen, jewel thieves, blackmailers, murderers, mobsters and drug smugglers. What an unsavoury bunch of villains—and they use our whole world as the canvas for their crimes. From Hong Kong's waterfront, to the Belanglo State Forest of New South Wales, and from Marengo County, Alabama, to a fishing boat in Devon, where the catch included a dead body.

It is impossible to pick my favourite from this rich mix, but one that stays in my mind is the thriller I commissioned from our Roving Editor, Tim Bouquet. He certainly lived up to his title as he roved the world in pursuit of the story, chasing the details across four continents, through the maze of drugs, corruption and international money-laundering. The villain in Tim's *Tracking the Fox* is a big-time drug smuggler who believed he was too smart to be caught by any police force anywhere. Not the first or last criminal to be brought down by overweening arrogance.

The styles of our writers are enormously varied. British writer David Moller creates immediate suspense with the opening lines of *Fear on the Highway*. "Concern pricked at Gill Walters's mind. It was now some weeks since she and her husband Ray had heard from their daughter Joanne." There follows a chilling tale of multiple murders of hitchhikers in Australia. In *Holly's Fight for Justice* Canadian Rick Mofina cuts straight to the action: "Holly Jill Desimone will never silence the sound of the rapist's zipper opening behind her." In *Free to Kill* American Henry Hurt fashions horror out of innocence, contrasting the converging lives of an 11-year-old girl enjoying an idyllic country summer and an itinerant farm hand who had spent much of his life defying the law. "The day-old black and white calf nuzzled its wet nose into Amy Jackson's hands as she reached over the wooden railing to rub its head."

Reading these stories again I was struck not just by the storytelling skills of these writers, but by the qualities of the everyday innocent men and women that they write about. Ordinary people caught up in extraordinary, violent events that changed their lives for ever. This collection is a testament to their courage and to the skill of the police who relentlessly seek out the perpetrators of crime. These stories of their lives serve to reinforce the belief that good will always triumph over evil. Eventually.

Russell Twisk
Editor-in-Chief
British Reader's Digest

THE CASE OF THE

ROLEX
MURDER

BY BILL SCHILLER

THE BODY OF A DECOMPOSED MAN IS FISHED

FROM THE DEEP. HE HAS A LARGE GASH ON

HIS HEAD AND NO ID. THE ONLY CLUES ARE

HIS WRISTWATCH AND A TATTOO ON ONE HAND.

At 5am on Sunday, July 28, 1996, fisherman John Copik and his son Craig set out from their home in Brixham, near Torquay in Devon, on board the trawler *Malkerry*. As they reached a rock behind a point called Hope's Nose, they shot a long trawling net out behind them.

After two and a half hours, the two men hauled up the cod end to check the catch. They found very few fish, so they released the gear again.

A few hours later things hadn't improved. Growing impatient, father and son shot the net a third time and turned for home.

It was almost 3pm and they were less than six miles from shore.

"Let's haul 'em in, mate!" John Copik called to his son.

When the cod end emerged from the water, he could see that their luck had changed. The net was loaded with fish, and there seemed to be an especially large one trapped inside. Probably a porpoise, he thought.

As the net drew closer, the sight sent a chill through Copik. A human face was staring at him through semi-liquefied eyes, its mouth slightly open.

The Copiks heaved the net on board and released the cod line to open the end of the net. The body and the mass of fish went slithering across the deck, wet and solid. Copik radioed the coastguard to tell them he'd found a body in his nets and was bringing it in.

As the *Malkerry* made its way into port, John Copik could see a police car waiting on the quayside.

After boarding the trawler, Detective Constable Ian Clenahan and police surgeon Nick Fisher bent down to examine the body. The dead man was fully dressed. On his right wrist was a stainless steel Rolex Oyster watch. The man's face was distorted and decomposed, and there was a large gash on the back of his head.

There was not a single piece of identification on the body. The only person in the area reported missing at sea was a 20-year-old student presumed drowned in a pedal-boat accident the week before. But this corpse didn't match the student's description. John and Craig Copik were openly sceptical and seemed convinced that the gash on the head suggested something sinister.

As the body was being taken to the mortuary in nearby Torquay, the Copiks walked back to the *Malkerry*, where they scrubbed down the deck and got everything back in order.

They hadn't been there long when another fisherman, Derek Meredith, came along and spotted an anchor caught up in the Copiks' nets. "Do you want it?" he asked, pointing to the anchor.

"You're welcome to it," said Copik.

Meredith climbed on board, untangled the anchor and sauntered off.

At 2pm the next day, pathologist Clive Hay and coroner's officer Robin Little donned white smocks and rubber boots and entered the post-mortem room. As Little undressed the chilled corpse, Hay began his examination, relaying his observations to Little, who wrote them down on a notepad.

Accompanying the two men was a police officer who took photographs and noted any significant details before placing each item in a separate plastic bag: the brown leather shoes; the green corduroy trousers; watch time and date—11.35, July 22; watch automatic and self-winding.

"He didn't like the sun," Little said. "Tan on back of hands only," he wrote. "Tattoo on back of right hand appears to be stars (five) joined together."

Hay then examined the gash on the back of the head. "Let's see what the police have got," he said.

Little handed him a form, a single sheet of paper labelled "Unidentified Male". It contained a brief paragraph compiled by the police in Paignton. There was precious little detail. To all intents and purposes it looked like a boating accident.

"I'm not satisfied," Hay told Little, and suggested they call in the Home Office pathologist. "I can't make a determination of cause of death based on this."

At 3pm the next day, Dr Gyan Fernando, the local Home Office pathologist, arrived and the whole process began again. Every major organ was removed, weighed, cut open and examined. All injuries were noted: a well-defined but inexplicable two-inch bruise on the left hip; an inch-long crack on the back of the skull that could have been sustained accidentally, perhaps as the man fell into the water; and minor lacerations on the chest and back that may have been caused by the body being dragged along the sea floor over sand and gravel.

None of these injuries, however, could have killed the man, Fernando determined. It was the condition of the lungs—laden with water—and the fact that the body had been found at sea that led the pathologist to make his final pronouncement: death by drowning.

THE INSIDE STORY

News about the mortuary's unidentified male spread quickly. On July 31, a friend suggested to Little that since every Rolex comes with a serial number, perhaps the Rolex company itself might help to identify the body. He dialled through to Rolex in Bexley, Kent, and explained the case to a Carol Hyland. His friend's information was indeed correct, she confirmed.

Since 1905 each Rolex watch has been made with a serial number inscribed on its casing. In this way, a record of every repair and service to a customer's watch could be obtained through Rolex's central registry as part of the company's pledge of quality control.

While he listened, Little slipped the watch out of its plastic bag and flipped it over. There was nothing to see. The watch, he concluded, must be a fake.

"The number isn't self-evident, of course," Carol Hyland explained. "It's on the shoulder of the casing, just where the bracelet joins the case. You can't see it without taking the pins out and removing the bracelet. Have a look and call me back."

With a small needle, Little nudged first one and then the other pin out and carefully removed the bracelet from the casing. There, inscribed on the side of the watch, was the number: 1544402.

Unfortunately, all Carol Hyland could tell Little was that the watch had been sold almost 30 years before by a jeweller in Germany. For its service history they would need to open up the watch itself. So Little obtained permission and the watch was sent to Bexley.

When Carol Hyland replied some days later, she told Detective Constable Ian Clenahan in Paignton that the watch had been serviced twice in the 1980s by an authorized Rolex agent in Harrogate, Yorkshire.

Clenahan phoned Harrogate and, with the help of local police, the owner of the watch was provisionally identified as Ronald Joseph Platt, born on March 22, 1945.

Using national and personal records, the victim was tracked from Harrogate to 100 Beardsley Drive, Chelmsford, Essex. Clenahan then asked police there to make inquiries about Platt on behalf of the Devon and Cornwall force. Sergeant Peter Redman found that the only useful piece of information the landlord had was the name and mobile telephone number of the reference Platt had provided six months earlier, when he'd moved in.

Clenahan dialled the number, and the phone was answered by a man.

"Hello?"

"Is that David Davis?"

"Yes, it is."

"Is that David Davis who acted as a reference for a Ronald Platt, who leased a flat in Chelmsford?"

"Yes. Who is this?"

"It's DC Ian Clenahan of the Devon and Cornwall police, Mr Davis. There's been an accident at sea and a body has been found."

"Oh, my God!"

"We believe that it may be the body of your friend Mr Platt."

"Oh, my God! Are they absolutely certain?"

"Apparently," Clenahan said. "But I don't think we should go into this on the phone. Could you come down to the local station in Chelmsford and lend us a hand? Perhaps tell us a little bit about Mr Platt?"

"Of course I will."

On August 22, Sergeant Redman welcomed David Davis to the station. "You knew Ronald Joseph Platt?" he asked.

"Yes, I did," Davis said, thoughtfully stroking his beard. "I've known him for a few years. He's a friend. A kindred spirit, really. Quiet. But I understood he'd left for France to set up a business. In fact, I'd lent him £2,000."

"When did you last see him?"

"June, I believe."

"Do you know where he was heading for in France?"

"He mentioned La Rochelle."

"Did he leave an address?"

"No. But I was anticipating hearing from him." Davis also said that before Ron Platt left, he had had his post redirected to Davis's address, Little London Farm, Woodham Walter, Essex.

Redman then suggested that Davis speak to Detective Constable Clenahan in Devon. He dialled Clenahan's number and handed Davis the telephone.

Platt's mother, Davis said, lived in High Wycombe. There were two brothers, but he wasn't sure where they lived. Also, Platt had served a stint in the army.

All interesting material, Clenahan thought. They were lucky to have found Davis. With a little more luck, they might be able to close the file on this apparent accident. The new detective chief inspector for Devon and Cornwall, Phil Sincock, had arrived and he was known to be a hard taskmaster.

MAN WITH A MISSION

Phil Sincock was settling in, getting to know his staff and having a look at ways in which he could improve efficiency, boost morale and keep his people keen.

Champagne lifestyle: "Is that David Davis?"

Sincock had come with impeccable credentials. Prior to this posting, he had won a special commendation for getting a conviction in a high-profile case in Barnstaple, north Devon. Police had convinced prosecutors to charge a man with murder before they had even found a body. Sincock had been that sure. Days later, the body did in fact turn up and the accused was sentenced to life imprisonment.

The Platt case, however, was just one of many, and it was still being treated as an accident. Army dental records had confirmed Platt's identity. Then the police managed to track down his brother Brian in Hay-on-Wye, on the Welsh border.

The dead man was definitely Ronald, Brian said. The tattoo on his right hand wasn't a five-pointed star, he explained, but a maple leaf. His younger brother had been brought up in Canada and loved the country. Brian also said that Ron had had a girlfriend named Elaine Boyes. They had lived together for more than 12 years, but three years ago, in 1993, they had broken off their relationship.

Brian said he'd pass the news on to his mother. He was the eldest in the family, so he'd look after that.

Two and a half months had gone by since the body had been found. The police had identified it, notified the next of kin and appealed through the media for extra assistance, but they'd come up empty-handed. At long last it seemed it was time to lay Platt's body, and the file, to rest.

But Coroner Hamish Turner, after talking to Ian Clenahan and his colleague Bill Macdonald, agreed that the detectives should pursue the lines of inquiry that were still open. Perhaps they could determine how and why Platt had come to be lying at the bottom of the sea. After that, they would reassess the situation.

Since David Davis seemed to have been the dead man's only friend, Clenahan wanted to arrange an appointment, but he couldn't reach Davis by phone. Once again, he appealed to Sergeant Redman in Chelmsford. Could he drive out and ask Davis to phone Clenahan in Devon?

On October 14, Peter Redman, dressed in civilian clothes, set off in an unmarked car for Little London Lane, Woodham Walter. There, he found four houses, but neither of the two that had signs on their gates said Little London Farm, Davis's house.

The odds are 50-50, Redman thought. As he approached one of the unmarked houses, an elderly gentleman answered the door.

"Sorry to bother you, sir, but is this Little London Farm?"

"You're barking up the wrong tree," the man said. "This is Little London House. That," he said, stepping into the porch and pointing next door, "is Little London Farm."

"Thank you very much," Redman said, and began to walk away. Then it struck him. He'd better make sure. He turned around.

"That is where Mr David Davis lives, isn't it?"

"My dear boy," the elderly man replied, "there's no Mr Davis who lives there. You're mistaken again. That is where Ronald Platt lives."

Sergeant Redman was stunned. "Ronald Platt?"

"Yes. And his lovely wife Noël. And their two children. Why? Is there anything wrong?"

"No, not at all. But may I ask what this Mr Platt looks like? I may have the wrong address."

"Oh, he's about 50. An American chap. Outgoing, friendly, dark hair, beard. A retired banker from New York. I can't think of anything else, really. Except that he's quite a nice fellow and he spends a lot of time on his boat down in Devon."

It was a precise description of Davis, Redman realized. He steadied himself. "Oh, I must have the wrong man," he said. Then he thanked the neighbour, got back into his car and drove to the police station to phone Clenahan.

"Good God," Clenahan said when he heard the news, his adrenalin rising. He hung up and went straight to Detective Chief Inspector Phil Sincock's office.

The next day Sincock convened a meeting with Clenahan, Macdonald and two other detectives. Orders were issued. Inquiries should be made about Little London Farm and its residents: local government records, banking records, even itemized telephone bills.

FIRST MEETING

Clenahan tracked down Platt's former girlfriend Elaine Boyes in Harrogate. On October 28, he showed her a photograph of the dead man's hand with the maple leaf tattoo. Yes, she said, it was Ron.

A David Davis, too, had been informed, Clenahan told her.

"How long has he known?" Elaine asked.

"Oh, a couple of months now."

Elaine Boyes froze. She had spoken to Davis only about a week ago, she said, and had asked him about Platt. All Davis told her was that he had seen Platt off to France.

Shaken by the news, she began to tell Clenahan all about her life with Ron Platt, as well as their connection with David Davis.

In the summer of 1990, 31-year-old Elaine Boyes was working as a receptionist at Henry Spencer and Sons Fine Art Auctioneers in Harrogate.

One day, a man walked in and asked to see some paintings. Just then the phone rang. Elaine answered several calls, dealt with tradesmen and handled queries from colleagues, now and then giving a nodding smile to the patiently waiting visitor.

"At last," she said, "how can I help you?"

"I've been watching you," the man replied. "You've got people traipsing through here, the phone's ringing, I'm waiting, and you treat everyone so well. I could use someone like you."

"I beg your pardon?"

"I'm planning on starting up a small fine arts and antiques company myself. I'm over here quite a bit now and I'll be moving permanently from America soon. I'd pay you well, you could travel, we could even take some courses together at Sotheby's in London. But working here, I'm sure you must know a lot already."

"Not as much as I'd like," Elaine said, still flustered.

"And I could teach you all about business and money. We could work together, I'm sure of it."

"But you don't even know me," she smiled.

"David Davis," he said, standing up to extend his hand, bowing slightly and smiling as he did so.

"Elaine Boyes," she said, shaking hands. "But this is ridiculous. I can't even think about changing jobs, Mr Davis. I've promised my boyfriend we'll move to Canada together. He grew up there and all he ever talks about is going back. It's his dream."

"Well, you can't blame a man for chasing a dream, can you?" Davis encouraged her, almost fatherly now. "Was he born there?" he asked.

The loyal servant: Elaine Boyes agreed to become Davis's special assistant.

"No, no. Ron's father was a teacher in Canada. They went over there from Liverpool when Ron was about ten. He came back in 1963, when he was 18, and joined the army later—that's where he learned about electronics—but we're planning to head off as soon as we have the money."

"Elaine," said Davis, dropping his voice to a confidential hush, "I could offer you enough money so that within a year's time, you could both go."

Davis saw Elaine again in February 1991. He also met her boyfriend Ron Platt, who approved of her decision to join Davis's new fine arts and antiques venture, Cavendish Corporation.

In April that year, Elaine formally accepted Davis's offer and became his special assistant. She was to act solely as Davis's nominee, under his precise instructions. Davis then confided in her about the "tragedy" of his first marriage and how his ex-wife, back home in the United States, was now pursuing him for alimony. His response was to move to London, he said, and one of his daughters, Noël, had chosen to come with him. It was absolutely vital, he told Elaine, that his name never appear on documents of any kind. Not even a cheque should be made out in his name. Security and secrecy were crucial.

Davis said it was good insurance, too, to have Ron Platt on the company board. "In case something happens to you," he told her. "Of course, nothing will, but it's good business practice." So Platt signed on as an unpaid director.

TERMS AND CONDITIONS

Elaine Boyes had a strong incentive in following David Davis's instructions to the letter, because by now his generosity far exceeded the original proposal. He not only paid her 50 per cent more than she had made at Henry Spencer and Sons, he also arranged for her and Platt to buy a smart two-bedroom flat in a modern building. "Mr D", as Platt now called him, had put up the money for the £55,000 purchase. More extraordinary still, Davis rented premises for Platt and set him up in his own television and video repair business. He had also lent Platt the £13,000 he needed for start-up costs.

As for the work Elaine had to do, it was hardly onerous, she explained to Detective Constable Clenahan. Davis would send her to France, Italy or Switzerland, where she'd take a look at this or that antique sale, these or those properties and—while she was there—deposit cash in different accounts she set up under her own name, as secretary of Cavendish Corporation. It was all sup- posed to be part of Davis's alimony avoidance.

Throughout 1991 and 1992 the operation worked smoothly. Elaine would return home after jetting across Europe, and a week later a deposit slip would arrive by post. She'd give it to Davis, who had by this time moved up to Harrogate from London, and he would tell her to transfer some of the same money back into Cavendish's accounts in town.

Not all transfers had to be made in person, Elaine told Clenahan. Davis some- times asked her to move money by fax or by post, which worked equally smoothly. In time, several accounts were set up, including two in Geneva and one in Paris.

Then, unexpectedly, late in 1992, citing "cash-flow problems" and referring to "money being tight", Davis told Elaine that the money he'd put up for the pur- chase of her flat had to be called in.

"Surely there's some kind of arrangement we could make, Mr Davis?" she asked.

"Elaine, I don't see any way around it."

"But Mr Davis, what if we let you rent out the flat? That way, we could hold on to the property and you would get all the income."

"It's not a question of income for me. It's a question of commitments I have to meet. It's time to start thinking about putting the flat up for sale. You and Ron will be going to Canada soon anyway."

"But what if we come back?"

"It would be prudent if you acted now, Elaine."

Davis's tone had turned serious and she knew the conversation was over. The couple put their flat up for sale.

A few weeks later, Davis also informed Ron Platt that he could no longer continue paying the rent on his shop. Platt would have to go it alone.

On Christmas Day, 1992, however, money no longer seemed quite so tight. Davis invited Elaine and Ron to dinner and presented them with a card in which he had written: "Two air tickets to Canada. Valid until the end of February."

"It's time you and Elaine seized the dream, Ron," he said.

The couple thanked Davis profusely. They were committed to going, although Elaine would later persuade Davis to give her a return ticket, just in case.

But Davis had a favour to ask in return. Since he still had to operate Cavendish Corporation and access his money, could Elaine and Ron make rubber stamps of their signatures?

The request didn't seem unreasonable, so they complied. Davis also managed to convince Platt to leave him copies of his birth certificate and his driver's licence.

On February 11, 1993, Elaine Boyes signed over a sweeping power of attorney to Davis, ostensibly so that he could finish up the sale of the flat after their departure. The document gave Davis the right "to deposit money, to draw money, to sign my name, to receive post on my behalf, generally to act in relation to my personal affairs in all respects as I myself do."

On the evening of February 22, 1993, after a farewell dinner in Harrogate, Ron Platt glanced down at his watch and looked up at Elaine's mother.

"By this time tomorrow I'll be there," he said. "I'm going home."

COLD COMFORT

It had been a rough landing in Calgary. When the aeroplane carrying Elaine Boyes and Ron Platt did finally touch down, the temperature was minus 34 degrees C [minus 29 F]. For Elaine, who had lived most of her life in gentle, leafy Harrogate, Calgary in February was a harsh introduction to a new country. As the jet taxied to the terminal, she peered out of the window and wondered what she had let herself in for.

Neither of them had jobs, so they were forced to look for cheap accommodation. It was a demoralizing experience.

"Well, it doesn't have to be Calgary, does it?" Davis asked Platt when he phoned them soon after their arrival to see how they were settling in.

"No, of course not," said Platt. "It's just that this is what I'm familiar with. Or was familiar with. It doesn't seem the same any more. We're thinking about driving to Vancouver."

"A great idea," Davis encouraged. "Give yourself time. It's a marvellous country, Canada."

But Ron didn't like Vancouver either. It was too congested, too expensive, and they drove straight back to Calgary.

The loner: like many before him, Ron Platt trusted Davis.

Eventually, they found a little basement flat. At night they lay awake and listened to the rumble of trucks on the Trans-Canada Highway just a few streets away. Calgary was not at all the wide-open, friendly frontier town of Ron's childhood memories. It seemed dark and cold now, and he began to brood and grow morose.

Elaine was worried. Ron's dark moods were beginning to drag her down, too. She was glad that she had insisted on having a return ticket before leaving England.

Her sister Gillian's wedding was due to take place in July and Elaine decided that if things didn't improve by then, she would return to England and stay.

At the wedding, Elaine announced to David Davis that she wasn't going back to Canada.

"What seems to be the problem, Elaine?" he asked.

"Oh, Mr Davis, if you only knew. It was terrible. Ron can't find work; I couldn't even look for work because I couldn't get a work permit. Then Ron got depressed. I just couldn't cope. I can't go back there, Mr Davis. It would break me."

"But what about Ron?" Davis asked gently. "He needs your support, Elaine. It sounds to me as though he's really trying. He just hasn't got a break yet."

Elaine grew silent.

"I think you should give him a second chance," Davis said.

But she would not be moved.

More than a year passed and in March 1995 it was Ron's turn to inform Davis that he was returning to England. He was living on odd jobs and little money and was fed up with Calgary.

In June, following Ron Platt's return, Davis found him a position at a security company just outside High Wycombe, Buckinghamshire, where Platt would be near his mother. But in December he lost his job. He said he wanted to move to Chelmsford to be closer to the person he now regarded as his only friend: Mr D himself.

INTO THE TRAP

By the last week of October 1996, DCI Phil Sincock and his team in Devon had gathered a fair amount of material. They had various pieces of paper bearing Ron Platt's signatures; some of them didn't match up with the ones being used by Davis. At the very least, they had built up a case for fraud.

A police raid on Little London Farm was planned for October 31. The day before, DC Clenahan finally obtained Davis's mobile phone records. They showed conclusively that he had made numerous calls from Devon between July 7 and July 23, placing him squarely in the area where Ron Platt's body was recovered. Sincock was now certain he had a murder case on his hands—even if he had almost no hard evidence. Come morning, he thought, we'll swoop.

At 10am, as the waiting police looked on, a taxi turned into the narrow confines of Little London Lane. It reappeared a few moments later, with David Davis sitting in the front seat.

One police car immediately followed and another intercepted the taxi, forcing it to pull over.

As the taxi driver wound down his window, a policeman walked up alongside. "Look in my eyes!" he shouted at Davis. "Keep looking in my eyes and get out of the car. Keep looking!"

Davis slid out, his hands up in the air.

"Up against the car!"

Davis stood spreadeagled across the rear window as two police officers frisked him for weapons. One constable snapped on a pair of handcuffs. Then a figure dressed in plain clothes walked into the circle of policemen that had formed.

"Good morning, Mr Davis. Do you remember me?"

It was Sergeant Redman.

"Yes, of course. What's this all about?"

"I am arresting you on suspicion of the murder of Ronald Joseph Platt," Redman said, then he cautioned Davis concerning his rights. That done, Davis was driven away.

Inside Little London Farm, Noël Davis, too, was told that she was under arrest. She asked one of the neighbours to look after her two-year-old daughter Emily, but nine-month-old Lillian was to go with Noël to the police station.

Once there, Noël's pockets and bags were emptied out. There were documents in Elaine Boyes's name: a telephone bill, a chequebook, bank and credit cards, and a National Health Service card. She also had a man's wallet containing Ron Platt's birth certificate, driver's licence, bank cards and various other papers.

At first, Noël Davis stuck stubbornly to what was obviously a well-rehearsed script: she was from Long Island and her husband David had been a friend of her father's. Sceptical, the police questioned her again and again until, finally, she admitted that David Davis was in fact her father.

It was after Platt and Boyes had left for Canada, Noël explained, that she and her father assumed their identities as Ron and Elaine and moved to Devon, where she gave birth to Emily. Soon, she said, her father suggested that because there was a baby, they should present themselves as husband and wife.

When asked who the father of her children was, Noël would not respond. As for the real Ronald Platt, she said, she hadn't seen him since they had eaten Christmas dinner together in 1995. She had no idea that Platt had been in Devon during July. In fact, she had no idea that he had even been confirmed dead. Not until now.

Questioned separately, Davis said nothing, only "I want to speak to a solicitor." As the result of a body search, the police found the birth certificate of David W. Davis, a credit card in the name of R. J. Platt, health club and museum cards in David Davis's name, as well as business cards in yet another name: James J. Hilton, 146 Avenue William Favre, Geneva, Switzerland.

Using Davis's personal telephone records and other documents already in their possession, Sincock had his team working around the clock. Fingerprints were sent to the US authorities via Interpol to see whether or not Davis was wanted there.

Davis's boat Lady Jane was impounded for forensic testing. The investigation was transferred on to HOLMES (Home Office Large Major Enquiry System), a computer database that would give every detective working on the case easy access to every piece of information available.

By November 3, police had gathered enough evidence and witness statements to warrant Davis's continued detention. Noël was released.

On November 4, Detective Chief Inspector Phil Sincock finally got his wish: David Davis was formally charged with the murder of Ronald Joseph Platt.

Ship of clues: Davis's beloved yacht, *Lady Jane*, is impounded by the police.

WEIGHING UP THE EVIDENCE

Meanwhile, the police investigation, now involving up to 70 officers, continued. When they raided Little London Farm, police found cash—more than £17,600 and 8,170 Swiss francs—and five gold bars. Among the mountain of documents seized was a receipt dated July 8, 1996, for the purchase of seven items, including a ten-pound plough anchor bought from Sport Nautique in Dartmouth, Devon.

Papers and keys led police to other locations. Fifteen miles away, in an office at Solutions in Therapy, where Davis was a therapeutic counselling partner, police found five more gold bars; at Genstar Storage in Northampton, more cash and gold, and a Global Positioning System (GPS) for navigation; at Chelmsford Storage, a set of suitcases filled with Ronald Platt's personal belongings.

In time, a couple of detectives were dispatched to interview John Copik. The fisherman went over every movement he had made on July 28, 1996, including the episode involving the anchor he had given to Derek Meredith.

The detectives tracked Meredith down.

"I gave the anchor to my girlfriend," Meredith said. "She and her mother Patricia Johnson put it in a jumble sale, I think."

Patricia Johnson confirmed that she had put the anchor in a sale, but hadn't sold it. The anchor, as police suspected, fitted the description of the one Davis had bought on July 8 at Sport Nautique. The other six items listed on the receipt were later found on the *Lady Jane*.

At the forensic laboratory, the yacht was thoroughly dusted for fingerprints and painstakingly searched for evidence. Incredibly, there was not a single print to be found—not even one of the owner's.

Eventually it dawned on the police to check the Sport Nautique shopping bag that had been found on board. There, they found the fingerprints of Ronald Joseph Platt.

Something else was also found: blood. There were three microscopic drops discovered on the rolled-up sails; and on cushions found in another investigation, there was a small bit of hair and scalp. All, tests strongly suggested, belonged to Platt.

Next, police looked at the Global Positioning System retrieved from Genstar Storage. They contacted the manufacturer, who explained that a feature of that particular model was that it stored the precise time and the last navigational reference point registered when it was shut off. When the police downloaded the data inside the GPS, the printout showed the time and date as 8.59pm, July 20, 1996; it placed the boat four miles from where Copik found Platt's body.

According to Noël Davis, on July 20 her father announced that he was heading out to sea alone. Noël and her two children stayed behind at The Old Brewhouse, a rented holiday cottage in Dittisham, on the River Dart.

The only other occasion Davis had gone sailing on his own, Noël said, he had returned by 6pm. But on that particular day, he hadn't returned by six in the evening. Noël prepared dinner for herself and the children, then cuddled up with them in front of the television. At 8.59pm, Davis still wasn't back.

At that precise moment, two and a quarter miles off the Devon coast, a hand gripped the control of *Lady Jane*'s GPS and switched it off. It was 15 minutes before sunset. In that light, and from that distance, the operator didn't need the GPS. He could easily see his way home.

It was well after dark when David Davis came in. Noël quickly prepared supper for him. He looked, she told the police, "scruffy and windswept".

The evidence against David Davis was mounting. On November 25, a second post-mortem of Platt's body was about to begin when something new emerged on the defrosting body: a bruise on the left leg, just above the knee.

With Platt's body stretched out on the examining table, a ten-pound zinc-plated plough anchor similar to the one retrieved from Patricia Johnson's house was brought in and laid out next to Platt's left side. There, for all to see, the two bruises—the new one and the one previously noted on his left hip—corresponded well with the contours of the anchor itself.

Dr Fernando, the Home Office pathologist, and a pathologist attending on behalf of the accused, cut into the newly discovered bruise and determined that the injury had been inflicted before death.

It looked as if whoever had killed Ron Platt, if he had indeed been killed, had fastened an anchor to Platt's left side. But how?

Sincock sent Platt's belt and the seized anchor for forensic testing. Near the base of the anchor's shank were fibrous deposits microscopically similar to leather. At the same time, some ten inches from the belt's buckle, several marks on the leather were found to contain zinc of the kind used to plate the anchor. The forensic evidence linked the belt and the anchor, supporting the theory that the anchor had been inserted under Platt's belt to keep the body submerged.

WANTED MAN

But Sincock was puzzled. He was certain David Walliss Davis, as Davis said he was formally called, couldn't possibly be the man's real name. They'd run a search and discovered only one David Walliss Davis born in Britain, and he had left as a child for parts unknown—in 1949.

So who was this Davis, who claimed to have been born here yet couldn't produce any convincing identification? He had portrayed himself to friends and acquaintances as an English Literature graduate, from the University of Edinburgh, who became a banker in New York, was posted to Geneva and later moved to England, where he retired from banking to become a psychiatrist. None of the details had checked out.

Sincock had two detectives go over every piece of paper retrieved from Little London Farm: bank documents, legal files, correspondence, old train tickets. The man is a hoarder, Sincock thought, yet nothing seems to go back beyond six years. Davis seemed to be a man without a substantial history. Who was he really? Definitely not Platt, or Davis.

"See what countries come up on the database," Sincock told his staff. An information circular on Davis, complete with his photograph and fingerprints, was prepared. This was passed to Interpol for distribution to Canada, because Platt had been brought up there, and to Switzerland, Italy and France, where Elaine Boyes said she had travelled.

On Friday, November 22, the National Criminal Intelligence Service office in London received a message from the Swiss office of Interpol in Berne. They were responding to the appeal for identification from the Devon and Cornwall police.

From the package that was before them, the Swiss said, David W. Davis looked a lot like someone

Canny cop: DCI Phil Sincock was convinced that the ten-pound plough anchor had been used to keep the body submerged.

26

they had on Interpol's most-wanted list. "We believe this man to be Albert Johnson Walker of Canada."

When the news reached Devon the following Monday, there was a celebration, albeit a brief one. They had caught what might be a big fish, but the investigation pressed on. Twenty-six days had elapsed since the arrest, and there was still more work to be done.

They discovered Walker's true identity soon enough. He was a Canadian financier from the town of Paris, in Ontario, who had fled from Canada some six years earlier, taking with him his 15-year-old daughter Sheena—also known as Noël Davis—and millions of dollars' worth of his clients' money, which Elaine Boyes had unwittingly helped to launder. Walker had eluded both his ex-wife and Interpol, by using a variety of aliases, reinventing himself over and over again.

David Walliss Davis, they learned, was indeed a British-born Canadian who had gone to Walker for help with a bank loan application and who, in the process, had handed over his birth certificate.

All in all, police estimated, Walker had stolen more than three million dollars. He had transferred almost one million dollars to his various European accounts, smuggled out as much as 700,000 dollars in gold, British pounds and French and Swiss francs, and probably spent much of the rest while financing his art acquisitions and bad investments.

EXPLOSIVE ACCUSATION

On December 9, 1996, Albert Johnson Walker was remanded in custody again, this time under his real name. By now the evidence against him was overwhelming, bolstered by an array of witnesses who said they had seen him together with Ron Platt in bars and hotels in Devon as late as July 10. One publican even remembered the two men checking out of his establishment on July 9, then coming back together the next day, when Platt had taken a room for another eight nights.

In stark contrast, Sheena Walker's statement to police said unequivocally that her father had told her he had seen Platt off to France in June. The statement suggested that Walker had tried to keep Platt's presence in Devon in July a secret from his daughter, a secret that, when seen in light of all the other evidence, might suggest a plot—perhaps even a murder plot. If allowed to stand, Sheena's testimony could be the most potent weapon in the prosecution's arsenal.

Sitting alone in his prison cell, Albert Walker must have suddenly realized this danger. On Sunday, February 2, 1997, he telephoned Sheena, who had now returned to her mother's house in Ontario, to ask her to say that she did know that Ron had been in Devon and on the boat with him.

Daddy's girl?: Sheena Walker's evidence condemned her father.

But shortly after that conversation, Sheena made her own long-distance call—to report to the Devon and Cornwall police that her father had directed her from prison to change her testimony. It was an explosive accusation. If true, Phil Sincock realized, it could be a trial clincher.

Meanwhile, at a committal hearing on March 24, during which a magistrate would decide whether or not there was sufficient evidence to warrant a trial, Walker's defence team was arguing a motion to dismiss the case.

The Crown didn't have enough evidence, barrister Gordon Pringle pointed out.

Without an eyewitness, he said, the Crown could not prove that Platt had actually been murdered. It could well have been a suicide. The Crown could not prove that the anchor retrieved from Patricia Johnson's house was the same anchor that was pulled up in John Copik's net. Nor could it prove the anchor was the same one Walker had bought on July 8, 1996. The manufacturer had made thousands and the retrieved anchor could have been any one of them.

More important, Pringle said, the Crown could not prove that Platt was on Walker's boat on the day the alleged murder supposedly took place. The Crown could not even prove that Walker himself was on the boat on that day. According to evidence, the last time anyone had seen them together was July 10. The death by drowning was said to have taken place approximately ten days later.

Finally, even the time of death could not be determined satisfactorily, Pringle stated. The watch had stopped at 11.35, but it was not clear if it had been am or pm. Hence, even if the precise specifications of the Rolex's self-winding mechanism had remained intact, shutting down the watch some 44 hours after Platt's arm ceased to move, there was still no way to go back in time.

The magistrate, however, was not convinced by Pringle's argument. "It is my considered view," he said, "that there is sufficient evidence here to commit the case to the Crown Court."

The trial was set for June 22, 1998.

"We find the defendant guilty," the jury pronounced on Monday, July 6, 1998. They had taken just two hours to reach their verdict.

The facts were overwhelming: Walker could not account for the whereabouts of the anchor he'd purchased on July 8; he could not explain why the GPS reading from *Lady Jane* showed the date and time that it did; and his alibis concerning his movements on July 20 at the approximate time of the murder were far-fetched and thoroughly incredible.

Added to all this was Sheena Walker's testimony, which exposed her father for what he was: a supreme manipulator capable of doing anything to save his skin, including telling his own daughter to twist the truth.

"What a job for a daughter," said prosecutor Charles Barton QC. "She came over here to nail the fundamental lie. Just imagine the scope of the story he could have constructed had she not come before us."

Albert Walker stood rigid and blinked, not once but twice, as though he wished to adjust his vision.

"This was a callous, premeditated killing designed to eliminate a man you had used for your own selfish ends," said Justice Neil Butterfield during sentencing.

"You are a plausible, intelligent and ruthless man who poses a serious threat to anyone who stands in your way," he continued. "And I shall have regard to that when making recommendations for the length of your sentence."

The judge then commended all the detectives for their painstaking work. "Everyone concerned," he said, "demonstrated true professionalism and should be congratulated."

Then Butterfield looked to the prisoner's box. Everyone expected him to gruffly say, "Take him down", as many English judges do.

Instead Butterfield gently said, "You may go down." It was entirely deferential and probably the last gesture of kindness Albert Walker would experience for a very long time.

Albert Johnson Walker is currently serving a life sentence at Long Lartin maximum-security prison in Worcestershire.

HOLLY'S FIGHT
FOR
JUSTICE

BY RALPH MOFINA

VICTIM OF A SERIAL RAPIST, THE YOUNG

WOMAN FROM RED DEER, ALBERTA, DETERMINED

TO BRING HER ATTACKER TO TRIAL.

Holly Jill Desimone will never silence the sound of the rapist's zipper opening behind her. "Count backward from ten!" he ordered, forcing her onto her hands and knees against a chair in her apartment in Red Deer, Alberta. Photographs of her seven-year-old son and five-year-old daughter smiled from across the room as the man assaulted her.

Holly thought of the butcher's knives in her kitchen. *Surely he will kill me. This is how I will die, 29 years old, studying to be a nurse, divorced, in the middle of a custody fight for my children.*

Three hours earlier that night of December 14, 1990, the delicious aroma of Iranian baking filled the air as Holly arrived at the home of her friends Albert and Celine Rasai. Holly had helped Albert find work as a hairdresser. Now he introduced her to his brother Ali, a polite, charming newcomer to Canada. Perhaps Holly could help him, too.

Barrel-chested with a thick black mustache, Ali, 37, said he was a former bodyguard to the Shah of Iran and a martial-arts expert. As he eyed the attractive young brunette, he regaled Holly with stories of his life as a globe-trotting refugee from Iran's civil strife. He did not reveal that he was a fugitive from an attempted rape charge in Australia.

When Holly offered to introduce Ali to club managers she knew who might need a bouncer or disc jockey, a grateful Albert insisted they use his car. Christmas lights twinkled in storefronts as Holly drove off with Ali. She took him to several clubs. By then it was late. "I'll just drop myself off at home," she told Ali. "You can come in and call Albert for directions to drive back. Or I can draw a map."

"That would be fine," he said.

Once inside, Rasai's charm evaporated. "You're very pretty," he said, pointing to a photo of Holly, whose slender figure had earned her modelling jobs. Rasai bragged about his martial-arts skills, insisting he demonstrate them. Holly grew uneasy.

"I'm tired and I have to get up early," she said. Rasai ignored the hint. Moving closer, he began touching her. He could kill using only two fingers, he boasted. Weighing 100 pounds to Rasai's 170, Holly was suddenly paralyzed with fear.

He told her to get on the floor. How could I have been so stupid? thought Holly. Then Rasai raped her anally.

When it was over, Rasai left. Holly staggered to her bathroom and collapsed to the floor. Bleeding and weeping, she struggled with shame, outrage and fear.

She showered, wanting to peel off her skin.

Holly phoned a friend and told her, through tears, what had happened.

"Never, ever tell anybody," came the reply. "No one will believe you."

Holly kept the rape secret, but the trauma was deep. She never felt clean enough. She showered up to three times daily, scrubbing herself until she was raw. Each time she passed a police building, she froze. She wanted desperately to report the crime, but she could not even say the words "I was raped."

At last Holly found the courage to go to the Red Deer RCMP. On March 1, 1991, Constable Rick Taylor tape-recorded her 90-minute statement.

The detective knew Rasai had been charged with sexually assault-ing another woman in Red Deer

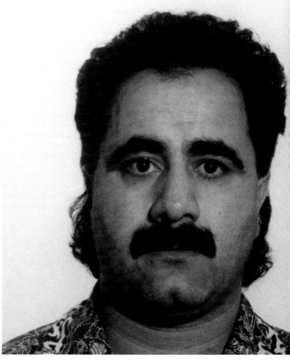

Dangerous deviant: just months after arriving in Canada, Ali Rasai had sexually assaulted three women.

and one in Edmonton. He had been charged, jailed, then released on bail in the Edmonton case. Rasai was arrested and jailed again in Red Deer.

Awaiting his preliminary hearing, Rasai sought bail. Unaware of the bail hear-ing, not one of the victims was present on June 10 when Edmonton lawyer Tom Plupek presented Rasai's case before Justice Robert Cairns.

Plupek urged Rasai be allowed to join his brother, now living in Edmonton. Rasai would find work to pay for his defence and support his pregnant wife, who would be arriving from Australia. Plupek portrayed his client as a struggling refugee whose martial-arts skills had led to some trouble. He made only passing reference to a sexual assault charge in Australia against his client.

But Crown prosecutor Roxanne Prior detailed the incident. In December 1989, Rasai lured a 19-year-old to his apartment, telling her he would give her karate lessons. Once there, he told her he was a medical doctor and that to ascertain her fitness level, he would have to give her a physical. He had "examined" her and was about to rape her when a knock on the door stopped him. Before his trial for attempted rape, he fled to Canada using a fake passport. Within three months of landing in Alberta seeking refugee status, he was charged with sexually assaulting three different women. Prior warned that Rasai could well flee Canada, just as he had Australia.

Nevertheless, Justice Cairns granted Rasai 3,000 dollars bail on the condition he live with his brother and report weekly to Edmonton police. A week later, stepping outside her Red Deer apartment, Holly froze. Nearby, a man was watching her. *Rasai? But he's in jail in Edmonton!*

Holly went to the RCMP. They told her Rasai had been granted bail. "No one told me!" she replied. Incensed, Holly went to lawyer Don Manning, who discovered that the restriction that Rasai not contact his alleged victims had not been made a condition of his bail. Pressing the oversight with the Crown, Manning got the condition applied. Yet Holly remained jittery. *Was reporting the rape worth it?* she wondered.

On August 9 the hearing against Ali Rasai began. Sitting alone in a small witness room, Holly nervously waited. And waited. At last Constable Rick Taylor entered. "Court's adjourned," he said. "Rasai didn't show up."

Within hours the court issued a nationwide arrest warrant for Rasai. Back home, Holly wanted to scream. A fugitive rapist enters Canada with a fake passport, assaults three women, gets bail—and skips court! But there was more. Days later Edmonton police revealed they were never told Rasai was to report to them.

As time passed, Holly's anger grew. If authorities were seeking Rasai, why hadn't they made his photograph public? She contacted the other Red Deer victim, and together they made their own "Wanted" flyer and alerted the media. Although their identities could not be revealed because of a court order, the two young women, reporters in tow, posted their flyer at airports, bus depots, car-rental outlets and corner stores across Edmonton and Red Deer.

Holly badgered local politicians for support. She got excuses—the file was a federal matter, or an immigration matter, or it was before the courts. Still, her persistence moved Alberta's then Attorney General Ken Rostad to demand an accounting of the bungling in the Rasai case. Shortly after, Rostad ordered changes to bail reporting. Victims of major crimes would now be alerted when their accused attackers sought bail.

Holly's rape was exacting a toll. She had to undergo an AIDS test, which proved negative. She could not focus on her studies or part-time jobs. Every time she entered her apartment she opened closet doors, looking for Rasai. He was lurking out there somewhere. *God, where is he?*

Rasai had slipped the law again. Using the alias Ali Basati, he landed in Oslo early in 1992, with his wife and new son, seeking political asylum. Rasai felt safe in Norway.

Meanwhile, on a visit to Calgary, Holly called the *Calgary Herald*. The Red Deer and Edmonton press had lost interest in her crusade. Would the *Herald* help? The newspaper assigned a reporter—me—to the story.

Holly looked frail in her full-length black coat. Snow fell as we drove back to the newspaper to copy her dog-eared folder of court papers.

Once started, I couldn't put the file down. By the summer of 1992 my story was ready to go. "The story would be stronger if she could be identified," said my managing editor. "Ask her about lifting the ban."

My jaw dropped. As a matter of law and journalistic practice, rape victims are not identified.

"I've been thinking about going public for a long time," Holly said when I called her. "I'll do it."

The court agreed to lift the ban, and days later, on August 2, 1992, the *Herald* published Holly's story. Her picture appeared in newspapers across Canada. Victims' groups called her courageous. A spate of press interviews followed the *Herald* story, but eventually public momentum stalled. Holly would have to keep fighting. "Why can't they find Rasai?" she asked again and again. "Nobody's looking. Nobody cares."

By March 1993 it had been a full year since Rasai sought political asylum in Norway. Officials processing the "Ali Basati" file were now asking questions, and Rasai grew nervous. On March 15, detectives arrived to search his apartment, and Rasai's wife admitted his true identity.

Rasai, however, had already fled, reportedly taking some 22,000 dollars from his bank account. Norwegian police confirmed Rasai's fingerprints through Interpol, the international police agency, and alerts were issued for him throughout Scandinavia.

Months later Holly was stunned to learn Rasai had been in Norway and escaped the police. Again, no official had informed her. "He just keeps walking through the system."

Nevertheless, Holly kept badgering the news media, and in September she appeared on "America's Most Wanted," a television show seen by an estimated 14 million people. Police followed up some 50 viewer tips, but none led to Rasai.

On December 8 a man identified by his papers as Fuat Yildiz tried to enter Istanbul with a woman and child. Immigration officials concluded the papers were fake. Yildiz was deported to Hong Kong. In March 1994 he again tried to enter Turkey. This time he was deported to Germany before Turkish police confirmed he was Rasai, wanted by Interpol.

Having no extradition agreement with Canada, Turkey did not rush to alert the RCMP. It was May before the Mounties were told. By that time Rasai, using aliases, had fled Germany, leaving no trail.

Holly took this latest news hard. Rasai was making a mockery of the justice system. She called Edmonton Liberal MP David Kilgour, who pressed authorities for information. He was told that Rasai's file had now been flagged arrest on sight.

But Holly had almost given up. She had no more energy to fight. It had been almost four years since the rape. Rasai, it seemed, had won.

On September 3, 1994, a flight from Hong Kong touched down in Amsterdam. Among the passengers at passport control was a clean-shaven, slightly overweight man named Fuat Yildiz. "In transit to visit a friend in Germany," he said. The Dutch passport officer entered the name Yildiz into his computer.

The file began flashing. It listed Ali Rasai's crimes and stated he was dangerous. The officer restrained Rasai. When police arrived, Rasai instantly requested political asylum.

When police told Holly of Rasai's arrest, she began shaking. Tears filled her eyes. "I never thought this day would come," she told me.

It took a year before Rasai lost his fight against extradition to Canada. In September 1996—nearly six years after the rape—he finally faced Holly in an Edmonton court. On September 11 a six-woman, six-man jury convicted Rasai of sexually assaulting Holly and two other women. He was sentenced to $4\frac{1}{2}$ years in prison and last June lost his appeal against the sentence.

Those who know Rasai's case attribute his arrest to Holly's fight not to let the file be forgotten. "Holly actually forced institutions to do their jobs," says Scott Newark, executive director of the Canadian Police Association.

Holly's case and others like it also helped change Canada's Immigration Act. Would-be immigrants like Rasai can now be turned away if officials believe they committed a crime outside Canada punishable here by a jail term of ten years or more.

Holly has since started a new life in a new city. Reflecting on her crusade, she says: "Either you're going to live with the pain and deal with it, or you're going to die from it. If I had not fought to see Rasai caught, I would have died inside."

BREAK-IN!

BY TIM BOUQUET

THE POLICE WERE UP AGAINST A WELL-ORGANIZED
GANG. HOW WERE THEY SELECTING THEIR VICTIMS,
AND HOW COULD THEY BE STOPPED?

Laura and Brian Mullin and their 18-month-old daughter Sarah* were looking forward to Christmas as they arrived to join Brian's family in Belfast on December 21, 1996. But next day, good cheer turned to numbing disbelief when a friend telephoned to tell them: "I'm afraid you've been burgled."

Back home in their comfortable 1930s house in an affluent Southampton suburb, they found their world had literally been turned upside down. No room was untouched. The intruders had systematically turned out drawers and cupboards, even emptied the tea caddy, looking for cash. The TV and hi-fi had gone. So had Laura's jewellery, much of it given to her by her grandmother and irreplaceable.

The break-in was one of a string of strikingly similar burglaries of well-appointed houses all over southern Hampshire since October 1996. Most had taken place while the occupants were on holiday. So far the thieves had plundered goods worth around £250,000. In eight cases they had even taken the victims' cars to drive away their haul. They hadn't left a single fingerprint.

Detective Inspector Dean Jones, head of Hampshire police's 30-strong Western Area Crime Unit, based in Southampton, had been called in to hunt down the highly professional gang. But the tough 37-year-old was baffled.

In his 19 years as a policeman, Jones had never come across a series of burglaries with no geographical pattern. Normally they happened in clusters in the same town or district, or strung out along motorways for a quick getaway. This gang seemed to be raiding at random.

Jones set a 12-strong team to study the police reports on all the break-ins, hoping to find a link that had been overlooked. It was like searching for a contact lens on an ice rink.

Then one detective spotted that two of the victims had flown on holiday from Southampton International Airport. "Is that just a coincidence?" Jones wondered aloud to Olan Jenkins, the 26-year-old constable co-ordinating the enquiry.

*An asterisk denotes names have been changed to protect privacy.

"Let's find out how the other victims travelled," Jenkins suggested. He went to see Brian and Laura Mullin. They had flown from Southampton. So had at least six others. And all had flown with the same airline: British Airways.

Olan Jenkins talked to airport director John Bullen and Roger Edge, general manager of Southampton Handling, the company sub-contracted to do BA's reservations, ticketing and checking-in. They were dumbfounded at the suggestion that BA passengers might be targets. "We'll give you every support," Bullen promised as the list of victims grew.

"It seems the same gang may have targeted as many as 30 passengers," Jenkins reported to Jones. All had booked privately, rather than via travel agents or tour operators, which meant they had given their addresses to BA's central reservations.

"There's only one way the gang could have got those addresses," Jenkins added. He asked Roger Edge for details of all staff who had access to passenger addresses.

Among those on the list was Katherine Woodward, an attractive 23-year-old blonde who had worked at Guernsey Airport before moving to the mainland in early 1996. That April, Edge, impressed by her efficient, friendly manner, had given her a job on check-in, processing departing travellers. After two months, she was promoted to the ticketing and reservations desk.

Nothing in Woodward's background suggested anything criminal. But one thing puzzled Jenkins. Her address was 2 Bishops Close, in the Totton district of Southampton—the home of 46-year-old Peter Harrison, a well-known criminal with a record for burglary, and his brash son Gary, 26, who had been released from an 18-month sentence for burglary just days before the break-ins began. How come a middle-class Guernsey girl is living with a couple of thieves? Jenkins mused.

The picture began to make sense when Jenkins found out that Woodward was the illegitimate daughter of Peter Harrison. Adopted as a three-year-old by a Guernsey family, Katherine had traced her father, turning up out of the blue at his house in early 1996.

With her access to thousands of British Airways passenger addresses, she was a serial burglar's dream daughter. All Dean Jones's team had to do now was prove it.

At 5.54pm on February 26 last year, Katherine Woodward, smart in her British Airways uniform, began to work on her computer screen at Southampton Airport, completely unaware that her every move was being tracked.

British Airways had hooked up a "clone" terminal and printer to her computer. Everything on her screen could now be seen simultaneously on a screen in an airport office manned by Dean Jones's team, and whatever she printed would print out in the observation room.

The police also had a security camera permanently trained on Woodward's workstation. And a record of all her computer time was being stored on BA's mainframe at Heathrow.

WPC Sheila Mason watched as Woodward scrolled names down the screen, homing in on passengers booked to fly on the weekend of March 8 and 9. First she picked out multiple bookings, where whole families would be leaving behind empty houses. Then she pulled out all passengers listing an address.

Forty-five minutes later Mason saw her print out a sheet of paper. As she came off shift, Woodward tucked it inside her BA hat, jumped into her white Golf convertible and drove to the Harrison house.

The gang had 11 new targets—and the police 11 chances to catch them in the act. Dean Jones put his officers into all the houses while their owners were away. At 7.30pm on Saturday, March 8, a white Volkswagen Golf drove slowly into a leafy cul-de-sac in Hedge End, an overspill town on the eastern edge of Southampton. Inside one of the target houses, Jones's men watched as two of the car's three occupants got out and counted the houses back from the junction, apparently double-checking for a later visit. Then they noticed the alarm box on the front of the house and drove off.

However, the police saw enough of the Golf's registration plate to run a check. They discovered it belonged to 23-year-old Jade Ifould, who lived in the Hampshire yachting town of Lymington. It was often driven by his closest friend—Gary Harrison.

The gang did not burgle any of the targeted houses that weekend. Dean Jones decided to step up surveillance. Airport security adapted Woodward's voicemail so that police could listen to and tape her calls. On March 12, she phoned her father: "I've got some bits and pieces for you," she said.

The police had established that the gang phoned all targets to confirm that houses really were empty. In the staked-out properties Jones's men left phones unanswered, hoping to prompt a visit. But again there were no break-ins. They seem to be getting very choosy suddenly, fumed Jones, whose team had now worked 28 days without a break.

"It's the tethered goat approach," explained burly 42-year-old Detective Sergeant Ian Bentall, an undercover specialist, handing Dean Jones a sheet of A4. It read like a script. "We'll give them something that is so tempting they can't resist."

Bentall's plan was for the police to rent a house. Then, having booked some tickets, he would visit the BA desk with a flight problem, posing as a rich antiques

Team leader: Detective Inspector Dean Jones.

dealer and making sure Woodward realized he had an unguarded house full of valuables.

"Better get some business cards printed!" smiled Jones.

By Monday, March 24, 1997, all was ready. Bentall had phoned British Airways central reservations and booked two tickets for New-castle upon Tyne, flying April 4. A four-bedroomed semi in Hedge End had become the sting house, its address logged on the BA computer. The police had arranged a new telephone number, removed the alarm box so as not to put the gang off and drawn the curtains to make it look as though the occupants were away.

Now it was down to Bentall.

At 9.15 he walked into the Southampton Airport terminal. He had dressed for the role in an expensive leather jacket, gold watch and cuff links—a touch of flamboyance to convince Woodward that he really was a prosperous antiques dealer.

He went straight up to her at the British Airways desk. "I've got a flight booked for the fourth of April," he began, then scratched his face. Watching via video, WPC Mason knew this was her cue. She rang Bentall's mobile.

"I'm just trying to get them sorted," Bentall replied to his imaginary wife. "Yeah, can you pack everything in a bag? If you put those watches and that bit of jewellery in my briefcase, stick it under the sofa, OK? Get as much upstairs as you can, and I'll give you a hand when I get back. All right, darling ..."

Appearing harassed, Bentall told Woodward that he had booked two return flights to Newcastle, paid for by credit card, but now his father-in-law had died and he and his wife had to fly north that day.

His mobile rang again. "Hello, James," he said, into his stride. "I've regilded one of them, so it looks pretty good. The other one's not going to be ready for a day or two. Look, I've got to dash off to Newcastle today ... I'll be back probably Wednesday night ..."

As Woodward tried to change Bentall's flights, she laughed: "Bet your wife's cursing!"

Bentall smiled. Here was a chance to unload more of the story.

"We've just moved house," he confided. "Closed my business. I've got a house full of junk."

Once more Bentall's mobile rang. "Hello, darling," he said to WPC Mason, "how are you getting on? I've just thought of something. Can you phone old Bill Burrows at the insurers and get some urgent cover for the contents, because we just haven't got time to move it. Can you see if he'll give us a two-day cover for about 180K? Cheers then. Bye."

Woodward handed Bentall new tickets. "No problems doing that," she smiled.

"Oh super," replied the cop. He handed her a business card for Eros Antiques. "If you fancy something special for your boyfriend, mum or dad, just give us a ring and I'll sort you out a deal. All right, love?"

"Thank you," said Woodward. "See you when you come back, then." As the detective walked away, she slipped the card into her bag.

Minutes later she picked up her phone and punched out a number she had rung more than 200 times.

"Eros Antiques?" asked Peter Harrison, puzzled.

"He's just sold a shop and everything is in his house."

"How long's he gone for?"

"Two and a half days," Woodward told him. "He's asked for insurance cover on his mobile phone. Gear worth 250K!" she continued, adding £70,000 to Bentall's valuation.

"Sounds interesting. Bring the address over and let's have a look."

Early on the evening of March 24, eight specially trained officers from the Divisional Support Unit, dressed in black clothes and balaclavas, moved into the sting house.

At 8.15 the phone rang and continued long enough to trace the call to a phone box about three miles away. It had to be the Harrisons. Only they knew the number. The phone rang again at 9.30, at 11.50 and at midnight. The policemen listened and waited. Nobody appeared.

Then at 12.50am on March 25, three constables on the ground floor saw two men standing by the front door. They heard windows and doors being rattled as the men made their way to the back of the house and tried the patio doors.

After 20 minutes the men appeared again at the front door. Just a sheet of glass separated them from arrest. Then they vanished.

It was 8.20 the next evening when PC Wilson, in the garage at Hedge End, heard voices and the sound of feet jumping over the gate into the alley between garage and house.

Peering through the half-glazed side door, he saw two men in hoods, staring back at him. He froze. *If they've seen me, we've had it.*

They tried the door. It did not budge. He breathed out slowly as they slipped round to the back of the house, slid open the patio doors and made their way gingerly through the sitting room into the dining room.

There was an almighty clatter as two policemen jumped them. The burglars hit out violently, kicking and wrestling to escape. Four more officers raced downstairs and forced one to the ground. "Were you expecting us or something?" sneered Jade Ifould as his hood was removed.

The other burglar ran down the garden, but was felled as he scaled the fence. It was Gary Harrison.

At 9.40 Peter Harrison and Katherine Woodward were arrested at their home. Inside, the search team found sophisticated electronic scanning equipment. While Jones's team had been eavesdropping on the Harrisons, the family that burgled together had been tuning in to 14 police radio frequencies all over Hampshire, trying to second-guess their every move.

In the face of overwhelming evidence, the Harrisons pleaded guilty. In January, 1998, Katherine Woodward began a three-year jail sentence for her key role in 22 burglaries. Her half-brother Gary went to prison for six years, her father Peter for four. Jade Ifould was jailed for two years.

"This is just about the worst breach of trust I have ever seen," said Judge Patrick Hooton. The sentiment was echoed by all the victims of the check-in thieves. "We were so shocked that we moved house," says Brian Mullin. "You just don't expect your home to be attacked by someone working for a respectable company."

WHO KILLED
MARGARET
WILSON?

BY IAN CUNNINGHAM

WALKING DOWN A QUIET YORKSHIRE

ROAD SHE WAS MURDERED AT RANDOM

BY A COMPLETE STRANGER.

Margaret Wilson dropped off a newspaper to a nearby housebound relative before returning home to prepare the midday meal for her husband Edwin. Her thoughtfulness and generosity were bywords in the small village of Burton Fleming on the eastern edge of the Yorkshire Wolds— the area where she had spent all her 66 years. She was always ready to go to the shops for the elderly or infirm, or to bake cakes for local events.

After lunch that afternoon of Thursday, February 9, 1995, the Wilson's daughter Heather, 39, dropped in for a chat. When Heather left shortly after 3pm, Margaret decided to accompany her for part of the drive, then walk home.

Farm workers Nigel Houseman, 30, and Martin Hornsey, 27, were in two tractors, ploughing a field near the road. They both noticed Margaret in her grey raincoat walking along the road a few hundred yards away.

As they turned at the end of the field, Hornsey spotted a white or silver Austin Montego estate car parked at the roadside. A man was walking away from it, in the same direction as Margaret Wilson. After a moment, he broke into a run.

Then Nigel Houseman heard Hornsey shout over the CB radio. "It looks like he's chasing Mrs Wilson."

Shocked, Houseman saw the man lunge at Margaret Wilson. She and her attacker disappeared behind the hedge. Moments later the man was running back towards the car.

By the time Houseman and Hornsey reached the spot where they'd last seen Mrs Wilson, the man had driven off at speed. Margaret Wilson was lying face down on the verge. She was already dead. Her throat had been cut from ear to ear.

Detective Chief Inspector Martin Midgley was in the CID room at Bridlington police station when the call came in. "A woman's been attacked in Burton Fleming," a colleague told him. "It looks like a murder." On hearing this, Midgley, thickset with grey, thinning hair, looked even more pensive than usual. Despite being born and bred in the area, he had to get out a map to remind himself where Burton Fleming was.

Midgley, a veteran of more than a dozen murder inquiries in his 28 years with the Humberside force, was aware that most victims knew their killer. But Margaret Wilson had apparently been killed at random by a complete stranger.

The first morning of the investigation brought one breakthrough. An officer saw something glinting on the verge near where the body had been found. A bloodstained knife.

A few hours later Midgley and his colleague Detective Constable Wally Youngman examined the knife at Driffield police station. Only about five inches long, it had a cheap-looking blade and a black plastic handle, embossed with the words "J. Adams, Sheffield, England".

"What do you make of that?" Midgley pointed to a dark stain, rather like a burn, over most of the middle of the blade. Youngman shrugged. Fit and muscular, with a formidable grasp of detail, he had been with Humberside police for almost 16 years, more than half of them in CID. But this was a new one on him. "Could be anything. Maybe forensics will tell us."

Forensic tests established that the blood on the knife was from the same group as Margaret Wilson's. As for the stain, the scientists were as mystified as the detectives. "Get on to J. Adams," Midgley told Detective Constable Nigel Ling. "We need to know who they sell these knives to."

Midgley also wanted to know if Heather's visits to her mother followed a set pattern. "Not really," Heather replied. So the killer could not have known that Margaret would be on the road that day.

"All we really know about the attacker is what sort of car he drives," Midgley remarked to Youngman. It wasn't much; tracing such a popular make would be virtually impossible.

A call to the DVLA confirmed that hundreds of silver and white Montegos were registered to owners within a 30-mile radius of the murder scene. Despite this, Midgley assigned officers to trace as many as possible.

Then a local woman, Elise Cundall, walked into the incident room in the grounds of Burton Fleming's village hall. Early on the afternoon of the murder, she told officers, she had set off to take her dog for his usual walk along the Bridlington road as far as the road sign, then home. She had actually seen Margaret and Heather leaving Margaret's house and had waved to them.

It was on her way back that she had heard a vehicle coming up very slowly behind her. As the car—a light-coloured Montego estate—passed by, the driver looked directly at her.

Black mark: the murder weapon had a strange stain.

"I've never seen anyone look so angry," she said. "Terrible piercing eyes as though they were going to come through the glass. They were horrible." Thankful that she had her dog with her, she had hurried home. *Was this guy cruising around*, Midgley asked himself, *looking for someone to kill?*

Another woman seemed to confirm precisely that. Around lunchtime on the same day, she told police, she'd looked out of her front-room window and seen a white Montego estate car drive slowly past several times.

"Let's not get too excited," Midgley told his colleagues. "The guy may be a completely innocent motorist. But somehow we've got to find this vehicle."

At the J. Adams factory in Sheffield, Detective Constable Nigel Ling showed the owner Jack Adams a photograph of the murder weapon. "We've made thousands of these over the years," said Adams. "They're mainly used in the vegetable-processing industry—cutting potatoes and so on."

"Who do you sell them to?"

"Warehouses, factories—they're not on sale to the general public."

Ling took away a list of Adams's main customers. There were hundreds of names. This investigation was going to be a long, hard slog.

The killer, the team agreed, must have a strong connection with the area. "Burton Fleming isn't on the way to anywhere—people don't just pass through it," said Midgley.

On March 16, 1995, five weeks after the murder, the case was featured on BBC TV's *Crimewatch* programme. The moment it ended, lights on the incident-room phones began flashing. Over the next three hours, 1,500 calls came in—*Crimewatch*'s biggest-ever response to a single item.

It would take months to check out all the leads. One call, however, promised to make Midgley's task easier. "My name's Alan Wirth," the voice said. "I'm a forensic specialist in metals at Sheffield Hallam University. I'd be happy to help you find out what that stain on the knife is." He would analyse the blade using the university's electron microscope.

Crimewatch yielded another, more unexpected result. The woman who had seen the Montego from her window, came to see the police again. "I watched the programme the other night," the woman told Midgley, by now exhausted from weeks of 15-hour days. "It must have been on my mind because that night in a dream I got the number of the car."

Fighting incredulity, Midgley took down the number. The police computer revealed that it belonged to a white Montego estate car—and the owner had previous convictions for violence.

The man freely admitted to owning the car. But on the day of the murder, he and a friend had been in Leeds, 60 miles away from Burton Fleming, doing building work on a house. The friend confirmed it, as did the owner of the house.

Midgley and Youngman made another visit to the woman who had given them the registration number. She had a confession for them: "I didn't have a dream. But I did see that car when me and my husband were on the Leeds ring road a few weekends ago. I told my husband, 'That looks like the man I saw.'"

For the life of him, Midgley couldn't understand why the woman had come up with the story about the dream. He was reluctant to dismiss her as a crank: she had, after all, seen the car in the first place, and the man did have a violent record. Yet his alibi seemed unshakeable. It just didn't add up.

But other developments were demanding his attention. Dr Wirth had identified the black stain. "The knife's recently been used to cut raw potatoes," Midgley was told.

Midgley's mind raced. One of the customers on Adams's list was McCain, makers of frozen oven chips. Their Scarborough factory was little more than ten miles from Burton Fleming.

Company records showed that the knife used to kill Mrs Wilson was one of a batch delivered to McCain within the last three years. Visiting the plant, Midgley and Youngman were taken aback to see so many of the knives in evidence that even a casual visitor could have taken one.

The police began interviewing the 900-strong McCain workforce, together with former employees from the last three years, to find out who had a light-coloured Montego and wasn't at work on the afternoon of the murder. One of the first to be interviewed was a 32-year-old man with long, dark hair. His name was Derek Christian.

Happier times: Margaret loved and cared for all her friends and family.

The murder squad had met Christian before. Right at the beginning of the inquiry, a car dealer had told officers that, for what it was worth, he had recently sold a silver Austin Montego estate car to one Derek Christian.

After finishing his shift at 3pm on the day of the murder, Christian had told police, he had driven straight back to his house in Driffield, arriving at 3.50. While he had no alibi, there was nothing, apart from owning a silver Montego, to make him a suspect, either. A check was made to see if Christian had a criminal record. Nothing.

But Midgley was intrigued. "He's cropped up with the car. Now he's cropped up with McCain. We need to find out all we can about him."

In the seven months since he'd given his statement, Christian had left the Driffield home he had shared with his wife and three young sons, and moved back to his parents' home in Bridlington. He appeared to lead an exceedingly dull life. He would leave for McCain at six every morning and set off home at three. He seldom went out; had no close friends; didn't visit pubs. His only real interest was in Sheffield Wednesday Football Club. He was a fanatical supporter.

Before starting work at McCain just two months before the murder, Christian had been a professional soldier, spending most of his service as a storeman. He was no seasoned killer—but no angel, either.

With the help of the Military Police Special Investigations Branch, Midgley discovered that a series of unpleasant assaults against women had punctuated his army career, earning him two spells in military detention. Yet on his discharge late in 1994, the army inexplicably described his conduct as "exemplary".

His 14-year marriage, already threatened by his frequent philandering and his failure to send money home when posted overseas, was soon in tatters. But he remained friendly with his wife's parents George and Jean Green, and was a devoted father to his three sons.

Surveillance revealed that Christian's route home from Scarborough was unvarying—and passed the end of the narrow country road that leads to Burton Fleming. Timing the route, police found that it would have been perfectly possible for Christian to have left work at 3pm, committed the murder and arrived home, as he said, at 3.50.

In March 1996, 13 months after the murder, Midgley brought Derek Christian in for questioning. The sweatshirt, jogging bottoms and fleecy jacket Christian had said he was wearing on the day of the murder were taken for analysis.

The police also found a copy of the *Hull Daily Mail*, printed two days before the anniversary of the murder, February 9, 1996, and open at the headline: "Who is hiding killer?" It was the only *Hull Daily Mail* found in the house.

Under questioning, Christian remained calm and consistent. He had not murdered Margaret Wilson. He had driven straight home from work. He had never even been to Burton Fleming.

Youngman placed the murder weapon, wrapped in plastic, on the table. "This is the knife that was used to kill Margaret Wilson. Have you seen one of these knives before?"

"No, I've never seen a knife like that before."

"You work at McCain, don't you?"

"Yeah, I work at McCain."

"And you use a knife in the course of your work."

"No."

"But all your colleagues say you need one to do your job."

"I don't use one."

"Derek," said Youngman patiently. "We've been to McCain. These knives are all over the place. We know you've seen them."

"I've never seen one of those knives before in my life."

And what of the *Hull Daily Mail*? The newspaper contained details of massage parlours, Christian explained; he'd kept it because he fancied working in one. "As you do," remarked Youngman sourly when he reported back to Midgley.

With no hard evidence against him, Midgley had to release Christian. But a few days later he had something else to tell the police.

In the interview room, Youngman asked briskly: "Right, Mr Christian, what would you like to say?"

In his rambling reply, Christian said that on the day of the murder he had not gone straight home, as he'd stated, but had visited his in-laws, the Greens, at their Scarborough home. He had loaded some linoleum and boxes into his car and they had all driven to the Greens' new home in Driffield.

Youngman and Midgley were instantly suspicious. Why had he changed his story? Christian shrugged. He'd simply confused the dates.

His in-laws backed up his story completely. They were palpably honest people, not the sort who would be prepared to give someone a false alibi. But as Midgley and Youngman cross-checked their statements, they realized the Greens' memory for dates was not infallible.

Jean Green had said that during the drive to Driffield on February 9, they had passed a serious road accident on the edge of Scarborough. Police checks showed that there had indeed been an accident—but not until March 10. Were the Greens confusing different journeys to their new home?

One detail in the Greens' statements caught Midgley's eye. George Green had said that on the afternoon of February 9, he had rung his son-in-law at McCain, asking him to come and collect the lino after his shift.

"We just need to get an itemized phone bill from BT," Midgley told Youngman. "If there wasn't a call to McCain that afternoon, bang goes his alibi." But, to Midgley's gloom, BT reported that the itemized bill for February 9, 1995, had gone missing.

Meanwhile, the forensic laboratory concentrated on analysing clothing fibres. By October 1996, it had some electrifying news. Fibres matching those from Christian's sweatshirt, jacket and jogging bottoms had been found on Margaret Wilson's clothing. In addition, a sharp-eyed member of the team had found a single fibre from Mrs Wilson's skirt on Christian's jogging bottoms. All told, forensics had matched 78 fibres—an astonishing number when a dozen matches is considered exceptional.

"But it's not enough to go to court with," Midgley said to Youngman. "The defence will just say: 'Yes, our client wears a fleecy jacket, sweatshirt and jogging bottoms. Thousands of people do. You haven't proved they came from our client.'

"We need to find out who makes these garments and check the fibres. If we can't find any that match Christian's, then we can go into court and say: 'Only Derek Christian could have been in contact with Margaret Wilson.' But it's going to be a long job."

The first task was to ensure that none of the 78 fibres found on Margaret Wilson had got there through "innocent contamination"—contact with someone at home, in a shop. Midgley ordered his team to trace every single person who had been in contact with her during the last two weeks of her life. Fortunately, Mrs Wilson had limited contacts. Fibres from garments they had been wearing were cross-checked. Nothing.

Officers turned their attention to the fibres found on Margaret Wilson's body. Over the next few months, Detective Constable Nigel Ling became a walking authority on fleecy jackets. Two ostensibly identical jackets from the same manufacturer could look totally different under a microscope if they were made in different batches, from different fibres.

Ling eventually traced almost every manufacturer of fleecy jackets sold in the UK. Then he eliminated all but one batch. The rest of the inquiry team concentrated on Christian's green sweatshirt, with its Carlsberg logo. Christian admitted to being given it at an army social evening in Germany. Travelling to the Carlsberg brewery in Denmark, Midgley and Youngman found that its computer system still held details of how many shirts had been dispatched and where.

A visit to the Portuguese manufacturer revealed that, as with the jacket, the fibres differed from batch to batch. The chances of anyone other than Christian wearing a German-batch Carlsberg sweatshirt and coming into contact with Margaret Wilson within a day of the murder were satisfyingly remote. The jogging bottoms yielded similar results.

In November 1996, Christian was arrested for the second time. He remained completely unruffled as Youngman set out the evidence against him: the car, the knife, the fibres. "Everything points to you. You killed Margaret Wilson."

Christian's reply was scornful. "I don't think so."

He was charged anyway.

One evening in October 1997, a couple of weeks before Derek Christian's trial was due to start, Youngman was talking to a BT worker on a separate inquiry. "By the way," Youngman said, "there's something else you might be able to help us with." He described Midgley's frustration over the missing phone bill. The man agreed to have one more look.

He rang the next day. "I've found it. Would you like me to fax it over?"

The evidence on the fax was damning. There had been no phone call to McCain on February 9. Instead, just after 4pm, a call had been made to a furniture shop in Scarborough. The Greens confirmed that they had made that call—so they couldn't have been travelling to Driffield that afternoon. Christian's alibi was dead in the water.

The trial began at Leeds Crown Court. Midgley continued to fret. The evidence, though overwhelming, was basically circumstantial. Midgley's cautious approach had become legendary over the last 30-odd months. A notice appeared in the incident room under the heading "Night Classes Available", with a list of officers and the subject they were teaching. Next to Midgley's name were the words: "Lectures in pessimism".

As it happened, the case had one more surprise to throw up. The woman who had seen the white Montego from her front-room window was called as a defence witness. Her testimony strengthened Christian's cause, reminding the court that on the afternoon of the murder another Austin Montego was in Burton Fleming.

However, after the woman's appearance on the witness stand, her husband phoned police with a bizarre story to tell. As he had been driving his wife home from the court, she had burst into tears. What she had told had been a pack of lies. She had seen no Montego that day. The car she had described had been one she'd simply happened to have seen on the Leeds ring road. She had intended merely to help the police, never dreaming she would end up repeating the story in court.

Prime suspect: factory worker Derek Christian.

The next day in court, the woman formally retracted her earlier story. On December 2, 1997, the jury unanimously convicted Derek Christian of murder. He was jailed for life.

One burning question remained: Why? Psychologists concluded that Derek Christian showed no signs of mental illness. And colleagues reported that he seemed perfectly normal on the day of the murder. "Maybe his obsession with Sheffield Wednesday triggered it off," Youngman suggests. "The night before the murder, they lost to Wolverhampton Wanderers in a vital FA Cup tie."

Martin Midgley laughs good-naturedly at this. "I can't go along with that, but so many questions remain unanswered."

Only Derek Christian has the answers. But for as long as he remains silent, he is unlikely to be considered for parole.

TO CATCH A
MAFIA
HITMAN

BY CHRISTOPHER MATTHEWS

THEY CALLED HIM THE PIG.
AND EVERY POLICEMAN IN ITALY
WANTED TO COLLAR HIM.

When the phone rang on Matteo De Santis's desk, the dark-haired, 28-year-old cop listened briefly, then walked briskly towards his boss's office in a concrete and bulletproof-glass building in southern Rome. Rino Monaco, newly-arrived head of Italy's elite Servizio Centrale Operativo (SCO), wanted to see him at once.

"I'm putting together a team for a top-priority mission in Sicily," Monaco explained on that October morning in 1994. How would you feel about going back?"

De Santis was surprised. He'd only just returned from months on the island, where he had helped track down a top Mafia boss.

"What's the job?" De Santis asked in reply.

"Giovanni Brusca," Monaco said. "Find him and bring him in."

De Santis's eyes widened. Everyone in Italy knew who Brusca was. And every Italian cop had him on his personal most-wanted list.

Nicknamed "U Verru"—The Pig—for his appalling manners, Giovanni Brusca was rumored to have killed 50 people, including the powerful businessman Ignazio Salvo. Brusca had shot away all of Salvo's face, except for one eye, testament to Brusca's sadistic streak, and to his skill with handweapons.

Brusca was one of the 475 Mafiosi who had been targeted by investigating judge Giovanni Falcone, and swept up into the so-called "Maxi-trial". But Brusca was freed on a technicality when the statutory two-year maximum period for which an Italian citizen may be jailed prior to sentencing had run out. By the time the sentence was issued Brusca had disappeared.

He would retaliate against the magistrates who tried to send him to prison. On the afternoon of May 23, 1992, as Falcone drove from Palermo Airport in a convoy of three armour-plated cars, several hundred kilos of high explosive concealed below the road suddenly went off.

The blast did more than kill Falcone, his wife and three of his bodyguards. Demonstrating that no one lay beyond the Mafia's power, the assassination stunned and humiliated every lawman in the country. And it was Brusca's pudgy finger, a snitch later told police, that had pushed the remote control button.

Nor was this the end of Brusca's vengeance. In 1993, he ordered the kidnapping of Giuseppe di Matteo, the 11-year-old son of a member of the Falcone hit squad who had turned informer. For over a year, Brusca kept the boy prisoner, allegedly torturing him and sending harrowing video cassettes to his grandfather to force a retraction. But it was too late for that. Finally, an enraged Brusca had the boy murdered.

As the trackers began their hunt, they took solace in one fact. An ordinary fugitive might leave Italy. But a big-time Mafioso's diversified business interests—which might be anything from extortion and usury, through drugs trafficking and money-laundering to rakeoffs on lush government contracts—meant he had to stay and "run the shop". Only in Sicily could he rely on mob protection. But the huge network was also an Achilles' heel.

San Giuseppe Jato, a grim hill village 30km southwest of Palermo and the Brusca family's "fief" for generations, was the logical place to begin. But, as he began the search, De Santis knew this could be no normal surveillance. Local traffic amounted to maybe a car every ten minutes, and the presence of a stranger would be immediately detected. Instead, unmarked vehicles—usually post-office trucks or delivery vans—would comb the area no more than four times a day. The most De Santis could hope for was a glimpse of a Brusca associate during a quick drive-by. To prevent the slightest suspicion, a different vehicle would be needed for each drive-by.

Soon after the surveillance was established, in June, 1995, local Mafiosi in a town just east of Palermo were observed taking elaborate security precautions. While walking they kept looking over their shoulders or checked their reflections in shop windows. While driving, they did repeated stops-and-go, or abrupt, tyre-screeching U-turns.

De Santis put surveillance teams in the town. He also hid a couple of prowl cars off the winding main road, just outside of the town. They were parked 300 metres apart.

On an early afternoon at the end of June De Santis was in the stakeout vehicle when an Alfa Romeo carrying two passengers drove cautiously towards him. Scouts, he thought. They would be looking for hazards, such as a police roadblock. He let it through.

Next, a small, red Lancia came into view. De Santis's heart was racing. Maybe the VIP himself. Once this car passed, they would have it boxed in.

Suddenly the Lancia did a high speed U-turn and roared off into the hills. Somehow, the driver must have smelt the trap.

As the car raced away, De Santis noticed a thick-set, bearded figure in the passenger seat. He thought it could have been The Pig himself. They were back to square one.

The following month two of Brusca's henchmen were noticed meeting at the curious hour of 6am. A couple of cops followed them out of town and watched them head down a country lane, but then had to stop. There was no cover, and to have trailed them any further was out of the question.

De Santis returned to the spot. The lane forked out into a bewildering maze of tracks, none of which appeared to lead anywhere in particular. If Brusca was indeed hiding out in the hills, he would be untraceable.

Summer turned to autumn, autumn to winter. Since entering the police academy at 18, De Santis had never known a single operation to go on for as long as this. *Be patient.*

Brusca, he knew, would be spending time with his girlfriend, Rosaria Cristiano, a good-looking brunette who had given Brusca a son, Davide, now four years old. In the meantime, De Santis had to sleep in a police barracks bed, separated from his wife and child in Rome. *Be patient.*

He got an unexpected break. A high-ranking Mafioso co-operated with the police and during his interrogation revealed that Brusca had moved into a new house in a Palermo suburb.

On January 12, 1996, De Santis, together with 150 police and a couple of helicopters, surrounded the dwelling. They battered down the freshly-painted front door. But The Pig was no longer there.

De Santis knelt down and picked up some newspapers scattered in the living room. They were dated some days earlier. "We missed them by a couple of days," he exclaimed, letting the papers fall to the floor. He could have wept.

But De Santis's months of patient work had not been in vain. Brusca had been rumbled from his lair and now he'd started to run. With all his cunning, he must soon start making mistakes. De Santis had flushed him out—and now the specialist Mafia hunters moved in for the kill.

At the Squadra Mobile (SWAT team) headquarters in downtown Palermo, Lorenzo Gentile, a tough 31-year-old with

On the run: Giovanni Brusca.

57

a handsome profile and a buccaneer's black beard was poring over the latest police report sheets. He was number two at the Mobile's elite Catturandi section, whose job was to track down and bring in wanted felons.

The Pig is cunning, Gentile thought, chewing on the end of an evil-looking, unlit Tuscan cigar. *But he's dependent on a lot of people. And that's where he's vulnerable. If we keep an eye on the little fish, with luck they will lead us to the big one.*

A breakthrough came a few months later when Palermo police arrested Salvatore Cucuzza, an old-style Mafioso who wouldn't talk. But his phone book did.

"How about this?" Gentile pointed to an entry in the I-J section that started with IGN.

Chances were that Cucuzza would know Brusca's alleged chief lieutenant, Ignazio Traina.

The number was in code, but the department's science lab eventually broke it. The number, they learned, had been disconnected within hours of Cucuzza's arrest.

But Italy's phone company keeps a record of all calls made to and from a cell-phone. They could still find out whom Traina had been talking to. The printout ran to several pages and hundreds of numbers. Gentile and his team started checking them, one by one.

The numbers corresponded to big and small-time Mafiosi, but one digital cell-phone number belonged to an 82-year-old peasant woman in the middle of Sicily who could barely read or write. "I'll get a tap on the number right away," Gentile said.

The team gathered in Gentile's office to listen in. The first call, relayed on a loudspeaker on Gentile's desk, appeared to be about a big public works contract. But the elderly woman had a deep and unmistakably male voice.

"I know that accent," a young detective exclaimed. "It's from San Giuseppe Jato." Someone remembered they had Brusca's voice on tape from the Maxi-trial days. It matched the old woman's.

Gentile sent out for spumante and cookies. "We've got The Pig!" he exclaimed, exultant.

But locating a digital phone signal is extremely complex, and it took several days before the Science squad brought them the good news—and the bad. They'd traced Brusca's calls to Cannatello—a resort town on Sicily's southern coast. But the exact location lay somewhere inside a one-kilometre square—an area roughly twice the size of the Vatican state.

Gentile picked his ten best men—professional chameleons who could stay invisible, and immobile, for hours. Under cover of darkness they assumed concealed positions in gardens, orchards and vegetable patches in Cannatello. All were equipped with night glasses, cellphones and infra-red cameras that took pictures even in pitch dark. Any villa where the light was on was considered a target.

There was no question of moving by day. Meals were a sandwich and a can of soft-drink thrown by Gentile from the window of an unmarked police car as he drove past.

Meanwhile, Gentile and his team monitored Brusca's phone calls night and day, catnapping at their desks, hoping that The Pig would betray his location. A week went by.

On Sunday, May 19, one of the watchers phoned in shortly after 11am. "There's a kid playing in the front garden of Via Papillon 34," he noted. At 7pm he called again. A bulky, bearded figure was outlined against a ground-floor window. It looked like The Pig.

The team held an emergency meeting.

"I think there could be a way," Gentile said, outlining his plan. The team would get ready to pounce and wait for Brusca to make a call. Then a powerful motorcycle would cruise past No. 34. If Brusca's phone picked up the noise of the engine, they'd know.

They had to be certain before making a move: a police raid on the wrong house would scare the real quarry away.

At 4pm on Monday, May 20, two unmarked vans came to a halt in the street parallel to Via Papillon. Concealed in each van were 15 policemen in full battle gear. Gentile led one of the squads, the second contained the top brass. Not far from them in a third van was De Santis. Further away, a force of 200 were ready to seal off the area the moment the operation began.

"Testing, testing . . ." Gentile adjusted the dials on the radio transceiver linking him to the other vans and to Palermo HQ.

"Reading you loud and clear," came the reply. Gentile then checked the device monitoring Brusca's cellphone.

Six pm. Brusca's line was silent. In the steambath of the third van, De Santis's shirt was soaked through. "Go on," he urged Brusca, "pick up that phone."

Seven pm. For the umpteenth time, Gentile checked his police-issue Beretta. He'd never had to fire his gun in anger. Now he prayed that tonight would be no different.

Eight pm. Still nothing. Could something have gone wrong, De Santis wondered.

Silently Gentile cursed The Pig and all Mafiosi. "Go on, pick up the damn phone."

9.15 pm. The monitor in front of Gentile came to life. The Pig was on the line at last. Gentile spoke urgently into his own handset. "Go with the bike!"

A police patrolman in civilian clothes pressed the starter on his big Japanese motorcycle and began moving towards the target house.

Brusca kept talking while a television blared in the background. *Don't hang up!* Gentile silently implored.

The bike was now 20 metres from the house. Ten metres ... five ... Theatrically, the patrolman gunned his engine. To make extra sure the bike was heard, they'd drilled a big hole in the exhaust pipe.

"Yeah, be seeing you." Brusca's last words were almost drowned out by the scream of an engine. "Let's do it," Gentile shouted into his microphone.

One team took the front door, Gentile smashed the ground-floor window on the left and another squad burst in through a window on the opposite side of the house. In a cascade of splintering glass and wood, 45 men, armed to the teeth and wearing black hoods over their faces, came storming into Brusca's living room.

The Pig was lounging in an armchair surrounded by Rosaria, Davide, Brusca's brother Vincenzo and his family, and another couple. Momentarily, they were startled. The only sound was that of the television which had covered the cops' approach. Then Brusca bolted for the back, simultaneously flinging his cellphone at the wall.

Beretta drawn, Gentile reached him in a few steps. Within seconds a dozen cops were upon him. With a muffled grunt The Pig dropped to the ground.

The women were screaming and the children crying, and with all that racket going on, Gentile went over to the TV and turned down the volume. His eyes narrowed to see what movie they had been watching. The irony of it! he reflected. The film was "Giovanni Falcone"—the story of the magistrate whom Brusca had killed. *The End*, Gentile thought as he flicked the set off.

Hunted down: anti-Mafia police, wearing masks to protect their identity, escort Brusca from Palermo's police headquarters to spend a life in jail.

HUNT
FOR THE
HOODED
RAPIST

BY DAVID MOLLER

HE HAD VICIOUSLY ATTACKED SEVERAL WOMEN;

THE POLICE FEARED HE MIGHT KILL.

COULD THEY STOP HIM IN TIME?

Detective Superintendent Duncan MacRae usually investigated murders. But on August 9, 1994, he was called in, as a member of an elite Metropolitan Police squad of senior detectives, on a series of other crimes—among the most puzzling and horrific known to Scotland Yard.

In the incident room at Harlesden police station in north-west London, the lean 49-year-old with wiry grey hair and soft Highland accent was briefed about a ten-month spate of violent late-night rapes and robberies of lone women. More than half had taken place within a mile of Willesden Green underground station.

Evidence suggested that some dozen assaults might be linked to the same man. But there was little to point to the actual offender. No victim had got a good look at her attacker's face.

Most had been grabbed in the dark by someone who approached silently from behind. Suddenly a large, gloved hand covered their mouth and throat, so they could barely breathe, let alone scream. Within seconds, they were pulled backwards into a car or a nearby garden.

Those who glimpsed the rapist could give only a sketchy description of a man in his late twenties, black, of muscular build, with a London accent. Estimates of his height varied from five foot eight inches to six foot. He wore dark clothing, including a tracksuit top with its hood drawn up tight, revealing just a patch of face.

Sometimes there was a stocking mask beneath the hood.

More than one victim had noted all or part of the registration number on the attacker's vehicle, but the car—when eventually recovered —always turned out to be stolen. *No chance of tracing the rapist that way*, concluded MacRae.

DNA tests on semen taken from three of the victims showed those assaults had been carried out by the same man. "But DNA will only help us if we pick up someone who provides an identical DNA sample," MacRae told his dozen-strong team. "So for the moment, we'll put all the DNA evidence aside, go back to the start, and research every last detail about the attacks."

A priority was to re-interview all the victims. Two women detectives, Louise Cherrington and Jeanette McDiarmid, were given that task. Louise Cherrington, 32 and married to a police officer, had acted as "chaperone" to nearly a hundred rape victims, comforting them, rebuilding their confidence and coaxing out of them evidence that could be used in court. Even so, she was stunned by these cases.

Two of the most vicious attacks took place in the six days before MacRae's team was set up. On August 3, 1994, a 25-year-old Asian woman had got off a night bus at Neasden Circle and was walking home when a car came past her, made a U-turn and stopped. A hooded figure got out and dragged her towards the car.

"Get in," he commanded. Thrown on to the back seat, she felt searing pain in her legs as the door was slammed on them. The man slammed it again, but she refused to draw in her legs. As he came angrily round the side of the door, she kicked him in the chest. He staggered back and she stumbled away, her legs bruised and bleeding.

She told police his dark tracksuit top had a red band round its middle. She also identified his car as a red Rover Vitesse, with G851 as the first part of its registration number.

Three nights later, the attacker struck again. As a 25-year-old New Zealand secretary was walking alongside a hedge at 3am, she was punched in the face. She regained consciousness to find herself, bleeding heavily from the mouth, in the back of a moving car.

She scrabbled for the door handle. "Don't bother," the driver said. "All the doors are locked."

The car was driven into a narrow garage. Grabbing her long hair with one hand, her attacker tore impatiently at her clothing.

Minutes later, he reversed out of the garage at speed, drove a short distance and stopped the car. "Get out!" he ordered. "Don't look back." He roared off into the night. The distraught young woman stumbled the short distance to her flat. Her flatmates called the police.

For hours, Louise Cherrington sat with her. The woman described a car that was probably the red Rover Vitesse used three days earlier. It had grey upholstery, and an extra layer of carpet matting in the back.

MacRae's team began contacting the registered owners of some 580 vehicles with the prefix G851 in London and the Home Counties. The police national computer listed 15 stolen cars with the same prefix. But none was a red Vitesse.

MacRae suspected that the car had been stolen and false-plated: given the same registration number as another vehicle of identical model and colour. Only in the unlikely event of both vehicles being stolen would it show on the computer as having gone missing.

"Get a message on the computer for us to be alerted if any vehicle with the same part registration number is found abandoned," MacRae instructed his team. A month later, they learned that a red Rover Vitesse, G851 WPM, had been recovered in north London. It had been stolen and false-plated—and it had grey upholstery and an extra strip of carpet in the rear.

There were no fingerprints on it, but on the back seat police scientists found strands of the New Zealand woman's hair, blood from her face wounds and traces of her attacker's semen. This matched DNA samples taken from earlier victims.

From other victims, Louise Cherrington had picked up more useful information. A year after her ordeal, the first victim was still obsessed by the rapist's sweet, sickly-smelling hair lotion. She had taken to smelling lotions in chemist shops and markets, until she identified the exact one.

She also recalled the precise route the rapist had taken her from Cricklewood Broadway after pretending to be a minicab driver. It intrigued MacRae. The rapist had cut across Willesden Lane, then down Brondesbury Park and Salusbury Road, past Kilburn police station. *He has got to be a local man*, MacRae told himself. *Someone who knows the area well.*

The police national computer provided a list of all sex offenders known to live in the area: about 120, excluding those in prison at the time of the rapes. Interviewing them would be a mammoth task.

As MacRae pored over the reports, he could see no pattern that might give a lead to the rapist's identity. The times of the attacks ranged from 11pm to 4.30am, on varying days of the week. The victims were of virtually all racial backgrounds and aged from 19 to 47. They had been attacked both in streets of detached private houses and among the terraced housing of bed-sitter land.

In early September, MacRae decided on a surveillance operation in the hope of catching the rapist on the point of attack. Officers set up observation points in houses and shops near Willesden Green underground station. Linked by radio to

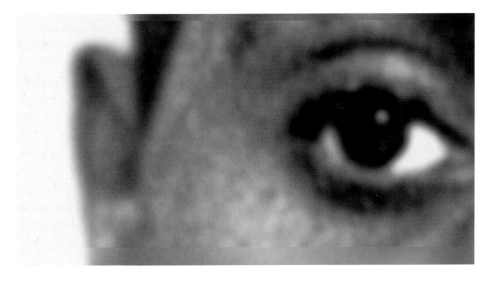

plain-clothes colleagues patrolling on foot or in unmarked cars, the observers could quickly direct attention to anyone taking an interest in a lone female. MacRae also put plain-clothes women officers on to the streets as decoys.

Night after night, the officers trudged the streets, stood at bus stops and telephone boxes, lingered at estate agents' windows. But the rapist made no move.

Until 5.30am on September 18. Sixteen-year-old Sandra Evans* was walking home from a party when a hooded man dragged her down an alleyway and raped her. "Don't look back at me," he ordered and melted away into the night.

MacRae intensified the surveillance: it now involved some 18 officers and six unmarked cars. But on September 29 the rapist struck again, slightly outside his normal area.

Mary Richards*, 17, had boarded a night bus in Finchley Road. She got off in Whetstone, north London, and was walking past a churchyard when a hand came over her face. "Don't scream. Don't make a sound," a voice murmured. She was pulled into the churchyard and raped.

Three days later came another attack, back in the area of the previous assaults. Alice Stevens*, a 22-year-old student, had gone for an early-morning walk. At 6.45am a hooded, masked figure grabbed her from behind and dragged her to the side of a house.

"If we don't get this man soon," warned Detective Sergeant Mick Freeman, MacRae's second-in-command, "he's going to kill someone."

At 3.45am on October 24, Freeman heard on his police car radio: "A green Rover, four-door, 800 series, registration number Golf eight four nine Whisky Papa Bravo, appears to be paying attention to the night bus on Cricklewood Broadway."

Moments later, the Rover did a U-turn and headed south towards central London. But 20 minutes later, it was spotted coming north again, behind another night bus making its way up the Edgware Road. When the bus stopped for passengers, the car would also halt, at a discreet distance. Two unmarked cars were now tailing it.

Suddenly, the Rover roared off at speed, but was soon seen parked by Willesden Green underground station. One unmarked police car parked behind it, the other went to pull up in front.

In the front car, Detective Constable Stephen Ward turned to look at the Rover's driver: a man of muscular build, with a pencil moustache. But before his car could block the way, the Rover shot off again. Heading north, it lost its pursuers.

Minutes later, another voice came over Mick Freeman's car radio. "Have sighted the Rover at Staples Corner ... He's veering on to the North Circular

*An asterisk denotes names that have been changed to protect privacy.

Road, travelling east ... He's approaching the junction with Golders Green Road ... The lights are red against him ... He's straight across ... Estimated speed 115mph."

Jumping another set of red lights, the car was lost, spotted by another patrol car, then lost again. Twenty minutes later, Freeman heard it had been found abandoned in Woodlands Avenue, N3. "No sign of the driver." He sped to the quiet residential street and organized road blocks.

Four dogs and their handlers set off through nearby gardens, without success. Freeman scrambled a helicopter, but it detected nothing. Whatever trail there had been was now lost.

The green Rover, it turned out, had been stolen and false-plated. At least there was Ward's sighting of the driver. *Now we've got a face*, thought MacRae, *maybe we can get a name.* The first stop was Golders Green police station, the one nearest to where the car had been abandoned, since the driver might live locally.

Two days later, Ward was leafing through one of its hefty volumes of photographs of local villains. "That's him," he exclaimed suddenly. "That's the driver." Victor Sylvester Willoughby.

With a name, police could obtain hard information on their suspect. MacRae could at last feel pieces of the jigsaw fall into place.

Thirty-year-old Willoughby had been repeatedly in trouble with the law from the age of 14, for burglary, theft and assault. In 1987, he had ambushed a young woman as she walked along the North Circular Road in Golders Green, and dragged her to a park. Spotted by two police officers, he had been arrested after a chase. He had spent five years in prison for attempted rape.

In March 1993, Willoughby was sentenced to 12 months for stabbing a man. He had been released in August 1993—two months before the first Willesden Green attacks. His last known address was in Lordship Lane, in Tottenham, north London.

MacRae's team learned that Tottenham detectives were well aware of Willoughby, but only as a thief who stole high-performance cars to order. Ostensibly keeping his various criminal activities separate—stealing cars in one part of London but attacking women in other areas, well away from where he lived—had helped him to evade capture.

A few days later in west London, Willoughby was picked up in a stolen car. MacRae's team immediately moved in to search the flat the man shared with his common-law wife and their two-year-old daughter.

In a cupboard, they found a tracksuit with a red band round its middle. In the bathroom was the hair lotion—Pink Oil—identified by one victim.

Since Willoughby refused to provide blood for a DNA check, the police exercised their right to take a hair and its root. Its DNA profile matched exactly the samples taken from eight of the rape victims.

At his Old Bailey trial in December 1995 Willoughby, a dapper figure in a grey double-breasted suit, admitted he was a car thief but said he didn't go around attacking women. The DNA wasn't his. Maybe the scientists had a problem.

The jury disagreed. They unanimously found Willoughby guilty of 17 charges of rape, buggery, indecent assault, false imprisonment, attempted false imprisonment, robbery, attempted robbery and dangerous driving. Given five concurrent life sentences, he will not be considered for parole until 2009 at the earliest.

For the Metropolitan Police it was a landmark case: never before had so many DNA samples been linked to one defendant in a UK criminal trial. For most of Willoughby's victims, who had suffered nightmares, periods of amnesia and a dread of going out alone, his conviction brought the beginning of the healing process.

With the aid of new technology, such crimes may be detected earlier. Now all Metropolitan Police divisions are linked to CRIS, an automated Crime Report Information System with 2,300 computer terminals in 270 police buildings.

At the touch of a few keys, detectives can find out about investigations into possibly related crimes in other parts of London, learn about criminals stealing similar types of car or using identical weapons, and ask for immediate help on specific clues.

Just as valuable is Britain's first DNA database, set up in Birmingham in April 1995. Since September 1995, police have been allowed to take samples from anyone charged with a recordable offence. Eventually the database will hold DNA profiles of virtually every convicted criminal. Rapists like Willoughby, with previous convictions of any type, could be picked up soon after their first assault.

But for MacRae, technology isn't everything. "DNA was certainly crucial in the conviction of this man," he says. "But getting him into court was the result of good, solid, old-fashioned detective work."

Willoughby: in trouble with the law from the age of 14.

DIRTY
DIAMONDS

BY DAVID KAPLAN & CHRISTIAN CARYL

COULD AN FBI AGENT AND A MOSCOW POLICEMAN
STOP THE AUDACIOUS SCHEME TO STEAL MILLIONS
IN PRECIOUS STONES?

"Can you take a look at this?" asked Joe Davidson's supervisor at the FBI, handing him a file. A year earlier, in late 1993, an informant had tipped the FBI that some Russian immigrants were throwing huge sums of cash around San Francisco.

The men, Davidson read, were diamond merchants who had opened a state-of-the-art diamond center called Golden ADA. Curiously, they had even attempted to give the police a gift—a Russian helicopter.

A veteran FBI agent, Davidson, 39, could see something wasn't right. First, San Francisco had never been much of a diamond center. Second, two of the three ADA owners had been painting sidewalk curbs just two years before. Davidson walked into his boss's office. "I want this case," he said.

BRIGHT BEGINNINGS

A Kamov Ka-32 helicopter was hardly the kind of aircraft one expected to see landing in downtown San Francisco. Yet here it was, the centerpiece of a gala rooftop reception in February 1994 to mark the opening of Golden ADA. Among the VIPs were Mayor Frank Jordan, his chief of police and local CEOs. They sipped champagne and dined on caviar while listening to speeches about how San Francisco would become a major player in the diamond trade.

The owners of the new company were a Russian named Andrei Kozlenok and his two Armenian partners, the brothers Ashot and David Shagirian. A slender, elegant fellow in his 30s, Kozlenok had peddled tires and cognac back home. Now he sported a 50,000-dollar watch, boasted of connections to high-ranking officials and wielded an apparently bottomless checking account.

In the Shagirians he had found partners who spoke fluent English and brought local contacts. Kozlenok offered each a 20 per cent stake in the company; he owned the rest.

Kozlenok often said that his mission was to punch a giant hole in the De Beers diamond cartel. The South African concern had long controlled the production and distribution of diamonds worldwide and, according to critics, kept prices artificially high. Since the 1950s, when huge diamond deposits were found in Siberia, Moscow had played along, contracting to sell most of its gems to De Beers. Now, diamond rich and cash poor, Russia wanted more control.

But the cartel needn't have worried. Apparently the men behind Golden ADA were after something other than market share.

The players: at first, Joe Davidson (right) was wary of Viktor Zhirov.

THE PLAN

Russian bureaucrats call it the Closet. It is the handful of heavily guarded underground repositories that hold the national treasury of the Russian Federation and the former Soviet Union. Unlike Fort Knox, which holds mainly gold bullion, the repositories contain vast stores of precious gems, rare coins and exquisite jewelry.

The man with the key was Yevgeny Bychkov, Kozlenok's mentor. According to the Russian press, Bychkov was repeatedly investigated for wrongdoing. But he survived, and President Boris Yeltsin, an associate since the 1960s, made him chairman of the Committee on Precious Metals and Precious Stones.

In 1992 Bychkov's agency proposed a plan to escape De Beers's control: Moscow would set up a diamond center in the United States and ship valuables from the state treasury to it. It would be collateral to obtain a 500-million-dollar line of credit for its entry into the diamond trade. That spring, Bychkov opened the Closet.

DISAPPEARING ACT

In San Francisco, Kozlenok and his men were soon opening pouch after pouch of polished Siberian diamonds. There were thousands of stones, 25,600 carats in all—enough to fetch nearly 20 million dollars. But diamonds were only part of the treasure. Crates arrived packed with fine silver and assorted gems—amethysts, topazes, emeralds. Others held antique artwork. And then there was the gold.

It arrived by the ton, thousands of collectors' gold coins—francs from pre-revolutionary France, hundred-year-old sovereigns from Britain and coins from Czarist Russia. All told, Golden ADA received a more than 90-million-dollar chunk of the Russian treasury as collateral for the loan.

Kozlenok, though, had other plans. He had a gold distributor melt down 5.5 tons of gold, which he sold for over 50 million dollars. Then he and his partners embarked on a world-class buying spree. One afternoon Kozlenok paid more than 1 million dollars for a Rolls-Royce and two Aston Martins. He and the Shagirians plunked down 1.2 million dollars for a trio of luxury yachts, 3.8 million dollars for three homes, and 20 million dollars for a twin-engine Gulfstream corporate jet.

In February and March 1994, Bychkov signed off on new shipments to Golden ADA, this time nearly 90,000 carats of uncut diamonds. By then, however, police on both sides of the world were asking questions.

LOST LOOT

Major Viktor Zhirov had spent much of his career in Moscow at the financial-crimes division of the Interior Ministry. To Zhirov, this new case had all the markings of, as he put it, "a swindling deal by thieves."

As Zhirov worked the case—largely alone—he found the going tough. Again and again Moscow officials assured him the diamonds were in good hands. Worse, he couldn't get key documents; everything tied to the company had been classified.

Still, police found enough evidence to raid Golden ADA's Moscow offices. They seized papers detailing the 89-million-dollar shipment of raw diamonds authorized by Bychkov.

So where was the loot now? Zhirov asked the FBI's man in Moscow.

That the Bureau even had a man in Russia was noteworthy. In the early 1990s, as Russian organized crime spread worldwide, the FBI realized it needed to find reliable partners in the former Soviet Union. The result was the formation of what might be called the Russian Untouchables—a small, elite group at the Interior Ministry with whom the Americans could work. Viktor Zhirov was one of them, so when he phoned, the FBI paid close attention. He was invited to fly to San Francisco as the Bureau's guest.

"THE CLEANER"

The diamonds Bychkov sent to ADA in California were enough to make 45,000 engagement rings. Most were quietly shipped to ADA's operation in Antwerp and sold for some 77 million dollars to a company reportedly controlled by De Beers.

Meanwhile, the situation at Golden ADA was growing increasingly chaotic. Kozlenok had a falling-out with the Shagirians. They claimed in court records that he had offered them 5 million dollars to leave or "a bullet to the head" (a threat Kozlenok denies). The brothers took the money.

Worried that Golden ADA would be taken from him, Kozlenok hired investigator Jack Immendorf, once a top mayoral adviser, to straighten things out as CEO. But Immendorf soon discovered sets of double records.

Teflon man: Yevgeny Bychkov, an associate of Boris Yeltsin, survived repeated investigations.

71

He hired a consulting firm, which found that ADA had disbursed over 130 million dollars with few clear records. After six months Immendorf quit, saying, "These guys were all stealing from each other. They thought they were still in Moscow."

The original plan, say authorities, may have been to pressure De Beers with Golden ADA, while skimming enough off the top to satisfy everyone. But Kozlenok seemed to have gone crazy. So Bychkov turned to Russian businessman Andrei Chernukhin, a man one FBI agent called the Cleaner. Chernukhin was a short, stout fellow whose business card read simply "Consultant to the Russian Federation." He began by installing guards at Golden ADA armed with semi-automatic weapons. Then he turned his attention to Kozlenok.

What happened next may never be known. Kozlenok claims he was lured to Mexico, where he was forced to sign over Golden ADA to one of Chernukhin's associates. Investigators, however, believe he was paid off. In October 1995 he made a hurried exit to Belgium.

CONSPIRACY UNVEILED

As Kozlenok was fleeing, Viktor Zhirov was just arriving. Joe Davidson knew how deep corruption was in Russia, so he watched the man's face and listened carefully to his translated words. He noted that Zhirov wore the same suit all week and brought snacks so he could keep the per diem from the FBI. He soon understood why: Zhirov made only 400 dollars a month.

In San Francisco, Zhirov found what he couldn't find in Moscow—property records, Customs declarations—proof of how much treasure had been squandered. And from Zhirov, Davidson began to understand the full scope of the case. His attitude toward Zhirov went from suspicion to trust—and then concern for his safety.

Returning to Moscow, Zhirov and his growing team raided offices tied to Golden ADA. Days later he was jumped by two men and savagely beaten. "Stop the Golden ADA investigation," one yelled, "or next time we'll kill you!"

THE COVER-UP

Undeterred, the Russian cop sparked probes at various government agencies. The pressure was building on Bychkov to explain the disappearance of almost 180 million dollars in state treasure. In late September 1995, Bychkov's agency filed

Social climbers: David and Ashot Shagirian (centre) and Andrei Kozlenok (far right) mixed with VIPs including Vice-President Al Gore (second from left).

suit against Golden ADA in US federal court, alleging that Kozlenok and the Shagirians had stolen the riches meant for its diamond-processing operation.

FBI wiretaps, however, suggested a different story. As agents listened in, Bychkov discussed with Chernukhin how to stop the investigations. The two men agreed that Chernukhin would get help from some of Russia's most powerful people: the mayor of Moscow, the head of Yeltsin's Presidential Security Service, and a deputy prime minister. Chernukhin's calls went to the executive offices of the president in Moscow—even to Yeltsin's dacha.

For the first time, FBI officials believed they saw evidence of a criminal cover-up reaching the highest levels of the Russian government (Bychkov and Chernukhin deny the allegations). Informants, meanwhile, said that the looting tied to Golden ADA might top 1 billion dollars. ADA had become a potential political scandal, with implications for the United States and the world.

The FBI-Moscow team pressed on, certain they were about to blow the case wide open. Then came some very bad news.

SURPRISE MOVE

"What do you know about the IRS raiding Golden ADA tomorrow?" asked Davidson's supervisor. Davidson was aghast. Without consulting him, prosecutors had approved a plan to seize ADA's assets. To him, this meant the end of the criminal case. Kozlenok had already fled. With tax agents on their trail, other Golden ADA figures were not likely to stick around.

The two men confronted the prosecutors. "How can you do this?" shouted Davidson's supervisor. But the attorneys wouldn't budge.

The next day, November 7, 1995, IRS agents seized Golden ADA headquarters and other holdings. They hit the company with the largest civil lien in the agency's history: 63 million for unpaid taxes. In all, authorities managed to grab shipments of gold, jewelry and diamonds worth 9,450,000 dollars.

Golden ADA was soon forced into bankruptcy. Of the original 180 million dollars in missing treasure, the IRS recovered 40 million dollars in assets.

POWERFUL EXCUSE

Still, Davidson and Zhirov refused to give up. After two more trips to San Francisco, Zhirov returned to Moscow with evidence that was hard to ignore. In February 1996, a surprised Bychkov was charged with "criminal negligence" and violating foreign-exchange law.

Facing a ten-year sentence if convicted, Bychkov was pardoned under a general amnesty for the 50th anniversary of World War II. Still a power in the gem industry, he blames his problems on Kozlenok, De Beers and political enemies. "To act as Golden ADA acted, either you'd have to be stupid or else somebody powerful must have led them to do it," he says without irony.

Ashot Shagirian was deported to San Francisco from the Caribbean and pleaded guilty to tax evasion. David Shagirian is believed to be hiding in Europe. Chernukhin is wanted for questioning in Moscow and San Francisco. And in June, Kozlenok, who denies doing anything improper, was extradited from Greece to Moscow, where the big question is whether he'll name names.

For his efforts in Golden ADA, Viktor Zhirov was promoted to colonel. He and his Untouchables—now numbering more than 50—have set an enduring precedent. "They've lessened the bleeding," a top FBI agent said.

But more troubles arrived last summer. With Russia's presidential election in 2000—and with possibly several contenders implicated—the case had become too sensitive to allow Zhirov's continued digging. After 18 years as a cop, Zhirov was fired and his investigation into Golden ADA quietly ended.

LICENSED TO *KILL*

BY TIM BOUQUET

POLICE KNEW THE SMOOTH-TALKING GUN-RUNNER

WAS LYING. BUT COULD THEY PROVE IT?

On a warm spring evening 29-year-old Devon Dawson was talking to another man outside a pub in Coldharbour Lane, Brixton, south London. Suddenly an argument broke out and the other man slid a small black object from underneath his coat. In an instant, bullets tore into Dawson's body, making him one of the first people in the UK to be killed by the Ingram-designed MAC-10.

No bigger than a box of chocolates, this American sub-machine gun is light and easy to conceal yet can fire an incredible 1,200 rounds a minute. Its devastating and indiscriminate power had made it standard issue for US drugs gangs.

Now this "spray and pray" killing machine had hit the streets of Britain and the hunt was on for its supplier.

RAT TRAP

It was May 1997, exactly a month after the slaying of Devon Dawson. Detective Constable Cliff Purvis of the National Crime Squad watched carefully as two cars drove in convoy along a tree-lined Islington road. One, a white Vauxhall Nova, pulled over to the kerb. Fifty yards further on, a cream and brown Nissan Prairie parked opposite a brick-built apartment block.

The balding, bespectacled man at the wheel was 67-year-old Henry Suttee, a semi-retired explosives and drugs dealer. His rat-faced passenger was 35-year-old Paul Ferris, malevolent king of Glasgow's streets. And thanks to a tip-off from Strathclyde police, Purvis, a walrus of a man, was in the command car of a 60-man armed stake-out.

The house that Suttee and Ferris then entered was the home of gun dealer John Ackerman. When the pair emerged 20 minutes later, Ferris was carrying a large Opal Fruits box. This he transferred to the boot of the Nova, driven by a bottle-blonde, and the two cars peeled off in opposite directions.

While one police team raided Ackerman's house, another tracked Suttee and Ferris to the West End. Heading north, Purvis led the armed response team after the Nova, boxing it in near the start of the M1. In seconds the firearms team dragged 29-year-old Mancunian Constance Howarth from behind the wheel and cuffed her. Inside the Opal Fruits box were three silencers, six magazines, 360 rounds of ammunition, four detonators and, wrapped in hessian cloth, three MAC-10s.

Spray and pray: the Mac-10.

MYSTERY CRAFTSMAN

"Where did you get the guns?" Purvis pressed John Ackerman.

Purvis already knew from forensics that the seized guns were deactivated weapons which had been restored to full operational use, their tell-tale serial numbers erased by sophisticated arc-welding equipment.

It was legal for Ackerman to import and sell as ornaments all sorts of guns whose barrels had been sawn and plugged, their firing pins removed or their breech-blocks rendered harmless. But reactivating them required engineering skills that Ackerman did not possess.

Whoever had done it was a craftsman. Not only had he given the guns a new breech-block—where every round is placed ready for firing—but he had also machined an angled slot into it. This allowed ammunition to be ramped into position even more quickly.

To Cliff Purvis—a former army firearms instructor—this modification was a sinister signature. But whose? Ferris, Suttee and Howarth weren't talking. But at only 55, Ackerman was a sick man with a chronic heart condition. Leaving prison in a hearse scared him more than gangland retribution: he turned Queen's evidence.

"I get them from a man called Robert Bown," he told Purvis. "I page Bown, he calls me on a secure line and I tell him: 'I need a new raincoat.'" This is how MACs are known in criminal circles.

"Bown's just the runner," Purvis suggested. "What happens next?"

"Bown contacts a man in Brighton called Mitchell. He's the armourer."

DISARMING CHARMER

Smooth-skinned Anthony David Mitchell, his dark, thinning hair slicked back to where it curled up over his collar, slammed the front door of his Brighton home and mounted his beloved Harley-Davidson motorcycle. But police were on his tail.

Out past the leafy villas of Hove, Mitchell pulled into Knoll Business Centre and went into Unit W11. When he left a few minutes later, the officers went into the bakery next door.

"He comes in for a pasty and he takes all our old Emerald margarine boxes," said a member of staff. "He says he uses them for bike parts."

Gregarious, popular, plausible, 44-year-old Tony Mitchell had used his redundancy package from a construction company to set up a business ostensibly restoring classic motorbikes. But back at Islington police station John Ackerman was painting Cliff Purvis a rather different portrait of Anthony Mitchell.

"We met in 1988 at the Stone Lodge shooting ranges in Dartford, Kent," he explained. "Bown was also a member." The three entered shooting competitions all over Europe.

With its club house and bar, the Dartford gun range was the hub of Mitchell's business and social life. It was here that he brought reactivated guns for members to try out—illegally. Deactivated weapons cost up to £300; reactivated, the price almost quadrupled. Mitchell was soon boasting of having earned more than £250,000. To the criminal world he was gold dust.

Mitchell had been seen at the ranges loosing off his prized Kalashnikov. But target practice was not enough. With Ackerman, Bown and about a dozen others, he formed a paramilitary group called the Black Shods. Dressing in black coveralls and police-style utility belts, restraint devices dangling from every loop, they had regular secret training exercises in unarmed combat, quick cuffing, using batons and sniping.

"Frustrated soldier?" Purvis asked.

"Ex-copper!" Ackerman replied.

A check with Sussex police showed that Mitchell had been a probationary special constable but had been thrown out after a year when he was caught trying to smuggle ammunition in 1993. Most frightening of all, he had since convinced the Home Office to grant him a licence to trade in legal firearms.

AWESOME ARSENAL

Police officers were crawling over every inch of his house but Tony Mitchell was a picture of unruffled calm, sitting in his living room. It was now July 18.

"Where's your firearms register?" Cliff Purvis asked.

"Not sure," said Mitchell.

The armoury he kept in the house was barred in accordance with the law and its 400 weapons securely racked and locked. However, there was no sign anywhere of the official register that should list all guns bought and sold and their serial numbers. Details should tally with the total housed in the armoury.

"By law you are required to have it ready for inspection at all times," Purvis reminded him. Mitchell just shrugged.

"Do you run a business from any other premises?" Purvis asked.

"No."

Purvis knew he was lying. At that moment, police were raiding Mitchell's 20-by-20-foot workshop at the Knoll Business Centre. But for now, an illegally loaded pistol found at his home was enough to hold him in custody.

Out of sight: Mitchell's workshop in Hove.

SEEKING EVIDENCE

"You don't believe Ackerman, do you?" Mitchell snorted at Purvis as next day they began two days of intensive questioning. "It's common knowledge that he's a liar—and a drug user."

Like Mitchell, the Crime Squad knew it could not build a case on the say-so of a self-confessed criminal like Ackerman. And Robert Bown, a vital link in the conspiracy, had disappeared after Ackerman's arrest.

Purvis found Anthony Mitchell an easy man to dislike. Arrogantly, he refused to answer all questions about making guns but was very happy to discuss his marksmanship and pseudo-military prowess.

Mitchell did not hold all the good cards, though. Two days after his arrest his girlfriend "found" the register of firearms in his house, but the weapons it listed bore no resemblance to the guns found in Mitchell's armoury.

And although the search of his workshop had produced no guns, it had turned up a TIG arc-welding machine—ideal for torching serial numbers off guns. There was also a four-inch tool comprising two flat calliper arms, hinged like a compass, with a small lug on the end of each. Known as a face-pin spanner, it was used for taking the front off silencers.

"By the way," said Purvis, who was known for his deadpan humour. "We had a look at your workshop next to the bakery." For the first time he saw Mitchell flinch.

But with Mitchell's barrister repeatedly applying for bail, the Crime Squad desperately needed to get its hands on some reactivated guns and prove they were Mitchell's.

They had put out a call to all other police forces in Britain asking for details of seizures, particularly MAC-10s. One of the first to respond was S011, the Organized Crime Group at Scotland Yard. It reported that in March 1997 it had found a cache of MAC-10s and ammunition in the boot of an Austin Maestro parked at the Tollgate Hotel in Gravesend. The guns were packed in Emerald margarine boxes and their serial numbers had been removed with a TIG arc welder.

Examination at the Forensic Science Service Laboratory in Lambeth proved that the breech-blocks were made in exactly the same way as those in the MAC-10s Ackerman had sold to Ferris. Like those, they were wrapped in hessian cloth, decorated with what looked like Cyrillic script in felt-tip pen. Language experts revealed the symbols could be read as 'TM'.

"It's like the Scarlet Pimpernel leaving his mark," Purvis observed.

More and more MAC-10s began to turn up. Of 20 or so examined, the Crime Squad could prove beyond all doubt that 15 were restored by the same person— including the gun used to murder Devon Dawson.

But they still hadn't actually found any similar guns on Mitchell's premises. In September, 1997, a judge decided there was insufficient evidence to hold him. With a smile and a spring in his step, gangland's favourite armourer was free on bail.

CLOSING IN

The two Crime Squad officers recognized a pallid, sunken-cheeked face on a street in Grove Park, south-east London. It was October 13 and Robert Bown had been paying a sneak visit to his family home. In a bag around his waist he was carrying a loaded Smith & Wesson revolver. In his coat pocket was a CS gas canister.

Later that same day, Cliff Purvis's men also searched the former builder's safe house in Chatham, Kent. Here they discovered not only eight weapons, but also six pounds of plastic explosive in some motorcycle panniers.

Mitchell had ordered Bown to remove these "bits and bobs" from the gun club before telling him to disappear.

Like John Ackerman, Bown agreed to testify. He told police about a lock-up domestic garage in Hove. There police found rifles, revolvers, silencers, MAC-10 breech blocks and 1,000 rounds of ammunition in an Emerald margarine box.

The garage was rented from an unsuspecting widow by "a nice gentleman who pays cash promptly". Anthony Mitchell. Since his release on bail, nice Mr Mitchell had been seen removing boxes.

To Purvis all was clear: this was where Mitchell had moved the guns before officers searched his workshop in July. Now he had been taking them back, confident that the police would never get enough new evidence to pay another visit.

Bown said Mitchell knew he was hiding out in Chatham. Detectives decided to flush him out with this item which hit the news wires on October 14:

"Police believe they have smashed a major weapons supply line to organized criminals. Bomb disposal experts were called in when police raided a house at Chatham, Kent. Police are questioning a 46-year-old man."

The conspirators:
Henry Suttee, Paul
Ferris and Anthony
Mitchell.

BANGED-UP

While most other residents of Baden Road were asleep on October 17, the lights were still blazing at number 30. Under 24-hour surveillance, Mitchell had been nervously active all day. He was up all night.

Early next morning he appeared and threw a bag into his red Ford Mondeo. Suddenly, Mr Cool was in a hurry. He was arrested before he could drive away. In his luggage were his passport and some foreign currency.

Over in Hove the staff at the bakery watched in amazement as the Crime Squad spent two days taking apart their neighbour's workshop. This time there was evidence everywhere. Inks from felt-tip pens matched those that made the 'Cyrillic' markings on the hessian used to wrap the guns found at the Tollgate Hotel. Yards of hessian were the same weave as that found at Ackerman's house. Ammunition matched that found at Ackerman's and supplied to Ferris. Best of all, in Mitchell's tiny office they found 40 deactivated MAC-10s and 25 breech-blocks identical to those already seized.

Then the forensic lab reported that minute indentations on the face-pin spanner found in the workshop matched exactly those found on the silencers Ferris bought from Ackerman. On top of all this, more Mitchell guns had turned up in Dublin. There were rumours he had supplied Loyalist and Nationalist terror gangs in Ulster and criminals in Cyprus. The total stood at more than 60, yet Mitchell still protested that he was just an honest craftsman gone a little astray. He had no idea, he said, what the guns would be used for.

Two days into his trial this January, facing an avalanche of evidence that he was the most prolific supplier of criminal guns in Europe, he pleaded guilty. Anthony Mitchell, the gold-dust armourer, was sentenced to eight years.

Following the National Crime Squad's investigation, which involved 150 officers, Paul Ferris was sent to prison for ten years—later cut to seven on appeal—and Henry Suttee and Constance Howarth for five years—cut to three on appeal. John Ackerman and Robert Bown are serving six years and four years respectively.

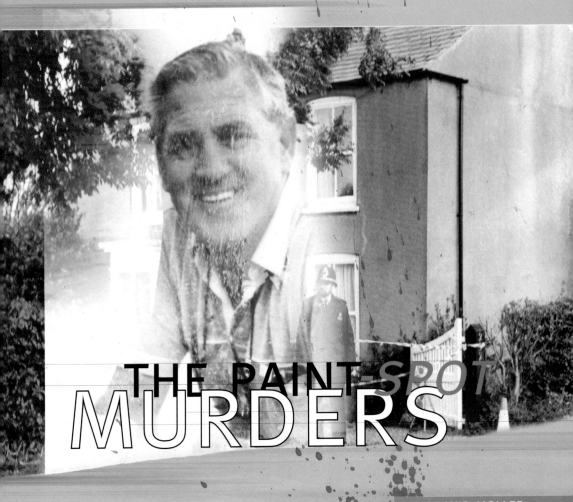

THE PAINT-SPOT
MURDERS

BY DAVID MOLLER

TWO ELDERLY MEN HAD BEEN SAVAGELY KILLED
AND DETECTIVES HAD NO LEADS—UNTIL FORENSIC
EXPERTS DISCOVERED A TINY CLUE.

The old man was still slumped in his favourite armchair—head tilted to one side. Three deep wounds on the skull of Fred Maltby, 75, ran some five inches from his hairline to the back of his head. Blood had soaked into the back and wings of the chair.

The blows must have been delivered with formidable force, thought Detective Superintendent Stuart Clifton. As he surveyed the shabby farmhouse living-room with watchful, brown eyes, he noted that blood had splattered the wall as high up as the ceiling. *Probably with the back swing of the weapon used to kill the old man*, he thought.

The 47-year-old detective, a tall, grey-haired veteran of some 40 murder inquiries, had seen the results of many forms of human savagery, yet was stunned at the force used against this weak and defenceless old man.

On a cushion on the living-room sofa, there was the outline—in blood—of an axe-like instrument. But as the burly detective moved cautiously through the house, he could see little else that might yield a clue to the crime.

There was no sign of forced entry. Nothing to indicate a struggle or search—no drawers pulled open, or objects knocked over. Just a quick, bloody killing.

It was an hour earlier—12.45pm on Wednesday, October 2, 1991—that his colleague Detective Chief Inspector Gordon Reedman had summoned him. "I'm at 292 Brant Road, Lincoln. We've a body in the house here. Looks like a murder."

Reedman, also 47, was a shorter man, but wiry and athletic. He had joined the Lincolnshire police just months before Clifton and the two moved up through the ranks together until Clifton had gone up to superintendent the year before. They had worked together on so many cases over the previous 20 years that they scarcely needed to exchange words as they moved round the murder scene.

In the kitchen, Clifton nodded at a couple of teacups on the sink draining-board. "Seems like Maltby might have had a visitor," he murmured. In the conservatory at the back of the house, Clifton noted there was a small black tin cash box with some coins inside. Something that might well have been scooped up by a burglar. Already, questions were beginning to pile up in Clifton's mind.

Upstairs, there were more indications of an old man living just above subsistence level. Frayed Carpet. An unmade bed. On a dressing table, a *Young Farmers' Guide* for 1957. At the end of their tour, Clifton paused and looked around him. He could hear an autumnal wind sighing through a rotting window frame. "I would say this one's going to be a long-runner, Gordon," he commented.

MURDER

Sometime between 7.00 pm and 12 midnight on Tuesday, 1st October, 75-year-old Fred Maltby was brutally murdered at his home at 292 Brant Road, Lincoln. He suffered severe injuries in what was a vicious attack with a heavy sharp instrument.

Lincolnshire Police need to hear from anyone who knows him or was a friend of his or saw him during Tuesday evening the 1st of October.

The Police would also like to hear from any person who saw a vehicle or people near Fred's house during the afternoon or evening of Tuesday the 1st of October.

PLEASE CALL IN CONFIDENCE
0522 558057
OR
CRIMESTOPPERS
0800 555111
— and you may qualify for a Community Action Trust Reward

ECHO
Lincolnshire Echo operating Lincolnshire Police

Hunting leads: Poster appeals for help to solve Maltby's murder.

THE HUNT BEGINS

Outside, it was a grey, overcast day. Branches on the ground gave a clue to the wild rainstorms of the night before. Clifton moved briskly into action. He instructed one uniformed officer to start a log of everyone who had so far been in the house—the neighbour who had discovered the body, the ambulance attendants who had been summoned, the doctor who had certified death. "No one now gets in the house," he commanded, "without the permission of either myself or the senior scene-of-crime officer."

Clifton briefed six detectives for a house-to-house tour of nearby homes. "Our first priority is to establish the time of Maltby's death. Find out from anyone who knew him when they last saw him alive. Ask about any people, vehicles or anything at all unusual seen near the murder scene."

Later that afternoon in Reedman's office at Lincoln's West Parade police station, Clifton sketched out on a blackboard their main lines of enquiry and administrative chores over the next few hours. Clifton would run the investigation from Lincolnshire police headquarters, at Nettleham, a village five miles north of the city. It had a room that could be devoted solely to the investigation. His team of 24 detectives would have to be drawn from all parts of the county. "We better start alerting people now," he told Reedman.

At 4pm, Clifton hurried off to a conference room to brief 20 officers for a search of the land behind the farmhouse. "We're looking for the murder weapon—an axe-like instrument—or for anything else that might have been dropped by the killer or killers fleeing the scene. I want you to search that whole area behind the house over the next 24 hours. Let's get moving."

Clifton later returned to the murder scene himself for an interview with the BBC's local radio reporter. On this case, he sensed that his team would need as much help from the public as they could possibly get. "Obviously, our inquiry is still at a very early stage," he told the interviewer, "but I would appeal for anyone who knew Fred Maltby or saw him after 5.30pm last night to contact us."

By the time Clifton had driven to headquarters, the first telephone calls were already coming in. In the long, low-ceilinged incident room, some dozen members of staff were feeding the first scraps of information into computer terminals linked to HOLMES: Home Office Large Enquiry System.

A massive computer database that had been refined over the years for just such a murder investigation, this would be used to store, correlate and cross-reference all the names, addresses and statement of witnesses, suspects and anyone else interviewed or involved in the case. Unlike many other senior officers who were baffled by the new technology, Clifton had taken a course on HOLMES and insisted on having his own computer terminal on this desk.

In the incident room, there was already building up the familiar hubbub of people, telephones, of fax machines and computer printers chattering spasmodically into life. Momentarily, Clifton glanced at the darkening farmland outside and, in the distance, at the floodlit, Gothic splendour of Lincoln Cathedral.

In the office designated for himself and Reedman across the corridor, he quickly riffled through a heavy, black notebook that held the messages and statements already accumulating for him as senior investigating officer.

He noted that at about 5.15pm the previous evening, Fred Maltby had gone to collect his evening paper as usual from the store across the road from his house. Shortly after 9pm he was seen walking back to his home, from a building site next door to his farm.

With the constant flow of telephone calls and administrative details to attend to, it wasn't until 9pm that Clifton was able to call his wife Marion. "It's another murder case, love. Don't wait up for me."

As he strode into the white-walled mortuary of Lincoln County Hospital, Clifton caught the distinctive smell of formaldehyde.

Fred Maltby, just over five foot tall, looked even more diminutive stretched out on the seven-foot-long white enamel mortuary table. The pathologist stood there dictating what he saw to his secretary standing by his side.

From the head injuries and gravitational flow of blood over the front of Maltby's right shoulder and down into the armpit area of his suit, the pathologist surmised that Maltby had been sitting down at the time of the attack. There had been three blows—any one of which could have caused death.

As the process dragged on, Clifton could feel the chill of the tiled mortuary floor seeping into him. "Any idea what the weapon was?" asked Clifton. "An axe?"

The pathologist was scrupulously non-committal. *A sharp, heavy instrument such as an axe, a machete or butcher's cleaver*, were the words he dictated for the official record.

HEAVY WORKLOAD

With the post-mortem concluded after midnight, it was nearly 1am before Clifton let himself into his home out in the country near Sleaford, some 15 miles south of

Lincoln. For a few moments, he knelt down as Pepper, the black-and-white family cocker spaniel, scrabbled excitedly over his knees and licked his hand.

Bone-weary, and too tired now to eat the dinner he had missed, Clifton sat at the kitchen table with a cup of coffee as Pepper scampered round on the lawn outside. He knew that his wife would have long gone up to bed and would be fast asleep.

But at 6.30 the next morning she was up with him. A slender woman, with shoulder-length dark hair, she knew that that was likely to be the only time she would see her husband that day.

It had been a rough six months. He had only just broken the back of another massively complicated investigation in which a young nurse on the children's ward of a local hospital, was charged with four murders, three attempted murders and attacks on another six children. She was later convicted.

As so often in the past, it had been a time of long, grinding hours and missed weekends, broken dinner dates, and postponed holidays with his wife. Ever since they had first met in their native Yorkshire—a hundred miles to the north— Marion had known him as a man who could work at only one speed: flat out. The son of a builder and without the means for full-time study, Clifton had had to slog through four years of night school courses to qualify as a building surveyor.

But then he had decided that he wanted something more out of a job. A career that would both stretch him more, and be of more use to the community. A switch to the police had suited him perfectly. But as he moved up through the ranks, it had meant some punishing hours.

"I don't suppose you know when you'll be home tonight?" Marion asked.

"Afraid not, love. You better expect me when you see me. At the moment, it's not looking like the most straightforward case I've ever worked on."

The next morning at police headquarters, some 40 officers crammed into a conference room for the first full briefing by Clifton and Reedman on the case. The conference room was absolutely quiet when a ten-minute video that had been made of the murder scene showed the deep wounds on Maltby's skull.

As Clifton took over the briefing again, he stressed, "We still don't have a motive for this crime. We've got to find out everything we possibly can about Fred Maltby. Who were his friends? Who visited him?"

By the next day, Clifton had some background on the man. With advancing age, Maltby had given up farming and, according to the police report, he sold fruit and vegetables—bought from a local wholesaler—and kindling wood from a shed on his farm to a core group of old, faithful customers. But apart from that he appeared to have little contact with outsiders.

Clifton and Reedman continued to explore the mystery of a man now emerging almost as a recluse. He went out little, had few friends. No known enemies, mused Clifton. So who on earth could have wanted old Fred Maltby dead?

Probably someone who knew him, suggested Reedman. The front door was always kept locked—and unless you knew the place, there was no obvious way in through the back.

An intruder would have had to push his way between bushes—and then along a narrow path that circled round to the rear of the house. From there a stranger would have to find his way through an unusual arrangement of corridors to the living room at the front the house.

"From everything we've heard," Reedman continued, "Fred Maltby wasn't the kind of man who would have had friends just dropping in."

The door to the living room would certainly have alerted him. A sliding door that ran badly on its top runner, it made a harsh, grating noise as it opened. "Yet all the indications are that he had been sitting calmly in his chair when he met his end," Reedman concluded.

"There were also the two teacups," added Clifton. "Old Maltby didn't seem the sort of chap who would have just anyone sharing his hospitality."

Both men were inclined to rule out burglary. Generally speaking, burglars don't kill, Clifton noted. They just want to get out of the place as quickly as possible. With someone Fred Maltby's age, they could have simply pushed him out of the way.

As far as the-scene-of-crime officers could establish, the only thing that was gone from the house was the brown wallet that Maltby kept in a breast pocket of his overalls. But those who knew him insisted that he never had more than about £10 or £15 in it.

STYMIED

Each morning, Clifton met up with his detectives in the busy office where they made telephone calls and grabbed a sandwich in between their outside enquiries. Shifting a pile of paperwork to sit on a table, he recapitulated all the indications that Maltby might have known his killer. "But the evidence that we have so far still doesn't make a great deal of sense," Clifton added. "An old man living on about the poverty line. Brutally murdered. So what was the motive?"

After several more days of hard digging, his team came up with a rumour. There was talk of a land deal that Maltby was meant to have pulled off several years before. It was at the height of the property boom in which he had negotiated the sale of some three acres of land to a builder for £500,000. In fact, before the deal could go through, the builder had withdrawn.

But rumours nevertheless persisted that old Maltby was rich, reported one detective. Some people seemed to think that he might have part of his wealth stashed away at home.

Another key issue that puzzled Clifton was the murder weapon. On a workbench in the conservatory at the back of the farmhouse, there was a jumble of old tools—but no axe. Yet Maltby would have needed one to cut up the kindling wood that he sold. Outside in the garden, an old wooden chopping block bore the indentations of an axe.

Clifton ordered that police dogs scour everywhere. Officers asked homeowners if they had any axes missing. Could they see the ones that they had? Some 40 axes were taken into police possession—but none fitted the outline of the axe-head left in blood on the cushion in Maltby's living room.

There was little better news from other parts of the investigation. An-inch-by-inch search of the house had not turned up much of interest.

Clifton refused to be despondent, knowing from past cases how often his best leads came from the public. It was just a question of keeping the case alive in the press.

In radio interviews, Clifton appealed, "Lincolnshire police need to hear from anyone who knew Fred Maltby or saw him during the afternoon or evening of Tuesday, October 1. Please come forward and talk to us." A local paper, the *Lincolnshire Echo*, produced posters seeking information on the murdered man and the weapon that might have killed him.

For the first five weeks of the case, Clifton worked for up to 16 hours a day, seven days a week, before he allowed himself a day off. At home, on a perfect autumn morning, he savoured the freedom of being at last outdoors, of digging vigorously in the garden he had neglected for so long.

His cocker spaniel, Pepper, scampered happily back and forth, as Clifton cleared the leaves that had fallen from the sycamore trees that crowded round his lawn. And with his police beeper carried, as always, on his belt, he yearned for some message from the incident room that might indicate a break in the case.

Nothing.

TWO SUSPECTS

Three days later, however, Detective Inspector Malcolm Vickers hurried into Clifton's office with a sheet of paper. "There's something here you ought to have a look at, boss."

It was a report of a telephone call just in from a motorist who had seen a couple of young men dashing from the direction of Maltby's home on the night of the murder at about 10pm.

That was about an hour after Fred Maltby had last been seen alive, Clifton reflected. For the first time on the case, he felt a faint glimmering of hope. His brown eyes glancing up at Vickers, Clifton asked, "How can he be sure it was the night of October 1?"

"The man remembered because he had been to see his mother and it had been a stormy night. He had had to brake sharply to avoid hitting the two men. He seems to have a good description of them," Vickers concluded.

"Right, let's get the police artists on to it straight away," Clifton instructed. With help from the motorist, Clifton's team produced a computerized drawing of the two—one taller than the other—and issued descriptions: *One is in his early twenties, of medium to stocky build, with light-coloured, collar-length hair. He wore an ear-ring, a brown leather bomber jacket, blue stonewashed jeans and a T-shirt. The second man is about the same age, six foot tall, slim build and he wore a designer T-shirt, blue jeans and white running shoes.*

A poster of the two was featured when Clifton appealed for help on the BBC's television programme *Crimewatch* a few weeks later. There was also a reconstruction of the crime—with two young men shown running across Brant Road on a stormy night.

Clifton urged anyone who had been in the area at the time of the murder to come forward. Someone must have seen something. He appealed for the two young men to contact the police—if only to be eliminated from the inquiry.

Following the programme, 129 calls came in from the public—but none that helped Clifton's detectives to trace the two young men.

By this time there were 2,500 names in the HOLMES system—people who had been interviewed or given information during the investigation. Late one night in early December, Clifton was tapping away at his HOLMES computer terminal when an idea came to him.

On his screen, he noted that the garage next door to Maltby's home had a shop. And that it was open until ten at night. The two runners could simply have been on their way back from the shop—recklessly dashing across the road because of the torrential rain on the night of the murder. Wearily, he retrieved his police beeper from the mess of coffee cups and papers on his desk and set off home.

The following evening, Clifton suggested to Reedman that they get away for a drink and a chat—well away from the distractions of the office. The Strugglers Inn in nearby Lincoln had long been a favourite pub. They found a table in a quiet side room.

Though Reedman was ostensibly more laid back, Clifton knew better than most about the tenacity behind his easy-going smile. Just five foot nine in height,

Reedman had nonetheless been a bruising rugby player who had captained the Lincolnshire police force team during five legendary years. He had given the game up only at the age of 35. And he brought the same full-blooded commitment to his police work.

On this case, Clifton had given it his all. Yet he knew he spoke for both of them when he admitted to feeling the trail growing very cold.

While most murder inquiries lasted no more than two or three weeks, this one had already dragged on for two months. "Is there anything we might have missed?" asked Clifton. "Anything at all that could give us a fresh line on this case?"

By mid-December, Clifton had to conclude that there was still nothing. He came to his office one afternoon with bad news. He had just been to see the top brass. The investigation was being scaled down. Reedman would return to normal duties at West Parade in Lincoln and Clifton would keep working with just a handful of officers.

Clifton felt bitter disappointment. "It will be the first unsolved murder case for the entire force since 1979," he pointed out. More than that, he felt that he'd not yet done his duty to a community that was appalled and still fearful in the aftermath of the horrific crime. And there was the question that lurked in both their minds: *Would the killer strike again?*

ANOTHER MURDER

Clifton took a couple of days off for the Christmas festivities. His younger son and daughter-in-law were visiting and he did his best to enter into the spirit of the occasion.

Occasionally, his mind would drift to memory of the old man—crumpled and bloody in his armchair. His wife Marion sensed his continuing preoccupation. "Don't worry about it, love. It'll come right in the end."

Then, on the morning of January 29, 1992, Clifton was in his office at police headquarters when he got a telephone call. It was Reedman. "There's just been a report of another body in the bookmaker's shop down the end of the High Street."

Victim 2: Rylatt and the betting shop where he was murdered.

"I'll be right with you," responded Clifton. He grabbed his coat and beeper from a chair. Soon he was manoeuvring

90

his car on icy country roads and through the early-morning traffic that clogged Lincoln's mile-long High Street.

In the back office of the betting shop, lay Alan Rylatt, 61, sprawled on his back. The carpet near his head was sodden with blood. The finger of his right hand were slightly clenched—as if in self-defence. Between his hairline and back of his head, there were the same kind of deep wounds—about eight this time.

Clifton noted that the door of the safe was open, with Rylatt's keys still in the lock. There were some cheques strewn around the floor. An overturned step ladder. In the cramped office, blood splattered the side of a desk, cupboards, a wall and door.

While the victim lay on his back, Clifton saw that the knees of his trousers were bloodstained. *Maybe Rylatt, in his death throes, had made one last floundering effort to get to his feet,* he wondered. But as with the Maltby murder, there were no signs of a real fight or a search.

"It looks like it's the same maniac who did in Fred Maltby," commented Reedman.

In the main office, Clifton walked over to the young man surrounded by a cluster of his officers. Twenty-three-old Edward Rylatt had discovered his father's body barely 40 minutes earlier. White-faced and clearly in shock, he nevertheless managed to give Clifton a coherent account of arriving for work through a side entrance. Finding something blocking the door to his father's office, he had gone round to let himself in through the main entrance on the High Street. That door was still locked. *That meant there was no forced entry,* noted Clifton.

Outside in the High Street, it was a miserably cold morning. There was snow on the ground, and wisps of mist from the fog that had shrouded the city the night before. Clifton knew that his first priority was to find the murder weapon. If it was an axe, it didn't seem likely that a killer would have carried it through a busy area like that. He would have tried to dump it as quickly as possible—maybe in a rubbish bin.

"What day are the bins emptied?" Clifton asked. Rubbish was being collected that morning. One refuse truck could be heard grinding away in the distance. "Tell them to stop collecting," Clifton instructed, "and get them to take the refuse that they have already picked up to some depot where we can have a look through it."

As more officers arrived, he dispatched them on house-to-house enquiries. "Ask if anyone has seen anything suspicious over the last few days. Find out when Alan Rylatt was last seen alive."

Pacing the area with Reedman, Clifton noted a closed circuit television guarding a garage across the road from Rylatt's shop. "We need to get hold of that video tape and see if there is anything on it," he told one of his officers.

Clifton also knew that there was another set of closed-circuit cameras at the nearby end of the High Street that were used to manage traffic through the city. "We ought to have the tapes off those cameras as well. It's just possible they might have picked up the registration numbers of cars driving along the High Street last night."

CHILLING SIMILARITIES

With his instructions at the murder scene under way, Clifton hurried to the city's West Parade police station. He had already decided that since it was just two miles away from Rylatt's betting shop, would provide a far better headquarters for what was now a double murder investigation. Quickly, he secured permission to expand the staff of this new incident room to 14 officers, and have 36 detectives on his outside team.

The next morning, all 50 officers crammed into the largest space available— the bar on the top floor of the modern, three-storey police station. Methodically, Clifton took them through the evidence gathered and the similarities of the two cases. "The post-mortem on Rylatt the night before had shown that in all probability both men had been killed by the same weapon—an axe-like instrument."

"Both victims," continued Clifton, "were older men who lived on their own— and in the southern part of the city. Both were people who others might have thought had a certain amount of wealth at home. Both were killed on a night of appalling weather, a Tuesday night—and we believe at about 9 or 10pm.

"In this case, as in the Maltby case, all the evidence suggests the victim knew his attacker and let him onto the premises. When the victim's son, Edward, came to work yesterday morning, he found the front door still locked. That means that the killer must have come and gone by the side door sometimes used by Rylatt's friends and visitors.

"All the indications are that Rylatt was sitting down at the start of the attack— suggesting that he was in his office with someone he knew and trusted. He was a big man. If he was given the chance to defend himself, that room would have been wrecked."

Edward Rylatt told police that some £3,658 was missing from his father's safe. That raised a mystery. There was another £800 in the safe that the killer had missed, and upstairs, in the flat where Rylatt lived, police had found a biscuit tin containing £13,000. "In both murders," stressed Clifton, "there appears to have been no determined search for money or valuables."

Briskly, Clifton now listed his team's immediate tasks. To contact the local bus company and taxi firms. "Ask about any suspicious persons picked up from near the murder scene." To check guest houses and hotels. "It's just possible that the killer decided to lie low nearby." To talk to dry cleaners. "Check if any blood-stained clothing has been handed in." To check Lincoln County Hospital. "In case the killer was injured in the attack." And to ask around local pubs and restaurants. "Find out about Rylatt's friends. Who did he eat and drink with?"

Clifton concluded, "We're dealing with a brutal killer. We've got to find him before he strikes again."

Clifton soon learned that while the two murders had many similarities, the victims could hardly have been more different. In contrast to the near-recluse Maltby, Alan Rylatt must have known half of Lincoln. With a sunny, outgoing nature, he was an avid golfer and president of Lincoln United Football Club. He had two betting shops, was a money-lender; rented out some half-dozen apartments in nearby Henley Street; and had an interest in a hairdressing business.

At his morning meeting with detectives two days later, Clifton pointed out that the divorced Rylatt had actively wined, dined and pursued women—some of them married to other men. "Rylatt was a man with any number of friends and associates—and maybe a few enemies. As far as is possible, we've got to trace and interview every single one of them."

Clifton split his detectives into teams: one group, to track down and question all those who had known or had business dealing with Joe Rylatt; another group, to interview those who had rented his property and might have unpaid debts.

He had the police drugs squad scour Rylatt's premises, to see if drugs might be in any way involved in the crime. He got an expert bookmaker to go through Rylatt's computer and accounts to find out if any illicit, off-hours betting could have led to a dispute.

On the Saturday following the murder, Clifton assigned plain-clothes officers to mingle in local pubs and betting shops, on what he knew would be their busiest day, to check for any particularly free-spending customers.

Next, he detailed a detective sergeant to scour the force's computerized records for burglars known to be active in the southern half of the city. There were about a hundred. "We need an account from each of them of what they were doing on the night of Joe Rylatt's murder."

But, as his teams enquiries got under way, Clifton saw a problem: tracing Rylatt's debtors. The core of his money-lending business was the biscuit tin—with its £13,000. There were few documents, however, to indicate how the money had been lent.

Clifton's detectives cobbled together a list of debtors from the odd IOU retrieved from Rylatt's bedside table; various chits and uncashed cheques found in other parts of his flat and at two betting shops. They also had to rely on the memories of his son Edward, brother Bruce and manager Mick Small. Bruce Rylatt described his brother's record-keeping as not that methodical.

Eventually, they came up with some 30 names. They included an accountant with a drinking problem, and electrician whose vanload of tools had recently been stolen, and a sheet-metal worker from a factory not far from Maltby's home. But each had an alibi for the night of Rylatt's murder.

Clifton was never convinced that the list of debtors was comprehensive. As he put it to Reedman, "The names of many of Joe Rylatt's customers were probably kept in his head—and went with him to his grave."

MORE DISAPPOINTMENTS

In their office overlooking a gloomy inner courtyard of the police station, Clifton and Reedman soon had a mass of eye-witness reports to wade through. A promising one came from a local garage worker who had spotted a brown Ford Escort, parked near the betting shop on the night of the murder. He specified it was Rio brown. "As the witness was a mechanic," Clifton told Reedman, "the information is probably good."

Clifton instructed an officer to contact the police national computer and the Driver Vehicle Licensing Centre for the names of registered owners of brown Escorts, the area of Lincoln and the East Midlands. There were about 200. Each was interviewed by an officer. Not one of them emerged as a suspect.

There were other disappointments. The search of the refuse collected on the day after Rylatt's murder, had revealed nothing. When they played the video tape from the garage camera, across the road from Rylatt's betting shop, they found that fog made it impossible to read any vehicle registration numbers. And the closed-circuit television camera overlooking the High Street hadn't been working on the night of the murder.

But as some leads went cold, Clifton's constant interviews with local press and television flushed out new ones. As with the Maltby murder, there was an eye-witness report on two youths seen running away from the area of Rylatt's betting shop at about 9.45pm. Again, one was noticeably taller than the other. And again, motorists had to swerve or brake sharply to avoid them.

One day, Edward Rylatt was going through his father's possessions when he came across a video cassette recorder that he had not noticed before. His father must have bought it just before his death. Clifton's detectives traced it back to the shop that had sold it—only to find that it had been bought by someone else.

A burglary had been reported from the purchaser's home ten days before Rylatt's murder. The recorder was among those items listed missing. Its serial number showed beyond doubt that Rylatt had acquired stolen property. *Could there have been some dispute over payment for the stolen goods*, Clifton wondered. *A fight that had led to Rylatt's killing?*

As he perused the list of other stolen items, he noted a decoder used to watch satellite television. Clifton's detectives had a stroke of luck. One of their regular criminal informants came up with the name of the man who had bought the stolen decoder: a local barman.

He named the young woman who had sold him the stolen item. She had no criminal record—but her mother worked in Joe Rylatt's betting shop. She was also the girlfriend of one of the two men she said had stolen the video and decoder.

Although both had convictions, there was no evidence against them. When Detective Constable John Taylor questioned the young woman again, she was adamant that there had never been any dispute about the money. "Joe paid me £80 for the video on Friday—four days before he was killed. We were all square."

Later, Clifton questioned Taylor, "Do you reckon she's telling us the truth?"

"I believe so, boss," said Taylor.

It was yet another crushing disappointment. Clifton knew that the two young thieves could not be regarded as serious suspects. But the incident raised a thought that had been niggling away at his mind for some time. It was a puzzle he tested on Detective Sergeant Richard Holmes, who had worked as a detective in Lincoln for ten years and had a wide range of criminal informants.

"Why is it," Clifton asked, "that we're getting so little feedback from our usual sources? We must have pulled in half the scallywags in town. There's a big reward going for information leading to the killers. Yet so far we have not had a shred of useful information."

Holmes had been pondering the same phenomenon. "I'm not at all sure it's local, boss. If it was, I think we would have got some whisper."

THE MURDER WEAPON

Clifton wasn't convinced. That night, in a pub on the hill above the police station, he and Reedman reviewed yet again what was known. With both murders, there had been no forced entry, no intense search for money. Both victims had given every indication of knowing their killers. There was no evidence of any fight.

"Who were their friends?" asked Clifton.

"They had to be local people," responded Reedman. "Neither of the two were sophisticates exactly. Maltby had hardly moved outside Lincoln in his entire

Murder weapon: DS Clifton with the axe.

life. Rylatt travelled abroad a bit, but we've searched his address books, letters, phone billing records. There's barely an acquaintance there outside the county."

"The killer could be someone right under our noses," said Clifton. "Maybe a suspect we've already had in for questioning?"

The two men were quiet for a while. Reedman finally broke the silence. "So where do we go from here? We don't have that many lines of enquiry outstanding. We're still trying to trace the two runners seen near both murder scenes. There's the spot of paint."

During the post-mortem on Rylatt, the pathologist had found a speck of paint deep in one of the wounds on his skull. There was a slightly larger spot on his left hand. Presumably, from the axe-like instrument with which he had been killed. If both Rylatt and Maltby had been killed by the same weapon, Clifton reflected, it might have been painted between the two murders.

Experts at the forensics science laboratory could tell police little about the paint— beyond it being grey and rich in zinc. But Clifton now assigned Detective Sergeant Holmes to find out more. Holmes consulted experts at the Zinc Association in London and a paint company in Harrogate, Yorkshire. All they could add was the paint was more than 80 per cent zinc.

"What that means is that it was a primer paint usually used in some sort of industrial process," Holmes reported to Clifton. "But that doesn't help us a lot as it could still be bought by anyone in hardware shops across the country."

Clifton was also aware that the amount of paint recovered from Rylatt's body, was so small there was a limit to the tests that could be done on it.

As winter turned to spring, his team were still no closer to identifying what the paint was—or who had made it. And there were no fresh leads. Once again, Clifton had that numbing sense of an investigation slowly bogging down.

At least now he could take the odd day off and join Marion out in their garden. Already, the sycamore trees round the lawn were coming back into leaf. He dug hard into the damp, clinging soil.

He was at his desk on April 3, 1992, when he got a telephone call. It was from a uniformed officer in the southern part of the city. "I've just had an axe handed in to me by four young lads."

According to the officer, the four teenagers had been paddling around in a boat on the lake in Boultham Park—no more than a mile from Joe Rylatt's betting shop. In the undergrowth on an island, they had found an axe. Remembering the publicity about the two recent murders, they had wrapped their find in a scarf and taken it to the police.

Clifton's heart was in his mouth as the young officer concluded, "It looks to me as if the axe has got blood on it."

He refused to allow himself to get too excited. There had been so many disappointments over the previous six months. "Get it up here straight away," Clifton instructed.

In the incident room, Clifton carefully examined the axe through its clear plastic bag. Careful not to touch it before it had been seen by forensic experts, he could see the blood quite clearly on one side of the axe-head near the shaft. The other side he guessed had been washed clean by the snow and rain of the previous few weeks. Luckily, the axe had been lying on it side.

He also noted that the axe-head had been freshly painted with what looked like a zinc-type paint. An impressively neat job. Not a speck of paint had strayed from the axe-head onto the shaft. Possibly the work of a craftsman, reflected Clifton. Someone trained to work with his hands.

He wondered whether at last they were on the way to solving the crime.

TELL-TALE PAINT

First there was a mass of work to do to gain forensic evidence from the axe, and if possible to trace its origin. "Lets get this axe to the lab," he commanded.

Scientists weren't able to get any fingerprints off the axe. Time and the elements had long since worn away any lacquer there might once have been on its 18-inch handle. But they established that blood on the axe-head matched that of Joe Rylatt. They also confirmed that the marks in the skulls of both murdered men were similar to this axe—and that the paint on the axe matched that found on Rylatt's skull and hand. The axe-head matched precisely the outline of blood found on the cushion in Maltby's home.

At a meeting with his detectives, Clifton determined, "The first thing we've got to do is find out who made the axe."

Fortuitously, Detective Constable Malcolm Soltysiak, before joining the police, had worked for a firm that owned a hardware store. Ringing his old boss there, Soltysiak found out within 40 minutes the name of the axe company: Skinner and Johnson. They had had a factory in the village of Ranskill, some 30 miles away. But it had closed down years before.

"Get over there," Clifton told Soltysiak. "There's bound to be some old employees in the area." The old brick factory had stopped making axes in 1949. But its last foreman—a man now in his 90s—was still living nearby. Shown a full-size photograph of the axe by Soltysiak, and comparing it with an old sales leaflet, he confirmed the axe as one of theirs.

"That means that the axe must have been made some time between 1860 and 1949," Soltysiak reported back to Clifton. "That fits in with the age of most of the tools found in the conservatory of Maltby's home." Days later, forensic experts were able to confirm that indentations made by the axe matched those found on the chopping block in the garden, where Maltby had cut up his kindling wood.

Clifton and Reedman began to speculate on what might have happened on the night of Joe Rylatt's death. In Boultham Park, they paced the winding path that bordered the lake under a canopy of beech trees. "Driving due south out of the city," suggested Clifton, "the murderer could have been here within minutes. He would have had to do a sharp right turn down Rookery Lane. It's got to be a local man, Gordon. It just isn't likely that a stranger would have known about such a convenient dumping place—a lake just 60 yards from the road."

"Standing on this footpath," continued Clifton, "he could have thrown the axe towards the water. But it was a dark, foggy night. He mightn't have seen the island—just 30 yards from the shore. A powerful man, maybe he didn't know his own strength."

"But he wouldn't have heard the splash of it hitting the water," interjected Reedman.

"No matter," said Clifton. "There was nothing he could do about it anyway. He couldn't wade out to the island. Maybe he didn't hang around to hear a splash. He would have just wanted to get away as quickly as possible."

But why had the murderer painted the axe between the two killings?

"Possibly to cover up any possible traces of the first murder," said Reedman.

Again the paint was a critical clue. But where had it come from? Even with larger quantities of paint on the axe now available for analysis, the Huntingdon scientists still weren't able to say. Again the investigation appeared to stall.

THE SCIENTIST-DETECTIVE

The only other hopeful lead that Clifton still had was the two runners seen near both murder scenes and still not eliminated from the inquiry. With all other avenues explored, he and Reedman in early June 1992 visited Professor David Canter at the University of Surrey in Guildford for an "offender profile" of the sort of person, or people, who could have committed the murders.

With a computer database of more than 1,000 murderers, rapists and other violent criminals, Canter had a reputation as the country's foremost forensic psychologist in being able to sift mounds of raw evidence for clues that could lead police to the type of offender capable of certain crimes.

In his book-lined office, the lean, 48-year-old professor viewed the videos of the two murder scenes. He suggested the possibility of there being two killers, of one being a much stronger personality than the other—possibly able to manipulate his accomplice. Clifton decided to scan the forces computer files for a few more suspects.

Later, as he was at the door and about to leave, Clifton mentioned their other problem: identifying the paint found on the body of Joe Rylatt. "Why not try the Paint Research Association?" suggested the professor.

The two officers looked at each other. This little-known private organization, serving the paint industry, was something they had never even heard of. Canter knew about it simply because it was local.

Within days, Clifton and Reedman were at the Association's headquarters speaking to head of research, Norman Falla. Clifton produced a small glass bottle with scrapings of the grey paint from the axe-head. "Is there any way you can identify the firm that made this paint?" he asked.

"Not a chance," Falla responded. "However, we can possibly tell you a little bit more about the ingredients of this particular paint."

A lean, balding 49-year-old with gold-rimmed spectacles and with degrees in chemistry and spectroscopy, Falla looked like the typical laboratory scientist, but he was a lot more than that. For the past ten years he had been a volunteer police officer in his spare time. He had also long taken an interest in the forensic evidence of murder trials.

Eagerly, he led his visitors up to his large, brightly lit, first-floor laboratory for a tour of equipment that might help solve their problem. Falla mentioned a couple of tongue-twisting processes: gas chromatography-mass spectrometry. "That's known to its friends as GCMS. The other one is called ICPAES—inductively coupled plasma atomic emission spectrometry. In essence, they simply subject tiny samples of paint to ferocious temperatures and then analyze the emissions produced."

In preparation, Falla had to spend some days setting up apparatus, dissolving the paint sample in acids. After the tests were run, a computer began printing out a list of the paints elements and their concentration. A high level of zinc—80 per cent came as no surprise.

Later that week, Falla was able to establish an important distinctive characteristic in the paint: its bonding agent—the ingredient that makes paint stick to surfaces. In the tests with his ICPAES equipment, Falla could tell that the bonding agent was an epoxy resin.

Next, he ran ICPAES tests on other zinc paints with known epoxy binders and scrutinized them. Finally, he had a near perfect match. The bonding agent was an unusual one: Epoxyester D4.

Sent a copy of Falla's report, Clifton again felt hope rising. On the phone to Falla, he queried, "Who makes this Epoxyester D4?" Falla couldn't say, but his association provided names of British paint manufacturers and component suppliers who might. Working their way through these lists, Clifton's team eventually got their answer. Epoxyester D4 was made by a firm called Condea, in Essen, Germany.

From Condea, detectives discovered that the bonding agent was supplied to 11 different paint manufacturers scattered through Germany, France, Belgium and the Netherlands. A team of officers spent several days on a mass of telephone calls and faxes to the paint companies.

They had three key questions to put to the companies: *Was their paint made with reconstituted zinc? Did it use the bonding agent Epoxyester D4? Was it grey in colour?*

In this way, they established that just two firms made paint that filled all those requirements: one in France, the other in the Netherlands. The French firm insisted that it had never exported its products to Britain.

That just left Rustoleum, a Dutch firm in Roosendaal, near the Belgian border. It made Rustoleum 2185, a grey, zinc-rich spray-on paint used mainly for touching up bare metal that was scratched in the course of a manufacturing process.

Supplied with samples, both Falla and forensic scientists at Huntingdon agreed that the paint had properties identical to those found on the axe and the body of Joe Rylatt.

HOLMES SPEAKS

Clifton's team now set out to trace the paint's distribution in Britain and found that Rustoleum had one agent operating from a warehouse in West Bromwich. From there they followed the trail back to Lincoln—to an engineering tool merchant who supplied the whole of the surrounding area: Hykeham Forum Supplies.

Police learned that Hykeham had only bought one consignment of 36 cans of Rustoleum 2185. A dozen were still on their shelves. The other 24 had gone to a nearby manufacturer of heating systems: Specialist Heat Exchangers, a company of 172 employees.

Clifton decreed: "If necessary, we'll interview every single person in that company." But as he scanned the accordion print-out of employees, he suddenly pulled up short. One name looked familiar: *Dennis Granville Smalley*.

Tapping the name into his HOLMES computer terminal, Clifton soon discovered why. His detectives had already interviewed Smalley five months earlier as one of those to whom Joe Rylatt had lent money. Quickly tapping more keys, Clifton soon had the interview report on his computer screen. Smalley had told police that on the night of Rylatt's murder he had been at home looking after his two young children while his wife was out at her cleaning job. *But was he telling the truth?* Clifton now wondered.

At the next morning's meeting, Clifton instructed his detectives: "Find out everything you possible can about Smalley—but without alerting the man."

Now living in North Hykeham on the southern outskirts of Lincoln, 47-year-old Smalley had been in trouble with the law only once, some 30 years before, when convicted of larceny. Of far more interest: Smalley was the only suspect to have emerged so far who was known to be connected to both murder victims.

Digging deeper, police discovered that Smalley had not only borrowed money from Joe Rylatt recently, but known him as a child. He was an almost exact contemporary of Joe's younger brother Bruce. They had all grown up in St Peter's Avenue—and often played together in nearby Boultham Park. And as a teenager, he had worked part-time for Fred Maltby for six months after leaving school.

In 1975, Smalley had borrowed £170 from Joe Rylatt to get married, and since 1977 been a steady, reliable sheet-metal worker at Specialist Heat Exchangers. But in 1987, he had been in a serious car accident that had meant him missing nine months of work over the next three years—and he had begun borrowing more money.

As Clifton read his detectives reports, he gradually realized that Smalley was a man drowning in debt. As police trawled through the judgments of the local county court, they discovered that various finance houses had not only sued him for unpaid loans, but that Smalley had even been defaulting in court-ordered repayments.

On the afternoon of July 27, 1992, Clifton summoned eight hand-picked members of his team to West Parade police station. He explained that the investigation had gone about as far as it could go without Smalley being brought in for questioning. "There are certain questions that we are going to have to put to him—formally and on tape. We are also going to search his house to try and establish the full extent of his debts and for any forensic evidence that might link him with the two murders. Who knows, maybe tomorrow we might at last start getting somewhere with this investigation."

In the frame: Dennis Smalley.

INTERROGATION

At 7.30 the next morning, two unmarked police cars pulled up outside 44 Elizabeth Avenue, North Hykeham—a two-storey brick house. Smalley had already left for work. While one team of police and forensic experts stayed to start their search of Smalley's home, another sped off to his workplace.

Smalley calmly agreed to accompany them to West Parade police station. Detective Constable John Taylor was struck by the composure of the man—very much the gentle giant. A hulking figure of six foot three, with short, greying hair and a moustache, Smalley walked with an almost shambling gait—yet nevertheless conveyed an impression of awesome strength.

In the police interview room suspect and detectives were completely cut off from the distractions of the outside world. Sound-proofed and air-conditioned, the room had no windows, no pictures, no adornments and pale grey walls. All the furniture—interview table, wooden benches either side of it—had been firmly anchored to the floor. Even the tape-recorder was bolted to the table.

Smalley answered the detectives questions with mild unconcern.

Asked about his whereabouts on the night of Rylatt's murder, he stuck to his original story. He had been at home looking after his two youngsters—9-year-old Andrew and Claire, 10. Challenged, Smalley insisted, "I did not go out that evening. I stayed at the house all evening with my kids. I never leave my children alone."

"And on the night of Maltby's murder?" He had been at home then as well. His wife, Gillian, couldn't confirm his alibi as she had been out at her job. She worked every evening except Sunday.

He admitted knowing Fred Maltby. "I used to do a bit of work down on the farm on a Saturday morning to earn a bit of pocket money."

"When was the last time he had seen him?" he was asked. A good 30 years ago.

"So you haven't seen him since then?" Taylor persisted.

"No, no."

Police knew that Smalley had large debts—but not how large. "How much do you reckon you owe in total, Dennis?" asked Westfield.

"About £7,000 or £8,000."

Yet police had discovered that within two weeks of Rylatt's murder, Smalley had been able to repay £2,500 of his debts. How had that been possible?

Calmly, Smalley explained that had been money he had managed to save. For the moment, there was nothing the detectives could do to disprove him.

From Clifton's extensive briefing the day before, Taylor knew that Smalley had been cashing his pay cheques with Rylatt—on 11 different occasions between January and October 1991. Why was that? "Because I sometimes used to work late and miss the bank late at night on a Thursday."

A more likely explanation, Taylor thought, was that Smalley owed his bank so much money that, had he presented a pay cheque, the money would simply have been seized by creditors to help pay off existing debt.

However hard Taylor probed, Smalley doggedly denied having any large debt with Rylatt. Yet in the month before his murder, he knew Rylatt had been down to see Smalley three times at his place of work—the last time the day before he was killed. Police had found Rylatt's name in the visitors' book at Specialist Heat Exchangers.

From other police investigations, Taylor already knew that the easy-going Rylatt didn't bother with a debt for anything less than £500. "How do you explain that, Dennis? Why would Rylatt have bothered to go four miles out of town for a small sum?"

Smalley shrugged. "Joe told me he had some other business in Doddington Road, so he had just sort of popped in like."

"The man's lying," Taylor reported back to Clifton. "I am convinced that he's been telling us one lie after another."

Clifton, however, had one good bit of news. In a shed at Smalley's home, his detectives had found five tins of paint. Three of them: Rustoleum 2185—the paint used on the axe-head. "Lets ask him about that," said Clifton.

Back in the interview room, Smalley remained unperturbed. He admitted that he had stolen the paint from his employers—but so had others. For many, it was almost a perk of the job.

THE TRIAL

To test the whole case, Clifton went to see prosecuting counsel, James Hunt, for a final, line-by-line perusal of the evidence. Hunt indicated one or two points that Smalley's defence might try to exploit and suggested some more detail on the household accounts produced by Smalley and his wife, and on the partial repayment of his debts so soon after Rylatt's murder.

After more than a year on the case, Clifton was ready to move. On January 7, 1993, police arrested Smalley and formally charged him with the murders of Fred Maltby and Joe Rylatt. Smalley seemed unperturbed by the charges.

His trial at Lincoln Crown Court began on June 8, 1994. Clifton, already working on another murder case, was only able to make an occasional visit to court. But for every day of its four-week proceedings, Gordon Reedman, now retired, took his seat amid the neo-Gothic splendour of No. 1 Court.

Unusual for British justice, the case relied almost exclusively on circumstantial evidence. Clifton, Reedman and their colleagues had done their work well. When Smalley took the witness stand, Reedman gazed at the large, powerful hands gripping the wooden rail of the witness stand and listened as Smalley, in a slow, even voice, struggled to explain how he had been able suddenly to repay substantial chunks of his debts; and where he had been on the night of Rylatt's murder. He remained as unruffled as ever, yet his answers to key questions sounded no more convincing than they had sounded to the police.

After six and a half hours' deliberation, the jury foreman announced the verdict. Unanimously, the jurors found Smalley guilty of both murders.

Awarding him two life sentences, the judge, Mr Justice Holland, told the convicted man: "Each man was known to you and had no reason to expect anything other than your affection and gratitude. My own and the public's reaction can only be one of revulsion."

Smalley stood in the dock without protest—or apparent remorse.

As Smalley was led off to his cell, Reedman felt a surge of relief. While the detective in him yearned to know what had gone through the mind of a man who could commit a crime of such unfathomable and unpredictable violence, at least he had the satisfaction of knowing the killer was now behind bars. Reedman knew that the anguish of the families of the murdered men could finally begin to ease. The time and effort that he and Clifton and their team had put in during the long months of the investigation now seemed of little consequence.

As Clifton himself put it later: "The most important thing was that a murderer had been brought to justice."

CRACKING THE
KILLER'S
CODE

BY PETER MICHELMORE

THE DETERMINED PROSECUTOR SUSPECTED THE

CRYPTIC MESSAGE MIGHT SPELL MURDER.

Slipping a cassette into a tape player in her office in downtown Baltimore, Assistant US Attorney Jamie Bennett listened in bewilderment to two men talking on the telephone.

"What's up?" said the voice of Anthony Jones, a 25-year-old drug lord and suspected killer. A grunt greeted him in reply. Then Jones said, "Go see that nergy bergy dergy and get them gergies."

On and on they conversed in a baffling mixture of English and ergy-talk. At one point Bennett heard Jones growl, "That nergy jergy gotta get wergy tergy."

Fellow prosecutor Robert Harding stood at the door listening. "There's something criminal going on here that we need to know about," Bennett said. Harding agreed. But not even these seasoned prosecutors could guess the full truth.

GANG WARFARE

Over the years Bennett had won dozens of convictions against drug dealers and gun traffickers, making neighborhoods safer, as she put it, for "people who don't want to live in fear." She had taken a huge pay cut when she left corporate law, but found her new work deeply satisfying. "I feel rich having a job I love," Bennett told friends.

In the spring and summer of 1996, she began developing a case against a drug organization headed by Daniel "Baby Dan" Ross. Harding, meanwhile, focused on a rival group led by Elway Williams. They worked together on the cases.

But the name Anthony Jones loomed large in both investigations. Baltimore police and Drug Enforcement Administration (DEA) agents counted him the biggest prize of all.

For years police had suspected Jones of terrorizing East Baltimore and hiring the toughest thugs to protect his drug-dealing business. They thought he and his associates had a role in at least ten killings, including that of an innocent bystander, a 20-year-old man.

In the violent world of inner-city drug gangs, Jones stood out; his reputation was that he was willing to kill *anyone* who stood in his way. One night in October 1994, a drug dealer, street-named Shugg, was shot 12 times. Police believed that Anthony Jones and a cousin, Darnell Jones, committed the murder, but the state lacked evidence to prosecute the case.

(Title page) **Gibberish**: Jamie Bennett (right) and Robert Harding had to decipher the strange language of taped calls.

According to Baby Dan Ross, he and Jones formed an alliance against Williams; then Jones gunned down Williams's partner. Almost a year later, in February 1996, Williams himself took two bullets in the back from three former cohorts, who, Ross would later testify, agreed to kill their former boss so that Jones would not kill them. But Williams survived; it was Jones's first big mistake.

The second mistake occurred a few months later when Jones was arrested for criminal possession of a loaded gun. After a court hearing in November 1996, he was sentenced to 37 months and sent to a prison in Allenwood, Pennsylvania.

WALL OF SILENCE

Meanwhile, DEA agents and Baltimore detectives were harvesting physical evidence—guns, narcotics and vehicles with secret compartments—and questioning key players. But Jones's men seemed to be more scared of him than the law. "I'm not talking," said one to Bennett. "You'll get me killed."

The prosecutors then made a major breakthrough. Ross and Williams, facing life in prison on charges of conspiracy and racketeering, agreed to plead guilty and become witnesses against Jones. They told what they knew, and in mid-December 1996 a sealed indictment was handed down against Jones and his gang. The case was shaping up, but prosecutors still needed cooperation from other witnesses. That wouldn't be easy. In the early weeks of 1997, police and DEA agents began rounding up suspected gang members and holding them in the Baltimore City Detention Center, where Anthony Jones awaited arraignment on the new indictment. Gang members would later testify that Jones warned them that if they talked, he would kill them—and their mothers.

Even though Jones was still locked away, Bennett felt the man's menace in interviews she conducted for grand jury hearings. "Jones's people would never admit it, but I guarantee they're all afraid of him," she told Harding.

One of the men Bennett had subpoenaed was John Jones, Anthony's brother. But Bennett came to like the young man for his easy laugh and self-deprecating manner. He was not a violent person, and she respected the fact that he was raising four children alone. John Jones testified that he knew nothing about Anthony's activities, although he did admit that his brother carried a gun.

Weeks later, on February 26, 1997, John Jones was murdered, shot three times in the head and once in the back of the neck, severing his spinal cord. "Anthony's behind this," remarked one officer.

"Let's not jump to conclusions," Bennett replied. "There may be no connection." It seemed inconceivable that Anthony would have his own brother killed. Why? And how could he dare to order a hit from prison?

CRYPTIC CODE

To help build her case, Bennett fetched tapes of dozens of telephone conversations Anthony Jones had with his henchmen on the outside. Inmates knew their phone calls were recorded, so Bennett didn't expect he would say anything incriminating. Still, she hoped he might let slip with a piece of information they could use.

On one of these tapes, Bennett heard him talking to his mother and his brother John in regular street language. Both explained they told the grand jury virtually nothing incriminating; John said he had mentioned the gun his brother carried, and Anthony's only response was to say, "Oh."

Bennett thought nothing of it, concentrating instead on Jones's unintelligible fergy-dergy conversations with his lieutenants. Refusing to give up, Bennett played the tapes over and over, even at home.

One morning she listened closely as a gang member referred to a newspaper story, and then went on with something about the "bergy cergy detergy cergy." Bennett recalled that the *Baltimore Sun* had printed remarks she had made about witnesses being threatened in the Baltimore City Detention Center.

That's when it hit her: "Bergy" meant Baltimore, "cergy" meant city. Jones and his men used the first letter or sound of a real word and added "ergy."

Jones habitually used the word nigger for black people. In the tapes, Bennett realized, "that nergy elwergy" must mean Elway Williams. When Jones said, "Go see that bergy dergy and get them gergies," he was, she guessed, telling his henchmen to go see Baby Dan and get guns.

Bennett replayed a tape and stopped at the words "That nergy jergy gotta get wergy tergy." Jones seemed to be giving an order. Then she had it: "That nigger John gotta get whacked tonight."

Bennett noted the date of the conversation, February 24—two days before John Jones was shot. A shudder of blame ran through her. The grand jury testimony she'd extracted from John Jones had cost him his life. *By having his brother killed*, Bennett thought, *he's sending a message that he'll stop at nothing.*

The prosecutors arranged to have cooperating witnesses transferred to different prisons, and moved the families of some to secret locations. Jones was also moved and denied a phone. But his ruthlessness was having an effect. Nine of the 17 men indicted in the case flatly refused to say a word about Jones, and one who had been talking clammed up.

SLIP-UP

One day that spring, Baby Dan Ross stepped out of a shower at the Charles County Detention Center in La Plata, Maryland, and stopped dead in his tracks.

There, sitting on a bench, was Anthony Jones. Jones spoke openly about the Shugg murder, Ross would testify: "I know they ain't got no witnesses because we were wearing masks when it happened."

In the transfer from Allenwood, Jones had accidentally been sent to the wrong prison. Ross figured that Jones didn't know he was talking to prosecutors. Prosecutors were horrified, but the mix-up had paid off. Bennett and Harding were now more confident that they would nail Jones for the murder of Shugg.

"DEVIL WOMAN"

The trial of Jones's confederates in October 1997 was conducted in an atmosphere of high tension. Jurors traveled to the federal building in escorted vans with tinted glass, and made rendezvous each morning at a frequently alternating, secret location. Even Bennett and Harding were forbidden to take public transport or to use public parking lots. They were to enter the federal building only from an underground garage. Ten defendants—watched over by 15 muscular marshals—sat in the front of the courtroom. Seven others had pleaded guilty and five of them would take the stand.

Jurors listened raptly when Bennett told them in opening, "This was all part of a war, a war about how Anthony Jones wanted to be the most feared and most powerful drug dealer in Baltimore."

Her compelling opening statement was followed by some unexpected fallout: One of Jones's lieutenants, caught on the tapes, changed his plea to guilty. He confirmed Bennett's translations of the code, thus allowing the tapes to be admitted as evidence. The recordings mesmerized the jury.

Although Jones was not there, Bennett could feel his presence. His henchmen glowered at her with hatred. "Devil woman," one hissed at her. "Black widow," snarled another.

The defendants seemed to grow increasingly desperate. At the end of a session in early December, a marshal had one handcuff on a burly thug when the man suddenly swung the free cuff at the marshal's face and lunged for his gun. Three marshals charged in with pepper sprays. Cursing and tearing at his eyes, the defendant was led away.

Three days before Christmas, after only a day's deliberation, the jurors reached a verdict. The defendants, fitted with electric-stun belts, didn't move a muscle as the foreman pronounced nine men guilty.

Bennett listened with the impassive face of a prosecutor who'd simply done her job, but inside she felt a surge of elation. The Jones gang had imploded. Its defiant members would go to prison—most of them for life.

FINAL VERDICT

Because Bennett and Harding were seeking the death penalty, Jones would stand trial alone. At a pretrial hearing in March 1998, Bennett watched Jones glad-handing his lawyers. It was his 25th birthday, and he acted as if he was sure to beat the rap.

During the trial he tried to strike up a conversation with Bennett. She ignored him. Despite the rebuff, Jones affected a glib, confident manner—even as witnesses described his grotesque crimes and tapes revealed his plot to kill his brother.

But in the end Bennett watched in quiet satisfaction as the jury foreman wiped the smile off the killer's face—speaking the word guilty. Anthony Jones closed his eyes.

The jury spared Anthony Jones the death penalty, but the judge gave him three consecutive life sentences. Forbidden contact with other inmates or anyone from the outside world, he is being held in virtual solitary confinement for the rest of his life. Jones is appealing his conviction and the conditions of his incarceration.

After the verdict, the mother of one of Jones's victims met Jamie Bennett outside the courtroom and clasped the prosecutor's hand. "Thank you," she said.

Face of defiance: Anthony Jones thought he was beyond the law.

JUSTICE
FOR-DIANE

MICHAEL WELZENBACH

THE MISSING WOMAN HAD SURELY
BEEN MURDERED, BUT BY WHOM? AND
WHERE WAS HER BODY? RICK PHILLIPS
WAS DETERMINED TO FIND OUT.

Constable Rick Phillips eases his patrol car to the side of Highway 518 and shuts off the engine. The road is hemmed in with tag alder, black spruce and birch, beyond which sprawl swamps full of cranberry and outcroppings of granite. A keen outdoorsman, Phillips knows the trackless bush of the Bear Lake region of northern Ontario well.

"You know," he says, "a person could fall off the roadside right here and break a leg, and never be seen again. People have just vanished out here."

The disappearance of Diane Chalmers is obviously on his mind. A plain, intellectually handicapped woman, Chalmers, 42, could neither read nor write. Like a number of residents of the remote townships of Bear Lake/Burk's Falls, she lived at the margins of Canadian society.

But for Rick Phillips, a sandy-haired 44-year-old with a ready smile, everyone is equal under the law, and Chalmers deserved justice.

"I'll take the memory of her to my grave," he says. That's partly because the bad guy got away—sort of.

Around 2pm on April 26, 1992, Phillips pulled up in front of a drab little cottage on Lot 24 of McMurrich Township. The square-jawed Ontario Provincial Police (OPP) officer was responding to a missing person's report filed at his Burk's Falls headquarters. It was a cold, bright afternoon, and rafts of stubborn snow still littered the woods and roadsides. In the car with Phillips was 32-year-old Ricky Cotter, common-law husband of the missing woman. They had shared the cramped residence for several years.

Diane Chalmers had not shown up as planned for Easter weekend in Fort Erie, Ontario, where Cotter was staying with his parents. In fact, Chalmers hadn't been seen by anyone for 12 days. Finally, late the night before, Larry Levinski, proprietor of the nearby Bear Lake General Store, had called the police on Cotter's behalf to report her missing. After asking Levinski to contact the cops, Cotter had driven up from Fort Erie.

Cotter seemed genuinely puzzled about his wife's whereabouts. The two were not terribly close, he admitted. Theirs was more an alliance of convenience: His part-time summer jobs were supplemented by Chalmers's welfare and tax-rebate cheques. But for her not to have contacted him for so long was highly unusual.

Phillips queried Cotter closely about Chalmers's friends and places she might retreat to if upset or lonely. The constable had never met Chalmers, but he knew she was in the habit of walking alone along winding, dusty Highway 518 to the Bear Lake General Store or to the Sprucedale Hotel for some company. While making his rounds, Phillips had often passed her—a slight, awkward-looking woman trundling along the road with a canvas bag.

As he and Cotter walked up to Chalmers's cabin, the constable saw a notice pinned to the inside door. On it was scrawled: "Diane, Rick phoned. Wants you to call his mom & dad. Will pick you up tomorrow. Fixed your door. Larry."

Apparently from Levinski, Phillips thought. He inspected the door. Sure enough, the hasp to the padlock had been pried and then roughly repaired with a couple of new screws.

The tiny living room looked recently occupied. The bed in the loft above was unmade. There were no obvious signs of intrusion or struggle. Maybe Chalmers had simply walked off.

"Is it normal for her to just disappear?" Phillips asked Cotter.

Cotter shrugged. "Sometimes." Then he stooped to pick Chalmers's purse up from under a table.

What woman would leave home without her purse? Phillips wondered. He began to inspect the cottage with renewed interest.

Chalmers's suitcase lay near the door, obviously packed for her trip to Fort Erie. Stranger still, her prescription glasses rested on the kitchen table, and two defrosted pork chops sat rotting in the sink. A pair of dark-brown slacks, panties still inside, lay half concealed by a blanket on the floor by the couch. Last, the bulky canvas bag Chalmers was never seen without rested against the wall.

Crime scene: Phillips at Chalmers's cabin.

From his car, Phillips radioed his partner, Constable Gary Alexander, asking him to start interviewing the missing woman's friends and neighbors. Then he called to request a crime scene officer to give the cottage a professional going over.

After examining Chalmers's home for two hours, Senior Constable Bill Belford and Sergeant Penny Barager called Phillips. "Could you return to the cabin?" Barager inquired. "And bring Mr Cotter with you?"

At the cabin, Barager walked out to greet Phillips. "I think we've got something more serious than a missing person's report," she said quietly.

The dingy living room was now brilliantly illuminated by a photo floodlight. "We've got blood here, Rick," Belford announced. He pointed out a small stain on a sheet covering the sofa. "There's also blood on the corner of the coffee table and a spatter pattern on the wall over here. And it looks like the area in front of the stove has been recently cleaned. We've also got several potential weapons," he said, pointing to a broken hatchet head and a curious-looking hammer he'd found buried under the stack of firewood.

Phillips went out to his car. "Ricky," he asked, giving Cotter a hard look, "is there any reason there might be blood in the house?"

Cotter frowned. "No," he said, obviously bewildered. Phillips believed him. "Come into the house for a second," he said.

Inside, Belford asked Cotter if anything looked out of place. Cotter gazed around. "The coffee table shouldn't be against the wall. Usually it's in front of the couch."

The misplaced furniture fitted with Belford's suspicion that someone had recently cleaned the floor between the sofa and the woodstove.

That evening, Belford found blood that had soaked through old hatchet cuts in the damp linoleum floor by the stove. An examination of the plumbing that ran from the kitchen sink turned up a sizable clot of congealed blood—about 500 millilitres. Enough, Belford thought, to have rendered unconscious the person who lost it.

Blood deteriorates quickly if moist. Retrieving viable DNA from these samples—almost two weeks old—would be difficult for experts at the Centre of Forensic Sciences (CFS) in Toronto.

A canine handler and his dog searched the immediate area the next morning but found nothing suspicious. Another team began combing the Bear Lake landfill just up the road from Chalmers's cabin.

Meanwhile, Detective Inspector Klancy Grasman of the Criminal Investigation Branch of the OPP in Toronto was driving north to Burk's Falls to co-ordinate the investigation. Given the wilderness terrain, the search would require a helicopter as well as numerous men on the ground.

Phillips and Belford were good officers, he knew. If they suspected murder, there had to be a body somewhere.

Grasman was flying over the bush in a helicopter the second day of the investigation when Phillips radioed that the search team had found a plastic bag full of blood-soaked clothing near the dump entrance. Jogging pants bearing the words Sprucedale Hotel appeared to be one of two pairs Chalmers had purchased the day she disappeared. The other was in her canvas bag at the cabin. Whoever murdered Diane, Phillips thought, must have used the pants to clean up the scene.

For the better part of a week, 30 police officers and a few locals fanned out to search the rugged bush around Bear Lake while helicopters skimmed the treetops. A police dog nosed through the frozen marshes, and divers searched lakes and swamps.

Without a body, it would be difficult to prosecute a murder case successfully, even if Phillips did come up with a plausible suspect.

As the investigation entered its second week, Phillips discovered that on the afternoon of Chalmers's disappearance, she had been seen drinking at the Sprucedale Hotel with Larry Levinski, then leaving with him in his Chrysler Laser that evening. That in itself was nothing strange. Levinski often gave Chalmers a ride home.

But that night, when Chalmers left with Levinski, she was carrying a paper bag containing the two new pairs of jogging pants—of which the blood-soaked ones were now being examined at CFS.

Chalmers's friend Judy Leigh's story of what occurred at Levinski's General Store later that night riveted Phillips's attention.

Leigh had gone to the store at about 9.30pm to wait for a phone call. She immediately noticed Levinski's wife, Pat, had been crying.

As the motherly Leigh chatted with Pat, Larry Levinski pulled up wildly in his Laser and screeched to a halt at the side door. Clearly drunk, he staggered out of the car with a container of furnace oil and headed straight for the basement.

Leigh watched as Levinski emerged from the basement and lurched into the kitchen to speak to his wife. She couldn't make out what he was saying but saw Levinski take off his glasses to examine them. They were bent and broken, with one of the lenses missing.

As the investigation dragged on, Phillips learned that Levinski and Chalmers had often been seen together. And the Laser had been observed at Chalmers's cabin, sometimes all evening.

Witnesses said the pair had left the Sprucedale Hotel around 7.45pm, and the hotel's cash register receipts corroborated that testimony. But Levinski claimed to have left the hotel about 9pm. So what happened during that unaccounted for hour and a half?

Finally, several people told police they had seen Levinski scrubbing out the back of the Laser in front of the store, using everything from baking soda to soap and cat litter. He told them he'd spilled fuel oil and was trying to get the smell out.

The contradictions in Levinski's account were piling up. After one local told police he had spotted the note on Chalmers's door days before she was reported missing, Phillips suspected Levinski had pinned it there to dupe investigators. The makeshift repair job on the door suggested a rushed job. Levinski could have returned to the cabin after the murder so he could clean up the blood and remove the body. There was also Levinski's statement that he had seen Chalmers getting the mail from her roadside mailbox as he drove past her place the day after their hotel meeting. But when Phillips checked the Sprucedale postal outlet, he learned her mail had not been picked up.

Looking into the 50-year-old storekeeper's background, Phillips discovered Levinski had a criminal history dating back to the early 1960s, having been convicted of crimes including conspiracy, theft, assault and gross indecency.

Phillips recalled the slacks found lying on the cabin floor. An attempted rape gone terribly wrong? If he could prove that, he'd have grounds for first degree murder charges against Levinski.

Bill Belford learned from an RCMP blood-spatter expert that the pattern of droplets on the wall at Chalmers's cottage suggested someone being hit by at least two powerful blows.

A piece of firewood could have done the job. All the killer would have had to do to dispose of the weapon was toss it into the stove, where Chalmers kept a fire going all day.

Phillips began to envision a scenario based on the physical evidence now assembled. Had Levinski bludgeoned Chalmers to death because she resisted rape, then gone back the next day to clean up and remove the body? Levinski claimed that the day after Chalmers's disappearance, he had taken his car to play bingo in a town some distance from Bear Lake.

But nobody at the bingo hall remembered seeing him.

Phillips discussed his hunch with Grasman, who instructed him to request a warrant to search the Levinskis' store and residence. On June 15, several items were seized from Levinski—including the clothing he was allegedly wearing the last time he was seen with Chalmers, his broken glasses and his car.

Phillips felt he was now beginning to draw the noose of circumstantial evidence tighter about his suspect. But he still had three towering problems: no

Searching for justice, and a body: Rick Phillips hunts for clues.

witnesses to a crime, no proof that the blood in the cabin and dump was Chalmers's—and no body.

At the CFS lab in Toronto, forensic scientist Keith Kelder had done some typing on the degraded blood from both the cabin and the clothes found at the dump. They matched, so he gave samples to Dr Wayne Murray for DNA testing. Now he had Levinski's car to examine for blood on the liner in the back. When he saw the vehicle, Kelder knew he had a tough job ahead of him. Although the liner had been soiled with fuel oil, cat litter, baking soda and possibly other chemicals, typing revealed that dried blood on the liner had the same origin as the blood on the clothes and in the cabin.

At Burk's Falls, Crown Prosecutor Don Upton impressed on Phillips that in the absence of a body, the Crown would be hard-pressed to convince a judge to commit Levinski to trial on a murder charge.

With Phillips pushing them hard, the search team continued combing the area. In late May 1992, they blew up a beaver dam to drain a small lake near Chalmers's cabin. In June they dug up some disturbed soil behind Chalmers's cabin that looked suspiciously like a burial site. It *was* a burial site—for two dogs. In July Phillips received a tip that Levinski had been seen tinkering with the septic tank of a cabin behind his lakeshore residence. Belford and Phillips spent an afternoon knee-deep in sewage, but found nothing.

Then Dr Murray requested samples of blood from Chalmers's ex-husband, her son, Lyle, and her mother, Alma. By taking their DNA profiles, he might be able to prove that the blood from the crime scene was Chalmers's. ·

As summer turned into autumn, Phillips stubbornly followed up all leads, no matter how vague. On October 27, Grasman got a call from Dr Murray at the Burk's Falls station.

"We've completed all of our probes," Murray told him. "The frequency with which the Chalmers's blood profile would be found in the population at random is at least one in 880,000."

"Cut to the chase. Is it Chalmers's blood?" asked Phillips.

"It sure is," said Murray.

"Come on," said Grasman. "Let's get ourselves a warrant."

The following morning, the two officers confronted their suspect. "Larry Levinski," Phillips said levelly, "You're under arrest for the murder of Diane Chalmers."

Levinski looked resigned as the officer read him his rights. Finally, Phillips had got his man.

But not for long.

At a hearing on November 30, the district court judge released Levinski on bail. An exasperated Phillips could only watch as the Levinskis packed up and moved to the border town of Welland, Ontario.

On May 10, 1993, Levinski was committed to stand trial for first degree murder, but his lawyer, Julian Falconer, was unimpressed. With no proof that Chalmers's murder had been premeditated, he knew that to make the charge stick, the Crown would have to prove Levinski had tried to rape Chalmers. Since there were no semen stains, he argued, the panties rolled up inside Chalmers's slacks did not constitute evidence of attempted rape.

The court agreed. Levinski would be tried on the lesser charge of second degree murder. Phillips and Upton would have to make the best of the circumstantial evidence and DNA matches.

After almost four years of legal wrangling, on April 15, 1996, Levinski's trial began in Parry Sound. Phillips spent gruelling hours on the stand, his meticulously compiled notes at hand. Thanks in part to his professionalism, incriminating statements Levinski made to police during the investigation were ruled admissible and presented in court.

Falconer knew if Levinski didn't plea bargain and the case went before a jury, he'd be looking at a lot of jail time. He convinced Levinski to tender an offer to the Crown: he'd take responsibility for Chalmers's death—on a charge of manslaughter.

During negotiations, Levinski admitted he had punched Chalmers during a drunken brawl after she accused him of stealing her tax-rebate cheque. She had hit him first, he claimed, breaking his glasses, and he'd lashed out in fury. Levinski further claimed he had no idea of the severity of her injury; Chalmers must have hit her head on the coffee table as she fell. He said he went home and fell asleep on the couch.

The following evening, he said, he began to worry about Chalmers and decided to stop by the cabin to see if she was OK. When he arrived, Levinski claimed, he found Chalmers dead in a pool of blood. He panicked, hastily cleaned up the blood, wrapped her body in a blanket and put her in the back of the Laser. The bloodied clothes, he shoved into a plastic bag that he threw into the dump. Then he drove off to toss Chalmers's body off a bridge into a nearby river.

Phillips was skeptical. Though Levinski was a big, strong man, a couple of blows from a fist couldn't possibly have resulted in so much blood loss. And Levinski's account of disposing of the body also struck him as dubious.

Levinski would have had to wrestle Chalmers's 125-pound body out of the side door of the cramped little Laser, then heave it up and over the metre-high guardrails.

Would a killer risk being discovered at such an act in the middle of a main road?

Nevertheless, Phillips and Grasman called out the dive teams. They found nothing.

The prosecution accepted Levinski's account of Chalmers's death and on December 2, 1996, he was sentenced to four years in prison.

Just four years! Phillips shook his head in disbelief.

For Rick Phillips the case isn't really over. He is haunted by the fact that someone was brutally killed on his watch and that the man who killed her will soon be free.

"I expect her body will turn up someday," he says, gazing out over the bush.

TRACKING THE *FOX*

BY TIM BOUQUET

UNDERCOVER POLICE HAD PENETRATED THE DEADLY DRUGS
RING AND MADE ARRESTS. BUT HOW COULD THEY TRAP
THE ENGLISHMAN KNOWN AS THE "FOX"—THE GANG'S
LEADER AND THE WORLD'S LEADING MARIJUANA SMUGGLER?

On a crisp April afternoon Larry Brant, a tall, craggy 44-year-old, stood on a small jetty in Hong Kong harbour, gazing in awe at the forest of high-rise temples to business that lined the waterfront. It was a world away from the sleepy town of Blaine, 6,500 miles distant in Washington State on America's north-west coast, which he had left two days earlier.

A keen sailor, Brant was captivated by Hong Kong's vast fleet of shipping, from tankers and luxury yachts to the ferries that ploughed their way over to Kowloon on the Chinese mainland. But he was looking for one boat in particular: a white launch. On board would be a gang of smugglers about to ship a massive load of marijuana from Vietnam across the Pacific to the US. They needed somebody to offload the drugs on to smaller boats which would then land the cargo north of Seattle.

Brant had to convince the smugglers he was that man.

He glanced at his watch. Then he saw her—a 50-foot motor yacht coming towards the jetty. *Right on time*, he thought as he went on board.

But Brant was no criminal. He was a US Drug Enforcement Administration (DEA) specialist in undercover busts. Posing as a drug runner, he had recently feigned sailing a cargo of marijuana from Thailand to Vancouver Island in a combined operation with the Royal Canadian Mounted Police. When dealers came out in small boats to unload his cargo, 14 were seized by the police SWAT Team on board.

Now the script was reversed. Accompanied by fellow DEA agent Helmut Witt, a ship-to-shore communications expert from Seattle, Brant was playing the offloader, a greedy small-town fisherman out for a big pay day.

The international undercover operation had started by chance. A few months before, DEA agents in Bangkok had picked up a small-time American drug dealer wanted in Florida. To save his neck, the dealer became an informant, promising to deliver a bigger prize—a major syndicate of expatriate Americans in south-east Asia who had been flooding the United States with marijuana for 15 years.

The informant reported that the shipment of marijuana was about to set sail from Vietnam. Back on America's west coast, the authorities set up a task force involving the DEA, the United States Attorney's office, the US Customs Office and the Coastguard.

First, the task force had to find out the precise spot where the marijuana was to be offloaded. Larry Brant was the ideal man for the job. Boats were in his blood. As a boy he sailed with his father. Between the ages of 18 and 21, when he went to college to study police science and criminology, he crewed on his uncle's salmon trawler. The stretch of coast where the dope was going was as familiar to him as his own back yard.

On board the white yacht Brant, armed with pictures of his "fleet"—snaps he had taken of six fishing vessels in Blaine harbour—nodded to the Chinese skipper. *Now we have no protection from our Hong Kong agents,* he thought as the craft headed out into the harbour. If their cover was blown, he and Witt could wind up at the bottom of the South China Sea.

In the comfortable cabin they were greeted by three men dressed in designer casuals who introduced themselves as Samuel, JT and Michael.

Brant immediately recognized Samuel Colflesh and his associate JT. In their early thirties, tanned, blond and good-looking, they had served in America's elite Special Forces in Thailand. Demobbed in the mid-1970s but hooked on adventure, they had turned to drug running.

But Brant could not place Michael. Standing six foot one and weighing around 13 stone, with a mop of mouse-coloured hair, he wore on his right hand a large jade ring in a gold setting. As Samuel Colflesh did most of the talking, he looked on in silence.

"So you can do the offload," said Colflesh.

"Sure, I've got the vessels," replied Brant, handing over his photographs. "We'll do the job."

While JT quizzed Witt on his knowledge of communications and encrypted codes, Samuel homed in on Brant's own supposed craft, a Delta 58. He already knew its engine size, storage capacity and sea-worthiness. *Thank goodness I ran through the technical spec with the boat's real owner,* thought Brant.

Then Michael spoke. He seemed bored by logistics. "On your previous offload missions you have *never* been intercepted by the Coastguard?" he asked. The accent was British, languid and well educated.

"Never," Brant assured him. "We have our own private dock." Michael nodded. *Maybe he's financing the operation,* mused Brant.

Colflesh was concerned that the mother ship carrying the marijuana, which he would be captaining, would be so much bigger than Brant's fishing boats it would crush them during unloading.

"How are we going to do this in rough seas?" he asked, then decided: "We'll tether you off the back on a line. My crew will load the product on to rafts and swing 'em alongside you. That way it should take about two days to offload." Brant realized that the cargo must be huge.

The meeting ended and the yacht turned back to shore. "What kind of boat do *you* have?" Brant asked Michael, hoping he might drop a clue to his identity. He said nothing.

Safely back in Hong Kong harbour, the two agents prepared to leave. Michael spoke again: "We're well known here. We'll stay in the cabin."

"Looks like we made it through the first hoop," Brant said to Witt as they watched the yacht head back out to sea.

Brant met Michael, Samuel and JT again a few weeks later in room 34 of Kowloon's spectacular Peninsula Hotel. They were joined by an American called Brian Daniels. A superannuated hippie married to a well-connected Thai, he was the supplier. The prime-grade Thai marijuana was on its way from the Golden Triangle on Vietnamese army trucks and would be loaded on to the mother ship off Da Nang. At 72 tonnes it would be the biggest-ever shipment into America's west coast.

"From now on," Samuel Colflesh told Brant, "you will be known as 'Gedo'. You'll call me 'Haig', and Michael is 'the Fox'."

Brant agreed to set up a private fax line by which they would let him know the ship was on its way. It led straight to a desk in the DEA's Seattle office.

But one question nagged at Brant: *Who is Michael the Fox?* Something told him the softly spoken Englishman had passed through his life once before.

Drug boat: *Encounter Bay* carried vast cargoes of marijuana.

Back in Blaine, Brant sifted through his old intelligence reports. Suddenly there it was. Two years earlier, Canadian customs had questioned Samuel Colflesh and an English companion in a routine stop. The two men had just delivered an 800-tonne ocean-going oil rig supply vessel called *Encounter Bay* into Vancouver for a million-dollar refit.

The report also contained the Englishman's passport photo. *That's the Fox!* Brant thought jubilantly. His full name: Michael Gleave Forwell, aged 43.

He was suspected of shipping marijuana into the United States for the past 14 years. But the American authorities knew little else about him. They had allowed him to go on his way.

Now Brant wondered: *Will we get the Fox this time?*

SHOOT-OUT

"Send the biggest boat you've got." In the Jackson Federal Building on Seattle's Second Avenue, Larry Brant was briefing the officers of the Thirteenth District Pacific North-West Region Coastguard. Their mission: to seize *Encounter Bay* and put Michael Forwell out of business.

"When Samuel Colflesh sees you and not me coming out to meet him, he's gonna take some irrational action," Brant continued. "If he runs, we need the speed to catch him wherever he heads. If he decides to ram you, we need any overpowering to be on our side."

Even though they had told him the shipment was due in early July, Brant had heard nothing from the Forwell organization since he had left Hong Kong. The fax in the DEA office had stayed silent. *Maybe they've guessed who I am and called it off.*

Then on June 25, 1988, the fax burst to life. It was a message from "Haig". Michael Forwell was on his way.

Brant jumped into his car. Half an hour later he walked into a bedroom at the Red Lion Hotel near Seattle's international airport. He had been told to expect Michael Forwell. But it was JT who handed him a VHF radio and a 15-page operational plan.

"The rendezvous with the mother ship is one of these six points 600 miles due west," Brant told his Coastguard colleagues. "The brief says that when we get to 100 miles from the ship we will get the exact offload point by radio."

The sleek 3,250-tonne Coastguard cutter *Boutwell* slipped from her berth at pier 36 on Seattle's Alaskan Highway South on June 28. On board were 20 officers, 148 crew, a helicopter and small boats. Soon she was surging out into the Pacific Ocean at 29 knots.

One of 12 cutters used by the Coastguard to hunt drug dealers over 74 million square miles of ocean from Alaska to Central America, the 378-foot *Boutwell* was armed with two 25mm laser-aimed machine guns and a weapons system for firing shells and tracers. On her bow was a 76mm gun used mainly as an anti-aircraft weapon.

Seven hundred and twenty miles away, Samuel Colflesh gazed down from the bridge of *Encounter Bay* over her ice-breaker bow. Even in 50-foot waves she could maintain 16 knots, and she had a back deck the size of a tennis court, ideal for shipping vast quantities of drugs.

Forwell had paid £2 million for her in the name of the Royalville Corporation, a Panamanian company incorporated in London, on behalf of Fox Marine International, based in the Cook Islands. Fox Marine also had a satellite Hong Kong office, care of a company in Aberdeen Marina called Trademax. But these were front companies, set up by Forwell. And if anyone did pry, between drug runs his flagship carried out legitimate business delivering marine equipment and towing battle cruisers for the Chilean Navy.

Encounter Bay's bridge was stuffed with the latest electronics and two state-of-the-art radar systems. A desalination plant and more than 500 tonnes of high-speed diesel meant Colflesh and his multinational crew could cross the Pacific without stopping. Covert antennas on masts and a sophisticated communications code helped her to hide in the vast expanses of the ocean.

Of the four days it had taken to prepare *Encounter Bay*, 17 hours alone had been spent loading bale upon bale of marijuana.

Now it was mid-afternoon on June 30, 1988. It would soon be time to call the fishermen and tell them the exact offload point. Samuel Colflesh looked up.

Above him a vivid orange, blue and white striped plane was circling. Colflesh swore. He knew exactly what he was looking at: *a C130 Coastguard surveillance aircraft, and it's not on fishery patrol!*

Instantly he turned course and yelled for full power from the engine room. An hour and a half later, Colflesh saw a boat on his radar screen. At 4.22pm *Boutwell* powered over the horizon. Twenty minutes on, she was 100 yards away and closing. Over the radio her skipper ordered Colflesh to stop.

The response was terse and dismissive. "You have no authority! I am a Panamanian vessel in international waters."

Once more *Boutwell* ordered Colflesh to stop and prepare for boarding. The cutter was now right up alongside the drug ship. But *Encounter Bay* still showed no signs of stopping.

Back in Seattle a teletype request from *Boutwell* arrived in the Coastguard office. "Permission to fire cannon over her bows."

Minutes later a large explosion shook *Encounter Bay*. Colflesh held his course. There was a rattle of machine-gun fire as *Boutwell* inched ever closer. Another shot thumped past *Encounter Bay*'s bow.

Just before 7pm a message echoed across the water from *Boutwell*'s tannoy: "Get your personnel out of the engine room! We're going to disable the ship."

Round after round of armour-piercing shells spat across the water, punched holes in *Encounter Bay*'s port side and ricocheted around the engine room. Forwell came on the satellite phone from his command base in Singapore. "Michael, they're shooting the life out of us," shouted Colflesh. "Any minute they're gonna hit the engines … What do you *mean* you don't believe me?"

Colflesh hauled back the bridge window and thrust the phone outside. The gunfire was headsplitting. *Boutwell* seemed close enough to touch. Colflesh pulled the receiver back inside. "*Now* do you believe me, Michael?"

But the line was dead.

THE STASH

Several days later, Larry Brant stood on top of 8,250 bales of marijuana. After the three-hour gun battle, during which his engine room and bridge were raked with 70 rounds, Samuel Colflesh had finally surrendered. On July 13 the crippled *Encounter Bay* was hauled into Tacoma Harbour, south of Seattle. Now Colflesh and his 17 crew were being taken into custody ashore.

Brant ripped open one of the bales, each wrapped in blue waterproof bags which were heat-sealed and secured with metal grommets. Every one carried a stamp of a blue eagle over a line of red type: PASSED INSPECTION. This was Brian Daniels's trademark.

Inside, Brant found a layer of polythene, well taped. Underneath that was a cardboard box. Inside were eight kilo-packs of prime-grade Thai grass, vacuum-packed on special machines imported from Germany.

Reloaded on to military trucks, the marijuana was taken under helicopter escort to the army's Yakima Firing Centre in eastern Washington. The bales took five days and five nights to burn.

The authorities had got the drugs and Colflesh, but they had not destroyed Forwell's organization—and they were nowhere near getting their hands on the Fox.

There was nothing to link Forwell to *Encounter Bay*, apart from those two meetings in Hong Kong where he had said little. Any smart lawyer would claim he was just a bystander.

Brant went back on board to nose around for clues. In Colflesh's cabin was a desk and a fax machine. Brant noticed a ball of paper screwed up on the floor.

He smoothed it out. It was a fax from Colflesh. It read URGENT: URGENT: URGENT: PLSE ASK FOX TO CALL US NOW. PLSE ASK FOX TO CALL US NOW.

Michael Forwell was now tied hard and fast to *Encounter Bay*.

KEY TO THE EMPIRE

"You don't need me to tell you that you're facing a long spell behind bars." Assistant US Attorney Mark Bartlett leaned back in his chair in the interview room at Kent Corrections Facility, south of Seattle, and stared at Samuel Colflesh. Next to Bartlett sat Larry Brant.

Bartlett, a dark-haired 32-year-old who kept fit by weightlifting, was a key player in the Organized Crime Drug Taskforce set up to hook Forwell, Daniels and Colflesh. To stand any chance of grabbing Forwell, Bartlett and Brant needed Colflesh to start talking.

"We're not drug runners, we don't just run marijuana," Colflesh told them defiantly. He launched into a rambling story about how the Forwell organization, refused financial help by the CIA, was only running drugs to fund its own private insurgency against communists in Laos and Cambodia.

Rich pickings: Larry Brant (centre) inspects 8,250 bales of marijuana, worth £300 million, found on *Encounter Bay*.

"We're going to need something a little less off the wall," Bartlett told him. "If you don't give us some real leads on Forwell's organization, you face a *minimum* of ten years."

Colflesh had run out of room to manoeuvre. He took a piece of paper and wrote down a set of numbers.

A few days later Brant punched the combinations into the door of a 5,000-square-foot warehouse in a light-industrial district in south San Francisco. "Looks like a commercial-vehicle showroom," said Brant to a colleague, eyeing three immaculate white Ford utility trucks parked inside.

The building, leased to Leading Sale Investment Company, a Hong Kong outfit set up by Colflesh, was the west coast distribution plant of the Fox's marijuana empire.

In one of the trucks they found a key which opened the door of a two-vehicle car carrier—a 40-foot enclosed trailer. This was where consignments of marijuana worth millions of dollars were broken down into smaller quantities before being loaded on to the vans and delivered to Forwell's dealer network.

"Wow!" Brant exclaimed as they walked towards two 40-foot racing power-boats, *Kimono* and *Mariposa*, moored on blocks. "Cigarette boats. They can do around 90mph."

As Colflesh explained later, Forwell had conceived the idea of catapulting the boats, loaded with 12 million dollars' worth of marijuana, straight off the back of *Encounter Bay*, like planes leaving an aircraft carrier.

Forwell volunteered to do it first. It worked! The 150-mile journey from ship to shore took Forwell and Colflesh eight hours. The two men dashed under San Francisco's Golden Gate Bridge at 60mph in broad daylight, and unloaded their cargo openly on to the white trucks at the city's best marina. Forwell even hired a helicopter and photographer to film their arrival.

"The more grandiose and visible Michael made himself, the less the authorities would see what he was doing," Colflesh told Bartlett and Brant.

Forwell backed up the bravado with meticulous organization. At any sign of police activity, watch teams on the coast would alert the cigarette boats to put into beaches where he and Colflesh would be picked up by E&E (Escape and Evade) teams. They would strip off their racing suits to reveal the business suits, shirts and ties they were wearing underneath. Jettisoning the drugs, they would escape on motorbikes.

But nothing ever went wrong. For two years Forwell shipped marijuana into San Francisco right under the noses of the Coastguard.

We'll find no fingerprints here, Brant realized as he read a sign on the warehouse wall: "Gloves will be worn at all times".

The Fox had left no traces in Hong Kong, either. Shortly after the seizure of *Encounter Bay*, police raided the offices of Forwell's company Trademax. They had been cleaned out.

Then the tide turned. Brian Daniels was arrested in Switzerland laundering his money. JT gave himself up, saving US authorities a lengthy extradition from Thailand. In Seattle he told Bartlett that a few days after the drugs were seized, Forwell had flown to meet him in Bangkok to discuss what to do next.

"I'm going underground," Forwell told him. "They're going to have to catch me."

While questioning JT, Bartlett received a message from the Australian police—Forwell was liquidating land and property worth £1 million. They were staking out his mother's house in Cairns, Queensland.

"Got him!" exclaimed the assistant attorney. But when police moved in, the Fox was gone again.

UNFINISHED BUSINESS

Four years after the *Encounter Bay* seizure, Mark Bartlett should have been a happy man. Yards of manila-bound evidence against one wall of his office had all but smashed the south-east Asian drug trade into the west coast. In addition to putting Brian Daniels, Samuel Colflesh and JT behind bars, Bartlett had successfully prosecuted 46 members of another Thai-based marijuana smuggling combine led by Americans.

But the Fox, with two federal indictments pending against him, was still on the loose. And the tidy-minded prosecutor hated cases that stayed stubbornly open.

Larry Brant had retired and most of the DEA's *Encounter Bay* team were busy on newer cases. Bartlett put in a call to the one man he knew had the tenacity to find Forwell and close the case.

"He's got to be out there somewhere," said Bartlett to the athletic, oval-faced man with thinning blond hair sitting opposite him.

Special Agent Fran Dyer, 48, an expert on drug runners, money launderers and fugitives, had begun his 26-year-career as a counter-espionage agent with the US Air Force Office of Special Investigations, tracking down global criminals in the Vietnam War.

He left the military to join the district attorney's office in Seattle as a corruption and fraud investigator, then moved to the United States Treasury Department as a special agent.

Unless I can find out everything about Forwell's habits and character, I've no chance of catching him, decided Dyer, starting to make a mental list. *Who are his friends?*

Vanity snap: Forwell could not resist having his powerboat *Kimono* photographed from a helicopter as it raced under San Francisco's Golden Gate Bridge.

The Fox at play: a photo from Forwell's private album.

What sort of places does he frequent? What are his strengths and weaknesses?

But here the paperwork went blank.

WHO IS MICHAEL FORWELL?

"How does it feel to be a free man?" Fran Dyer smiled as he rose to shake hands with Samuel Colflesh. It was now December 1992 and he had been released from jail the day before on condition he help the US authorities. He looked fit, but seemed disorientated by the subdued atmosphere of Seattle's Justice Building.

"Must feel good starting your life over," Dyer continued. Colflesh nodded sullenly. Dyer carried on breaking the ice.

"I know it's difficult for you," Dyer told him, "but I can help you put your life back together." He paused, watching his words sink in. "In return, I'm asking you to give up your friend and co-conspirator. I need to find Forwell."

Colflesh thought he might still be in south-east Asia. But there had been no sightings. Then Colflesh, who knew Forwell better than anyone, said: "It's not so much, where is Michael? It's more a question of who is Michael?"

Dyer waited. He felt he was through the first gateway.

"You want it from the beginning?" asked Colflesh.

"You bet!" replied Dyer.

"Michael comes from a well-off British family," Colflesh began in his meticulous way.

Born in Burnham, Buckinghamshire, in 1944, Michael Gleave Forwell was the son of an RAF Flight Lieutenant who emigrated to Queensland, Australia, after the Second World War. Forwell's father flew for the Royal Flying Doctor Service, then as a commercial pilot before he was killed in a flying accident.

Forwell, who was just a boy when his father died, was brought up in Australia and Singapore, where generations of his family had business interests. He was sent to Scotland to board at Gordonstoun, where Prince Charles was educated, but spent only two years there.

"Michael is a highly creative person who was born with a powerful desire for excitement and adventure," explained Colflesh.

In 1973, on a headland on the Queensland coast, Forwell, aged 29 and an under-achieving free spirit, bumped into a globe-trotting American called Robert Lietzman.

Dyer's ears pricked up. Lietzman, who had died mysteriously in a helicopter crash in 1985, had been one of America's most notorious drug runners.

When Lietzman met Forwell he was wanted by the Australian police and needed to get out of the country fast. Forwell had a sailing boat called *Diana*, and Lietzman asked for his help.

Forwell sailed Lietzman to Thailand, where the American owned a go-go bar in Bangkok's red light district. It was a front for a much more profitable business: drug smuggling. In no time, Forwell became his partner. His sailing skills, combined with Lietzman's ability to procure marijuana from all over south-east Asia, made them a formidable pairing.

To fool police Forwell set up a company called Dari Laut, Malay for "from the sea". He sailed marijuana from Thailand to Singapore, where it was packed inside crates of live fish which were air-freighted to San Francisco, apparently bound for restaurant aquariums.

"If it had been up to Lietzman they would have used fake fish," Colflesh said. "But just to make sure, Michael insisted on the real thing and taught himself to become an expert on exotic tropical fish varieties." It was this perfectionism that enabled Forwell to stay ahead of the authorities.

As the money rolled in, Forwell bought a house in Singapore. He called it Dari Laut, too. He and Lietzman bought a 180-foot flat-top barge on which they built a luxury residence three decks high. They were so competitive that she had to be fitted with two of everything: two cigarette boats, two landing craft and two seaplanes.

By the time Colflesh and JT entered the conspiracy in 1980, Michael Forwell was worth millions. He ditched Lietzman and broke up his organization into independently operating cells.

Bangkok, where the drugs were procured, became Command Control North, or CCN. Command Control South (Singapore) and Command Control Central (Hong Kong) organized shipment and money laundering. Only Forwell, Colflesh and JT knew exactly what was going on throughout the organization. During operations they talked in code on secure mobile phones which they junked after one call.

Soon Forwell had a small navy, including a landing craft and a freighter. Off duty, he flitted between his flats and houses in Singapore and Hong Kong. He even had a crayfish farm in Australia.

In 1979 he married May Yoong Ong, a 26-year-old Chinese sales assistant in a Singapore department store, and showered her with jewellery and diamonds.

They had a daughter and two sons but it was never an even-keel marriage. "Alcohol played a major role in all our lives," Colflesh told Dyer. "Michael drank at least a bottle of gin or vodka a day, usually more."

At one dinner party the Forwells had a row in front of their guests. Michael whipped the tablecloth, cutlery, china and food off the table and threw it all out of the window. The flat was on the sixteenth floor.

A WORLD OF HIS OWN

"Michael behaved like an aristocrat," Colflesh said. "He smoked cigarettes in a holder and wore this large jade ring. He also designed a jade Buddha brooch encrusted with diamonds, worn peeping out from under his lapel so people would ask what it was. He had his suits and shoes handmade in London. He was a member of the Royal Melbourne Yacht Squadron.

"He taught me how to order in the world's best restaurants. I was a wide-eyed, blue-collar kid from Philadelphia who had just come out of the army. To me Michael was like royalty."

Forwell was impetuous. One night in New York, he was flicking through a boating magazine when he saw an advertisement for *Delfino II*, a 130-foot motor yacht costing one million dollars. He picked up the phone, dialled the owners and said, "I just bought your boat."

Berthing her on the seafront at Miami Beach, Forwell had the en-suite bathroom kitted out in marble and glazed tiles imported from Italy. The fittings were finished in 24-carat gold.

Four million dollars later, *Delfino II* could stay self-sufficient at sea for up to six months. She had jet skis, sport boats, fishing and scuba gear, a landing pad and a five-passenger helicopter.

"To Michael, money was always easy come, easy go," said Colflesh. When he suspected pilfering, Forwell lined his crew up on deck and tossed 5,000 dollars in 100-dollar bills into the sea, yelling that money meant nothing compared with the loyalty he expected. Once in Miami he was having such a good time dancing with friends in a restaurant that he hired the house band to come on board the yacht to play through what was left of the night.

Then Forwell got bored. He sold Delfino II for 3.5 million dollars and bought *Encounter Bay*. It was time to get back to work.

Within a year he was some 15 million dollars richer. He switched his focus from San Francisco to the east coast, using *Encounter Bay* to ship marijuana from Indonesia via Sri Lanka, Rotterdam and London into New York. It was hidden inside five-tonne steel spools around which were wound British-made ships' towing cables. He gambled that US Customs would never stop a cargo from the UK marked "maritime supplies in transit". They waved it through.

One thing still intrigued Dyer. He asked Colflesh: "You got the dope in. How did you get the money out of the States?"

Forwell set up a company in the US called Fast Lane Express. Every year it entered a car for the Macau Grand Prix. It looked like a Formula One car, but inside there was only a go-kart engine. All the unused space was stuffed with dollar bills. The car was air-freighted to Hong Kong, but that was the closest it got to the starting grid. It was withdrawn from the race and the money removed.

More cash left the US in Louis Vuitton cabin trunks bound for Hong Kong's best hotels, where they awaited Forwell's arrival. Inside were his hand-made suits, lined with hundreds of pockets stuffed with cash. Even the pedestal of the captain's seat on *Encounter Bay* was specially designed so that 750,000 dollars could be stashed inside. Forwell laundered the cash through bank accounts in Switzerland, Hong Kong, Singapore and the Cook Islands.

"We created our own world," said Colflesh, "with our own rules."

"It amazes me he hasn't tried to see his children," Dyer said.

"Who says he hasn't?" Colflesh replied. "Maybe you should be looking for Michael Stocks, Richard Attenborough, Rodney Wayne Boggs, Michael Escreet or Wayne Bernard."

Forwell had adopted this cast of characters from the duplicate birth certificates of dead people which he then used to acquire passports. These identities appeared on the paperwork for the web of shell companies he had set up. He used to blur his tracks by entering a country as one person and leaving as another.

"Michael never travels without at least two passports, with credit cards and driving licences to match," Colflesh told Dyer. "He buys his first-class tickets six months in advance, and often switches at the last minute to other airlines which issue replacement tickets with new serial numbers. How do you track someone like that?"

CALL TO THE YARD

It was no more than a scrap of information, but Fran Dyer knew it could be vital. In January 1993 Australian Federal Police told him one of their informers reckoned Michael Forwell might be in London. He called the Extradition Squad of Scotland Yard's International and Organized Crime Branch and was put through to Detective Sergeant David Jones. "We have information that at one time Forwell may have been living in north-west London under the name Michael Charles Young," Dyer briefed him. "Can you check it out?"

"Tell me exactly what Forwell is like," Jones responded. "Everything you've got."
*Fake passports, yachts, love of money, Chinese wife...*Jones began jotting down a CV.

Like Dyer, 40-year-old Jones was a policeman who thrived on detail. A combative sportsman who had only recently been forced to retire from rugby by a cracked skull, Jones had spent much of his 20-year career solving murders before coming to the Yard in 1992.

A short, broad man with a laconic sense of humour and an attractive Welsh burr in his voice, Jones had also witnessed his share of drug-related robberies, muggings and killings during an 18-month operation that had smashed Asian organized-crime and drug gangs in Southall, west London. They, like Forwell, had obtained passports by deception—which is why Jones knew his way around the British Passport Agency's record office at Hayes, Middlesex.

It was a daunting task. The 3.5 million or so passports issued each year were listed by name and date of birth only. Worse still, before 1988 the archive was not computerized.

Jones and a colleague began searching the records of all the passports issued in 1988, looking for Young's. The year yielded nothing. Jones ploughed on into 1987. Again he drew a blank. By the time he reached 1986, two years before *Encounter Bay* was seized, he had been scanning applications for seven days.

As he thumbed through January, Jones felt like a marathon runner who despairs of ever finishing the race. Then a name in a clear black hand woke him up. *Michael Charles Young!*

Young was listed as born in Preston in 1947, his profession as civil servant. Jones turned quickly to the next page. A black-and-white photograph stared back at him. The slightly fleshy face bore the trace of a smug smile. Jones compared it to the colour photograph of Forwell that Dyer had sent him.

He phoned Seattle. "It's definitely Michael Forwell," he told

Card sharp:
Forwell's fake ID.

Dyer. "Now all we have to do is find him." But, with the passport issued in 1986, Forwell already had a six-year head start.

Manchester Street runs down one side of London's renowned Wallace Collection museum. Number 18, which Forwell/Young had given as his home on his passport application, was a five-storey Georgian house. Beside the large black-panelled front door was a video entryphone and 13 entry buttons set in a brass plate. The Fox was not at home. *It was probably only a correspondence address anyway*, thought Jones.

Next he ran a credit card check, turning up a Visa card in the name of Michael Charles Young. The billing address, in St John's Wood, yielded nothing. Jones ran his eye over Young's recent transactions. One of the most recent was for petrol. Once more, Jones reached for his A-Z.

A few hundred yards south of Chalk Farm underground station in north-west London, Jones drew into a garage. In the forecourt shop, he asked if the video footage still existed for the day on which Young's Visa card had been used.

As the videotape flickered, Jones noted down the registration numbers of cars using the same pump as Young. One was a silver Volvo Estate. The camera had even captured the driver. The facial features were blurred but, from the jet-black shoulder-length hair, it was clearly a woman.

When Jones fed the Volvo's registration number into the Driver and Vehicle Licensing Authority's computer in Swansea, out came an address: 351 West End Lane, London NW6.

"Maybe we're getting somewhere," Jones reported to Dyer in one of his daily calls to Seattle.

STAKE-OUT

Jones turned right into West End Lane, West Hampstead, a tree-lined street of large houses, shops and mansion blocks of flats. On the corner of Cannon Hill, just where the street got steeper on its way up to Finchley Road, he spotted the silver Volvo, parked outside a four-storey house.

The ground floor of number 351 was a shop. Above the four large plate-glass windows, the name "Dream Street Designs Arts and Antiques" was picked out in ornate gold script against the bottle-green livery. The address puzzled Jones. *I expected him to be living somewhere much grander.*

He drafted in a couple of plain-clothes men to help him watch the house. Next morning after breakfast the front door opened and three small children came out. The girl looked about ten. The two boys were younger. The woman shepherding them towards the car was Asian, in her thirties. Jones recognized her shoulder-length raven hair from the forecourt video.

"I'm going after her," he radioed his colleagues. "You stay put."

For 20 minutes Jones tailed the Volvo as it navigated its way north and east through rush-hour traffic. At 9am they were approaching Hampstead Heath when the Volvo indicated right and pulled into a drive. Jones watched it disappear into a collection of buildings set in several acres of park and woodland. A call to the bursar of King Alfred School confirmed that the Young children had been attending the £1,700-a-term private school since September 1992.

Over the line to Seattle, Jones heard the anticipation in Fran Dyer's voice. "Great work, Dave! From your description and the ages of the children, it sounds as if you've found May Ong Forwell. If Michael is not living at 351, he's going to be pretty close by."

Jones stepped up his surveillance. He and six colleagues watched 351 West End Lane 24 hours a day, seven days a week. Nothing happened.

They took turns to shadow May Forwell. Most days after dropping the children she went into the West End, giving Jones a guided tour of some of London's best clothes shops and restaurants. Of Michael Forwell there was no sign.

Jones was getting frustrated. *Forwell is supposed to dote on his children*, he thought. His absence for almost three weeks from what was obviously the family home was baffling. *Maybe he's not even in the country.* Jones could not keep this level of surveillance going indefinitely.

At lunchtime on the twentieth day, a large white Transit van parked outside number 351. A tall, well-built man in jeans and sweatshirt jumped down from the cab.

Jones fixed his binoculars on him but could not get a full view of his face. The height and build were spot-on. So was the man's hair colour. *Is it him?*

The man went into the shop. Now the van stood between Jones and a clear sighting. A few minutes later the man came back out again. As he climbed back into the cab, Jones still could not get a good view of his face.

He had a split-second decision to make. What if it really was Forwell? *We might never get this close to him again* ... But dare he risk jeopardizing the whole inquiry by going in and possibly arresting the wrong man? He radioed his men: "Stay where you are!"

Jones clenched his fists as the van drove away.

Two days later it was back. This time the driver was an Asian man in his thirties. As it left number 351, Jones went after it. It pulled up outside a large detached house just north of Finchley Road, about half-way between West End Lane and King Alfred School, in just the kind of well-heeled suburb Jones had imagined Forwell would be living in.

But instead of going inside the house, the driver made off down an alleyway. Leaving two officers to watch the house, Jones hurried after the Asian on foot. For ten minutes he pursued the man through a maze of suburban streets.

Then he was in a road he recognized—back where he started, in West End Lane. The Asian went through the door of 351 and pulled it shut.

"We're chasing shadows, Fran," Jones admitted.

"If he's been there once," Dyer assured him, "he'll be back. By the way, Dave, I've got something that might interest you. Samuel Colflesh tells me that one of the ways Michael Forwell laundered his drug money was buying and selling antiques. Forwell's collection of oriental porcelain is worth hundreds of thousands of pounds. As far as we know, he still has it with him."

Jones sent a female detective posing as a shopper into Dream Street Designs. What she found inside the shop was not oriental porcelain but English oak and stripped pine furniture.

If that's the kind of stuff he's dealing in, where's he buying it? Jones pondered. He decided to shift his search.

FACE IN THE CROWD

"If you see him don't do anything, just radio for assistance," Dave Jones told the three colleagues whom he had persuaded to sacrifice a sunny Sunday.

It was only 9am but already Camden Lock, just north of Regent's Park, was its usual frenetic mosaic of clothes stalls, bookshops, tarot readers, pavement artists, New Agers, punks and drunks. But what draws many of the 200,000 visitors a week to its cobbled alleys and old converted warehouses is antiques.

Jones shouldered his way slowly through the crowds. Sometimes he went with the flow, in and out of shops and stalls. Then he stood back, trying to pick faces from an ever-changing vista.

It was hopeless. His feet ached. After an hour he forced his way back out of the maze and on to Chalk Farm Road. He spotted an arch on which "THE STABLES" was emblazoned in gold capitals, and walked under it into a cul-de-sac of Victorian warehouses.

A large sign on a warehouse wall announced: "Restored Oak Furniture". The cavernous ground floor was divided into lots. Standing on tiptoe, Jones gazed around. On the far side he saw a tall man with a mop of hair.

He had only seen him side-on before. Now for the first time he saw him full face. Relaxed and smiling, the man looked as though he worked there. He was talking to another man.

Dave Jones was looking at Michael Forwell.

Happy days: May Ong and Michael Forwell. She was spotted outside their London house. Was there more to her than met the eye?

He backed quickly outside and used his radio. A few minutes later four policemen were in the warehouse. As Jones made his way towards the big man, he thought: *I'm not letting on that I know who he is. I don't want anybody here calling West End Lane before we can get there.*

"Michael Charles Young?"

"Yes," the man replied with a puzzled smile.

"Detective Sergeant David Jones, Scotland Yard. I am arresting you for possession of a forged passport." Forwell seemed unconcerned. He shrugged and followed Jones out to the street.

Jones had radioed Scotland Yard for three uniformed officers and a WPC to meet him at Forwell's house. Forwell stared out of the car window and said nothing.

In the large living room at West End Lane they found May Ong Forwell, the children, and another Asian couple. Jones recognized the man he had followed in the van.

Jones told May Ong he planned to search the house. There was not a flicker of emotion on her face.

The detectives began their search. The house was furnished well but not lavishly. Jones found no clues in the shop. He moved downstairs.

The basement covered the entire area of the house and ran out underneath the pavement. It was an office-cum-den. Children's bicycles were parked next to a large oak desk heaped with paper, ledgers and files. This looked more promising.

Forwell draped himself against a steel filing cabinet and smoked a cigarette. His expression hovered between faint amusement and studied boredom.

In the bookcase, Jones noticed a badly folded map jammed between two volumes. As he touched it, he noticed Forwell's eyes suddenly fix hard on him, almost willing him to pass on to something else.

Jones pulled it out. It was a map of Queensland's Gold Coast, where Forwell had been brought up. It felt strangely heavy. Jones unfolded it carefully. Inside were 11 variously shaped passport stamps. Brilliant forgeries, they were well-inked and had been used frequently.

With half a smile on his face, Jones looked up and stared at the fugitive. "Michael," he said, "I know exactly who you are. I'm arresting you for drug trafficking."

Forwell's shoulders slumped. But by the time they reached the interview room at Bow Street police station, the Fox's arrogance had surged back. He turned down the chance to call his solicitor and refused to answer questions. "I've got nothing to hide, Jones, so I've nothing to say," he smiled dismissively. "You have just made a very big mistake."

Within hours, Jones received a tip-off of a plot to spring Forwell from the cells at Bow Street. He was swiftly transferred to Belmarsh top security jail in southeast London to await extradition.

At 4.30am Seattle time on March 1, 1994, Dyer was woken by the phone. As soon as he heard Jones's voice he knew.

"You got him!" he shouted, hauling himself upright. He showered, dressed and drove to his office. As he began the paperwork to extradite Forwell, he thought, *I can't wait to tell Mark Bartlett.*

But there was still one more twist in the tale of the Fox.

FULL CIRCLE

The doors of the panelled lift slid open on the second floor of the Washington Athletic Club, a 22-storey art deco sports club and hotel in Seattle's business district. Fran Dyer saw a man about his own height step out carrying four well-stuffed cabin bags.

"Dave Jones!" he said, stepping forward to shake the Welsh detective's hand for the first time. "What have you got there?"

"Evidence!" said Jones as the two men went in to breakfast.

The day of Forwell's arrest, Jones had removed a van-load of paperwork from 351 West End Lane. Back at Scotland Yard, he could not believe his luck as he thumbed through the fake passports for Young, Stocks, Escreet and Boggs which Forwell had used to make around 500 journeys to and from the UK since 1990. He had forged the counter-signature of an MP on his passport application forms, so they would not be checked so rigorously.

The deeper Jones ploughed into the paperwork, the more convinced he became that May Ong Forwell was not the innocent housewife she appeared to be.

The house, bought in 1991 for £350,000 in cash, was in her name. There were scores of letters from May, using her maiden name, to solicitors in London, Hong Kong and Singapore, instructing them on money transfers and setting up companies in Asia and the British Virgin Islands.

Jones faxed many of the documents to Dyer, who told him that these were shell corporations designed to launder money. From bank statements it looked as though it was May, not Michael, who had been shifting millions through 30 bank accounts around the world.

May was not in court when her husband faced extradition charges. Jones discovered she was booked on a flight that evening for Singapore.

"We had to act fast," Jones told Dyer over breakfast. Before she could leave the country, Jones arrested and charged May Ong Forwell for money laundering. She won bail, pending trial, but crucially Jones now had her passport.

"If we can only get enough hard evidence to prove that May knew how Michael made his money and that she was actively involved, then we can convict her for benefiting from drug trafficking," Jones explained to Dyer.

The two officers had switched roles. It was now Jones who needed Dyer's help. Even though Jones had brought with him one of Scotland Yard's top money-laundering experts, Detective Sergeant Keith Butler, he still did not fully understand the evidence he had found at Forwell's house.

After his breakfast with Dyer, Jones had an equally warm welcome from Mark Bartlett. "We are beyond ecstatic with the work you have done finding Forwell," the assistant US Attorney told him.

Dyer and Bartlett shared all their evidence. Then Dyer said to his colleague, "There's somebody else I'd like you to meet."

At Dyer's behest, Samuel Colflesh had flown in from Singapore, and he was carrying a very large black plastic case.

Jones showed Colflesh two pieces of paper he had taken away from 351 West End Lane. They looked like balance sheets with lists of names, but they didn't mean much to either of the detectives.

"These were the profit and loss accounts I prepared for our 1987 project, shipping the product into San Francisco," Colflesh explained. The code names referred to drug dealers on the west and east coasts who distributed the marijuana and to crew members on *Encounter Bay*.

Even better was to come. Colflesh opened his case to reveal stacks of A4 brown envelopes. Inside them were files of correspondence, faxes and other documents, all arranged carefully in date order.

For a day and a half Colflesh briefed Jones on the Forwell organization and May's role in it.

Colflesh had been at the Forwells' house in Singapore when crates of cash had arrived. He had seen May counting it. She had knowingly paid it into bank accounts.

"May was Michael's downfall," explained Colflesh. "She knew exactly what Michael did. Her only concern was getting her hands on enough of his money to buy jewellery, property, anything to safeguard her future. If it wasn't for May bleeding Michael, he could have retired years ago a rich man."

"Would you go into court and say that?" Jones asked him.

"Yes, sir."

"Excellent," said Jones.

Back in London, Jones interviewed May Ong Forwell. "I am just an innocent housewife," she repeatedly told him. "I had no knowledge of my husband's business dealings. I just did what he told me to do."

But Jones had discovered that May had instructed her sister to transfer 390,000 Hong Kong dollars from a bank account in Hong Kong to one in Singapore.

An informant had told him how May had attempted, without success, to get a firm of lawyers to fake documents to show that 351 West End Lane had been bought with inheritance money from Michael's Scottish grandfather. And Forwell's business partner in Camden Lock, who claimed he had no idea who Michael really was, told Jones how May, days after the arrest, had used him to ship all her husband's Chinese porcelain collection out of the country.

In April 1994 May Ong Forwell went on trial at Southwark Crown Court. Fran Dyer gave evidence. Samuel Colflesh spent two and a half days in the witness box, detailing May's money laundering and the mechanics of international drug running.

There was a third American testifying: Special Agent Larry Brant, five years retired. It was the first time Brant had met Samuel Colflesh since he had interrogated him in 1988. Now on the same side, the two men shook hands.

On July 29, 1994, May Ong Forwell was sentenced to three years' imprisonment. Assets worth £747,220, including the house in West End Lane, were forfeited.

Dyer called Jones from Seattle to congratulate him, then added: "There's only one piece still missing from our jigsaw. We need to get our man out of your jail."

PAYING THE PRICE

The escort helicopter hovered over Belmarsh jail. A heavily armed detachment of the Special Escort Group was on hand for the trip to Heathrow. Having lost his fight against extradition in the High Court Michael Forwell had thrown in the towel.

On the nine-hour flight Forwell said nothing to Jones. Two days after Jones had handed him over at Seattle Airport, Forwell walked into an interview room at the US Marshal's office at nearby Tacoma wearing blue overalls. Emblazoned on his back was the word PRISONER. Mark Bartlett and Fran Dyer were waiting for him.

"Michael," Dyer began, "you don't have to say anything, but you are going to have to listen to me." As he and Bartlett began detailing the case that would be presented against him in court, Forwell interrupted: "The amount of money has been exaggerated."

He was lying. In the file was a copy of a letter found at West End Lane, written while Forwell was on the run, in which he had stated he wanted to invest £400,000 cash in property in Singapore.

Forwell changed tack. "It was only marijuana," he said.

"You're a major drug dealer, Michael," Dyer shot back. "You made bad choices, now you are going to pay the price. You have two options. You can plead not guilty, waste a lot more public money and get 25 years. Or you can plead guilty."

He let Forwell think this over, before adding: "Samuel Colflesh will be giving evidence for us."

Forwell went pale. His lawyer spoke. "Is there any information my client can offer to reduce the sentence?"

"He has nothing left to offer us," said Dyer.

On March 15, 1996, Michael Forwell pleaded guilty in Seattle to aiding and abetting the unlawful importation of more than 1,000 kilos of cannabis into the US, and was sentenced to 15 years in prison. Detective Sergeant David Jones and Detective Sergeant Keith Butler were awarded special commendations by the Metropolitan Police Commissioner for their part in bringing Forwell and his wife to justice. Special Agent Fran Dyer still is hunting down international drug smugglers.

TO CATCH A

BLACK*MAILER*

BY DAVID MOLLER

FIRST CAME THE THREATENING LETTERS, THEN THE POISONED CANS OF DOG FOOD. HOW COULD SCOTLAND YARD CATCH THE BLACKMAILER WHO WAS ALWAYS ONE STEP AHEAD, IN WHAT BECAME ONE OF BRITAIN'S LONGEST AND MOST COMPLEX INVESTIGATIONS?

First came the threatening letters demanding money. Then poisoned tins of dog food showed up on the supermarket shelves. And suddenly, a mother feeding baby food to her young daughter was fishing glinting pieces of a cut-up razor blade out of the child's mouth.

Somehow the unknown blackmailer always managed to keep one step ahead of the police, cashing in on a scheme that was about as close to the "perfect crime" as Scotland Yard ever wanted to see. Even as the investigation spread to different police departments, building societies and computer systems, detectives found themselves turning up more questions than answers. Who was this fiend? Where did he get his uncanny ability to anticipate their next move? How many innocent people would die before they caught him ... if they caught him?

Here, from the annals of Scotland Yard, is the story of one of the longest and most complex investigations in British criminal history.

The morning of August 3, 1988, was sunny and warm. But as Leslie Simmens, managing director of Pedigree Petfoods, surveyed the package his secretary had just brought him, he felt a sudden chill.

There on his desk at company headquarters in Melton Mowbray, Leicestershire, lay a tin of the company's own dog food, Chum, and a letter warning that it had been contaminated with chemicals that were "colourless, odourless and highly toxic ... virtually undetectable by a pet owner before feeding the contaminated product to their dog."

The letter demanded an annual £100,000, to be paid for the next five years. "If payment is not forthcoming; large numbers of similarly contaminated tins will appear on retailers' shelves throughout Great Britain."

Blackmail is a familiar threat to major manufacturers, yet Simmens sensed that this case was different. In most extortion plots, the weak link is the actual collection of the money. But this blackmailer had worked it out carefully. He described how the money was to be paid into building society or bank accounts, which he would specify later, so that he could withdraw it with cash cards through any one of thousands of dispensers around the country.

He had, he explained, opened these accounts in false names "a long time ago". The cards and personal identification (PIN) numbers had been sent to accommodation addresses—offices which take in mail for businesses and individuals unable or unwilling to give a permanent address. Since such offices receive anything up to 60 callers a day, the chances of staff remembering one man from two years before were nil. Clever.

"When your company agrees to pay, it will place an entry in the personal column of *The Daily Telegraph* which will read, 'Sandra, Happy birthday darling. Love John.'" The advertisement, stipulated the blackmailer, must be placed by September 1, 1988.

Cool, brisk, confident, the letter appeared to have covered every angle. A worried Simmens pondered its implications. He had spent 30 years with Pedigree, helping to build up the company's petfood products and image. Now one cunningly directed contamination scare could send sales plummeting and mean laying off hundreds of good workers.

Quickly summoning a "crisis committee" of sales director John Dale and publicity chief William Duncan, Simmens stressed the importance of keeping the threat under wraps. "Obviously we've got to alert the police, but we mustn't meet them anywhere near Pedigree premises. If staff get wind of what's going on, indiscreet talk could put the press on to us."

Later that day, Dale and Duncan drove to a supermarket car-park in Melton Mowbray to meet Detective Superintendent Ian Leacy, second-in-command of Leicestershire police CID. Leacy, a slim, grey-haired 42-year-old who had spent the bulk of his 23 years' police service in the CID, was impressed by the letter. "A real professional," he murmured. "It's almost as if he knows what we will be thinking and has closed off possible avenues of action. There's not a lot to go on here, but maybe forensic will come up with something."

But examination of both letter and tin by police forensic laboratories at Huntingdon revealed nothing. The chemicals were exactly as the writer had described them—and lethal. The letter had been printed on a widely available type of dot-matrix printer and then photocopied; it showed no fingerprints.

Nor was there a chance of any help from genetic finger-printing—a technique which helps to trap criminals through analysing the unique chemical sequences of DNA (deoxyribonucleic acid) found in an individual's blood, sweat or saliva. Instead of licking the stamp, which would have left DNA clues trapped between stamp and envelope, the writer had moistened it with water.

A few days later, John Dale and William Duncan had another meeting with Leacy and a colleague, Detective Chief Inspector Tim Garner. They thrashed out all aspects of the threat. Despite his company's vulnerability, Duncan stressed: "There is absolutely no way we are going to buy off this blackmailer."

Leacy pointed out: "We have to face the fact that we haven't got a single lead. If the culprit writes again, we may well have to put money into the accounts he specifies and let him draw it out from cashpoints. It could be the only way of making contact with him. If we can drag out the withdrawals, he's bound to make a mistake eventually."

Dale nodded thoughtfully. "If the blackmailer comes back to us," he agreed, "we'll take him on."

Leacy had already alerted Scotland Yard's criminal intelligence section, SO11; provincial forces must report all cases of blackmail and food contamination, in case they tie in with incidents being investigated by other forces. Although the inquiry remained firmly on Leicester's "patch," he now travelled to Scotland Yard in London to confer with Detective Chief Superintendent Patrick Fleming and other senior detectives.

Fleming, then 47, a lanky six-foot-three with fair hair and watchful grey eyes, was in charge of the Metropolitan Police's 100-strong regional crime squad, part of a national detective network handling crimes that overlap normal force boundaries.

After long discussion, the detectives decided that since the demand letter gave a deadline of September 1 for *The Daily Telegraph* advertisement, it made no sense to rush matters. "Let's make him sweat it out," said Fleming. "Make sure he has to buy the newspaper every day."

In fact, they left it until the last possible date, August 31, before placing the advertisement. And they included a deliberate come-on—a telephone number for the blackmailer to ring—in the hope of drawing him into the open. "Sandra, Happy birthday darling. Want to help, must talk, phone 0664 500065. Love John."

OPERATION ROACH

For five weeks, there was no response. Leacy, beginning to hope that the case had gone dead, fixed what he saw as a debriefing session with the Pedigree men on October 7, in a country pub in the depths of Leicestershire. But just as the meeting was breaking up, William Duncan got a bleeper call to ring his office at Pedigree. The second blackmail letter had arrived. "Your reply has been seen," it stated bluntly. "We will not telephone, there is nothing to discuss."

It went on to give details of accounts, in the names of John and Sandra Norman, with the Halifax, Nationwide Anglia and Abbey National. These were to be credited with a total of £100,000 by November 1, "otherwise the threatened action will begin during that month."

Again Leacy played for time, waiting until October 28 before paying in £5,000 of Pedigree's money. To limit costs, the money went into just the Halifax and Nationwide Anglia accounts.

There was one piece of luck. "Only the Halifax account turns out to be fully active," Leacy told Garner. "Because the Nationwide Anglia and Abbey National have had so much mail returned, uncollected, from our friend's accommodation addresses, they've put a stop on withdrawals. But it's no bad thing to put funds into the Nationwide account. The blackmailer might use his cash card to check his balance or make some other query, and it's just possible he might give something away."

Apart from this small break, the blackmailer appeared to hold most of the winning cards. Through the Halifax account he could draw up to £300 a day, from 1,066 cashpoints countrywide—impossibly widespread targets for the police to keep under constant surveillance.

At 9.29pm on November 4, the blackmailer drew his first £300, from a Halifax cash dispenser in Reading. Over the next ten days he made eight withdrawals from such widely dispersed points as Walsall in the West Midlands, Gillingham and Ashford in Kent, Liverpool, Southend-on-Sea, Bournemouth, Haywards Heath in Sussex, and Newcastle. With no other means of keeping in contact with the blackmailer, Leacy advised Pedigree to top up the accounts with another £11,000 over the next month.

But after the initial flurry of countrywide withdrawals, a pattern did begin to set in. More and more, the blackmailer was using cashpoints in a wedge of south-east England stretching from London's eastern edge to Southend-on-Sea in Essex and Ashford in Kent. It was time to mount a surveillance operation.

Jointly, Leicestershire police and Scotland Yard began planning Operation Roach, a huge night-time watch on selected cashpoints, in the hope of catching the blackmailer, or an accomplice, in the act of drawing money.

"We can be practically certain that the blackmailer won't use his cash card during business hours, because a computer alert on the card could tip off Halifax staff," Leacy told a small gathering of senior officers at Scotland Yard. "So far, virtually all the money has been drawn in the late evening. By watching Halifax cashpoints from close of business in the afternoon until they stop operating at midnight, we've got a good chance of nabbing someone."

Surveillance teams, in radio contact with police at the building society's headquarters in Halifax, Yorkshire, could be alerted at the precise moment the blackmailer's card was being used in a nearby dispenser.

Operation Roach went into action on November 28, with 150 officers—three to a team and three reserves—lying in wait near 49 carefully selected cashpoints in east London, Kent and East Sussex. Uncannily, that was the very night that the blackmailer chose to start drawing money well away from the south-east, in Doncaster, Poole and Oxford, where they had no surveillance teams.

On the night of December 1, Leacy was in an operations room at Scotland Yard with an open line to the Halifax computer headquarters. He felt like a gambler awaiting the start of play. Sooner or later, with such an extensive surveillance operation, surely his number *must* come up.

Stomach churning, he gripped the phone as a contact at the Halifax told him: "He's playing. He's playing ... He's at Blackpool."

Leacy swore. Once again, they had no team near by. Quickly his team asked Lancashire police to log the registration numbers of vehicles leaving on the town's main exits. At 7.15 on a December evening, there couldn't be that many. Through the Driver Vehicle Licensing Centre in Swansea, they could trace the registered owners and check what anyone who normally lived in the south-east was doing in Blackpool that night.

"At this stage of the game," Leacy told Garner, "we're into trying anything." But their enquiries produced no names that raised even the remotest suspicion.

By now the blackmailer had drawn £7,800, but he still wasn't satisfied. On December 5, he wrote to Pedigree demanding that the Nationwide Anglia and Abbey National accounts become fully operative. Clearly he wanted the safety of a wider choice of cashpoints.

"The demand has now increased to £50,000 to be paid into each of the three accounts annually for five years. Just pay up; otherwise we will not hesitate to place contaminated tins of Pedigree Chum in five retail outlets throughout the country."

To underline the threat, the first tin of contaminated dog food appeared the following day. An anonymous caller, using the code words "Romeo and Juliet" specified in the blackmailer's letters, directed police to a supermarket in Basildon, Essex. There they found a tin of Chum dog food, poisoned with the same lethal chemicals used in the tin sent to Pedigree the previous August.

THE NET WIDENS

Fleming's regional crime squad detectives were being drawn more and more into the investigations. Asked by Leacy to track down how the blackmailer had originally opened his building society accounts, Fleming assigned the task to the Metropolitan police's regional crime squad office at Barkingside. One of four dotted round the periphery of London, it was the closest to Southend, where the postal orders used to open the accounts had been issued.

Soon Barkingside's 24 detectives were working full-time on the case, under their "governor", Detective Chief Inspector Gavin Robertson, a cheery, broad-shouldered 41-year-old with the neat hair and suit of a bank manager.

On the case: detectives Fleming (left) and Robertson.

Fleming and Robertson, with something of a common background, had always got on well. Both were the sons of police officers and, unlike most of their CID colleagues, neither was from London. Fleming hailed from Norfolk; Robertson still had traces of a Somerset accent.

Robertson's team, more accustomed to carrying out undercover surveillance of known criminals, threw themselves with vigour into the novel assignment of investigating a crime by "persons unknown." On a map in their operations room, they tried to pinpoint where the blackmailer would make his next cashpoint withdrawal. They even opened a book on it.

Every morning, each detective would throw 50p into a hat and guess a likely location. Next day, whoever came closest would scoop the jackpot. But Detective Sergeant Len Hynds was one of several who never came close to winning. "Picking the right place was a bit like hitting the bull's eye at darts—but blindfolded."

Another demand letter, on December 15, lent urgency to their quest. Stung by the slowness with which his accounts were being topped up, the blackmailer increased his demands to £200,000 a year for five years.

"You should have met the deadline … We have been planning this enterprise for several years and our commitment is total. We are very much prepared to progressively contaminate your entire product range … Effecting the threat will provide us with the opportunity to demonstrate how effective we are to our next 'customer'."

Over the next two days, anonymous calls guided police to five more tins of contaminated dog food in Bexleyheath and Welling, in south-east London. On December 19, on police advice, Pedigree paid another £8,000 into the blackmailer's accounts.

Using every trick of their trade, the detectives had moments when they felt they were closing in on their quarry. From Halifax computer printouts, they found out the names and addresses of account-holders who had used a cash dispenser just before or after the blackmailer. A dozen detectives fanned out to homes across the country, trying discreetly to glean a description of the suspect.

From a man who had withdrawn money in Derby on December 21, they eventually got some details: "A man wearing a black or dark-coloured crash helmet and an olive green, thigh-length army coat … Five foot eight tall, medium build."

Police had installed video machines at several cashpoints to photograph everyone withdrawing money outside business hours, and Leacy's hopes soared two days later when police in Ipswich, Suffolk, telephoned: "We've got your man on video."

But as soon as Leacy saw the video, his hopes collapsed. Under the helmet and visor, the man's face was completely invisible.

With no other leads, the police had little alternative but to mount another, even bigger surveillance operation. From mid-January, 2,000 officers from forces across Britain would watch 700 cashpoints—nearly three-quarters of all Halifax machines in the country.

Then, just after the operation started, the blackmailer again suddenly and bafflingly changed his pattern of behaviour. On January 18, he made his last withdrawal for more than five weeks.

Meanwhile, he and the police continued to play a sinister game of cat and mouse. Police and store staff, acting on a series of coded anonymous telephone calls, scooped contaminated tins from supermarket shelves in Luton, Cambridge, St Albans, Royston, Birmingham. Clearly angered by his failure to get publicity, the blackmailer kept changing the demands in his letters; on the instructions of the police, Pedigree paid just enough to keep the game in play.

The case was becoming an almost obsessive topic of conversation for the Barkingside detectives, as they were increasingly posted on surveillance duties around the Home Counties. "I suppose one day I might have supper with the wife again," sighed one officer. "She probably wouldn't recognize you anyway," a friend retorted.

"It's definitely a job where we could do with your superior brain-power," commented another officer to Rodney Whitchelo, a recently retired colleague who frequently returned to the office to collect documents before giving evidence in cases still outstanding from his police days.

Whitchelo smiled non-committally. Eager to gain help from whatever source he could, Robertson frequently called his team together to see if they had any leads or clues. After yet another late-night discussion Detective Inspector Tony Drain noted wearily, "A thoroughly modern criminal—so far, he doesn't seem to have put a foot wrong."

LURKING HORROR

On March 20, the case took an even more chilling turn when a package arrived at Charles Street police station in Leicester. Inside were a jar of Heinz cauliflower cheese baby food and a letter.

"It is now clear to us that there will be no publicity (or payment) until someone suffers ... The enclosed sample has been contaminated. Fumes are barely noticeable under the strong natural smell of the baby food ... One spoonful to a three-month-old child will render it in need of urgent medical attention and possibly surgery. It is quite probable that the mother will continue to feed most or the whole of the pot without noticing the contamination.

"We will look for your entry, 'To Sandra from Bob' in the usual column on March 27. If there is no entry indicating the accounts are to be each credited with £100,000 and made available to us, we begin. When Heinz pay up ... that will be the end of our demands for all time."

The managing director of Heinz set up a three-man management team to deal with the threat. One person was briefed to keep in close contact with the police and various people at Pedigree.

Because H. J. Heinz, now the main target, was based in west London, and because the growing scale of the threats required the greater resources of Scotland Yard, it was decided that Fleming should take over command of the whole inquiry.

In his fourth-floor office in the Met's 19-storey headquarters, he reviewed the investigation with Robertson who, as his deputy on the case, had moved up from Barkingside. On hand, he knew he had some of the world's best police computer and information retrieval systems, surveillance equipment, forensic and scientific back-up. But would they help?

As a veteran of 25 years in CID, some 40 murder investigations and myriad other major inquiries, Fleming had never known a case like this one. So far, the culprit had given absolutely nothing away. Letters were always photocopied. The warnings they had found in contaminated tins were punched out on widely available black plastic labelling tape. There was a complete absence of fingerprints or other forensic clues.

"Our friend has already extorted nearly £18,000 from the food companies, yet we haven't had even the faintest whiff of his identity," exclaimed Fleming in exasperation. "And we're not really getting any closer. Somehow, we've got to double our chances."

At the detectives' suggestion, the Halifax machines were programmed to seize the blackmailer's card the next time he made a withdrawal. There was just the off-chance they might get a fingerprint from it, or provoke him into showing himself in some other way. At 9.44pm on March 28, the blackmailer's card slid into a cashpoint in Chelmsford, Essex—and was held. But there were no fingerprints. Another dead end.

A week later, in a letter to the Charles Street police station in Leicester, the blackmailer declared:

"You've now ... forced us to put poisons on the shelves ... You have made it clear that you will not pay us. We are making it clear to you that Heinz and Pedigree Petfoods will lose more by not doing so."

Quickly, the horror escalated. On Saturday, April 8, Robertson was gardening at his Essex bungalow when he received a call from Fleming. "We've got another contamination that looks like it's down to him. It's a bad one. Could you go and have a look?" It was at Rayleigh, not far away.

In her mobile home, Mrs Jennifer Bosson told Robertson how she had been preparing a meal for three orphaned bichon frise puppies. As she scooped the contents of a jar of Heinz baby food into a bowl, some spilt on her hand. It stung. Even *after* she rinsed it off, it left an angry red weal.

Stung: victim Jennifer Bosson.

She caught a whiff like ammonia, and her eyes began smarting. Then, poking about in the dog bowl with a spoon, she found two drawing pins and a strip of labelling tape; it read:

"Poisoned, 3 more Heinz products in the store unmarked ..." and went on to specify the poison used.*

Before leaving, Robertson asked Mrs Bosson about a red mark on her cheek. It had come from holding her hand against her face—after she had tried to rinse off the poisoned baby food. "You can imagine what this stuff would do to a baby's throat," remarked Robertson to Fleming. "I'd say we've got a maniac on our hands."

Child at risk: Helen Coppock found glass in her baby food.

Forensic analysis later established that the jar of food contained 27 grammes of the poison—enough to kill 27 babies.

There was worse to come. On April 16, Mrs Helen Coppock of Cowley, Oxford, was spooning Heinz pear yoghurt baby food into the mouth of her nine-month-old daughter Victoria when she noticed her child chewing on something hard.

Putting her fingers into Victoria's mouth, she brought out a piece of razor blade. In horror, she saw that other fragments of razor blade had fallen on to the floor when she opened the jar.

Victoria was rushed to hospital, where examination showed she had not swallowed any pieces of blade, though her mouth was cut. Police laboratory investigation established that the jar had contained eight fragments of a Boots razor blade and, again, a plastic strip message: "Poisoned also Heinz ketchup and beans in store contaminated."

TIME OF ANGUISH

After both incidents, the police issued warnings to local press and radio. But would more contaminated items appear—without telephone warnings? Fleming faced an agonizing decision: should police now issue a national alert?

It would send the sales of Heinz and other baby food manufacturers plummeting. What's more, any public announcement was likely to be followed by a wave of hoax and copycat contaminations which would threaten more injuries, swamp his inquiry and reduce even further his chances of catching the elusive, evil blackmailer. But public safety had to be the prime concern.

*For security reasons, details of poisons have been omitted.

On April 18, Fleming held a press conference at Scotland Yard to alert the nation. He warned the general public "to check their purchases with care before feeding … The contaminants used can be potentially harmful but have been detectable by sight and smell."

Within days, panic gripped the country. In the House of Commons, Home Office minister John Patten spoke of the government's determination to resist all attempts at "consumer terrorism". But each morning brought newspaper pictures of young children who had been rushed to hospital after their baby food had been spiked with glass, wood, metal, pins, razor blades, in copycat contaminations.

In the three weeks following the Scotland Yard press conference, Fleming's investigation was knocked sideways by 1,300 reported cases of food contamination. Many were perpetrated by cranks, or by sad, lonely people craving any publicity that would get their pictures into the papers. A few were the work of opportunists hoping to blackmail the food companies into a quick pay-out in return for keeping quiet about self-inflicted "injuries". The police later brought a handful of prosecutions.

As public, press and politicians clamoured for action, the pressures on Patrick Fleming were intense. A father of four himself, he could well understand the tension and anxiety felt by parents around the country. Yet few men could have been better qualified to lead the investigation than the calm, unflappable Fleming.

One of the Met's senior negotiators in hostage cases, he had undergone FBI training in Quantico, Virginia, and had been involved in some dozen major hostage incidents. He understood well the time-consuming, give-and-take process by which a criminal could be induced to reveal clues to personality and motivation, to be enticed little by little into a dialogue with police. But in this case, he was having to do everything at one remove—through the cashpoints, demand letters, advertisements.

JULIET · Very worried about the babies. Must talk privately. H.

Eventually he and Robertson hatched a scheme, concentrating on Heinz since the blackmailer no longer appeared to be targeting Pedigree. "We'll try to make contact with the blackmailer again by masquerading as Heinz," said Fleming. "It will be easy enough to make it seem that they are so worried about their enormous losses that they are prepared to do a deal behind the backs of the police."

They placed another advertisement in *The Daily Telegraph* personal column, using a name close to the blackmailer's original Romeo and Juliet code words: "JULIET - Very worried about the babies. Must talk privately. H."

The advertisement ran twice before the blackmailer nibbled at the bait. In a letter addressed to Heinz's chief security officer on April 17, he acknowledged he was responding to the personal column entry and wrote:

"DO NOT inform the police that you have received this letter ... If you want to talk to us privately, credit the accounts and make them available to us. We would then be prepared to enter a 'private' (NO POLICE) dialogue."

The police then ran two personal column advertisements, using new code words supplied by the blackmailer and suggesting he and Heinz must make contact in some way other than through the newspaper entries.

But any hope that Fleming was about to make contact with his hidden opponent was dashed by a letter to Heinz on May 25. "We are about to return with a vengeance ... If we are to be prosecuted for murder, we might as well deserve it, but we are confident we will never be caught. An infant's death will be another statistic ... but will ensure that we are not ignored."

To avoid the ruin of their company, Heinz must open eight building society accounts in new names he supplied, credit them with £50,000 and have the cash cards and PIN numbers sent to eight specified accommodation addresses.

Heinz again went through the motions of secrecy while keeping the police informed. With the accounts opened, credited with £19,000, and the cash cards sent out, the police placed another advertisement in *The Daily Telegraph* using the code words and message specified by the blackmailer: "MARIAN. We have made the home ready for you. Please come back. Love Arnold."

MARIAN · We have made the home ready for you. Please come back. Love Arnold

MORE THAN LUCK?

On June 19, police mounted Operation Stab—a complex and costly surveillance operation on all eight accommodation addresses, four of them in London, the others at Quorn in Leicestershire, High Wycombe, Birmingham and Warrington. Each needed up to 20 officers, from Barkingside and other regional crime squad offices, to keep watch inside the building and to follow the collected mail.

Nothing happened. It was uncanny. Indeed, it was one coincidence too many. To Robertson, Fleming now voiced the niggling doubt that was becoming a conviction. "Do you think we've got a leak? How is it that every time we make a move, he keeps away? No one deserves that much luck."

Robertson, too, was worried. "But how on earth do you set about looking for a leak? There are 29,000 officers in the Met, 1,800 in the Leicester police, and about 20,000 civilians in the two forces. If you include people in Pedigree, Heinz and the building societies who might somehow have become aware of an entrapment operation, you're looking at about 100,000 people. How do you screen that lot?"

For the moment, the two men had little option but to push doubt to the back of their minds and plough on. If they needed any reminder of their opponent's callousness, it came on June 29. Mrs Lynn Bradbury was stirring a saucepan of Heinz Weight Watchers' minestrone soup in her Croydon home when she spotted pieces of razor blade and noticed the soup was foaming. The poison it contained was strong enough to strip the lining from the pan and leave it a misshapen lump.

A report on this contamination joined others flooding in to the major incident room at Scotland Yard. There, for up to 12 hours a day, 25 typists and police officers fed into computer terminals the details of statements from victims, cashpoint witnesses, detectives, shop staff, laboratory personnel.

The terminals in turn fed HOLMES—Home Office Large Major Emergency System—a massive database that stores, correlates and cross-references names, vehicle numbers and other scraps of information. By the end of the inquiry, HOLMES would contain 8,000 vehicle numbers and the names of 20,000 suspects, witnesses, victims or people who had given information. Again and again Fleming urged his team to go back over every clue. "There's got to be something we've missed."

Studying the incident-room maps of the blackmailer's cashpoint withdrawals, Robertson noticed that on November 18, 1988, the blackmailer had drawn money from a Halifax cashpoint in Aberystwyth. He was intrigued: virtually all the early withdrawals had been close to a motorway. "Why a two-and-a-half-hour detour into the Welsh hills?" he asked Fleming. "Does he live there? Did he go there for a particular reason?"

From detectives' enquiries, two intriguing leads emerged. On the night of November 18, there had been a conference of British Telecom employees in Aberystwyth, and a television team had also been in the town, filming a money-raising telethon for charity. Could someone connected with either event have slipped off to the cashpoint? Dozens more names were checked for criminal records and to see if their movements over previous weeks matched those of the suspect.

Then Robertson got a telephone call that set his pulse racing. "I think we've hit the jackpot, boss," Detective Sergeant Hugh McDowell told him. He had learned that, in a separate operation to keep watch on arsonists who were burning down homes owned by the English, local police had logged the registration numbers of vehicles going in and out of Aberystwyth on the night of November 18.

Thousands of licence numbers were checked with the DVLC in Swansea to find out the registered owners, then double-checked with the police national computer to see if the vehicles had been lost or stolen. Finally, the results were fed into HOLMES to see if people or vehicles matched any already logged. Nothing.

The checks were still under way when another loose end appeared. At 5.40pm on January 18, the blackmailer had drawn £300 from a cashpoint near the port of Dover. There had been no more withdrawals until February 26. Could he have caught a ferry that night, and been on the Continent for the next five weeks?

For several days, desks in the incident room were heaped with shipping manifests showing the licence numbers of vehicles that had left Dover and Folkestone by sea on January 18 and 19. Detectives toured the country to interview the owners. Stacks of statements were processed into the computer. But HOLMES could come up with no licence number that featured in both the Dover and Aberystwyth inquiries.

By now the investigation had become one of the largest in British criminal history. To get away from the mountainous paperwork and constant telephone calls, Robertson and Fleming occasionally spent lunchtime walking round nearby St James's Park, cudgelling their brains over puzzling aspects of the case.

"You realize we don't know a single thing more about the culprit than when we started nine months ago," said Robertson. "We don't even know whether we're dealing with a lone criminal or a gang."

"I'd say he's a loner," said Fleming. "The way the letters keep referring to a gang makes you think it might be only one person. He's trying too hard. And that withdrawal in Aberystwyth—it could have been made simply to give the impression of a gang spread out across the country. In fact, there would have been time for one person to draw the money in Aberystwyth and still get to Bristol for the withdrawal that was made next morning."

There was something else that strengthened Fleming's supposition. At the end of April it was agreed that a reward should be offered for information leading to the arrest and conviction of the blackmailer. Fleming urged that it should be a large one. "If it's big enough, it's bound to tempt someone on the edges of a gang." £100,000 was put up. But there were no takers. Gloomily, Fleming concluded that he was up against just one twisted individual—a needle in a very large haystack.

As the two men strode across the park, the smell of new-mown grass made Robertson suddenly long to be out in his own garden, kicking a ball with his two boys. He had just heard that he had passed a promotions board to go up to superintendent. But was any job worth missing so much of family life? Ben was already nine, Adam seven. Just occasionally, he wanted to be there as they were growing up.

At least the boys had plenty to keep them amused. A few weeks earlier, his former colleague Rodney Whitchelo had turned up in a new red Peugeot to bring them a stack of computer games which he no longer used as he had bought a new, different kind of home computer. The boys had been ecstatic.

was taking something from the front passenger seat. A white crash helmet. As he left the car-park, he was putting it on. "Why would a motorist want a crash helmet?" Kearton whispered. The detectives trailed him.

In nearby London Road, they could see the man at the Woolwich cashpoint. For a few moments he pressed buttons on the machine, then turned away empty-handed. The two detectives, clutching empty beer cans as though they were a couple of lads who had been at the pub, walked right past him, scanning the street for accomplices. No one. Turning round, they briskly retraced their steps to the car-park.

The man had just taken off the white helmet when Kearton opened the car door and showed his warrant card. "Don't move your hands. Keep them on the steering wheel," he instructed. "What's the crash helmet for?"

The man, bearded and stocky, looked stunned. Finally he stammered, "To stop me getting wet."

Holding the man's wrists, Kearton told him: "I want you to come out of the car. We're going to search you in connection with articles for serious crime."

In the very first pocket he tried, Donnelly found a cashpoint card. He held it up to the dim car-park light. A Woolwich card—in the name of Ian and Nina Fox. Swiftly concluding his search, he announced, "I am arresting you on suspicion of blackmail."

"No problem, guys," blustered the man. "I know what this is about, but I'm innocent." Then, as he was being handcuffed, he slumped to the ground in a faint.

CASE CLOSED

Robertson could hear the phone ringing as he pulled up outside his Essex home. It was McDowell. "Governor, I think they've nicked somebody." He had just received a call from north London: it seemed a prisoner had been taken to Enfield police station.

Ringing Enfield, Robertson was told by the duty sergeant: "We've got a man who's trying to say he's an ex-policeman and used to work for the regional crime squad. His name's Rodney Whitchelo."

Robertson reeled. Whitchelo! A man he had entertained in his home—who had befriended his own boys. At last, everything fell into place. A frequent visitor at the Barkingside regional crime office, Whitchelo hadn't even needed to ask questions to find out what was going on.

Robertson rang Fleming and they arranged to meet at Paddington Green police station, one of the most secure in Britain, where Whitchelo was being taken. At 4.20am they began to interview the suspect.

Robertson felt cold, dead, flat. With Fleming asking most of the questions, he studied his former colleague's face as if for the first time: the beard flecked with grey, the cold, calculating blue eyes. Why him?

For three hours Whitchelo, never admitting an iota of guilt, stuck rigidly to the line that he was just a go-between. His story was that he had been paid £5,000 to act on behalf of the informant, whose name he refused to give, saying he had given his word he would not do so. He had taken on the job only reluctantly, in the hope of unmasking the blackmailer. There was nothing he wanted more than to help the police find the man behind the conspiracy.

But more and more inconsistencies appeared in his tale, and when he had finally been taken away to a cell, Robertson shook his head. "I can hardly believe it, but he's the man."

Later that morning of October 20, Whitchelo was taken to Marylebone Magistrates' Court to be remanded in custody. At about the same time, he should have been appearing at Snaresbrook Crown Court as a prosecution witness in an armed robbery case; until the moment of his arrest, he had access to the very police unit which had been investigating his crimes almost from the start.

Party animal: the many faces of Rodney Whitchelo.

It was only the final covert Operation Agincourt that threw him off the trail. And it was only because the Woolwich computer went down that night that, having tried unsuccessfully to draw money at Uxbridge, he tried again later at Enfield.

At Whitchelo's home in Hornchurch, Essex, police recovered poisons, equipment used for contaminating products, and pieces of the same make of razor blade that could have killed little Victoria Coppock. They also found Woolwich cashpoint receipts relating to a John and Sandra Norman account.

Caged: the hunt is over.

From a former girlfriend they discovered the whereabouts of a typewriter that, unknown to her, had been used to type some of the demand letters, and the shredded remains of cashcards in the names of John and Sandra Norman. From the home of another friend, they recovered a dot matrix printer of the type used to print the first blackmail letters to Pedigree.

When police found out that Whitchelo used a mobile telephone, they were able to gather even more damning evidence. The telephone hire company was able to produce not only numbers he had rung—mostly those of his mother and girlfriends—but also the locations and times at which he had made calls. These coincided almost exactly with the times and places of cashpoint withdrawals.

At his trial, Whitchelo appeared far cooler and more forceful than his colleagues had ever seen him in court. And he had yet one more surprise up his sleeve. He suddenly changed his defence, and desperately accused Gavin Robertson of being the mastermind behind the conspiracy.

The trial lasted ten weeks. When it ended on December 15, 1990, Whitchelo was found guilty on 11 out of 16 charges of blackmail, food contamination, attempting to obtain property by deception and making a threat to kill.

It is estimated that his actions led to baby food manufacturers destroying 100 million jars and tins of food, with a retail value of £32 million. Of the £3.75 million Whitchelo tried to extort from Heinz and Pedigree through 18 blackmail letters, he actually obtained £32,000, which has not been recovered. As one of the Heinz team concluded: "The case certainly proves the need for the food industry to keep on its toes and to be prepared for trouble *before* it strikes."

Whitchelo was sentenced to a 17-year prison sentence. The case, a classic in the annals of police detection, has had wide repercussions. Heinz and other manufacturers accelerated their plans to introduce various types of tamper-evident packaging. It is at least partly responsible for spurring banks and building societies into tightening up procedures when opening accounts. Identification such as a full passport, UK driving licence or armed forces identity card must be produced in person.

SECRET OBSESSION

Why did Whitchelo do it? Since he has never admitted his guilt, we can only speculate.

He had passed out top of his intake at Hendon Police Training College and was a competent detective, in many ways the intellectual superior of his colleagues. But the 42-year-old bachelor was something of a loner, never really fitting in well with the macho detective elite with whom he worked. He lived with his widowed 69-year-old mother, and rarely joined his colleagues for a drink after work, preferring to spend his time on his all-consuming hobby of computers.

There were tales of a man who had a succession of girlfriends, with whom he could latterly gain sexual satisfaction only by being beaten until he bled. His girlfriends recall an element of fantasy in much of his talk. Among other tall stories, he claimed that he had infiltrated the IRA and that he had met the Queen while investigating a break-in at Buckingham Palace.

Looking back over the year when they overlapped at Barkingside, his old boss Gavin Robertson believes that Whitchelo felt a growing disenchantment, possibly the frustration of a man not getting the acclaim he felt he deserved. With hindsight, he finds it easy enough to diagnose an intellectual arrogance that could have made Whitchelo delight in outwitting his former colleagues.

Robertson recalls with some bitterness that when Whitchelo was leaving to take early retirement because of his asthma, he had invited the man to dinner at his home, to thank him for all he had done during his 13 years with the Met. That was the very day—August 3, 1988—when Whitchelo dispatched his first blackmail demand to Pedigree.

Robertson also remembers an incident that took place in March 1987, shortly after he had taken command at Barkingside. Scotland Yard had just decreed a massive cut in overtime, and his crime squad team were in ugly mood.

Late one night, Whitchelo rang Robertson at home, insisting that he had to talk about something so urgent that he must see him immediately. "You'd better come up to my place, then," said Robertson. When Whitchelo arrived, he told Robertson that almost his whole squad had gone off to the pub to discuss the overtime issue and what they could do about it. Robertson's wife Jenny could see the two men talking as she worked in a nearby room.

"That was weird," she told her husband after Whitchelo had left. "Why would anyone want to come up here to tell stories about their colleagues behind their backs? You ought to watch out for that bloke." Robertson shrugged his shoulders and forgot all about it.

Anyway, by then the seeds of Whitchelo's crime had been sown. Almost a year earlier, in July 1986, he attended an advanced surveillance course in Derby, at which he learned the inside details of a food contamination inquiry. In that case, the criminals had been caught—but Whitchelo became obsessed with going one better, with committing the "perfect crime".

Within three months, he had opened the secret and virtually untraceable building society accounts in the names of John and Sandra Norman. With a journalist friend he even began working on a draft of a book about ways to commit the perfect crime.

He followed most of its advice, but this evil man "became complacent and lazy, and began playing too close to home," says Fleming. "Like others before him, he became so certain he could go on making fools of his former colleagues that he was eventually trapped by his own arrogance and vanity."

MANHUNT
ON THE *HEROIN* ROAD

BY NATHAN M. ADAMS

NICKEL-AND-DIME DRUG BUST, THOUGHT ED MADONNA.

WHAT BEGAN AS A ROUTINE INVESTIGATION LED HIM INTO

THE SHADOWY WORLD OF A SINISTER CHINESE CARTEL.

Edward Madonna, a 33-year-old special agent in the Seattle office of the US Drug Enforcement Administration (DEA), was looking forward to an uneventful Sunday working in his garden. But a few minutes after midday, the pager clipped to his belt started bleeping. He dialled his office number, listened briefly, then slammed down the phone.

"Customs have just picked up a couple of drug couriers on a flight from Tokyo," Madonna told his wife. "Sounds like small-time stuff. Probably just a few ounces of dope."

An hour later, special agent Madonna watched as American Customs inspectors at Seattle-Tacoma Airport drilled through 138 metal ice buckets that two passengers had declared as product samples. The inspectors drained 212 pounds of pure heroin from the hollow sides of the buckets. It was June 23, 1985, and the largest single shipment of East Asian heroin ever seized in the United States.

But there was more bad news. Before Madonna arrived, one of the couriers—a thin, mustached Hong Kong Chinese identified as Fang Han-sheng—had been allowed to go to the toilet unaccompanied. After a few minutes, inspectors went to check on him. They found a false mustache lying on the floor, and the small window thrown wide open. The smuggler had vanished.

The remaining passenger was under close guard in a detention room. He claimed that he was an electrical engineer on a business trip. "I know nothing about heroin," he said in halting English. "I'm delivering the ice buckets for a friend. I'm supposed to take them to Chicago and wait for a phone call."

Special agent Madonna asked the Customs inspectors to leave him alone with the suspect. He read his passport.

"You're Chen Tsung-ming?"

The man was in his early thirties, small and wiry. "Yes," he replied. "I am Tommy Chen." Beads of sweat began to form on his forehead.

Madonna, a former police sergeant from Vermont, had joined the DEA only eight months earlier, hoping to make a difference in the drugs war. But his cases had been limited to local cocaine and marijuana investigations—the small change. Until today. He studied the courier for several moments. The man was clearly terrified—but of whom? Chen's eyes darted around the room as if searching for some hidden threat.

"Relax, Tommy," said Madonna. "Nobody's going to hurt you. But we have a big problem with the ice buckets. I see only one way out."

Then Madonna offered a deal: Chen would go ahead and deliver the buckets to Chicago. And he might just avoid spending the next 20 years behind bars—if he also identified the owners of the shipment and testified against them.

"No," Chen shook his head. "No way I can do that."

Madonna glowered at the man, telling him again and again that he had no choice. *How can he not know the game is up?* Madonna wondered. Finally the courier agreed to go to Chicago and await the call he had been told to expect. But that was all. He would not testify. "Otherwise, they will get me. My family too."

"*Who* will get you?"

Chen said no more.

Two hours later Madonna was accompanying the courier on a flight to Chicago. Following instructions Chen said he had been given, they checked into the O'Hare Hilton. Three DEA agents were posted in the corridor and one guarded Chen in his room. Madonna was set up in an adjoining room.

Just before 11pm Madonna's phone rang; it was a call for Chen's guard. Madonna knocked on the wall, and the agent slipped into the room.

Chen had been alone just seconds when Madonna heard a loud noise. "Get in there!" he yelled to the surveillance team as he raced into the next room. Chen was gone. The smuggler had forced open a sealed window and stepped out—falling six floors on to a concrete canopy. He then jumped another two storys to the street below. Incredibly, he not only survived—he had disappeared into the night.

As Madonna radioed Chen's description to the police, hospitals and transport terminals, he felt a chill. What kind of fear would induce someone to jump out an of an eight-story window?

Half an hour later, a cop at the coach station spotted the bleeding Asian about to board a bus for New York. The man had suffered a fractured ankle and severe internal injuries. Yet somehow he had managed to hail a passing taxi near the hotel and, fighting back excruciating pain, had almost made his escape.

The following morning, Madonna was at the courier's hospital bedside. "Twenty years is a long time, Tommy," he reminded him.

Chen stared vacantly at the wall. He had made his decision. He would go to jail rather than talk. Clearly, he was fleeing a terror Madonna could only guess at.

SHOT IN THE DARK

Back at the Seattle office, Ed Madonna wrote up his report, noting Chen's astonishing escape attempt and his refusal to cooperate. The clues went nowhere: 138

ice buckets, 212 pounds of heroin and one crippled courier. Madonna had no idea whether the huge shipment was a one-off or one of many; more frustrating, he had no idea who sent it.

Again and again, as the summer of 1985 wore on and Tommy Chen remained silent, Madonna worked his way through Chen's tickets and personal papers. Photocopies of his address book, a gibberish of names and phone numbers, were sent to DEA offices around the world. They produced no leads. Nobody had ever heard of Tommy Chen or Fang Han-sheng, the courier now at large.

But Madonna couldn't let it go. Using the travel documents confiscated at the airport, he drew up a "profile" of the episode: two males, both Chinese, flying together from Bangkok or Tokyo with metal artefacts and staying at Hilton hotels. Then Madonna called the Customs Service databank.

Every visitor to the United States is required to fill in Customs and immigration forms which can be accessed through a computer program called the National Narcotics Border Interdiction System (NNBIS). Could the NNBIS isolate the people who matched his profile?

It would be a monumental task, he knew. Hundreds of thousands of immigration cards and Customs declarations would have to be checked. But the NNBIS intelligence coordinator said he would get the system working on it.

By the end of August, NNBIS notified Madonna that it had a list of 19 visitors who matched the profile. Madonna was cautioned, however, that they were only "possibles" and might be of no help at all.

Hunched over his computer in Seattle, Madonna tapped the keys to access the NNBIS data he had stored and peered at the names crawling across the screen. The visitors' travels had been so extensive that it took nearly an hour to view the arrival and departure dates, flight numbers, countries of origin and addresses in the United States.

By the end of the transmission, Madonna was sitting bolt upright. His shot in the dark had scored a bull's-eye.

Each of the suspects shared remarkable similarities. Many had made at least a dozen trips since 1983, and they often arrived with ice buckets or metal vases declared as "sales samples." Their final destination rarely varied: a Hilton hotel, usually in New York City.

Fang Han-sheng had made four such previous trips. Tommy Chen had brought in 98 ice buckets just a month before his arrest. Both couriers had traveled with others whose names appeared on the computer. They seemed to be coming from every corner of the Far East.

Madonna leaned back in his chair, stunned. The NNBIS database suggested that he had uncovered an immense, complex drug operation. Finally, after months of dead ends, he could move.

Madonna requested a Customs and immigration "look-out" for all the suspects in case they re-entered the country. Then he ordered records of every long-distance call dialled from the suspects' hotel rooms on their visits to the USA. There were hundreds, to places as far away as Hong Kong and Taiwan.

Madonna also sent a report to DEA headquarters in Washington, DC. His evidence suggested that Chinese suppliers might now control the US heroin market, he wrote—as much as 65 per cent of it through a single organization.

Madonna next contacted the DEA in New York. It quickly became clear to him that any investigation into oriental drug traffickers was not one of its priorities. Indeed, they would assign only one overworked agent to assist him, and he could be of little help. For the time being, Madonna was on his own.

On August 30 the telex machine in Madonna's office clattered out a brief but urgent message. Drug squad officers in Bangkok had pinpointed the whereabouts of Fang, the missing courier. He was a victim of what the DEA believed to be a professional assassination.

He had been shot through the heart.

HEROIN ROAD

Madonna guessed that the pieces of his puzzle were scattered on the opposite side of the world. And he would have to go there to find them. He arranged to meet with the drug enforcement team in Thailand and, since he suspected a Hong Kong link, also got the Royal Hong Kong police to send a detective.

Guidebooks describe Bangkok—the City of Angels—as an enchanting capital of 5.5 million, whose peaceful waterways shimmer with the reflections of golden pagodas. Temple bells and wind chimes tinkle softly in the night; the haunting chants of Buddhist monks announce the dawn. The dense, sticky air is perfumed by orchids and incense. For tourists, it is the acme of intrigue and exoticism.

But picturesque as it is, Bangkok also serves as the terminus of the Heroin Road: 700 miles of paved roads, jeep tracks and steep jungle paths which connect the hidden poppy fields of Myanmar (Burma) to the Gulf of Thailand

and the South China Sea. In a secret world behind saffron-robed monks and graceful Thai dancers, there is corruption, greed and sudden death.

For Edward Madonna, who had never set foot out of North America, it was simply hot. On the morning of November 12, 1985, he walked into the drug squad office and met several agents and analysts. "I'm John Pritchard," said the detective inspector from Hong Kong, an Englishman, extending his hand.

Madonna listened closely as Pritchard described the structure of Chinese trafficking groups in Hong Kong. Unfortunately, he said, none of the overseas calls Madonna had identified could be traced to any known crime organization.

"Whoever we're dealing with," said Pritchard, "is very clever."

Pritchard and Madonna leafed through the eight passports and other documents Thai authorities had discovered after Fang's murder. One of the passports was from Hong Kong, another from Singapore, a third issued in La Paz, Bolivia.

"A man of many parts," Pritchard said. "Hold on. What's this?"

Pritchard was peering at the Hong Kong passport. It was faded, but he could see that the photograph did not resemble Fang. "I know this one," he told Madonna. "He calls himself Lee Kwun, alias 'Tiger.' A former Red Guard. We're watching him."

The year before, in November 1984, a Hong Kong Customs boat had intercepted a fishing trawler loaded with 295 pounds of Thai heroin packed in fuel drums—as well as a small arsenal of automatic pistols. Narcotics officers learned from the ship's navigator—the only crewman willing to cooperate—that the organizers of the shipment were Hong Kong residents. But before they could be arrested, they all fled the territory. Tiger Lee was among the fugitives.

Madonna fingered the passport. Finally, he had a piece of evidence linking the Fang murder, the Seattle case and Hong Kong. Madonna had also found an ally.

Like Madonna, Pritchard had begun his career as a uniformed policeman, a constable tramping the beat back in Bedfordshire, England. He had joined the Royal Hong Kong police in 1981, but had been assigned to the Narcotics Bureau only eight months ago. Now it was his assignment to probe the connection between local heroin rings and Madonna's case. His one advantage: he could speak Cantonese.

"The blind leading the blind" was how Madonna put it as they stood in the sticky heat outside Bangkok Airport preparing to leave.

"Mind yourself, Ed," Pritchard warned him. They both knew that drug squad officers were marked men, targets of a violent drug culture every day they worked the streets.

"Count on it," said Madonna. Then he shouldered his bag and headed into the terminal.

BIG CIRCLE GANG

When John Pritchard arrived back at his office overlooking the sampans and junks that bobbed at anchor in Victoria Harbour, a thick stack of surveillance reports greeted him. They represented hundreds of hours of work his unit had put in since the DEA had notified him of the June ice-bucket seizure and the suspected Hong Kong connection.

His team had located the Bangkok travel agency where the airline tickets used by the Seattle couriers were purchased. But the tickets had been paid for in cash, leaving no credit-card receipts. He would continue to check phone calls to Hong Kong and Taiwan numbers copied from Tommy Chen's address book.

But now he went through records of the fishing-trawler investigation, indexing and cross-referencing late into the night. One report drew his attention: a top-secret analysis describing activities of a new crime cartel in Hong Kong.

It was called the Big Circle Gang, an alliance of some 350 hard-core criminals once based in Canton in the People's Republic of China. They had shifted operations to Hong Kong in the late 1970s. But evidence suggested they remained in close touch with groups on mainland China and used them to bring in heroin from Myanmar. Tiger Lee was one of their leaders.

Pritchard continued his search. An earlier reference to the Big Circle Gang appeared in another file—a November 1983 Canadian case. Toronto police had arrested two men with eight pounds of heroin, hidden in false-bottomed luggage, destined for New York. Records showed that the couriers had stopped in Singapore before flying to Canada. And there was something else. While in Singapore one of them made a call to a Hong Kong fur trader. Name: Kon Yu-leung.

"I'll bet you trade more than furs, Mr Kon," Pritchard said aloud. He dug deeper into the file.

According to a detective sent to question him, Kon Yu-leung, known as Johnny Kon, claimed to be a simple exporter. Born in Shanghai, he now lived with his wife in a luxurious high-rise flat across the bay from central Hong Kong.

Police didn't believe Kon's story that the call from Singapore was from someone trying to reach one of his house guests. But they had no real evidence to connect him to the Toronto shipment.

Pritchard put aside the file and took a bite from the remains of a stale sandwich. Kon Yu-leung. Johnny Kon. The name tumbled through his memory. It nagged at him like an itch he couldn't quite reach.

He found the reason as he reread the debriefing of the fishing trawler's navigator. Kon was identified as one of the paymasters of the voyage—now a fugitive, gone to Taiwan.

He grabbed the next file. Police had obtained a search warrant for Kon's flat and had removed box-loads of records that exposed the workings of a half-dozen companies Johnny Kon controlled in Hong Kong. Pritchard felt a growing shiver of excitement as he pored over the documents.

Ledgers revealed hundreds of thousands of dollars in deposits that could not be accounted for by Kon's fur sales. There were payroll records for 60 employees, many of whom had been mentioned in previous files as members of the Big Circle Gang. Among them was Tiger Lee.

It all fitted together like an intricate mosaic. Madonna and Pritchard had uncovered a vast operation smuggling heroin into the United States. They were now pursuing some of the most dangerous drug dealers in the world.

CHAIN OF EVIDENCE

In December 1985 John Pritchard flew to Seattle to present evidence at the trial of Tommy Chen. He would testify about the courier's airline tickets and a stop-over he'd made in Hong Kong on his way to America with Fang Han-sheng.

Madonna was waiting when Pritchard arrived. "John, we're not getting any closer to Kon or the rest of these guys," he said dejectedly. "They could have moved a ton of heroin in here since the ice buckets and we'd never know it."

"We *are* making progress," said Pritchard. "And we're not done with the numbers from Chen's address book. They could be our answer."

During the trial, Pritchard noticed a thin Chinese man aged about 40, dressed in an expensive suit, sitting among the spectators. One of his eyes was so askew that it appeared to stare at the ceiling. He sat by himself taking notes, and spoke to no one. Pritchard watched him closely. He noted a flicker of recognition as the stranger exchanged glances with Chen. Or was it an exchange of messages?

Pritchard edged nearer. The stranger had placed a folder beside him, and there was a name printed on top of it. Pritchard managed to read it upside-down: So & Karbhari, Solicitors, Kowloon, Hong Kong.

Pritchard recalled that the same lawyers had represented the courier in Canada *and* the trawler case defendants. Now they were following the case of Tommy Chen. A coincidence?

On December 23, Chen was convicted and sentenced to 20 years in prison. By Christmas, Pritchard was back in Hong Kong.

The more he read his detectives' reports, the more convinced he was that they were on the right track. Kon had sold smuggled gold jewelry, furs and watches to US servicemen in South Vietnam in the late 1960s. He began trafficking heroin in Thailand in 1974, and by 1980 his companies in Hong Kong alone employed 300, in mainland China another 150. He also owned two firms in New York—a fur dealer's and a real estate agency in Chinatown.

These days Johnny Kon, 42, wore hand-tailored suits of the finest silk and dined at the most exclusive restaurants. A 30,000-dollar diamond-studded watch glittered on his wrist; his nails were manicured and buffed. And yet, for all Kon's apparent polish, Pritchard knew that he and his henchmen were ruthless. His lieutenants were former Red Guards who specialized in heroin trafficking, armed robbery and assassination. Pritchard suspected that Kon himself had given the order to eliminate Fang Han-sheng.

Well into January 1986 Pritchard toiled every night alone in the office, in the pool of light cast by a desk lamp. He cross-checked every call made by Kon or his associates from the boxes of phone traces for numbers taken from Chen's address book. Sooner or later, the search would have to end.

One night in late January, it finally did. In 1983 a single call had been placed to Taipei, Taiwan, from a Hong Kong phone registered to a top Kon lieutenant. The identical number also appeared in Tommy Chen's address book.

Bingo!

He reached Madonna at DEA headquarters in Seattle. "I told you to be patient," he said as he passed on the news.

It took Pritchard until dawn to finish typing up an official report. The chain of evidence was clear: the organization led by Johnny Kon was responsible for the record heroin shipment to Seattle in June—and probably many more US shipments since.

The unmasking of the Kon syndicate was in itself a victory over all the odds but it was only a beginning. There was just one witness, the trawler navigator. Unless other witnesses were found, charges, arrests and convictions were mere pipe dreams. *As the Yanks might say*, Pritchard thought, *where is the cavalry?*'

An ocean and a continent away, it had just arrived—in the unlikely guise of a callow DEA enforcement unit called Group 41.

THE DIRTY DOZEN

"I don't give a tinker's damn what you were before I got here," snapped special agent Richard LaMagna. "Group 41 is going to be the best enforcement group in the DEA!"

LaMagna, 37, stood in an office of New York's Federal Building and stared at the agents. He had been ordered to take over the group early that January, and he was appalled by what he discovered. Group 41 did not even have a surveillance car. Created to uncover drug conspiracies, Group 41 had accomplished almost nothing. Arrests were rare. In reality, it was an orphan among enforcement groups, pushing paper rather than working the streets.

Morale was at rock bottom. Of the five agents assigned to the unit, three wanted out. Lawyers in the building regularly drafted the agents to serve as personal security guards instead of encouraging them to pursue cases.

The fact was, the DEA had little defense against the deadly threat of Asian heroin. But it had at least picked the right man for the job. LaMagna was the only Caucasian investigator who could speak both Cantonese and Mandarin. He had spent six and a half years in the Far East, first in Hong Kong, then Bangkok. He was a man who held tough standards—and was determined his agents would do the same.

"I want to know the minute any US attorney orders you to pull guard duty," he told the agents. "You work for me, not them. Now, let's make some arrests."

But LaMagna was not content to leave it at that. He beefed up his forces, recruiting additional agents from DEA outposts in Brooklyn and Queens. Someone who caught his eye was a streetwise 29-year-old named Kevin Donnelly, whom he put in charge of the Kon investigation. After meeting his new colleagues, Donnelly jokingly described them as "The Dirty Dozen."

They had been together less than a week when the unit received its first alert. At 8pm on January 19, 1986, LaMagna got news that Customs inspectors at New York's JFK Airport had arrested a Chinese woman with 44 pounds of heroin. The drugs had been packed inside several large metal picture frames, and agents were attempting to make a controlled delivery at a Manhattan hotel.

LaMagna joined them and he questioned the woman in Mandarin. She had arrived from Tokyo, she said, and had been asked to bring the frames for a friend. She claimed to be unaware that they contained heroin. Someone would contact her at the hotel to collect them.

"OK," said Richard LaMagna. "We'll wait."

The woman—her passport showed her to be a 52-year-old Taiwan resident—was well-dressed and educated. She was also very anxious.

The phone rang two hours later. LaMagna told the woman to answer in Mandarin and speak calmly as though nothing had happened. Instead, she broke into a rapid-fire Chinese dialect that he recognized but could not understand. She was clearly warning the caller of her arrest and that others were present.

LaMagna grabbed the phone from her and hung up. "That's it. The game's over," he angrily told Kevin Donnelly. "We've been had."

The woman would say no more, and she was led away. But LaMagna couldn't shake the feeling that there was something familiar about the arrest.

At his office the next day he read through DEA background reports. He came across the Seattle ice-bucket seizure seven months earlier—there were startling similarities between the two cases. Both involved Chinese couriers and metal objects cleverly designed to hold drugs. Was there a connection? LaMagna put in a call to Seattle.

Ed Madonna took down the details. He asked about the woman's travel pattern, her itinerary before she arrived in New York.

"Non-stop out of Tokyo," LaMagna replied. "But her tickets show she started from Bangkok."

Madonna knew this was the same route taken by Fang Han-sheng and Tommy Chen. Then he asked, "Do you know the hotel the woman used in Thailand?"

LaMagna consulted the courier's statement. "The Montien," he said. The Montien was the same Bangkok hotel that Tommy Chen had stayed in. "This is another Kon load," said Madonna. "It's got to be."

The Seattle agent then brought his New York counterpart up to date on the investigation, plus what he had learned from John Pritchard in Hong. But unless they got support, Madonna stressed, they could not take it much further.

"Let me talk to headquarters," replied LaMagna.

TIP OF THE ICEBERG

Three days after the seizure at JFK Airport, LaMagna went to meet Catherine Palmer, an Assistant US Attorney attached to the Justice Department's Eastern District. At the age of 30, she had little experience in the specialized field of drug-conspiracy prosecutions. The word was that she had recently joined the department to escape the boredom of a large city law firm.

LaMagna was in for a shock. Catherine Palmer would be unlike any federal lawyer he had ever met.

He looked around the office in amazement. Baseball memorabilia occupied every inch of wall space. There were rows of pennants, caps and team photographs. A bat leaned in one corner; a ball autographed by legendary slugger Carl Yastrzemski was balanced on the edge of her desk.

"I see you're a fan," observed LaMagna.

"Boston Red Sox," she answered. "What can I do for you, Rich?"

They went over the cases. LaMagna told her about the identical courier routing and similar techniques of the Seattle and the JFK Airport cases. He pointed out how Asian traffickers were on their way to dominating much of the New York heroin market. The JFK and Seattle seizures, he believed, were just the tip of the iceberg.

LaMagna pressed on. Only a unified strategy stood a chance of succeeding against this network. He needed more support. Group 41 was only a Class C team playing in the big leagues. They needed a cleanup hitter. Could he count on Catherine Palmer?

"What are we waiting for?" she answered with a smile.

LaMagna knew he was asking Palmer to take a chance in supporting the case now, because neither he nor Madonna could promise a thing. Yet he wouldn't get very far without the cooperation of the US Attorney's office. It's the Assistant Attorney who shapes the investigation and gets the search warrants. In the end, the charges and trials were hers—to win or lose.

Two weeks later, Ed Madonna flew to New York for a council of war. He brought along his addresses and telephone numbers, as well as Pritchard's notes on the Johnny Kon organization.

Madonna could see that the JFK picture-frame-delivery seizure echoed the *modus operandi* used by Chen and Fang. A joint investigation between LaMagna and Madonna, spearheaded by Group 41, was now rapidly gaining strength. Their group would seek to turn theory into prosecutable reality.

Through March, April and May of 1986, Group 41 continued to trace phone numbers looking for leads—and witnesses. Again there were no breakthroughs. Then, on the night of June 18, the telephone at Madonna's bedside in Seattle roused him from sleep. Pritchard was on the line from Hong Kong. "They got him," he said.

"Who?" Madonna asked groggily.

"Our witness."

A professional hit-squad had tracked down the navigator of the fishing trawler. He had been shot in the back with a .45-calibre pistol. As his family looked on, one of the gunmen calmly bent down and put an insurance bullet in his brain. The killers had escaped. In an instant, the case against Johnny Kon had collapsed. "I'm sorry," Pritchard told Madonna. "We're right back where we started."

For LaMagna and Group 41, things were not going well in New York either. Every day, Donnelly led his agents out on to the streets. They were learning the ropes of the Asian underworld, recruiting informants, adding more agents. But there had been no progress locating Johnny Kon's local distributors.

PENETRATING THE CIRCLE

In Seattle, Madonna was under increasing pressure to devote more time to a swelling backlog of less important cases. So was Pritchard in Hong Kong. The investigation was now 15 months old and getting cold. Then, on September 22,

Home turf: Hong Kong, where Kon frequently operated.

they finally got a break—Madonna's computer profiles scored a hit.

An immigration inspector at the Seattle-Tacoma Airport had detained a Taiwanese whose passport contained what appeared to be a forged visa. But unless the DEA expressed interest, the Taiwanese would simply be deported.

"His name?" Madonna asked, reaching for the printouts. His eyes ran down the list—and stopped.

"Keep him right there!" he ordered. "I'm on my way!"

Yin Cheng-ling, a.k.a. Ah-ling, a South American adopted by Chinese parents whose passport showed various birth dates and nationalities, had—according to NNBIS computers—visited the United States on nearly 20 occasions since January 1984. Twice he had declared large quantities of metal vases on Customs declaration forms; twice he was accompanied by Fang Han-sheng and once by Tiger Lee.

He was a small, dapper man not quite 40. His hair was outlandishly groomed, tinted with blue rinse. Costume jewellery adorned his fingers, and he wore traces of make-up. The overall effect was clown-like, but he was supremely confident, displaying none of the fright they'd observed in others before him. There must be some mistake, he kept insisting. He was Ah-ling, a businessman, a trader in export goods. Here. His card. Madonna glanced at the Taipei address, then threw it on the table.

"I've got an indictment here, and your name's on it," Madonna said. "So let's talk about ice buckets and vases you delivered for Mr Kon."

Madonna read off the dates of each trip Ah-ling had made to New York and Chicago, which hotels he stayed in and when he departed. "We know all about you," snapped the DEA agent. "See for yourself. It's enough to put you in jail for life." It was a bluff, but Ah-ling bit.

Catherine Palmer came up with a solution. She knew that anyone taking more than 10,000 dollars in cash out of the United States, even if it's just a stop-over, is required to report the sum to Customs. Failure to do so is a federal offense.

"I'll bet you a season box at Yankee Stadium that he didn't report," she said to Richard LaMagna.

"Easy enough to check," replied LaMagna.

A phone call determined that Chin had made no declaration.

"Then I'm going to play a little hardball," Catherine said.

It took her less than a week to badger American officials into negociating an agreement under which Chin would be expelled from Paraguay—and into DEA custody. Meanwhile, Chin would be only too happy to escape his South American jailers. He was prepared to tell all.

On March 9, 1987, Chin was turned over to DEA agents and flown to New York. The next day, he was seated in Catherine Palmer's office revealing the extent of Kon's financial empire and the location of his properties in the United States.

With the enrolment of Chin, Catherine Palmer was now a short step away from a formal charge. Suddenly Madonna, LaMagna and Group 41 could do no wrong. For the Seattle special agent, who had suffered through the long months of a frustrating investigation, it almost seemed too good to be true.

FACE TO FACE

In April, Madonna and LaMagna learned that Ah-ling had heard from Johnny Kon for the first time in more than five months. Ominously, Kon had phoned and ordered him to fly to Singapore.

"Tell him to be careful," Madonna warned.

On April 14 Ah-ling arrived in Singapore and took a taxi to a luxury hotel. Johnny Kon greeted him at the door of his suite and directed him to an empty chair. Several aides fell silent when he entered the room. Ah-ling accepted a cup of tea. Kon studied him through a haze of cigarette smoke.

"There is a traitor among us," he announced suddenly. "Can you guess who that might be?"

Ah-ling felt fingers of ice curl around his throat. The world stood still. "I agree," he managed to say. "There has been too much bad luck lately. Whoever it is must be found."

Kon reached out his cigarette and pecked at an ashtray. His men had been so cautious, but they were getting caught. He had lost face with his suppliers. They would no longer sell heroin to him on consignment. Every shipment now had to be paid for in advance, in cash. Kon could take no more chances.

His sources had already informed him that Chin had been taken from Paraguay, and they suspected that he was cooperating with a prosecutor in New York. But Chin was not beyond reach. They would learn from informants where he was being held. If so, Chin would die, like the others.

If Kon already knew about Chin, Ah-ling wondered, what else had he found out? Was Kon toying with him? Would he leave this hotel suite alive?

Kon smiled at him slowly. None of this, he said, was why Ah-ling had been asked to come to Singapore. Chin's arrest had forced them to shut down operations through Panama. New methods and routes would have to be devised. "You will play a more active role from now on," he confided.

Ah-ling sagged in the chair with relief. Shipments of heroin were still planned, explained Kon, in amounts as large as a ton. However, purchases would take much time and preparation. The drugs were to travel from Thailand by container ships, first to Manila, then the West Coast of America. When all was ready, Ah-ling would assist in leasing warehouse facilities in Los Angeles. "We are counting on you," Kon said. Then the meeting was over.

"I MAY BE A DEAD MAN"

Throughout July, Ah-ling continued to report on Kon's preparations for one-ton shipments of heroin. Twice that month, he was flown to New York to brief Catherine Palmer, LaMagna and Madonna. Ed had himself made two trips to Hong Kong to tie up the loose ends with Pritchard in anticipation of an appearance before a grand jury, now only weeks away. Ah-ling told them Kon was still completing heroin deliveries to New York and Miami.

On August 29, Ah-ling met clandestinely with Hong Kong agents and reported that Kon had started to purchase and store heroin in Thailand for his latest shipment. Ah-ling would be paid one million dollars for helping complete the delivery. Kon had also confirmed to Ah-ling that heroin was being sent regularly to Europe and the United States from the People's Republic in 80- to 100-pound loads, once a month. Meanwhile, the liquidation of Chin had become Kon's obsession.

Aware of the danger, Catherine Palmer and Richard LaMagna were doing all they could to protect their witness. Chin was placed under protective custody.

By early September, Catherine Palmer was ready to apply the finishing touches to her grand-jury presentation. She hoped to secure charges against Kon and at least a dozen of his Big Circle Gang.

Another witness fell into her lap on September 23, 1987. Lau Shu-ming, a powerful Big Circle council aide, decided to moonlight a shipment of his own into the

United States. He was caught in Los Angeles with 12 pounds of heroin hidden in his luggage.

Madonna flew in from Seattle. Lau turned out to be the well-dressed stranger Pritchard had pointed out during Tommy Chen's trial nearly two years before. One eye was still fixed skyward, the other blinking rapidly with nervousness.

"I'm told you're anxious to help us," said Madonna. "Is that so?"

Indeed he was. Lau had no intention of going to prison. He disclosed how organization assassins tracked witnesses through corrupt police officers worldwide and a network of private detectives worldwide. "I myself sent a message to Tommy Chen after his trial that his wife and family would be killed if he talked." He paused. "I also may be a dead man now."

Then Lau spoke of yet another recent murder. When one of Kon's rivals in the Big Circle attempted to break away, he was traced to Paraguay where assassins crushed his skull with a hammer and then incinerated his remains.

"You agree to testify?" Madonna asked.

"Yes."

Madonna's first phone call was to Pritchard to break the news, the second to LaMagna in New York.

Two days later Lau was seated before Catherine Palmer repeating his story. On December 15 a grand jury met in New York. Kon was placed behind five drug shipments beginning with the trawler delivery and the Seattle ice buckets. On December 21, Catherine Palmer made her presentation.

Two days later, the grand jury returned indictments against Kon and 14 of his comrades. The formal charges were sealed and held under the strictest secrecy so that Kon and the others would not be aware of them until their arrest.

SETTING THE TRAP

The hunt for Johnny Kon intensified. Drug-enforcement police in at least a dozen nations were put on look-out. But Kon remained elusive. Only Ah-ling was in touch with him, usually through cryptic late-night phone calls.

Then on February 25, 1988, Kon ordered Ah-ling back to Tokyo. The first installment of heroin—nearly 900 pounds—was set to leave Bangkok for Manila. But Kon had a problem that would require Ah-ling's attention. It had to do with cash.

The enormous expense of the heroin purchases had sapped Kon's resources. Kon would have to sell some of his property in New York and San Francisco. He estimated he would net nearly 20 million dollars. Ah-ling was to fly to the United States and find buyers.

"That's going to mean a hell of a lot of dope," LaMagna told Catherine Palmer. Then, together with Kevin Donnelly, and Madonna in Seattle, he drew up a plan. The cover story would be that real-estate attorneys were demanding that Kon himself be present to sign the contract. Once he was lured into the United States, officers would arrest him. Meanwhile, Pritchard's men could swoop down on other members of the Big Circle Gang in Hong Kong.

Ah-ling was briefed by Pritchard about the plan. Ah-ling would follow Kon's instructions and travel to New York. Upon his return, he would explain that the buyer insisted the property owner attend the closing formalities in person.

Kon was suspicious. Was there really no alternative? What did he pay lawyers for? But finally he agreed. The money drew him like a magnet. In a guarded phone conversation he ordered Ah-ling to meet him in the bar of New York's Hilton Hotel at 8pm on March 13.

Ever cautious, Kon refused to disclose how he would arrive, when or from where. Indeed, warned Ah-ling, Kon still might not even come at all. "He is always suspicious," Ah-ling told the agents.

Two days before Kon's anticipated arrival, Madonna flew in from Seattle to attend the pre-arrest briefing at DEA headquarters on West 57th Street in New York. None of the agents had ever seen Kon, a chameleon of several disguises.

Madonna and LaMagna circulated the few photos that were available. "Memorize them," LaMagna ordered the agents. "And be careful. He rarely goes anyplace without somebody watching his back."

Madonna called Pritchard in Hong Kong. The timing would have to be split-second. As soon as Kon was in the bag, they would signal for the arrests to begin. Did Pritchard have any questions?

"Piece of cake," was the answer.

"LET'S TAKE HIM"

The evening of March 13, a Sunday, was cold and gusty. The Hilton was cordoned off by Group 41 agents hidden among the shadows of doorways along the Avenue of the Americas opposite the entrance.

Seated at a table in the bar, Madonna checked his watch. It was a few minutes before the hour. LaMagna waited on the opposite side of the room. His lead agent and point man, Kevin Donnelly, sat near by, idly drumming the table-top with a swizzle stick. Inside, his stomach was in knots. He recalled the warning about Kon's well-armed backup. Were they already there and, like him, watching and waiting?

Eight o'clock passed.

The lounge filled, but no one joined Ah-ling, seated alone in the corner. Images of the investigation flickered through Madonna's mind like a grainy newsreel: how it had all begun at Seattle-Tacoma Airport; the computer profiles and endless research; the improbable baseball-mad attorney; the ex-constable in Hong Kong who had become his best friend.

With the exception of LaMagna, they had stated the case as novices, taking on one of the world's largest and best-organized drug-trafficking rings. Each had since matured into an accomplished professional, and Madonna had grown with them. He could hardly believe it was about to end.

His thoughts were interrupted by a well-dressed Chinese man who strolled past the bar as though searching for someone. He was compact, but fleshy. A heavily jeweled watch glittered on his wrist. His eyes were quick, dark.

Madonna held his breath. Was he just a businessman or ...? He could see no bodyguards, no sweepers lurking to warn the stranger of danger. Madonna was uncomfortable. Kon never travelled far without his gunmen. Donnelly looked up, winked, and went on tapping.

The man returned moments later. Catching Ah-ling's attention, he beckoned and pointed toward the restaurant. Madonna felt a flush of excitement.

Ah-ling rose and left the bar. The three agents followed seconds later. They selected a table near the entrance of the restaurant where they could cover the doors, yet far enough from Kon and Ah-ling for them to escape attention. Madonna watched from the corner of his eye as the two discussed the property sale. After an hour, Kon got up and slipped on his overcoat. He left by the street exit.

"Now!" said LaMagna. "Let's take him." Outside, Kon was already a block ahead of them, striding briskly under the street lamps, heading south along the Avenue of the Americas. The agents caught up quickly near the corner of 52nd Street. As they did, Donnelly drew his revolver.

"Federal agents, Mr Kon," LaMagna announced. "You're under arrest!"

Johnny Kon turned slowly, his face empty of expression. "You are mistaken," he said quietly. "I am Mr Wong."

A police car pulled up alongside. "Get the cuffs on him and we're out of here!" LaMagna shouted. An agent handcuffed Kon's arms behind him.

Still protesting that they had the wrong man, Kon was bundled into the back of the car. LaMagna read him his rights as they drove to DEA headquarters.

It was nearly midnight when LaMagna phoned Pritchard and told him of Kon's arrest. In less than two hours, a return call informed him that Hong Kong police had detained nearly all the local targets.

Catherine Palmer prepared Kon's arraignment for the following morning. Then she edited final drafts of the extradition papers for Kon's lieutenants picked up in Hong Kong. Exhausted, she fell asleep on the couch in her office amid the bats and balls.

At 10am on March 14, 1988, Johnny Kon was led into the federal courthouse in Brooklyn. He appeared confident as he posed for courtroom artists—until he heard the list of charges against him and learned of the other arrests. There would be no bail. As he was escorted back to a holding cell, Kon turned to Kevin Donnelly. The drug dealer's lifeless eyes narrowed to pinpoints. "Others will die," he hissed. "Then you!"

Donnelly shrugged it off. An empty threat, he thought. Later, however, the DEA would learn of a plot to kidnap the agent and inject him with a lethal dose of heroin. And Catherine Palmer narrowly escaped the revenge of Asian drug traffickers when agents stopped her before she opened a booby-trapped briefcase delivered to her office. It contained a sawed-off rifle rigged to fire.

YEAR OF THE DRAGON

Without its leader, the Big Circle Gang scattered like a house of cards in a gale. On March 18, a key deputy was picked up by Pritchard when he arrived in Hong Kong from Manila. He was extradited to the United States on March 25, and later hanged himself in his jail cell. Meanwhile, the DEA ran to ground another Kon distributor in New York's Chinatown, and a third was learned to be in China.

The DEA redoubled security on witnesses Chin and Ah-ling, constantly moving them to different locations. Agents had intercepted several letters that Kon had written from prison, offering large sums for the murders of those who were to testify against him. But the fear he once instilled among the Big Circle Gang had evaporated. Even Tommy Chen, the Seattle courier, had agreed to co-operate in exchange for leniency.

Finally, after more than a year of pre-trial maneuverings, Johnny Kon pleaded guilty to each count of the indictment. On September 29, 1989, he was sentenced to 27 years in federal prison.

Group 41 did not await the final outcome before celebrating. Two days after Kon's arrest, LaMagna, Madonna and Group 41 agents took over a small Irish bar on Manhattan's West Side for a victory party. Catherine Palmer was the guest of honor. They could not have done it without her, said LaMagna. Word had even reached Chinatown, where people were calling her the "Dragon Lady."

Catherine Palmer would later be cited for distinguished service by the US Attorney General, Richard Thornburgh, the highest honor awarded by the department. Now Detective Chief Inspector, Pritchard received both Hong Kong's prestigious Governor's Commendation and the US Justice Department's Public Service Award—one of the few times it has been presented to a non-American police officer.

Catherine Palmer and Richard LaMagna would continue to spearhead the assault against Asian drug traffickers, and today, thanks to their efforts, nearly all major Asian heroin-trafficking rings have been uncovered. Rarely does a shipment arrive in the United States without DEA agents knowing its exact source and going on the counterattack.

That spring, Ed Madonna enjoyed a less boisterous reunion with John Pritchard, who had flown with his new wife to Seattle on their honeymoon. The two agents sat in Madonna's living room, drinking champagne.

Pritchard extended his glass for a refill. "Cheers," he said. "To the case, and the Year of the Dragon."

"What's that?" Madonna asked.

Pritchard drained the champagne. "Nothing really," he said. "Except that Chinese fortune-tellers say it's very good luck."

Captured: Greed became Kon's final downfall in New York City.

CAR-
JACKED!

BY ANITA BARTHOLOMEW

SHE HAD TWO DESPERATE CRIMINALS IN
HER CAR AND A GUN POINTING AT HER HEAD,
YET SHE KNEW SHE HAD TO STAY CALM.

The steamy air hung thick over Florida's Interstate 75. But in her new green BMW convertible with the top down, Edith Silver, 59, barely noticed the heat. Carefree, the wind mussing her short, blond hair, she was about to go on vacation before starting a new career as a real-estate agent.

This afternoon of July 8, 1997, she was heading to Bonita Springs to pick up her new business cards. A couple of miles before her exit, she passed a highway patrolman who had pulled over a sport-utility vehicle. She paid it no notice.

Even in this heat, Trooper Tom Roderick of the Florida Highway Patrol wore his bulletproof vest. After 15 years on the force, he had learned that you never know what might happen out here, about 40 miles from Everglades National Park.

The brown-and-beige Chevy Blazer that Roderick had pulled over for a cracked windshield held two very jumpy young men. The driver, whose license identified him as David George of Greenville, South Carolina, said they had borrowed the Blazer from a friend. But when Roderick asked for the friend's name, the men could not remember.

"I need you to turn off your vehicle," the trooper said. Instead, George mashed the accelerator to the floor and took off.

Roderick ran to his car and followed the speeding Blazer. Suddenly the driver stuck his arm out the window and pointed a semi-automatic pistol at the trooper's car.

Bullets ricocheted off the front bumper of the patrol car, and it swerved as a tire was hit. The trooper struggled for control.

Now the Blazer's passenger aimed at Roderick's windshield.

Ka-ping! Bullets caromed off the front of the patrol car, and smoke billowed from its right front side. Reluctantly, Roderick pulled off the road, already calling headquarters.

As Edith Silver slowed for the Bonita Springs Boulevard exit, a Blazer whipped past on the grassy shoulder and then snapped around, blocking the offramp. Worried that the brown car had spun out of control, Silver pulled over to make sure everyone inside was OK. But before she could move, two young men jumped out and ran to her convertible. "Do what we tell you," one said, aiming a semiautomatic at her heart. "If you don't, you're dead."

"Please," Edith cried, "you can have the car."

"No, lady, you're driving. Move!"

Commercial diver Wil Killmer, 30, was heading down I-75 on his way to his job in Key Largo when he saw the curious scene: the Blazer blocking the exit; two men jumping out and into a convertible without even stopping to open its doors. Suspicious, he watched the BMW head back onto I-75. Slowing to let it pass, he could see its occupants clearly. A blond woman was driving. Next to her was a lean young man with bleached hair; behind them sat a huskier young man with light brown hair. Killmer noted the license plate: EDY SWTY.

At the next exit the BMW pulled off I-75. As it disappeared from view, Killmer reminded himself that he still had a long drive to work and that the woman might have picked up the men by pre-arrangement.

Could he take that chance? No. He would have to be late for work. At the next exit he turned around and headed back to the abandoned Blazer.

Billy George and his brother, David, told Silver that her choice was simple. She could do exactly what they ordered and live, or she could hesitate for an instant and die. She spent no time ruminating about her choices. She wanted to see her sons and grandchildren again.

David, 27, sat in the back. Billy, 30, sat in the front passenger seat, ordering Silver to weave in and out of traffic. Then, apparently realizing that they could be identified more easily driving in an open car, he made her put up the top and roll up the windows.

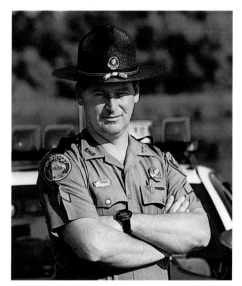

Sergeant Roden: patrolling the lonely road, he saw the car and acted quickly.

The Bonita Springs Boulevard exit swarmed with troopers who had responded to Roderick's call. Killmer approached. "Excuse me, but the guys you're looking for—they're nowhere near that car," he said.

When he told them what he'd witnessed, Highway Patrol notified all Florida law enforcement: "Be on the lookout for a green BMW convertible, tag E-D-Y-S-W-T-Y."

Smoking one cigarette after another, Billy seemed hyped up. But Silver realized he had intelligence. He wanted to keep her just scared enough to obey his orders but not so scared she would be unable to drive.

David wanted to listen to the radio, but Billy overruled him. "Don't you want to hear if …" David began excitedly. Billy cut him off and said, "No." Apparently Billy didn't want Silver to know too much.

"We've been accused of something we're not guilty of," he told her. "But no one believes us."

"Well, then, let me get you an attorney," Silver said, putting as much sympathy into her voice as she could muster.

Billy shook his head. "We've had one."

"I know a real good one," Silver replied.

Billy then spun a long tale about being chased by a white Jeep filled with bounty hunters who had falsely accused the brothers of destroying a hotel room. Silver didn't believe the story, but it didn't matter. She wanted to keep them talking.

From her years in sales, Silver knew how to talk to people. She had to assume these men planned to kill her; she could identify them. But if she could get them to see her as an ally, maybe they'd let her live.

With David George's driver's license in hand, Roderick contacted the Greenville, S.C., sheriff's office. He learned that the George brothers were wanted for a long list of violent crimes, including kidnapping and bank robbery. They'd allegedly stolen the Blazer from David's employer. And there was one more disturbing wrinkle: the previous November, their grandparents had been murdered. Police suspected David and Billy of the killings.

Turning on the charisma that had led her late husband, Ernie, to nickname her Edie Sweetie, Silver humored her abductors.

"So, boys," she asked with a lightheartedness she did not feel, "who do you want to play you when they make a movie of this?"

David chose Nicolas Cage; Billy wanted John Travolta. He decided Rue McClanahan of television's "The Golden Girls" should play Silver, explaining, "I think you're like her in real life. You've got lots of energy and zest."

Silver's strategy seemed to be working. They were calming down. Billy told her she reminded him of his mom and scolded her for driving alone with the top down, telling her that's why they'd chosen her car. But, throughout, he kept his gun pointed at her.

They were now driving on Highway 41, a lonely two-lane road through Everglades National Park. Silver hoped the monotony might work in her favor. Maybe her kidnappers would relax enough to fall asleep—giving her the opportunity to flag down another driver for help.

Right then, as if reading her mind, Billy said, "Don't even think about jumping out of the car because I'll kill you. Understand?"

Don't let him get to you, she told herself. She watched as he caressed his gun, checked its ammunition, aimed and mock-fired. Satisfied, he lit another cigarette.

They had been following a tanker truck for a few miles. Billy told Silver to stay on its tail. Then a Florida Highway Patrol car drove past in the opposite direction.

Billy bolted to attention. "That cop eyeballed me!" he spat out.

It has to be them, thought Sergeant Michael Roden. How many green BMW convertibles could there be around the Everglades?

He waited for a couple of cars to go by before turning to follow. If they spotted him, he knew things could get ugly very quickly.

As the BMW pulled out to follow the tanker around another vehicle, he saw the tag: EDY SWTY. Dispatch told him his backup team, troopers Andy Smith and Orlando Saavedra, was two minutes away. "Let's stop 'em right here," Roden radioed.

"Whatever that truck does, you do," Billy repeated to Silver. But the truck was moving between lanes as it passed slower vehicles.

"There are cars coming right at me!" Silver cried as she dodged oncoming traffic.

"I said do whatever he does," Billy shrieked. "Now do it!"

Ahead, at an intersection, Silver saw a patrol car with lights flashing. There was no longer any point in trying to cajole the brothers. All she could do was obey—and pray.

"When we get to the red light, I want you in the left lane," Billy commanded. As her eyes met David's in the rearview mirror, she saw he had a gun to her neck.

Then she saw another patrol car approach from behind. *Oh, no*, Silver thought, *I'm going to get caught in the cross fire.*

Billy checked his weapon. "When this light turns, go as fast as you can," he said.

Suddenly the patrol car that had trailed them rammed the BMW from the rear, sending it into a slight skid. Troopers ran toward them from front and behind. Billy yelled, "I'll kill her!" Then he swung halfway out the window, aiming his gun at police. "Step on it!" he screamed at Silver.

She took off, bullets ricocheting off the bumper. One whizzed by her ear, the most frightening noise she'd ever heard. Billy hung out the passenger side as David fired through the back window.

The BMW was flying now, weaving in and out of traffic at around 100mph. Then Billy leaned inward, his shirt soaked a bright red. "I've taken a hit, man," he groaned to his brother. "I ain't gonna make it."

Badge of Courage: Edith Silver clutches her Civilian Award for her bravery.

Silver saw her last chance. "Why don't you guys just give yourselves up?" she called to David. "He's dying, and you're not going to get away!"

"She's right," David said, and Billy weakly agreed. Silver slammed on the brakes, and the BMW skidded sideways. The two patrol cars smashed into it, blocking it in. Silver dropped as low in the seat as she could.

Billy started to climb out the window. Saavedra, the first trooper out of his car, grabbed him. Wounded as he was, Billy kept fighting. "I'll kill you," he screamed.

The troopers heard a shot. Fearing the fugitive was shooting at Saavedra, Roden fired. Billy slumped over the window, dead.

At the edge of the woods, Trooper Smith was on the ground, struggling with David George. Grabbing his pepper spray, Roden blasted the criminal in the face. He was handcuffing David when he looked up and saw her for the first time.

Edith Silver. Edie Sweetie.

"Are you OK?" he asked.

After two hours of trying to charm the devil for her life, all she could do was nod. It was over—and she was still alive.

David George is serving a life sentence in prison for kidnapping and other crime associated with the carjacking and abduction of Edith Silver and the shoot-out with Florida Highway Patrol. In South Carolina, charges are still pending against him for kidnapping, home invasion, bank robbery and auto theft, and for acting as an accessory after the fact in the murder of his grandparents.

A TRAP

FOR

MR
UNTOUCHABLE

BY TIM BOUQUET

HE WAS EUROPE'S TOP DRUG TRAFFICKER—
AND FOR FIVE YEARS HE LAUGHED IN THE
FACES OF POLICE AND CUSTOMS.

Beyond a passion for £40,000 cars and helicopter lessons, there was nothing about Curtis Warren to suggest that he was enormously wealthy. The chirpy Liverpudlian, himself a teetotaller, was happiest in a bar, regaling his mates with witty stories. But by 1997 Warren, who called himself a company director, was at number 461 in *The Sunday Times Magazine*'s annual list of Britain's richest people.

The magazine estimated his wealth at £40 million and described him as "a major property player and trader in the North-West", who also had "extensive interests on the Continent".

Warren, bull-necked, five foot eight and prematurely balding at 34, did indeed own 250 properties in north-west England; two petrol stations in Turkey were among his other investments. But what *The Sunday Times* list didn't say was that Curtis Warren was also Europe's number one drug trafficker.

Head of an organization thought to be worth £400 million, he was importing a ton of heroin a week from Afghanistan and Pakistan, industrial quantities of cocaine from South America, cannabis from Morocco and Senegal, Ecstasy and amphetamines from laboratories in the Netherlands.

Interpol dubbed him "Target One". Yet less than ten years ago he was no more than a minor criminal and street-corner drug dealer in run-down Liverpool 8, better known as Toxteth.

Curtis Francis Warren was born in 1963 to mixed-race parents. He started bag-snatching in his teens, went on to car theft, built a reputation for ruthlessness and violence, and was sent to Borstal for assaulting a policeman. Despite prison terms for crimes ranging from robbery to blackmail and possession of firearms, by 1989 the police regarded Warren as little more than an annoyance.

Warren's life changed when he met a Liverpool millionaire businessman with underworld connections. In him, Warren, ambitious and quick to learn, found a mentor who introduced him to a better class of criminal, to protection rackets and to "thugs who would beat the hell out of anybody who stood in his way", as one local journalist put it.

But operating through the drug-supply chain was not enough for Warren. If only he could cut out the middlemen, he could get very rich. He started dealing direct with the Colombian cartels.

In September 1991 he and Brian Charrington, a former car dealer from Middlesbrough, flew off to the Venezuelan capital of Caracas to strike a deal.

Rich and ruthless: Curtis Warren.

On September 23, the MV *Sierra Express* sailed from Caracas for Felixstowe in Suffolk. On board, impervious to X-rays, were 50 lead ingots containing 1,500 kilos of Colombian cocaine with a street value of around £230 million.

At Felixstowe, Customs officers tried drilling the ingots to see inside, but the drill-bit broke. Warren retrieved his drugs, distributing 500 kilos worth £83 million in the UK, and shipping the rest to Greece and the Netherlands.

In January 1992 another 32 ingots docked at Felixstowe. This time, officers from Operation Fullbloom-Singer, a massive investigation by Customs and the Midlands and Liverpool regional crime squads, put them under surveillance. Warren was arrested and charged with importing 900 kilos of cocaine worth £138 million, the biggest haul ever in the UK.

At his trial at Newcastle Crown Court, Warren, who audaciously claimed to be working for a government agent, looked relaxed.

Charges against Charrington, in whose house Customs had found £2.5 million in drug-contaminated notes, had been dropped when at the eleventh hour two detectives revealed that he was an invaluable informer. The police, under the cloak of public interest immunity, suppressed all documents concerning Charrington's relationship with their detectives.

Warren's QC argued that without such important evidence he could not conduct a proper defence. Then the judge ruled that crucial surveillance against Warren was inadmissible.

The Crown's case was now in ruins and Operation Fullbloom-Singer a total fiasco.

As he walked free from the court, Warren paused to confront waiting police officers. "I'm off to spend the £83 million from the first shipment—the one you couldn't find," he beamed. "And you can't touch me!"

In August 1993, two months after Warren's acquittal, a lorry from Turkey drove off a ferry at Dover, carrying fresh diced tomatoes bound for Suffolk. Customs officers who stopped it for a check discovered, under the truck bed, steel trays crammed with loaf-sized, plastic-wrapped packages—178 kilos of heroin worth £18 million.

The lorry was allowed on its way, tailed by a Customs surveillance team. After unloading the tomatoes in Lowestoft, the lorry headed for Liverpool, where the driver made a call from a payphone. He then drove towards Burtonwood services, ten miles east on the M62 and often used for drug drops.

But the lorry didn't stop there, and the surveillance team realized they'd been spotted. Staking out the service station, Customs officers saw a familiar stocky figure standing on the restaurant balcony watching his load disappear south—to be seized on the M1 at Scratchwood services.

Curtis Warren, too greedy to retire, had given police and Customs a second chance.

Top Customs investigator Colin Gurton, a methodical, cagey 49-year-old with a dry sense of humour, was put in charge of a new task force, Operation Crayfish, to try to nail Warren. With rumours of police corruption on Merseyside, he insisted that his team be based at a secret location well away from any canteen gossip.

"Nibble at the edges of the empire and we will reduce the confidence of those at the centre," Gurton told the team of 16 Customs men and nine police officers. "That's when they'll start to make mistakes."

Crayfish gradually built up an intelligence profile of a big drugs combine. They seized 22 kilos of Warren's heroin, "but Curtis reckons to lose one consignment in four", warned Detective Chief Inspector Mike Keogh of the North-West Regional Crime Squad, senior policeman on the team, who had followed Warren's "career" from the start. "If we're only getting a quarter of what he's importing, it's terrifying." Then, in May 1995, their efforts were stalled. A turf war broke out between rival gangs in Liverpool. Fearing for his safety, Warren vanished.

Within weeks, Crayfish officers at Manchester Airport noticed Warren associates making frequent flights to and from Amsterdam. Dutch police traced Warren to a villa in Sassenheim, a small town between Amsterdam and The Hague.

"Damn!" snapped Gurton. "We can't touch him."

Christmas came and went. Easter too. Mr Untouchable remained out of reach.

"It's Tony," said the Mancunian voice on the other end of the long-distance call.

It was late May 1996 and Curtis Warren was agitated. "Are you sure we're dealing with the top guys?" he demanded. "If not, I'm out of it."

"Don't worry," Tony reassured him. "No Neck is talking to Mr L."

Warren was not the only one listening as Tony Farrell made his daily call from Colombia. So too was Tom Driessen, 40-year-old chief of the Prisma team—70 specialist detectives based in The Hague, who target Latin-American criminals using the Netherlands as a drugs artery.

Driessen had launched a major investigation into Warren and Farrell. As he explained to Dutch public prosecutor Willy Don: "Mr L is Arnaldo Luis Quincena Botera, alias Lucho Palmeria, alias drugs supplier. No Neck is also known as Michael and, like Farrell, is working for Warren."

If Driessen could link Warren directly to a drugs consignment, it would be Willy Don's job to prosecute him. Don had already convinced a judge that Warren was such a major player his telephone calls must be intercepted.

Ten Prisma men were now tuned in to Warren round the clock. But in spite of their impeccable English, they couldn't understand his thick Scouse slang. Gurton had to send four officers to translate.

It became clear that Botera and Warren were setting up a direct "cocaine line" from a South American cartel into Europe. "It sounds like a very big deal," said Driessen. "The first shipment is due in three or four months."

By September there was no sign of it. But the Crayfish team was busy taking out other Warren cargoes. At Dover, they found 54 kilos of heroin in two holdalls on board a tanker from France. The bags had begun their journey at a Warren safe house in the Netherlands known as "The Shed", guarded by three Englishmen. The house was put under 24-hour surveillance.

Nine Warren men were arrested at an end-of-terrace house in Peckham, south-east London, unloading a van full of video display screens. Behind the screens, officers found 400 kilos of Moroccan cannabis worth £1.2 million. The Prisma detectives and their English translators smiled when they heard an angry Warren complaining that he'd "lost a commodity".

Warren had other problems at home. In July his brother-in-law Philip Glennon had been arrested for shooting at a nightclub bouncer and a Merseyside policeman. In order to scupper Glennon's trial, Warren needed to know details of the police case. Who better to ask than Detective Chief Inspector Elmore Davies?

Already suspicious of Davies from Dutch intelligence, police bugged his flat. Davies was recorded agreeing to pass on details about the chief prosecution witness PC Gary Titherington, including his daughter's nursery, to Warren's muscle-bound go-between Mike Ahearne, better known to millions as "Warrior" from TV's *Gladiators*.

Hard evidence: drilling into the seized aluminium ingots (above), police found 317 kilos of Warren's cocaine (below right).

Warren was ahead on points, but on October 1, 1996, Driessen got the call he'd been waiting for, from a Dutch officer in Caracas. A shipment of cocaine was on a freighter bound for Rotterdam—hidden in a cargo of aluminium blocks.

Colin Gurton could not believe it. "Warren's pulling the ingot trick again!"

"Can't he do anything right?" Warren yelled down the telephone to Tony Farrell in mid-October. "Tell No Neck to come and sort it."

Driessen heard a new tone in Warren's voice. Gone was the bravado. In its place was fear.

No Neck had given Farrell a copy of the Venezuelan freighter's bill of loading. But Warren needed the original to give to Dutch Customs if his ingots were to stay safe in transit before going on to their destination—Varna in Bulgaria, where he had a wine business as a front.

On October 23, the freighter docked in Rotterdam, its paperwork still incomplete. Driessen immediately ordered the ingots to be warehoused. "We must move," he urged Willy Don.

Bang! At 5am Warren was woken by the sound of stun grenades as a 12-man SWAT team came crashing through his windows. They found him in bed with a prostitute. Simultaneously, teams arrested four of his sidekicks in two other houses near Amsterdam.

In Warren's sparsely furnished house, Driessen's men found little of interest except the guarantee and operating instructions for a Smith & Wesson pistol. The gun itself turned up, fully loaded, under a pillow at "The Shed", where detectives also

found hand grenades, rifles, cartridges, cash, forged passports, driving licenses, hashish and thousands of Ecstasy tablets. In a lock-up garage they seized 67 kilos of heroin.

Later that day in a police garage, a man in overalls, helmet and visor crouched on a large aluminium ingot, bracing his legs against the hammer of a road drill. In three hours, Driessen's team retrieved 317 kilos of cocaine with a street value of £46 million.

A fingerprint check revealed that Tony Farrell was really Stephen Mee, a violent Manchester drug dealer whom Colin Gurton had arrested in October 1991 only to see him sprung from a prison van two years later, escaping a 23-year sentence.

At a court in The Hague, defence lawyer Han Jahae urged the examining magistrate to throw out the case. "This was a vindictive operation mounted by the UK against Mr Warren," he argued.

Slick and accomplished, 36-year-old Jahae had won a reputation for exploiting points of law to get drug dealers off. He claimed that the British tip-off which had sparked the Dutch investigation was based on contaminated evidence, collected by bugs, telephone taps, hidden cameras or coercion, all illegal in the Netherlands.

Forbidden under Britain's Interception of Communication Act to reveal how the evidence had been obtained, Colin Gurton now risked imprisonment for contempt.

Once again it looked as though Warren might wriggle free. Then Nick Baker, head of intelligence at British Customs, arrived in court. With Home Office clearance, he was able to reveal: "Our evidence came from telephone intercepts."

The British had not broken Dutch rules. Warren's defence was shattered.

In June 1997, Curtis Warren was sentenced to 12 years' imprisonment in the Netherlands' toughest jail.

The Crayfish team has charged 129 people and the guilty have received prison sentences totalling 568 years. Drug seizures total nearly 13,000 kilos, worth £120 million.

In September 1998, Detective Chief Inspector Elmore Davies, who had been promised £10,000 by Warren for passing inside information, was sentenced to five years for corruption and attempting to pervert the course of justice. TV Gladiator Mike "Warrior" Ahearne was sent down for 18 months.

FEAR
ON THE
HIGHWAY

BY DAVID MOLLER

TWO LIVELY YOUNG BRITISH BACKPACKERS DISAPPEARED WITHOUT
TRACE IN THE AUSTRALIAN OUTBACK. BUT WHAT BEGAN AS A
ROUTINE INVESTIGATION SOON BECAME A HORRIFYING TRAIL OF
DISCOVERY WITH A HUGE MANHUNT TO CATCH THE BRUTAL KILLER.

oncern pricked at Gill Walters's mind. It was now some weeks since she and her husband Ray had heard from their daughter Joanne. The dark-haired 22-year-old had left their house in Maesteg, south Wales, almost a year earlier to travel round the world. A trained nanny, she had had no difficulty in picking up jobs in Australia—working with children, as a waitress, fruit picker, crew member on a yacht cruising to the Great Barrier Reef.

Joanne was an assiduous letter-writer and always rang home every other weekend. But since mid-April 1992, there had been no word from her. Finally, towards the end of May, Ray contacted Joanne's bank. No, the account hadn't been touched since April 15.

Rural idyll: Belanglo State Forest.

Ray spent his evenings on calls to Australia—to people for whom Joanne had worked, backpacker hostels, police stations. He and Gill wracked their brains for contacts. During their last chat, Joanne spoke of leaving Sydney to pick melons in Western Australia. "She said she was with an English girl called Caroline," Ray now recalled.

From a farm in the state of Victoria, where he knew the two girls had worked earlier, he got Caroline's surname, Clarke, and a telephone number for her in England. She was the daughter of a senior Bank of England official living in Slaley, Northumberland.

Ray felt his hands turn to ice as Caroline's father Ian related a pattern of events identical to his own. Caroline, a tall, fair-haired 21-year-old, had set off in September 1991 for an extended trip round the world.

Ian and his wife Jacqueline had been surprised to hear nothing from Caroline on May 8, her sister Emma's birthday. When there was no word on May 24, Ian's birthday, they became seriously worried. "Caroline isn't the best of correspondents. But she would never miss a birthday."

Ian Clarke contacted the Northumbria Police. Within an hour, Detective Sergeant Tony Noble was at the Clarkes' home, noting details of Caroline's possessions that could help in a search.

In Sydney, Detective Sergeant Neville Scullion and a small team began tracing the girls' last movements. Leaving their accommodation in the Kings Cross area of the city on April 18, the girls had apparently taken the train to the southwestern suburb of Liverpool. From there, it was just a short walk to the Hume Highway, the traditional setting-off point for backpackers hitch-hiking south.

Throughout the summer, Ray Walters and Ian Clarke kept in contact. They helped make up posters with photographs of Joanne and Caroline, which were sent to backpacker hostels round Australia. At home in Maesteg, Gill Walters clung desperately to the hope that Joanne was in some remote settlement where communications were difficult—an outback sheep station or an Aboriginal reserve. People couldn't just disappear in a country like Australia.

But as the summer drew on, Ray realized that they'd know no peace until they visited Australia themselves. He got time off from his job as a paper-mill engineer, and on August 24, 1992, they left for Sydney with photographs and other material that might help identify the girls. At a press conference at New South Wales Police headquarters, the couple made an impassioned appeal for help. "I just hope that somebody out there has some information," implored Gill. They then toured the country, visiting anywhere that might have some tenuous connection with their daughter's travels. But they turned up nothing and by mid-September were back in Sydney.

Saturday, September 19, was a beautiful Australian spring day with luminescent blue skies. Conditions seemed perfect as members of the Scrub Runners Orienteering Club split into pairs and began an exercise in the 9,000-acre Belanglo State Forest, some 85 miles south-west of Sydney and seven miles off the Hume Highway.

Keith Siely and Keith Caldwell made their way through a clearing of eucalyptus trees towards their next marker: a large outcrop of grey sandstone. But as they approached the rock, they became aware of the stench of decaying flesh.

They knew that the forest abounded in wildlife, yet curiosity drew them to an overhang on the far side of the rock. At first, they could see only branches. But, peering closer, Caldwell made out a patch of hair, what looked like an elbow and part of a T-shirt. His eyes travelled the length of the barely perceptible six-foot-long mound, then noted the unmistakeable outline of a boot.

After warning their companions not to come any closer, Siely used a mobile phone to call police in the nearby town of Bowral. "I'd like to report a body in the Belanglo State Forest." It was the start of the biggest murder investigation in Australia's history.

THE FULL HORROR

By the time crime-scene investigator Senior Constable Andrew Grosse arrived in the Belanglo forest, it was dark. Emergency lighting cast a harsh, silvery light on the forest floor as the 26-year-old began the hunt for clues within a cordoned-off area.

Each layer of leaves and branches had to be meticulously scrutinized and photographed before being removed. Gradually, Grosse made out a body lying face down, wearing jeans, walking boots and a navy T-shirt. It had been pulled up around the shoulders.

Next morning, police found another body up against a log just 30 yards away. A maroon cloth, stiff with congealed blood, covered the head. With no sign of backpacks or other possessions, the victims were identified from clothing, jewellery and dental charts.

That Sunday, September 20, Neville Scullion was trying to locate Ray and Gill Walters when Ray made one of his periodic calls to ask if there was any news. "Whereabouts are you, Ray?"

"We're down at the Sydney Opera House."

Within minutes, Scullion was hurrying through the crowd on the famous waterfront. As he approached the Walters he noted their look of grim anticipation. "It isn't the news you want to hear," he began. "We've found a body and it's Joanne's. She's been murdered." Gill Walters gave a scream and collapsed against her husband, unleashing the pain that had been clawing at her for over five months.

Ten thousand miles away, Ian and Jacqueline Clarke were on their way home from a wedding in Surrey when their car phone rang. It was Detective Sergeant Noble of the Northumbria Police.

"Pull into the side," said Noble. "I'm afraid I have some bad news." He paused. "Two bodies have been found in a forest. It looks as though it's the girls."

What neither police nor parents yet knew was the full horror of what the two young women had been through. Intimations of that would emerge only in the autopsies scheduled to start the following day at the New South Wales Institute of Forensic Medicine.

For seven hours forensic pathologist Dr Peter Bradhurst, at 57 a veteran of 200 homicides, examined the decomposed remains of Joanne Walters. She had received 14 stab wounds in the chest. One blackened cut in the partially mummified, orange skin indicated a blow so strong it would have cut her spine—causing paralysis.

Joanne had been gagged and a ligature tied loosely round her neck. The pathologist examined her hands for "defensive" wounds, indicating that she'd had a chance to deflect the blows. There were none. And, five months on, there was no conclusive way of establishing if death was by stabbing, strangling or suffocation.

Painstaking search: police comb the Belanglo forest area for clues.

On Caroline Clarke, Dr Bradhurst found just one stab wound to the right side of her chest. Was that done simply to incapacitate her? After removing the blood-matted cloth from her head, he noted ten separate shots in the skull, any one of which would have proved fatal. It's almost as if the head had been deliberately turned and used as target practice.

LOOKING FOR LEADS

Detective Inspector Bob Godden of the South-West Region Major Crime Squad had worked on more than a dozen murder inquiries during his 27-year police career. But as he read the pathologist's report, the 48-year-old father of four knew this was going to be one of the worst.

In addition to the variety of weapons used—guns and knives—and the victims' apparent helplessness, there were the signs of sexual molestation. Caroline's breasts had been exposed. All but the top button on her jeans had been undone. It was the same with Joanne, except that she was also missing her underwear.

In the Belanglo forest, a massive search was under way. For five days, 40 officers scoured a great swath along two miles of fire trails. There was no trace of the victims' possessions, or a murder weapon.

The only substantial leads were three bullets recovered from the soil where Caroline Clarke had lain and, near by, ten empty cartridge cases. All were from a .22 Ruger semi-automatic rifle.

Since the bodies had been found deep in the forest, Godden speculated that the killer was likely to be local. "I reckon he's also likely to have access to a four-wheel drive," he remarked to his second-in-command, Detective Sergeant Steve McLennan. "Those fire trails are too steep and rocky for standard vehicles."

Godden's team of 14 detectives started trawling through computer lists of four-wheel-drive owners, noting anyone convicted of a violent or sexual offence. Investigators visited local gun-holders, began gleaning information about campers who used the forest. The case's high media profile brought in a stream of leads. Two women reported picking up a pair of hitch-hikers south of Sydney, three days after Joanne and Caroline were known to have left Kings Cross.

One girl had said she was from Wales, the other from northern England. After a 25-minute drive south, they had been dropped off at a service station near the coast at Bulli Pass. Employees there had seen two British women getting into a truck that same day.

There was another sighting inland, at the Blue Boar Hotel in Bowral. Two British girls had arrived at about 10pm, entertained customers with Welsh ballads and brought the house down singing to a karaoke machine. Police focused on reports of vehicles that regularly travelled between Bulli Pass and Bowral.

Then a Canberra policeman reported seeing two young women getting out of a white Volkswagen Kombi van at a picnic site in Mittagong, not far from the Belanglo, on April 26. The driver was about five foot ten, athletically built, with cropped hair. Godden put out an appeal for him to come forward. His team also began tracking down every white Volkswagen Kombi in Australia.

MORE SAVAGERY

The first anniversary of the victims' discovery loomed, but there was still no suspect. Apart from the van owner whom the police were still trying to trace, there were few leads. Detectives returned to other duties, leaving only four on the case.

Yet those living near the Belanglo continued to feel alarm at the possibility of a killer in their midst. One in particular, 42-year-old potter Bruce Pryor, was mystified by the complete absence of the victims' possessions. Pryor often visited the Belanglo to collect firewood, venturing deep into the forest in his utility truck. He was convinced that one day he would come across a backpack or some other clue. As the father of two young girls, he knew there would be no peace for the victims' families until the killer was behind bars.

On Tuesday, October 5, 1993, Pryor was driving to do some "fossicking"—picking over old gold mine workings—at Nowra, when an idea crossed his mind. *The Morris fire trail. That's the one I've not been down.* He turned and set off back towards the Belanglo.

An hour later, he was inching his vehicle down a rock-strewn track. When the view opened out, he stopped and strolled down a clearing among the eucalyptus trees, his artist's eye feasting on the distant hazy-blue wooded hills. Suddenly he stopped in his tracks. On the forest floor was a large bone. He picked it up.

He had learned some physiology from his wife, a radiographer. He turned the bone in his hand. A femur. The top end of the bone shaft wasn't wide enough for the muscle attachment of a kangaroo. It had to be human. He measured it against his own thigh bone. Someone about his own relatively short height. A woman?

Searching the area in a grid pattern, he spotted other whitened bones. Half an hour later, any lingering doubts vanished. Upside-down on the forest floor was a human skull.

Within hours, the Belanglo was again swarming with police. Just 35 yards from where the skull was found, officers glimpsed the outline of sand-shoes. Removing twigs and leaves, they uncovered jeans and a green T-shirt. Inside was a skeleton lying in a foetal position.

Both bodies had been there for some years. Only half a mile of dense bush separated them from where Joanne and Caroline had been found. And there were signs of the same calculated savagery. Near one body, police found a pair of tights, with each leg tied into a slip-knot to form a loop with two further knots—perhaps used to bind a victim's hands and feet.

This time Peter Bradhurst had only skeletal remains to work on; all soft tissue on the bodies had gone. But by examining the bones minutely for chips and cracks, he established that the victim found in a foetal crouch had been stabbed seven times in the chest with a blade just under one and a half inches wide—about the same as the one used on Joanne Walters. Another grim clue linked the two murders. The top button of the victim's disintegrating jeans was still done up, but the zip was down.

On the remains of the other body, Bradhurst found clear signs of multiple injuries. Marks on a lower left rib showed that a stab wound would have penetrated the lung. The skull bore evidence of four shallow cuts on the forehead, two fractures on the right side and a broken lower jaw.

From their clothing, jewellery and dental records, the two were identified as backpackers from Melbourne: James Gibson and Deborah Everist. Both 19, they had last been seen on December 30, 1989.

Deborah, an attractive, blue-eyed girl with an engaging smile, had been studying for an arts degree at Monash University in Melbourne. James, a gangling youth of over six foot, had taken time out while studying art at college. The two had known each other just a few months, and were still living with their respective parents.

After seeing friends in Sydney, they'd planned to hitch-hike to an environmental meeting in Albury on the New South Wales (NSW) border. They were expected to be away for no more than a week.

As soon as they got to Sydney, Deborah rang home. "Just calling to say hello and that we're all right. I'll call you tomorrow or the next day, Mum, to let you know what our movements are."

The call never came. Every few days, Patricia Everist rang James's mother Peggy Gibson to ask if she had heard anything. On January 15, the two women reported their children's disappearance.

It was nearly four years before police came to break the news: Deborah and James would never come home.

TASK FORCE AIR

Within hours of Pryor's discovery, the police murder hunt went into overdrive. Far greater resources would now be needed to solve the brutal serial killings. NSW Assistant Police Commissioner Bill Galvin put a call through to Superintendent Clive Small, patrol commander in Liverpool, the Sydney suburb from which all four victims were believed to have started their journey. His message was brief: "They've found another body in the Belanglo. Could you go down and have a look?"

Clive Small, a dynamic 47-year-old, had made a name for himself by cracking several big money-laundering and drugs operations. A man of diamond-hard integrity and keen intellect, he bristled with diplomas and degrees.

Now appointed to head the beefed-up investigation Task Force Air, Small could think of no case in which he had started with fewer advantages. Seasoned detectives had worked tirelessly for a year, making little headway. There was the remoteness of the crime scenes, the lack of witnesses.

Small refused to dwell on the setbacks. Far more important, a brutal killer was still at large. Energetically, he set about appointing his team. Bob Godden was made chief investigator of operations, and brought with him Steve McLennan. The immediate task of organizing a Sydney headquarters fell to Small's deputy, Detective Superintendent Rod Lynch, who set about equipping some disused offices with wiring for 30 telephones and a dozen computers. Crucial was the computer link to Bowral police station, where Clive Small had a base from which he ventured daily into the Belanglo.

Small took a bold decision to make friends of the media. As hundreds of reporters from round the world converged on the area, he conducted a briefing in the forest at eight each morning, and one in Bowral each afternoon. "We've got to shake out every scrap of information that might help," he said to Rod Lynch. "Who knows, some foreign backpacker who has long gone home might know something useful."

It was a decision that nearly sank the investigation. A telephone hotline received over 2,000 calls in the first week. Within a few days, 2,500 people were nominated as possible suspects. Every single one had to be scrutinized, and many interviewed personally, for possible links with the murders—or with the other missing young people whose photographs were displayed in Small's command post.

Among those pictures was one of Simone Schmidl, a 21-year-old from Regensburg in Germany. A seasoned traveller, she had already explored Canada, Alaska and New Zealand before arriving in Australia for a second visit on January 19, 1991. That night, Simone—known as Simi—stayed with friends in Guildford, not far from Liverpool. They had heard some disturbing stories about backpackers and begged her not to hitch. But Simi, heading for Melbourne airport to meet her mother Erwina, was adamant.

Tall, sturdily built, resourceful, she had never had any problems on her travels. Hoisting an enormous backpack to her shoulders, she cut a distinctive figure in her yellow singlet and green shorts, her dark dreadlocks held back with a purple headband. As she enveloped her friend, another German traveller, in a farewell hug she promised to phone her from Melbourne.

As soon as Erwina arrived, friends informed her that her daughter was missing. She stayed on in Australia for six weeks, while back in Germany her ex-husband Herbert, an adoring father of their only child, struggled to carry on his job as a bus driver. Worst of all was the anguish of not knowing as the weeks turned into months.

Meanwhile in the Belanglo forest, up to 300 police continued their search. Shoulder to shoulder, often on their hands and knees, they scoured great swaths on either side of the fire trails, sieving hundreds

In command: Superintendent Clive Small had never headed up a case with so few leads.

of square yards of earth and ground cover. On a gorge known as Executioner's Drop, officers rappelled down 150-foot cliffs to search ledges for evidence.

At 3.15pm on November 1, 1993, a shout of "Find!" suddenly halted a line of searchers. Three miles further into the forest from the place where Deborah Everist and James Gibson had been found, an officer had spotted what might be a human leg bone.

From under the mantle of leaves, crime-scene officer Andrew Grosse uncovered another large bone, then a hiking boot. A decaying yellow singlet and faded green shorts suggested that the remains had been there for two or three years. Round the skeleton's skull was a greying purple band with the word "Compact-O-Mat" on it.

In his autopsy room in Sydney, Peter Bradhurst listed two stab wounds in the spine and six in the chest. He removed a beaded chain from the neck. This, together with a ring and a leather neck-band with a Maori carving found near the body, helped identify the victim as Simone Schmidl.

As news of Simone's murder was broadcast on the German media, it brought renewed heartache for Manfred and Anke Neugebauer, living near Bonn. For nearly two years, they had heard nothing from their son Gabor, 21, who had been touring Australia with Anja Habschied, 20, a fellow student at Munich University.

Gabor had phoned home on Christmas Eve, 1991. He was planning to visit Darwin before leaving for Bali. Later, his father discovered that mail sent to the young couple at Darwin post office had not been collected; plane tickets to Bali were not used. Desperately concerned, the Neugebauers, too, had gone to Australia with Anja's brother. For four weeks they searched, travelling several thousand miles—before forlornly heading home.

Three days after the discovery of Simone Schmidl's body, the forest revealed more dark secrets. A mile east of where she had been found, searchers were again stopped by a cry of "Find". An officer had caught the gleam of a whitened skeleton. Just 60 yards away, on the other side of a fire trail, was another body. They were identified as Anja and Gabor.

Some 160 yards from Gabor's remains, police found a mass of .22 cartridge cases, along with tangled electrical tape, white sash cord and a leather strap that could have been used as bondage restraints. Broken pieces of a silver-coloured necklace, given to Anja for her eighteenth birthday, suggested a ferocious struggle.

In Sydney, Dr Bradhurst recorded a variety of horrific assaults. Anja had been decapitated. He believed she had been kneeling, almost as if in a ceremonial execution, with her chin resting on her chest. A sharp, heavy instrument had slammed downwards, slicing cleanly near her fourth cervical vertebra. Her skull was never found.

Gabor had been shot in the head six times with a .22 calibre weapon. A piece of cloth had been stuffed into his mouth to gag him. Another piece of material had been tied round his mouth, perhaps to stifle his cries further. There was also a fracture of the hyoid bone at the base of his tongue, which suggested that he had been strangled.

Anke Neugebauer travelled to Australia to bring Gabor's body home. Bob Godden, now working a punishing 18-hour day, nonetheless insisted on accompanying her to the clearing where her son had been found. Among the eucalyptus and wattle trees, she sat and wept quietly. Then she asked Godden, "I know your time must be precious. But could you let me have one hour here by myself?" Telling her to take as much time as she needed, he walked away into the forest.

UNDER PRESSURE

By mid-November, 1993, the search of the Belanglo was completed. As Clive Small's full team joined forces in their Sydney headquarters, the city was beginning to swelter in the humidity of early summer. Dust hung heavy in the operations room, where walls were being pulled down to create the single working area that Small wanted for a close, fast-communicating team. With calls still pouring in, there would be a mass of work for his 38 detectives and 20-odd computer analysts and support staff.

But at last they might have one or two solid leads. The .22 calibre bullets used on Gabor Neugebauer appeared identical to those found in Caroline Clarke. Distinctive crescent-shaped markings on the cartridge cases found near both bodies showed they had been fired with the same firing pin—that of a .22 Ruger 10/22 made before 1982.

From the gun's American manufacturers, police learned that 55,000 Rugers of the suspect type had been imported into Australia between 1964 and 1985. They set up a computer database with details of all 55,000 weapons. Using the manufacturer's records, they would trace every single gun through distribution outlets to rifle clubs and individual purchasers. They would appeal for all owners of Ruger 10/22s to come forward and sift gunshop records to pinpoint those who had brought Ruger 10/22s in for repairs. It was a massive undertaking.

The task force, however, had made one find that quickened Small's blood: near Gabor's body, an empty Winchester-brand cartridge box had been picked up. It could have held the .22 calibre bullets used on Gabor and Caroline Clarke. It had the batch number ACD1CF2. At the Winchester factory in Geelong, Victoria, officers discovered that that particular batch of ammunition had been relatively small—just 320,000 bullets—but they would not have been sold in any specific order. After a week combing through several boxfiles of sales invoices and stock records, they established that the batch had left the factory between June 2 and November 30, 1988.

Detectives would now visit wholesalers and gunshops, starting with local ones, to try to find out who had bought the ammunition. Meanwhile, other investigators were trawling databases of sex offenders and of people convicted of abduction or crimes of violence.

Given the number of circumstantial links between the murders, Small and Lynch were working on the assumption that one person was likely to have killed all the victims. "If we alibi a person for one crime," said Small, "that will have to take them out of the inquiry for the moment."

State police forces across Australia alerted the task force to possible suspects. In all, six convicted killers were scrutinized, but in every case their alibis checked out.

As the investigation ground on towards the end of 1993, Small felt mounting pressure. Apart from Joanne Walters and Caroline Clarke, all the victims had gone missing around Christmas and the New Year. Is the killer poised to strike again? He increased police patrols and stepped up the covert watch on those still hitching from the Sydney end of the Hume Highway.

Another concern was the sheer volume of information pouring into the inquiry. As more bodies had been found, Small's team had had to absorb all the data from previous police inquiries into their disappearance. In almost every case, even where the same software packages had been used, classification of the material varied.

By January 1994, the system was fast approaching breakdown, with nearly 1.5 million pieces of information on computer. Rod Lynch warned Small that investigators were simply not getting the data they needed: "We might have to start again, almost from scratch. But we'll end up with a much better system."

Gloomily, Small stared out of the window at what he could see of another golden summer evening. At 7pm it was still sweltering in the grimy building. He wasn't going to get home, again, in time to see his daughter Amber, 11, or 14-year-old Joshua. These days even he and his wife Alison met only briefly.

For a few moments, he pondered. A whole new computer system? Only he could make the decision. "All right," he concluded. "Let's do it."

Rod Lynch and a team of computer analysts worked almost round the clock to put the new technology in place. But still Small worried that in the mountain of data, some minute clue might somehow have been overlooked.

Are there people in our system that we've already looked at who should be ringing a few bells?

To help produce a psychological profile of the killer, he set up a panel of outside experts. At their first meeting on January 28, 1994, Small, Lynch, two officers from the NSW police intelligence group, an educationist, a computer expert, forensic psychiatrist Rod Milton and Richard Basham, a specialist in psychiatric anthropology from Sydney University, brainstormed for several hours.

Basham offered the view that, given the ruggedness of the terrain in which the victims had been buried and the "macho" nature of the killings, the murderer might also own a motorcycle. Rod Milton suggested that, since none of the victims' possessions had been recovered, the killer could well have kept "souvenirs" of his crimes.

Sexual assault was considered a possible motive, although not the major one. There were clear signs of sexual interference to four of the victims. The improvised restraints found near the bodies of Deborah Everist and Gabor Neugebauer implied an interest in bondage. And the remains of camp fires near two of the burial sites suggested that the killer had lingered at the scene of his crimes.

The group came up with a profile of a killer in his forties, who might have been in trouble at school. A man not good at forming relationships; who perhaps killed for the pleasure of exerting power; who had a strong interest in firearms and knives; possibly dominant within his own family.

During a break, Small decided to test a hunch on Basham. He explained that enquiries had brought into the frame a family group, several of whom lived in isolated hamlets or ramshackle farmsteads. Big purchasers of ammunition, between them they had notched up a variety of offences. Basham's response was swift. "Clive, that could be what you are looking for. You've got to watch that family."

A SINISTER BUNCH

Small deployed a team to delve into the Milat family—a task complicated by the fact that some of them used several different names and owned vehicles and held firearm licences in each others' names.

Stijphan, the father, had emigrated from Yugoslavia after the First World War. He married an Australian girl half his age and they produced a family of 14—four daughters and ten sons. Stijphan worked seven days a week in back-breaking labouring jobs to provide for his family in their weatherboard home in Moorebank, near Liverpool. Hard on himself, he was also harsh with his children. As one son put it, "If you came home and you'd been in any sort of trouble, he'd just whack you to the ground."

Nevertheless, in time four of his sons had brushes with the law for theft, breaking and entering, stealing cars, illegal possession of firearms. One daughter was killed in a car driven by her brother Walter; another brother, David, lost the use of an arm and was seriously brain-damaged in two other accidents. Michael Milat served a long prison sentence after being involved in several armed robberies.

Besides their interest in firearms, the family had come to the notice of the task force for one other reason. Among the flood of statements made to the police was one from a member of the Bowral Pistol Club, located in the Belanglo Forest.

Leaving the club at about the time that Joanne Walters and Caroline Clarke had disappeared in April 1992, he had passed two vehicles turning on to the forest's access road. One was a brown Ford Falcon, the other a beige and brown four-wheel-drive utility van—possibly a Holden Rodeo. In the Falcon were four men, and between two of them in the back was a woman gagged with "a length of honey-coloured material which was wrapped around her head across her mouth". There was another gagged woman in the second vehicle. The informant was a 52-year-old former miner who at the time lived in the Belanglo area. His name: Alex Milat.

Detectives returned to his home several times to check his statement, but Alex Milat simply supplied more detail, even describing calluses and tattoos on the hands of one of the men. But could anyone passing a car on a dusty lane have noticed such detail?

Clive Small felt nonplussed. Why had Milat waited more than 18 months to report such a menacing incident? *Is he deliberately trying to throw police off the scent with misleading details? Or is he trying to let us know, in a very oblique way, that something horrifying is going on in his family?* Small instructed his team to keep digging.

Attention was soon focused on a younger brother: 49-year-old Ivan. In his youth, he had acquired several convictions for car theft and breaking and entering. A short, stocky man with piercing blue eyes and formidable strength, he had developed into a model employee as a roadworker for the Department of Main Roads at Liverpool; one of his previous employers described him as "honest, courteous and reliable".

At home in Eagle Vale, near Liverpool, where he lived with his sister Shirley, he was seen as an ideal neighbour, always the first to get a neighbour's car started or help cut down a tree. He maintained his garden in picture-book condition; spent hours polishing his four-wheel-drive Holden Jackaroo and his prized Harley Davidson motorcycle; kept an eye on his ageing mother and brain-damaged brother David, who lived with her in nearby Guildford.

But further digging revealed a darker picture. Years earlier, over Easter 1971, Ivan Milat had picked up hitch-hikers Margaret Patterson and Greta Pearce on the Hume Highway. Turning on to a dirt road, he had stopped the car and said, "Either one of you have sex with me or I will kill you both." Then he'd produced two knives and some cord, evidently prepared in advance to tie up his victims.

Margaret eventually agreed to have sex, so long as he later drove off and left them unharmed. At one stage, Greta made as if to escape. In an instant, Milat grabbed her leather choker, whipping it tight with horrifying strength. He then tied her up.

Brazenly, Milat later drove them to a petrol station for Margaret Patterson to buy them drinks. Once inside the garage shop, she told the staff: "There's a chap in the car. He has a knife and he's raped me." A small crowd hurried outside. Greta Pearce, who'd been untied, escaped from the car just as Milat drove off. In a chase at speeds of up to 105mph, he outran the police. He was stopped later only when they set up a roadblock.

Out on bail, Milat fled to New Zealand. He slipped back after three

A darker side: Ivan Milat seemed to be a model employee and ideal neighbour.

years, but by the time he was arrested and tried in December 1974, memories had dimmed. The jury, persuaded that sex had taken place with the woman's consent, as Milat insisted, acquitted him.

On his return from New Zealand, Milat was also tried for the same armed robbery that had sent his brother Michael to prison. But again he walked free.

Small's team then heard from two women, Mary Tregillas and Therese Tran, concerning another incident. As teenagers in 1977, they had accepted a lift near Campbelltown on the Hume Highway. When the driver turned on to a road leading to the Wombeyan Caves, one of the girls protested, "This isn't the way to Canberra."

"No, don't worry, this is a scenic short cut."

After a while, the road became a dirt track through dense bush. Finally, the car halted in a clearing. "Why are we stopping here?" Therese Tran asked. "Nature calls," the man reassured them.

But as the driver got back into the car, he leaned over to grab Mary Tregillas. "OK girls, which of you wants it first?" Desperately, Mary fought to break away from her attacker. "Run!" she screamed. As the two sprinted from the car, Therese yelled, "Hit the ditch." They raced down the ditch beside the track, then dodged into the bush. Time stood still as they huddled, terror-stricken, while their enraged pursuer drove back and forth, looking for them.

Although the two women did not report the incident to the police, they had never forgotten their ordeal. But would they be able to identify the man? Therese Tran, sitting in the back, never saw his full face, but said she'd never forget his cold, steely eyes.

Shown a series of photographs, she selected two. One was of Ivan Milat. Mary Tregillas chose just one photo—of Richard Milat. Small realized that their testimony would be of little use in court. The incident had happened 17 years ago. Identification was uncertain, the link with the Belanglo killings circumstantial. Once again, Ivan Milat appeared to have slipped the net.

Intensifying their scrutiny of Milat, police located his ex-wife Karen. Traumatized by the verbal abuse and violent behaviour she had endured while living with him, she had changed her name and moved to a secret address.

She told police how he was so gun-obsessed that he often stuffed a small handgun down the side of his boot. He kept another revolver either in a case under their bed or under the driver's seat of his car. His guns, like many of his other possessions, were often marked distinctively with his initials—an M intersected with an I.

She and Jason, her son by another relationship, had made several trips with Milat to the Belanglo forest. On one, she had been stunned when he had shot a kangaroo, then slit its throat.

Finally, on St Valentine's Day, 1987, when her husband was away for a few days, she left him. On his return Milat, incandescent with rage, stormed off to her parents' home demanding to know her new address. But even after a fire mysteriously burned their garage to the ground, they refused to say where she had fled.

For a couple of years Milat took up with one of his brother's ex-wives, but that relationship ended in 1989, just a few months after an acrimonious divorce from his wife was finalized. Was that the trigger for the killings? Small pondered.

With Milat now a prime suspect, checks at his workplace established that he had been on holiday, or taken days off, on each of the occasions that the seven backpackers had gone missing. Small set up covert surveillance on Milat and his home in Cinnabar Street, Eagle Vale, to see if they could glean any direct evidence linking him to the Belanglo murders.

"Everything we have so far is circumstantial," Small remarked to Lynch. "There is really nothing with which he can be charged."

"HE'S GOT A GUN!"

Then investigators working their way through the mountain of leads came to the record of a telephone call from a woman called Joanne Berry. In January 1990, she had picked up a terrified backpacker who had been attacked by a driver who had given him a lift on the Hume Highway. She had driven him to nearby Bowral police station. The victim was Paul Onions, a 24-year-old air-conditioning engineer from Britain.

But Bowral police had taken no statement from him about the attack; there had been no follow-up interview. There was only a rough entry in the notebook of the officer on duty when Onions arrived at the station. This calamitous failure in police practice meant that Small's team, who'd spent weeks checking out every attempted or successful abduction in the area since 1985, had had no chance of finding what could have been their best lead.

Another check with Milat's employers established that he'd been away from work on the day of the attack on Paul Onions: Thursday, January 25, 1990. On the phone to Onions, now living back in Britain, police at last got a full account of what had happened.

Onions, a slim man just five foot six tall, had taken a train out to Liverpool to start hitching down the Hume Highway. At 1pm, still without a lift, he was trudging along in the heat of the Australian midsummer, when he came to a row of shops in Casula. As he bought a cold drink in a newsagent, a stocky man with a bushy moustache standing next to him asked genially, "Need a lift, mate?"

"Do I ever!" replied Onions. "I'm heading for Mildura, but anywhere along the way will do."

As they came out of the shop, the man indicated a silver four-wheel-drive vehicle. Onions pushed his backpack over the back of the passenger's seat and settled into the sheepskin seat cover. "My name's Paul," he introduced himself.

The driver responded with a smile, "Mine's Bill." As they travelled through the parched, rolling hills of NSW's Southern Highlands, they exchanged a few more sketchy details about their lives. Bill worked on the roads, based at Liverpool. He was divorced. His family came originally from Yugoslavia.

But after about half an hour, Onions noted that the warmth had gone from his companion's voice. Somehow, the conversation veered to the presence of British troops in Northern Ireland. "I reckon they ought to get out. They've no right to be there. What do you reckon?" Onions began to feel uneasy. *Is this man trying to pick an argument?*

From time to time he noticed the vehicle slowing down. "What's happening?" he asked.

"No worries, mate," said Bill. "We're getting out of range of the Sydney radio stations. I'm just looking for somewhere to pull over so that I can get some tapes." Onions glanced down. Several cassettes were within easy reach between the seats. When the vehicle finally halted, he was glad to step out to stretch his legs—and shake some of the uneasiness from his mind.

As he got back into the car, Bill was fumbling under his seat. Seconds later, Onions found himself staring down the barrel of a small black revolver. Just inches from his face, he could see copper-tipped bullets in the chamber. *This isn't happening. It's a dream.*

Suddenly, Bill's voice boomed, "This is a robbery." Again he fumbled under the seat. As he brought out a bag, rope dangled from it. Stark terror now flooded Onions's mind. *A gun might be used as a threat. A rope is for real.*

Whipping off his seat belt, Onions flung himself out of the car. Half-falling to the road, he began running. He heard a cry, "Stop or I'll shoot." Cars flashed by. There was the crack of gunfire.

Onions dodged across to the grassy central reservation separating the two carriageways. Frantically, he tried to flag down a passing vehicle. No one stopped. Bill was right behind him. Powerful hands gripped his T-shirt. Onions dropped to the ground, and the two men rolled over several times. With terror-driven strength, Onions yanked himself from Bill's grasp and dashed on to the road. If the next vehicle didn't stop, he would throw himself at it.

As a van lurched to a halt, Onions was at the driver's window. "Please let me in. Please ... help ... he's got a gun!"

"Go away!" yelled the woman driver. Joanne Berry, travelling south with her sister, had seen part of the struggle. But in the back of the van were four of her children and one of her sister's.

"Please let me in. Please." Joanne Berry saw the terror in the man's eyes. He was trembling, close to tears. She pulled over and Onions slid open the door, stumbling in among the youngsters. Locking the door behind him, Joanne gunned her vehicle in a bumpy arc across the central reservation to head back towards Bowral.

Now, as the detective checked key points over the telephone, Onions reflected on his escape. The attack had taken place just half a mile from the turn-off to the

Vital witness: Paul Onions had a lucky escape.

Belanglo forest. With icy certainty, he realized that that was meant to be the end of his journey.

Clive Small already knew that Bill was one of the aliases used by Ivan Milat—and the details of his life he had related to Onions fitted him like a glove. If Onions could identify his attacker, they could at least charge Milat with attempted abduction.

On May 5, 1994, at NSW police headquarters, Paul Onions viewed the identification video showing 13 photographs, all of men with moustaches. After several replays, he paused on frame four. "That's him. He's got the same face and moustache." It was the photo of Ivan Milat.

Small and his team now had enough evidence to charge Milat with attempted abduction. What they still didn't have was sufficient evidence linking him to the Belanglo killings.

From Milat's previous brushes with the law, Small and Lynch knew that he was extremely unlikely to be panicked into making any incriminating admissions. It could all depend on what they found in his house. Three hundred police were briefed to search it and seven other properties owned or used by members of the Milat family.

Before making his final move, however, Small decided to dispatch Detective Senior Sergeant Bob Benson to ask Alex Milat, now living on a small farmstead in Queensland, about his sighting of the gagged women. But Alex still stuck to his statement; the police never did discover what lay behind it.

As Benson chatted to Alex and his wife Joan over a cup of coffee, she suddenly asked the detective the colour of the victims' backpacks. When Benson described them, Joan left the room to return minutes later carrying a lilac, pink, grey and black backpack. Benson could hardly believe his eyes. It appeared to be identical to one owned by Simone Schmidl. Joan said that her brother-in-law Ivan had given it to her before they moved to Queensland. Nodding nonchalantly, Benson inspected the backpack's inside flap. It bore Ivan's initials—an M intersected by an I.

When he heard the news, Rod Lynch exulted, "We've got him."

THE NET CLOSES

At 6.40am next morning, Sunday, May 22, a convoy of vehicles blocked off Cinnabar Street in Eagle Vale. They left just enough space for a van with members of the commando-style State Protection Group to speed through.

Inside Milat's bungalow, the telephone rang. "Police are around your premises," a police negotiator told a sleepy-sounding Milat. "They're in possession of a search warrant to search those premises in relation to an armed-robbery matter."

"No joke."

"I want you to come outside for the safety of yourself and whoever's in the house with you. I want you to come out the front door. Turn left. You'll be met by some State Protection Group police who'll be dressed in black. They will be armed and I want you then, at their direction, to lay face down on the ground."

"Okey-dokey." But Milat did not appear. When police called again they got his girlfriend Chalinder Hughes. After a brief conversation, Milat himself was back on the line. He claimed that he thought it was some friends from work, winding him up as a joke.

"No, mate, this is the police. It's no joke."

Finally, Milat emerged in checked shirt and jeans. "Turn to your left, get down, get down," yelled police. As soon as Chalinder appeared, she was whisked away to a waiting car.

Police now poured into Milat's home. For Andrew Grosse it had been a long wait—nearly 20 months since he had bent over Joanne Walters's body in the Belanglo. As he and others fanned out through the house, they saw signs that items had been hurriedly concealed.

Milat, utterly calm, was handcuffed and brought back into the house for questioning. He was told he was being arrested for an armed robbery and asked if he understood what was going on. "Yes, but it wasn't me." Detective Sergeant Stephen Leach, a large, bearded figure, asked about the backpackers and the Belanglo forest. Milat replied, "I don't know what you are talking about."

"Have you got any firearms in the house?"

"No."

"Have you ever been to the Belanglo State Forest?" asked Leach.

"I've driven up the dirt track that goes past it—a long time ago, in the mid-eighties."

In Milat's bedroom, police found dozens of .22 cartridges, rolls of black electrical tape and a driving licence in the name of his brother Michael, but with his own photo. There was also a postcard from New Zealand which started with the words, "Hello Bill." Asked by Leach, "Have you ever been known by the name of Bill?" Milat shook his head.

Leach showed him the card. "It must've been a mistake."

Hidden beneath the washing machine was a .32 Browning pistol. In the spare bedroom, police found more .22 calibre ammunition and a plastic bag with a used .22 Winchester cartridge case (later found to have the impression of a Ruger 10/22 firing pin). A book on road surfacing concealed an instruction manual for a Ruger 10/22.

"Have you ever had in your possession a Ruger 10/22?" asked Leach. No, said Milat. If he wanted to use firearms he borrowed them from his brother Alex, who'd just gone to live in Queensland.

In the hall cupboard, part of a Ruger 10/22 was stuck in a boot. Later, groping through the roof and wall cavities of the house, police found more parts for the same weapon, plus a spare magazine.

Elsewhere in the house they found sleeping bags identical to those once owned by Simone Schmidl and Deborah Everist; an Olympus camera similar to Caroline Clarke's; and a cooking set like the one used by Simone. A water bottle bore the scratched initials IM, but examination under ultra-violet light showed that someone had attempted to scratch out another name: Simi—Simone's nickname.

A green tent in the garage was tied up with a purple band that stirred memories for Andrew Grosse. It was an exact match of the Compact-O-Mat band found round Simi's skull. Also in the garage was a green-striped pillowcase with five lengths of sash cord, one stained with blood. Later DNA testing of Caroline Clarke's parents showed that the blood was 118,000 times more likely to have come from one of their children than from anyone else.

time in their Northumberland garden—not far from Caroline's final resting place in the churchyard of St Mary's, Slaley.

Deep in the Belanglo State Forest, next to the boulder where Joanne Walters's body was found, there is a plaque inscribed to her:

> Keep your arms around her, Lord,
> and give her special care,
> make up for all she suffered,
> and all that seems unfair.

ZERO HOUR FOR
THE ZODIAC

BY BOB TREBILCOCK

A STRANGE TWIST OF FATE GAVE

THE POLICE A CRUCIAL LEAD.

Star team: Joey Herbert (center) with Tommy Maher (left) and Danny Powers

On June 18, 1996, Sergeant Joey Herbert was wolfing down a sandwich at his desk at Brooklyn North Homicide, in one of the most crime-ridden areas in New York. On a shelf behind him sat a row of books on serial killers—a nagging reminder of a wrenching unsolved case that had absorbed the energies of Herbert and his colleagues for several years.

Despite the frustrations that went with unsolved murders, Joe Herbert loved police work. He had become a detective in 1986, then gone on to train as a hostage negotiator in the early 1990s.

Suddenly the phone rang. "We've got a situation in the 75th Precinct," the dispatcher told him. "A guy's got a hostage, and officers are pinned down under fire. We need a negotiator."

"We're on our way," Herbert said. Grabbing a blue jacket with "Hostage Negotiation Team" written on the back in white letters, the stocky 38-year-old detective stepped out into the midday heat and headed for his car.

Crime scene: Highland Park in New York, one of the places where the killer struck.

As Herbert pulled up to the hostage scene, Emergency Service Unit support teams were erecting a bulletproof barrier in front of a block of flats. Police helicopters hovered above and marksmen were staking out positions.

Herbert strapped on a bulletproof vest and donned a helmet. "There's a man called Eddie on the third floor," an inspector briefed him. The man, Heriberto "Eddie" Seda, had shot his sister, who'd escaped from the flat. But he was now holding her boyfriend hostage in a bedroom.

Herbert had never heard of Seda, but the police who patrolled East New York knew him well. A tall, dark-haired 28-year-old loner, he carried a Bible with him and preached about good and evil to drug dealers, while supplying their names to the police.

Joe Herbert approached the bulletproof barrier and took a deep breath. Then he did what he was trained to do: he attempted to establish a dialogue. "Eddie," he called out.

A long gun barrel poked through the kitchen window and Seda stood in full view. "Get out of here," he cried; then he disappeared.

"Eddie, my name's Joey," Herbert shouted over the din of whirring helicopters. "Listen, there's been enough bloodshed." He paused. "We want you to surrender."

Seda reappeared in the window. "Get everybody out," he screamed, "or I'll start shooting again."

For the next two hours Seda paced with gun in hand between the front and back windows. He threatened to start shooting but didn't fire. A good sign, reflected Herbert, his shirt and tie soaked with perspiration.

By 2.30 Herbert had climbed in through a window and made his way to the third floor, where he crouched in the hallway. "Eddie," he called. "It's Joey. I came up to talk to you."

"How's my sister?" Seda asked.

I've got him now, Joe thought, sensing concern in Seda's voice. "She's gonna be OK," he said.

233

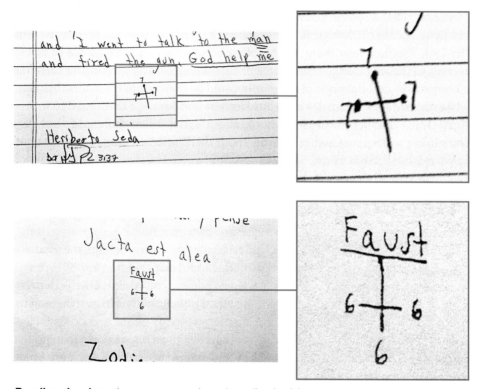

Reading the signs: the statement made to the police (top) bore an uncanny resemblance to one of the Zodiac killer's letters (bottom).

"I don't know what you're talking about," Seda said.

"We've got your prints, Eddie," Herbert added. "They're a match. You're the guy."

For two hours Eddie would talk only about religion. Then the detectives taped ten of the grisliest Zodiac crime-scene photos to the wall.

"Who speaks for these people?" Savarese asked Seda. "Somebody has to speak for these people."

As Seda stared at the lifeless bodies, the veins in his neck pulsed. Herbert knew they were getting to him.

"I know what you've been going through, Eddie," Herbert told Seda gently.

"What are you talking about?" Seda asked.

"You've been going through cycles," Herbert began, drawing on all the books he'd read about serial killers. "You start getting the feeling; you think about it. Then you seek out your victims. The next phase is the murder. Then, Eddie, you get depressed because you didn't achieve that feeling and it starts all over again."

Seda was silent.

"Eddie," Herbert pushed on. "Who's the Unabomber?"

"Ted Kaczynski," Seda replied.

"The Milwaukee Cannibal?"

"Jeffrey Dahmer."

"The Nightstalker?" Herbert asked, trying to think of more famous serial killers.

"Richard Ramirez."

"Who is the Zodiac?" Herbert asked finally.

Seda was silent again.

"It's Eddie Seda." *You've made the big time*, Herbert thought, *just like your heroes.*

Finally, at 1.20am, more than 13 hours after the siege in the flat began, Savarese pointed to the photo of Patricia Fonti's mutilated body. "Eddie, who speaks for this person here?" he asked solemnly.

"I met her at the YMCA," Seda began. For the next two hours he explained how he chose his victims and wrote letters to the *Post* to increase the public's fear of him.

Final destiny: Heriberto "Eddie" Seda, clutching a Bible, had toyed with the police for six years.

Meanwhile, the ballistics department had matched the crime-scene bullets to one of Seda's guns, dispelling any lingering doubt.

On June 24, 1998, Seda was found guilty of three murders and one attempted murder. Later he was sentenced to life in prison. The Zodiac may have fallen into their laps, Joe Herbert liked to say, but the evidence that convicted him was the result of old-fashioned detective work.

Joe Herbert, Louie Savarese, Danny Powers and Tommy Maher were all honored for their role in the Zodiac investigation.

FREE TO

KILL

BY HENRY HURT

TWO LIVES WERE ON A CONVERGING COURSE, LEADING TO
A VICIOUS CRIME AND THE DEATH OF AN INNOCENT YOUNG
GIRL, IN A TRAGIC CRIME WHICH COULD HAVE BEEN PREVENTED.

Short tail swishing, the day-old black-and-white calf nuzzled its wet nose into Amy Jackson's hands as she reached over the wooden railing to rub its head. Smiling, the young girl looked into the little Holstein's huge, black eyes and straightened the feeder attached to the side of the wooden pen. Moments later, prancing on the fresh straw, the wobbly calf again knocked the feeder loose and pressed toward Amy, licking the girl's hands and fingers. She laughed with delight and rubbed the calf's ears.

Amy was 11, a happy child with brown hair and brown eyes. She lived with her brother, Bobby, 13, and their father, Robert, in the rural North Carolina town of Yanceyville. Home was an old house trailer at the Shumaker Dairy, where their dad worked as herd manager.

This summer of 1995 had been a fairly happy time for both Jackson children. Amy's softball team, the Ace Hardware Bullets, was having a great summer, with an 11-1 record.

Other important things were going on, too, such as the birth of six kittens to Samantha, Amy's gray cat. And newborn calves arrived almost every day for Amy to visit at the dairy barn across the field from her home.

These pleasant events, however, were unfolding beneath the shadow of a great sadness hanging over the Jackson family. Six months earlier, the children's mother, Shana, had walked out on her 14-year marriage.

Shana said she loved the children but was sick of the daily grind—often a seven-day workweek. Her husband, Bob, left home each day at 2am, worked six hours, then went out again at 2pm for another six hours.

These days Bob and the children rarely heard from Shana, even though she was living only about an hour away. The Jacksons did not have a phone in their trailer. They had to use the dairy phone.

In addition to causing the children sadness, Shana's absence devastated Robert Jackson. Hazel-eyed with a lean, ruddy face, high cheekbones and a prominent nose, Jackson did not mind his brutal work schedule. He was an accomplished herdsman born into the business on his parents' own dairy farm 32 years earlier in upstate New York.

Now, working directly with dairy owner John Shumaker, Jackson oversaw the milking of the herd twice a day. Jackson and Shumaker, a second-generation dairyman himself, had known each other since they were teenagers.

Jackson took care of medicating the 150 cows, scheduling the breeding and making sure the milk met the dairy's prize-winning standards.

Notwithstanding Shana's complaints, Bob Jackson was dedicated to much more than his work. He wanted Amy and Bobby to have better lives than his 365-day-a-year regimen. The only dairy work he let his children engage in was the part that was fun: occasionally feeding the new calves. He found spots for his son and daughter on the local ball teams. Though he had to get up at 1.30 each morning for work, he still spent his evenings at the games.

"When I was a kid, I never got to do anything like that," Jackson says. "All I ever did was work. I wanted Amy and Bobby to have something more."

His two children got along well, with Bobby occasionally taking care of Amy's kittens and Amy watching over the miniature rabbits her brother was raising. They had their separate interests as well. Bobby loved riding his bicycle along the back roads, fishing in the farm pond and going "hunting" with his BB gun.

Shy and a little awkward, but a big boy physically, Bobby seemed to depend upon his more purposeful little sister to take charge of things. "Amy would set the alarm clock on school days and get me up," Bobby says. "She'd fix breakfast and make sure we were on time for school."

The devotion between Amy and Bobby was touching to friends and neighbors, never more so than during the period after their mother left.

"Every morning I'd see them waiting for the school bus," says Jo Page, a high-school teacher who lived across the road from the Shumaker Dairy. "It was so funny to watch the way they got along: sometimes acting just as sweet as can be, sometimes teasing and fussing with each other."

Amy loved school and nurtured ambitious dreams. In a school essay she wrote of her hopes for the future: "I plan to go to college to be a nurse and [hope to have] a handsome husband who's a Christian and has a lot of money. And I hope I can have a car and a two-story house and two children. And when I die I want to go to heaven."

That summer what Amy was most excited about was turning 12 in August

Amy Jackson: a young girl with big dreams.

240

and buying a purse-style book bag, one like the other girls had. And so Amy took her savings to Wal-Mart and bought the burgundy book bag of her dreams.

Bob Jackson says with a little smile, "Sometimes I think the main reason she was looking forward to the school year was so that she could get on the bus with that bag."

Whether feeding newborn calves or tending rabbits or simply cherishing a book bag, Amy and Bobby Jackson lived lives that echoed an earlier and more innocent time in rural America—when fear was not a factor in raising a family, and horrifying violence was something that happened only on television or on the mean streets of distant cities. As many of the people living along the rural road near the Shumaker Dairy would have said in the summer of 1995, nothing bad could happen here.

At work on the farm: Bobby Jackson idolized his sister.

NIGHT TRAVELER

The Statesville *Record & Landmark* newspaper had help-wanted ads for everyone from metal fabricators to vinyl-siding installers. But it was an ad for a dairy worker that caught the eye of Archie Lee Billings, 21, as he sat in his mother's living room near the small town of Harmony in western North Carolina.

Squatly built with a moon face sprouting a scraggly beard, Billings had powerful hands and forearms that came from years of manual labor. His black hair and quick, dark eyes were in sharp contrast to his dough-white skin.

He liked to work at dairies because the job was outside and usually involved tasks he enjoyed. He even liked the early working hours because they gave him time to roam rural neighborhoods in the middle of the night, usually traveling noiselessly by foot or on a bicycle.

It was John Shumaker who had placed the newspaper ad in February 1995. The new man's job would be to assist Shumaker's herd manager, Robert Jackson.

Archie Billings picked up his mother's phone and called the number. He spoke with Shumaker, a direct, businesslike man who reviewed Billings's work experience and carefully wrote down the young man's references. With his wife and four young daughters living on the farm, Shumaker made sure to check out all the men he hired.

When Billings finished talking, he told his mother he was glad the Shumaker Dairy was so far away—about 120 miles—from his home in Iredell County, where his troubles with the police made it hard to find work. If he could just get this job, Billings told his mother, no one would know of his past.

Born into a cradle of lawlessness, Archie Billings was an illegitimate son of a notorious mountain bootlegger named Harvey Cass, who was nearly 70 when Archie was born. Cass had 12 legitimate children, but he never saw fit to give his name to Archie and the two other boys that he fathered with Archie's mother, Ozell. Billings was her maiden name.

The log house on Brushy Creek where Archie was born had a kitchen, two rooms and no plumbing. When Archie was six, Ozell moved her family to slightly better quarters in Union Grove.

Even though their new home was right next to a schoolhouse, this did not change Archie's negative notions about education. Nor was he often exposed to much religion.

It is ironic, then, that a religious symbol was indirectly responsible for one of Archie's powerful aversions. At age 13, he used a needle and some blue ink to inflict a small tattoo of a cross in his left hand. After that, he swore off needles—even for the drugs that he soon used. "I just couldn't stand the pain," he said.

A fear of the law, however, was not among his aversions. Archie quit school after ninth grade. By then he was drinking and smoking marijuana, occasionally with his mother, and getting into trouble.

Soon Archie moved in with his brother Keith and Keith's girlfriend. One night in June 1991, Keith was awakened by her screaming. He jumped up, flicked on the light and found that Archie had crawled into her side of the bed. "I beat the hell out of him," Keith recalls, "and threw him out of the house." Some months later Keith gave Archie a second chance and invited him back.

One of Billings's first serious exploits with a car happened less than a month after his 18th birthday, in February, 1992. He refused to stop for a police officer, and by the time police caught him, he faced eight charges, including reckless driving and possession of marijuana. Billings had no driver's license for the court to suspend, but he was fined 200 dollars and given a six-month jail sentence. That was suspended for two years on the condition of good behavior; the term of his two-year unsupervised probation began on April 9, 1992.

Despite a blizzard of subsequent convictions for both misdemeanors and felonies, this probation would never be revoked.

Late on the night of April 19, 1992, Keith heard a noise outside his bedroom. As he walked down the hallway, there was a loud blast, and he felt a sudden force that slammed him against the wall. He turned on the light. Before him stood his brother holding a sawed-off shotgun.

Without a word, Archie had fired one shot into Keith's chest. "Archie then threw down the shotgun and picked up a .22 rifle and shot again," Keith recalls.

Even as a .22-caliber slug tore through Keith's left wrist, he lunged for the rifle and wrenched it away from his brother. Keith's girlfriend got him to the hospital where, after extensive surgery and a long recuperation, he survived.

Since the brothers had not been arguing that night, Keith speculates that Archie intended to kill him so that he could rape the young woman.

Davie County Deputy Sheriff John Coley investigated the shooting. Arrested and jailed overnight, Billings was charged with "assault with a deadly weapon with intent to kill and inflicting serious injury." He was released the next day on an unsecured bond of 500 dollars. Eight months later the charges were dropped after Keith and his girlfriend did not testify.

Even though the assault was committed just ten days after Billings's probation began, records show no attempt by the court to revoke probation and put him in jail.

In May 1993 Archie Billings was again in serious trouble that, if prosecuted aggressively, might also have taken him out of circulation. After a fight at a convenience store, Billings was charged with beating a man in the head several times with a hammer. Precisely what happened in this case has been reduced in court records to a plea-bargain agreement reached five months later. The felony charge was dropped, and Billings pleaded no contest to a misdemeanor charge of simple assault. His only punishment: he had to pay court costs.

While he was waiting for the disposition of his hammer-assault charge, Billings got into more trouble with his car in September 1993. For him it was a routine infraction: no driver's license, no registration and no insurance. The judge fined him 25 dollars and gave him a 30-day jail term, which was suspended. Instead, Billings was placed on a year's unsupervised probation without so much as a mention of his ongoing probation.

He was "riding high and laughing loud," according to his brother Keith. "No matter what he did, he'd go to court and they just let him go."

Billings's legal infractions continued, and so did his luck. He began 1994 with another arrest for driving without a license. In August 1994 he was arrested for trying to outrun a police officer, resisting arrest and not having a driver's license.

But by the time a 60-day jail sentence was finally handed down in January 1995, Billings had already turned an ominous page in his life. Finally, it looked like he was up to something even the careless legal system could no longer overlook.

CROSSING THE LINE

In the 34-month period between February 1992 and November 1994, Archie Billings was employed by at least two local dairies. In his off hours, he prowled country roads terrorizing a local family.

Between one dairy where Billings worked and where he lived, there was a farm and nursery operated by Carolyn and Daniel Allen. They had two daughters, ages 12 and 17. In November 1994, while the family was at church one Sunday night, someone broke into their home by smashing open a basement door. The Allens called the police.

An investigation revealed that things had been disturbed in both daughters' bedrooms. Even more distressing was the discovery of marks indicating someone had placed a ladder against the side of the house just under the girls' second-story bedrooms.

This was chilling. For months the two girls had been hearing vaguely suspicious noises outside their windows. In their innocence they had dismissed these as normal night sounds of the countryside.

Daniel Allen and the county sheriff's office would ultimately learn that more than a half-dozen families in the surrounding area had complained about a particularly aggressive peeping Tom.

Though deputy sheriffs investigated, Allen was not happy with what he felt was the scant attention they gave the matter. "It may have been a little thing for them," he says, "but it was a pretty big thing for us. I decided I had to protect my family."

Two nights after the burglary, Allen walked around in the dark, armed with a shotgun, watching his house. When he saw and heard someone lurking in the shrubbery beneath his daughters' bedroom windows, he called out, then fired three shotgun blasts at the fleeing intruder.

Later that night the family found a jacket in the yard, obviously dropped by the person who had fled. Inside the collar were inked six letters: ARCHIE.

But even being shot at did not seem to discourage the interloper. The next night the Allens thought they heard strange sounds again. "We felt like someone was still watching us and waiting," says Carolyn Allen.

Still fearful for his family, Daniel Allen poured sand around the area where the intruder had been. Next morning he discovered footprints. The intruder had returned.

This guy wasn't going to stop until somebody killed him or caught him, Allen recalls thinking. So he began his own investigation. He was able to track the jacket to a nearby dairy and was soon talking with Iredell County Detective Sergeant

Ronald Wyatt. When Wyatt heard the story, he suspected this "Archie" just might be the young man he'd been having run-ins with for years: Archie Billings.

Wyatt questioned him, and during the interrogation Billings told the detective: "If I was there, that ain't against the law. Look, we both know what I did, but it's stupid for me to tell on myself."

Despite his initial denials, Billings ultimately pleaded guilty to two counts of secret peeping and was given 45 days in jail.

Soon after Billings was released, he appeared in court to plead guilty to the separate charges of breaking and entering and larceny at the Allen house. No stranger to the legal system, he managed a good deal without a lawyer.

Superior Court Judge Catherine C. Eagles imposed "a community punishment" on Billings. This meant that he would serve no time at all on the two charges of breaking into the Allens' house and stealing various items. The judge gave him a sentence of eight to ten months, suspended for 36 months.

Judge Eagles also placed Billings on supervised probation, ordered him to pay 137 dollars in court costs and to make restitution to the Allen family of 928 dollars, to be paid at the rate of 50 dollars per month.

Moreover, Billings was ordered to report to a state mental-health agency for evaluation, which he did on March 7, 1995. He was interviewed by primary therapist Loy W. Devine, who concluded that Billings was not a danger to others and that no follow-up sessions were necessary.

On the night in March 1995 when Archie Billings called John Shumaker to answer the newspaper ad, the dairyman knew none of this. He was merely impressed by Billings's experience and was interested in hiring him.

While one of Billings's references checked out satisfactorily, that was not the case with Barry Myers, who runs a 650-cow dairy where Billings had also worked. Myers declined to comment to Shumaker on anything about Billings, saying his lawyer had warned him against providing any references, either good or bad. (In fact, Myers had fired Billings; his son had spotted Billings looking through a bedroom window, and other employees also suspected the young man had been loitering around their homes.)

Shumaker did not like the noncommittal response from Myers, but he remained interested in Billings. Shumaker asked him to come for a personal interview with him and Bob Jackson.

Confident that he would land the job, Billings packed and got one of his brothers to drive him to Caswell County. Among the few possessions he took along was a rusty ten-speed bicycle for transportation. Apparently, Billings had finally become chary of tempting fate by driving without a license.

245

After the interview with Shumaker and Jackson, Billings got the job. With the post, he was given a place to live, a house trailer Shumaker owned about a mile from the dairy. It was a pleasant bicycle ride along Yanceyville's County Home Road, over which Billings made his way to work in the dead of the night.

WELCOME TO CASWELL COUNTY

"I think most of us try to see the good in others and assume somebody is OK until we know otherwise." High-school teacher Jo Page reflects the common view of Archie Billings in Caswell County.

Billings established himself as an excellent worker and quickly fit into his new surroundings. Acting friendly, he soon got to know the people in the neighborhood, including the Shumakers' four girls and Bobby and Amy Jackson. He often had candy in his pockets for the children.

"He'd stop by the house now and then," recalls Bob Jackson. "We tried to be neighborly. The children were nice to him. I remember once when he needed to get some things at Wal-Mart. I drove him there, and Archie bought us lunch. Amy was with us."

Another time when Jackson planted a big garden near his family's trailer, he told Billings he could take what he needed if he'd do some of the work. Billings agreed and spent some time at the plot, tilling the soil.

The face of a killer?:
Archie Lee Billings.

Sarah Shumaker, John's wife, remembers once having all the dairy employees to the house for a cookout. "Archie fit right in," she says. "He was friendly and playful with the kids and an excellent employee."

Sarah's daughter, Lucia, 15, was raising steers that summer to make money for college. She kept them in a remote part of the farm and was often working there alone when Archie would come by. "I never once felt uncomfortable around him," Lucia says.

Amy Jackson, however, seemed to sense something amiss. Her Little League coach, Garry Chandler, remembers a night when he drove her home after a late game: "She asked me to wait while she went in to be sure her brother was home. She said there was a new man working on the farm and that he'd been hanging around the house."

By most people's accounts, Archie Billings did all right in Caswell County during his first months. He regularly checked in with his local probation officer as required by the court. Says Shumaker: "Archie told us he'd gotten in trouble over racing cars and that's why he was on probation. There wasn't any reason to doubt him."

As his probation officer would later say, everything was just fine, even when Billings checked in with him on June 23, 1995. But it was that night when Archie Billings's life took another violent turn. He and a woman he knew were at a Yanceyville bar. Billings became provoked over something. He quarreled with the woman's father and her boyfriend and then hit her in the face.

"Yes, I heard about it," recalls Robert Jackson. "Archie might have even told me himself. But we never once smelled alcohol on him. Besides, by then we thought we knew him."

NIGHT OF THE KNIFE

On the late afternoon of Thursday, July 6, 1995, Billings mentioned to Jackson that he wanted to hear a band that night at a Yanceyville beer joint called Country's Place. Jackson offered to drop him off there. Billings put his bicycle in the back of the truck, and they drove to the saloon.

"See you in the morning," said Jackson as Billings unloaded his bicycle. Then Jackson drove away.

Country's Place is owned and operated by a middle-aged, pony-tailed man named Brodie "Country" King. He remembers Billings as a quiet guy who stopped by now and then for a beer.

King also remembers Billings on that particular Thursday night: "He sat at the bar and ordered a draft beer. Drank it and left. He didn't say anything. I remember thinking he had one of them 'ain't nobody home' looks on his face."

Archie Billings's face may have looked like nobody was home, but someone was there—someone known only too well by several judges, prosecutors and policemen in Iredell and Davie counties 120 miles away.

Billings finished his beer at Country's Place, then hit another joint in Yanceyville. Accounts of what he did next conflict. Some say he drank a little moonshine whiskey and may have smoked some drugs. But of those people who saw him that night, no one thought he was drunk or out of control.

What is known for sure is that in the dead of night, Billings headed east along County Home Road. The night was steamy and the ground wet from days of rain. He was going toward the Shumaker Dairy and the trailer where Amy and Bobby Jackson slept. Billings knew at that time of the early morning their father was at work in the barn.

Billings also knew the noise made in the barn by the milking machines would make it impossible for the father to hear any sounds from the trailer. Moreover, from

"I'm surprised to see you too," Billings replied cheerfully. Shumaker was rarely in the barn this early in the morning. At that moment the dairy owner noticed that Billings was wearing a pair of trousers left in the barn long ago.

Shumaker told his employee that something had happened over at Bob Jackson's trailer and that he would like to drive Billings there. The police needed to talk to him. Billings calmly went along.

Even as Amy Jackson's body lay in the woods 1,000 yards away, Billings insisted that he knew nothing. He said that he had been out drinking all night and had simply come to work early. After a few minutes of questioning, Billings was taken into custody.

What he did not know was that two things had gone very wrong with his plans. First, Bobby Jackson, despite 23 stab wounds, had refused to die. Second, Robert Jackson had installed a phone in his trailer a few days before the attack. Moments after Billings disappeared into the night, Bobby had crawled to the phone and dialed 911.

Four minutes later, a remarkable response time for a rural area, Sarah Clayton and other EMS technicians entered the Jackson trailer. The scene, the medics later said, was horrible—blood was smeared on walls, all over the floors, the furniture, the beds. Sarah Clayton put Bobby on oxygen and gingerly covered the slash across his neck so that doctors could repair it. By 5.19am they were on their way to the hospital, 12 miles away. They got there in 11 minutes.

"He was fighting with everything he had," says Robert Jackson, who reached the emergency room before 7am.

Jackson stood there, convinced his son could not survive. Suddenly, from a few feet away, Jackson saw Bobby's eyes open. Then he heard the most wonderful words of his life.

"Hi, Dad," said a very small voice.

Twelve hours later, after a massive search effort, a bloodhound located Amy's body. As a lead for her scent, the tracker had given the dog Amy's new burgundy book bag.

THE TRIAL

By May 22, 1996, nearly a year had passed since the murder of Amy Jackson and the brutal attack on her brother. On this day, coincidentally Bobby Jackson's 14th birthday, opening arguments began at the jury trial.

The next day District Attorney Joel H. Brewer's steady voice rang through the Caswell County courtroom: "The state of North Carolina calls Bobby Jackson." This was the prosecutor's star witness, left for dead by the man who murdered the boy's sister. Bobby's savage neck scars were visible as he shyly took the oath and settled into the witness chair.

Less than 20 feet away sat Archie Lee Billings. He was well represented by two defense lawyers, who were assisted by a professional jury consultant and others, all paid for by the state of North Carolina.

The defendant sat at the defense table wearing a blue blazer, gray slacks and a striped, clip-on necktie. Cocky in his manner, he twiddled his thumbs and flicked at bits of lint on his tie.

Killer evidence: D.A. Joel H. Brewer (left) meticulously presents his case with the help of sheriff's investigator Keith McKinney.

Across the courtroom Brewer, 45, a prosecutor for 15 years, sat alone. With dark eyes and close-cropped, salt-and-pepper hair, the Georgia-born Brewer was calmly and softly reassuring his witness.

Behind him sat Robert Jackson and his wife, Shana, now reconciled. Beside them were the Shumakers and other neighbors from County Home Road.

As Brewer laid out the state's evidence, Billings rocked back and forth in his high-backed leather chair, looking on.

The prosecution's case was straightforward: that Billings had devised a carefully laid plan to rape and murder Amy Jackson while she and her brother were alone, asleep and defenseless. According to Brewer, Billings's plan was also to murder the only eyewitness, Bobby—now in court to point out his sister's killer.

A powerful part of the evidence against Billings had been introduced the day before: the recording of Bobby's 911 call. It was logged at 4.51am. The child's voice was calm but barely audible. The boy's words sketched out the horrendous crime: "A man came in here … he had a knife … his name was Archie." At this point the breathing became so heavy, the voice so weak, that it was unclear whether the boy would live long enough to finish.

Dispatcher David Vernon is heard calming Bobby.

"He took my sister. My dad. He's in the barn. …"

The courtroom was cloaked in silence, broken only by the sobbing of Shana Jackson. Others wiped away tears. The playing of the 911 tape was one of the only times any color came to Billings's dough-white face. Slightly flushed, he looked down and flicked at his tie.

Now, sitting in the witness chair, Bobby Jackson, poised and confident, calmly pointed to Archie Billings as the man who had stabbed him and abducted his sister.

The mother is asked if she's ever noticed how in all these pictures, Archie is never smiling, how he just looks angry.

"No," she says. "I never noticed." Ozell Billings stares at the pictures and gently pops her knuckles.

DEATH ROW

Central Prison in Raleigh is where those sentenced to die in North Carolina are taken for their appointment with the death chamber. Death's menu here offers inmates execution by either gas or lethal injection.

The interview with Archie Billings takes place just off death row in the presence of a prison official. Wearing a red jumpsuit, Billings is polite but wary; his handshake is firm. Sitting at a conference table, he is asked how he feels about spending much of his life laughing at the law and society, and how only now he is being held accountable.

Relaxed, unshackled, Billings looks down as he twists a pencil stub between his powerful fingers. "I was always lucky nobody did much to me," he says. Then he looks up. "But maybe I'd be better off if they'd made me go in [prison] sooner."

When it's suggested that the Jackson family might have been better off, too, Billings rubs the little pencil nub back and forth across the table and says nothing.

What about the Jackson children, he's asked.

"I liked them," Billings says. "Bobby, he was sort of quiet and happy. I could tell he liked his family. And Amy, she was a good kid. She was happy, too, and liked her daddy and brother. All of 'em was nice to me."

Asked about the oddness of his comments in light of what he did to Amy and Bobby, Billings smirks. "Now you're talking about my case. And we ain't gonna talk about my case for legal reasons. But I'll tell you I don't blame what happened on nobody but me."

With good appeals lawyers, Billings knows he may not be executed for ten or 15 years. But he says he will not drag out his fate. After one appeal he'll be ready to die. He says he'd rather be dead than cooped up like this.

Asked about his death sentence, Billings says, "I think about it all the time." His eyes becoming more intent, he adds, "Much as I hate needles, I'll probably have to go with that. The guys here say the gas takes 18 minutes, and I couldn't stand that."

Then, without prompting, Billings observes: "This will be an easy out for me. What happened to Amy was a lot more painful. If I should die, I guess I should be tortured the way the evidence shows Amy and Bobby were."

Then his eyes dart up wildly from the table top, his voice edged with fury: "But I ain't scared of nothin' or nobody, and I sure ain't scared of dying."

PEACE AT LAST

Today life goes on in Yanceyville. More than two years have passed since death cast its shadow upon this gentle neighborhood. Crops are planted and harvested regularly. The cows "freshen," bearing the calves that keep the milk cycle going.

Like black-and-white boxcars, the huge Holsteins lumber in and out of the milking parlor at the Shumaker Dairy. Robert Jackson knows each cow, and each cow knows him.

In a barn near the milking parlor, the new calves frisk in their pens, stretching toward any hand that might harbor a snack. This is where Amy Jackson might be if she had stopped by to visit her father.

On this day, Bobby Jackson carries milk and feed to the 14 new calves. He enjoys caring for them, but he doesn't want to be a dairyman. "I'd like to be a police officer," he says with his shy smile. Bobby has a lasting impression of the warm professionalism of the police officers who worked so carefully with him to develop the case against Billings.

Bobby's mother and father, reunited by the tragedy, remain together. They are now living in a house in town and have a new baby girl. "I feel like God just sent her to us," Bob Jackson says, his voice breaking.

Amy's death has had several repercussions. In the wake of her murder, the North Carolina legislature enacted a sex-offender registration provision called the Amy Jackson Law. It makes available the records of certain sex offenders to prospective employers. Ironically, peeping Tom crimes are not included, so the law still would not have done any good in the case of Archie Billings.

"But it's a step in the right direction," says Robert Jackson hopefully.

Today many people look back with their private regrets. John Shumaker still grimaces when he thinks that he's the one who hired Archie Billings; but he isn't sure what he might have done differently. "We never saw any sign that we had such a monster among us."

Keith Billings wishes that he had pressed charges against his brother. "May God drop me dead," he says. "I wish Archie had killed me if that meant he wouldn't have killed that little girl."

Shana Jackson also fights the demons of recrimination. "I'll never get over it," she says, weeping, as she holds pictures of her children as babies, and her own wedding pictures with Bob. "If I'd been there where I was supposed to be, it never would have happened."

And Barry Myers, who refused to discuss Billings when John Shumaker called him, says he'll always wonder whether he did the right thing in sticking by his lawyer's advice.

Reunited in grief, hope and love:
the Jackson family today.

One of the cruelest ironies to emerge from the entire case concerns probation. The fact is Billings got away with flouting the law and never had any of his probations revoked. By the time the state of North Carolina finally terminated Billings's last probation, he had been on death row nearly six months.

After Amy's murder the neighborhood rallied around the Jacksons in a magnificent affirmation of America's best traditions. More than 50,000 dollars poured into a trust fund that the neighbors set up, and they found a house in town for the family. The fund also provided Bobby with a long-dreamed-of computer that he uses in his schoolwork and to play chess.

Robert Jackson is proud of his courageous son. Bobby showed such an extraordinary will in surviving and doing his best to protect his sister. His physical scars will be visible for the rest of his life. But the unseen scars are the ones that most concern his parents. About those, only time will tell.

Jackson thinks about Amy often and how she was, in his words, "taken into the arms of the Lord."

He pauses and makes an important point: as long as Billings is alive, he can relive what he did to Amy. For that reason, there can be no true peace, Jackson says, while Billings can still remember. It is only when the executioner's poisons flow through a hated needle into his body and Archie Billings goes gently into the night that his vile memories of this atrocity will be deleted forever. That, Robert Jackson believes, will bring peace.

For his part, prosecutor Joel Brewer has proved that Archie Billings was solely responsible for Amy Jackson's death. But he believes that if there is any greater lesson to be learned, it is that the key to stopping horrors such as what happened to Amy lies in a stronger sense of community responsibility. If more people at different points along the way had noticed a few things about Archie Billings, it is possible that the tragic death of Amy Jackson would never have occurred. Those small lapses of attention had a cumulative and lethal effect.

"The community has elected me to enforce their laws," Brewer says. "That's my duty, but I can't do it without the community's support. People must care about each other."

INTRUDER IN THE
NIGHT

BY JIM HUTCHISON

FOOTSTEPS APPROACHED HER BEDROOM, THEN
PAUSED IN THE PASSAGE. SHE KNEW HER LIFE
DEPENDED ON HER COURAGE AND WITS.

Although the night of Saturday, March 4, 1995, was hot and humid, Marjorie Tidman left her 36-year-old husband, Peter, and their three-year-old daughter, Natasha, in the air-conditioned comfort of their back-yard cottage. She had chosen to sleep in the main house with their five-month-old son, Raymond, because her asthma, worse than usual lately, was aggravated by the air-conditioning. "Give me a yell if you get too lonely," Peter said with a grin as he kissed his wife and son goodnight.

The Tidmans had moved to the coastal town of Carnarvon in Western Australia from Perth 11 years earlier and Peter, an optometrist, had started his own practice. They soon discovered that there was corrosive racial tension in Carnarvon, and set out to do what they could to build bridges between Aborigines and other groups in the community. Peter visited remote communities to test eyes and prescribe glasses. Marjorie, 36, a family counsellor with a doctorate in educational psychology, had for a time helped out at the Carnarvon youth centre, a haven for over 600 Aboriginal youths.

The couple's philanthropy was grounded in their Baha'i faith, a religion that embraces the underlying principles of all the great religions. When Marjorie had been introduced to Peter 13 years earlier in Sydney, she had been attracted at once to the big, bearded man, also a Baha'i. Beneath his huge frame, she discovered, lay a similar empathy for others and a desire to help people in need.

As Marjorie snuggled close to her baby and began drifting off to sleep, she heard a noise somewhere in the house. The petite blonde's hazel-green eyes flew open, and she listened intently. Then a light snapped on in the hallway. She stared at her watch, and a deepening dread crept over her. Peter would never turn on the light and wake her at 2.30 in the morning.

Footsteps approached her room, then paused in the passage. On the other side of the wall, someone was rustling through cupboards. Surging adrenaline slammed Marjorie's mind to full alert and her heart began to pound. *There's an intruder in the house!* She forced herself to calm down. Think your way out of this.

She resisted the urge to scream for help. No one would hear her: the neighbour's house was separated from theirs by a garage and Peter was 30 metres away in the cottage with the noisy air-conditioner running.

For two minutes, Marjorie lay still, her mind racing. Her only chance was to persuade the intruder to leave, she decided at last. Gathering her sleeping child in her arms, Marjorie stepped into the hallway.

A young Aboriginal man with short, curly hair, dressed in dark trousers and a nylon jacket, crouched in the passage, searching through clay pots. Standing barefoot in her white-and-red pyjamas, Marjorie took a deep breath and said quietly, "I don't know you. Just leave and I won't call the police."

The intruder jerked upright, spilling a handful of coins on the floor as he spun to face her. Marjorie did not recognise him, but Matthew Jennings (not his real name) knew her. The muscular, 175-centimetre-tall 17-year-old had seen the Tidmans before and, with several other youths, had stolen their car four months earlier, dumping it at a service station. Tonight, Jennings had jumped their property's one-and-a-half-metre-high fence and, with a screwdriver stolen from their car, had forced the front door lock.

Jennings's crimes were not limited to car theft. In late 1993, he had sexually assaulted a 16-year-old girl sleeping on the back veranda of her Carnarvon home. Earlier that same night, he had entered another house where a horrified mother discovered him sexually assaulting her three-year-old daughter. For the sexual assaults, he had served ten months of an 18-month sentence in a juvenile detention centre.

Lunging forward, the intruder grabbed Marjorie's wrist, shoving her back into the bedroom. The smell of alcohol was on his breath as he pushed her down on the bed.

No way he's going to rape me, Marjorie thought. Quickly she rolled Raymond out of her arms against the wall. In one, swift movement she brought her legs up and snap-kicked her assailant hard in the stomach. He reeled backwards and fell as Marjorie leapt from the bed. Calling for divine protection, she cried, "Yá Bahá'u'l-Abhá! (O Glory of All-Glorious!)." Seven more times she intoned the Baha'i invocation. Stunned, Jennings stood frozen, then ran down the hall towards the kitchen.

He was back almost instantly, pushing her towards the bedroom once again. Marjorie resisted, but her 165-centimetre tall, 50-kilo body was no match for her attacker's strength. Get him talking, she thought desperately. "You must know my husband Peter," she babbled. "Do you have family here?"

Jennings said nothing. Then, without warning, he swung his left arm over his head. In the pale light, Marjorie glimpsed the chilling gleam of a carving knife he had brought from the kitchen. Jennings stabbed down hard at her face.

Instinctively, Marjorie's free hand flew up, grasping the 20-centimetre-long blade, not even noticing as it sliced through her palm just below the thumb. She refused to let go, and tightened her grip. The blade snapped and she was left clutching the broken two-thirds in her right hand. Strangely, she felt no pain.

her face. She was covered in blood. Now she fully understood how badly she was injured. She knew she had little time left.

Marjorie faced a terrifying dilemma. She must get to the hospital immediately. Yet if she left her sanctuary, she feared Jennings would be waiting outside to finish her off.

She quietened the baby and cocked her ear, listening intently. There was no sound in the house. Waves of blackness again threatened to overwhelm her as she prayed for guidance. *Please God, is it safe to leave?*

Soon she heard an inner voice. Go now, it told her. "Trust in God," she murmured. Tottering to her feet, she pushed the door open. With Raymond in her arms, she crept down the corridor. No one was there. She went to the kitchen and reached for the phone to call police. The line was dead. *He's cut the wire.*

Marjorie retraced her steps to the side entrance. Managing to wipe some of the blood from her hand this time, she turned the handle and stepped out into the humid night. She resisted a temptation to cross the lawn directly to the cottage. Her assailant might be watching for her. Instead, she crept along close to the fence, hoping she would not be seen.

At the cottage, she pounded on the locked door. No one stirred. She banged harder, terrified that Jennings would loom out of the darkness. Still nothing. Peter can't hear me over the noise of the air-conditioner, she realised.

Reaching up to the fuse box beside the door, she flicked the mains off and on several times, hoping the sound of the air conditioner stopping and starting would wake Peter, then went back to hammering on the door.

Finally, Peter Tidman stirred himself from deep sleep. He rose groggily, opened the door and looked at her blankly. At first Peter's sleep-fogged mind did not comprehend what he was seeing. Marjorie stood swaying on the veranda, clutching Raymond. Both seemed to be covered in a black substance. "I've been hurt," Marjorie sobbed. "I've got to get to the hospital."

Three doctors at Carnarvon Regional Hospital worked on Marjorie Tidman for over an hour, administering two-and-a-half litres of intravenous fluids to replace her lost blood and stitching her multiple wounds. They agreed that her infant son had probably saved her life. Clutching Raymond close to her had prevented Marjorie from bleeding to death.

"Please tell our Aboriginal friends to come and see me," Marjorie asked Peter the next day. "We mustn't let anyone think this has anything to do with race."

As word spread, cards and flowers from well-wishers poured in and a steady stream of Aborigines visited the hospital. "We feel deep shame," one said. "I would have gone through it for you," said another as tears ran down his face.

Marjorie's problems were far from over. Each night that followed, she woke in the early hours and wailed uncontrollably, assailed by grief at what had been done to her. Peter held her tight and prayed as she sobbed, images of the attack replaying over and over in her mind with terrifying clarity. Peter called it the "hell hour".

After six days Marjorie went home, determined to get on with her life. But that night she felt too frightened to sleep. Nightmarish delusions raced through her mind. She began to believe she was dead. A week after her return home, a doctor gave her an antipsychotic shot and sedatives, diagnosing severe post-traumatic psychosis.

Face what happened and find a way to move forward, Marjorie resolved finally. After six weeks, she began to regain some of the emotional and mental stability stolen from her by the attack. Aboriginal people who met her in the street hugged her, expressing their sorrow without words.

Eight months later, Marjorie was called to testify at the trial of Matthew Jennings, who was arrested when he sought hospital treatment of the wounds Marjorie had inflicted on him. The thought of facing her attacker again was terrifying, but Marjorie was determined. "I can't let this happen to someone else," she told Peter. In the Carnarvon Children's Court, she testified against Jennings, who was convicted of several charges, including attempted murder, and sentenced to 11 years in jail.

The Tidmans now live with Marjorie's parents in Karratha, north of Carnarvon. Make-up hides most of Marjorie's physical scars, but emotional pain lingers. She still has difficulty sleeping in a house alone and always checks locks before going to bed.

Determined to turn her ordeal into a force for good, Marjorie counsels women struggling to overcome the trauma of violence. "My faith in God has been strengthened by what happened to me," she says. "I can use what I've learned to show others that no matter how bad things get, there's always hope, and healing is always possible."

Hope and healing: make-up now hides most of Marjorie Tidman's physical scars.

TERROR AT THE DOOR

BY DAVID MOLLER

THE RUTHLESS GANG SPREAD FEAR THROUGHOUT
SOUTHERN ENGLAND. THEY HAD TO BE CAUGHT
BEFORE SOMEONE GOT KILLED.

It was 7pm and Lord McGowan was watching TV when the dogs began barking. The 58-year-old City stockbroker didn't pay much attention. Living in Lower Froyle in the heart of rural Hampshire, he was used to his dogs barking at countryside sounds. It was his wife Gillian who eventually interrupted her jam-making on that Saturday of October 26, 1996, and opened the back door to investigate.

As she did so, three men burst in. All in black, they wore balaclavas and gloves. One manhandled her back to the kitchen. Two others were in front of her husband before he had time to stir from his chair. "We've got a gun to your wife's head," one of them yelled. "Where's the safe?"

They made Lord McGowan kneel on the floor, hands manacled behind his back. "Don't move. Don't look at us. Look at the floor."

The shouting was constant. "Where's the safe? We'll shoot your wife if you don't tell us." He was cuffed on the head and frogmarched along a passage to show them the safe's location. He heard his wife cry out in pain as a raider struggled to remove a gold ring from her hand, breaking her finger in the process.

After showing his captors the safe, he was bundled into the kitchen, forced to his knees and blindfolded. "If you move, you'll be shot," a raider warned him. Lord McGowan felt no inclination to move. *This is about property. They just want to get in and out as quickly as possible. They're slick. They've done this before.*

"Tell them where the safe keys are," he told his wife. Two raiders led her away to retrieve them. Seconds later, she was brought back, handcuffed, blindfolded, gagged. Then the two were manacled to the kitchen radiator. In 12 minutes, the gang had invaded their lives—and departed with £50,000 worth of their jewellery.

Detective Sergeant John O'Leary worked his way through a three-foot pile of chilling reports and witness statements. It was early January 1997, and the 37-year-old, a member of the crack 25-strong team provided by the South-East Regional Crime Squad (SERCS), which is drawn from 13 forces, had been called in to help solve a series of horrifically violent robberies.

On a large wall map in the Peel Centre, a Metropolitan Police building in Hendon, north London, pins showed the location of 24 raids across the Home Counties in 16 months, the first on September 12, 1995. Most had been close to the network of motorways around Greater London.

"The robbers could have come from practically anywhere—and got back pretty quickly," said O'Leary to the team leader, 48-year-old Detective Chief Inspector John Morse.

Few of the raids lasted more than ten or 15 minutes, and all had taken place when householders were at home and internal security systems were likely to be switched off. Then the raiders could terrorize their victims into revealing the whereabouts of money and jewellery. In all, some £5 million worth of cash and valuables had been stolen.

Several victims were convinced that the raiders were in contact, by two-way radio or mobile phone, with others stationed outside. "Everything we know suggests that the raids were professional, well planned," O'Leary said. "But we've got practically no solid leads."

Always masked and gloved, the raiders left no fingerprints and had few distinguishing characteristics, though several victims had described one man as short. Few words were spoken in the course of the raids, and those were often shouted, presumably to terrorize householders and disguise accents. When accents could be discerned—Scottish, Irish, German —they were so pronounced as to be obviously misleading.

The raiders had beaten one man with a stick, threatened to brand others with an iron. Brandishing a baseball bat and knife at one robbery, they told victims, "You'll never look the same again after tonight."

Even the elderly were handcuffed to banisters or radiators. Children had been dragged from their beds to be manacled. One man, not discovered until the day after a raid, nearly lost his right hand. With the handcuffs fitted so tight, it was beginning to turn black. Twice the raiders had shot dogs that were menacing them.

"Unless we nail this lot soon, someone is going to get killed," O'Leary commented to Morse.

With the SERCS team, they could tap into a formidable range of police intelligence. Was there anyone, they wondered, with the background of

Former boxer: Ronald Shinkwin.

burglary and violence, the working methods, psychology, who might measure up for these crimes?

Several names emerged. One was Ronald Shinkwin, 31, from Bushey, Hertfordshire, a former amateur boxer who was serving a community service order for assaulting a policeman. His older brother Shaun, 33, who lived in Watford, had also been a boxer, and had much the same record of minor convictions for theft and violence. "Not major criminals," mused O'Leary, "but certainly worth keeping an eye on."

Fraternal fighter: Shaun Shinkwin.

One night in the car park of the New Victoria inn in Watford, the two brothers were spotted conferring with a much shorter man. A SERCS photographer managed to sneak two sideshots of a man no more than five foot six tall.

Several days later, two undercover SERCS officers followed the short man into the pub and heard him speaking in a Liverpool accent.

O'Leary showed the photographs of the unknown man to Merseyside detectives. As they studied them, an officer remarked that Liverpudlian criminals often refer to rich targets as "hob nobs". The raiders became known as the "Hob Nob Gang".

At last one of the detectives came up with a name: Peter Champion. A 28-year-old painter and decorator from Liverpool, he had a string of convictions for assault, theft, burglary. Height: just five foot five.

By now, Morse's team had established that Champion had taken a room at the New Victoria and was meeting the Shinkwins regularly. They began keeping the three men under almost constant watch.

On February 18, their efforts were rewarded. As Ronald Shinkwin left his terraced home, a surveillance team spotted him putting a half-filled bin liner into the back of his van. Later that day, they saw him slip the bag into a rubbish bin in the New Victoria's car park.

The bag, recovered by police, contained a pillowcase and four pairs of barely worn trainers. "Why would anyone throw away almost new trainers?" O'Leary

Small but nasty: serial criminal Peter Champion.

asked Morse. It seemed that, after each raid, the robbers were dumping any footwear that might link them forensically to the offence.

The night before, there had been another raid, in Northwood, north-west London. Four masked figures had terrorized and handcuffed an Asian businessman, his 12-year-old daughter, his elderly mother and his cook, then made off with £20,000 in money and jewellery.

It was virtually impossible to link the trainers to the scene. But the pillowcase was one of a matching set at the Northwood house. Better still, a scrap of paper found in the bin liner was part of a receipt for currency exchanged by one of the householders.

"We can definitely establish that Ronald Shinkwin was in possession, within hours, of items connected with the Northwood raid," said O'Leary. "But if we pick him up, he could simply claim he was dumping rubbish for a friend and didn't know what was in the bag." All they could do was watch and wait.

On the afternoon of Thursday, February 20, three men in rough working clothes arrived in a grey Volvo at Ronald Shinkwin's house. An hour later, they reappeared with Shinkwin—but smartly dressed.

From his unmarked car, O'Leary listened on the SERCS radio channel as several other vehicles trailed the Volvo. It met up with a dark blue Ford Mondeo containing Shaun Shinkwin and Peter Champion. The two cars then set off for an affluent nearby suburb.

For an hour, they drove round and round, perhaps looking for a house that might yield rich pickings. *But*, thought O'Leary, *they're also making sure no police are taking an interest in their movements.* He knew it was just a matter of time before the gang noticed one of the police number plates once too often. *Then the whole operation will be blown.* Reluctantly he announced, "OK, let them go."

At 10pm, the Volvo was driven back to Bushey and parked some distance from Ronald Shinkwin's home. No vehicle with this number plate had been reported lost or stolen. But it was shown as registered to a titled owner in London—an unlikely associate of Shinkwin.

O'Leary guessed that the car had been stolen and "false plated"—equipped with false number plates for an identical car. Inside it, two officers checking by torchlight could see a scarf and a road atlas.

The police national computer revealed that a Volvo of that year, model and colour, registered to an owner in nearby Hemel Hempstead, had been stolen two weeks before. Early next morning, two officers went to the owner's home to ask about items left in the vehicle. He mentioned a scarf and an atlas.

The gang's Volvo was certainly stolen. Yet O'Leary and Morse agreed that an early arrest would be absurd. "Maybe a £150 fine," said O'Leary, "and they could all be back on the street that same day."

At 5.56pm that Friday, the three unidentified suspects returned to the Volvo, this time in a white Ford Escort. A computer check revealed that the car was registered to a Paul Clarke of Liverpool. It had not been reported lost or stolen. And Paul Clarke? A 27-year-old, he had convictions for burglary, theft and violence going back 14 years. *Another Merseysider*, thought O'Leary. Pieces of the jigsaw were falling into place.

Clarke and the two others transferred to the Volvo—and again set off in convoy with the Mondeo containing Champion and the Shinkwin brothers. At 6.15pm, O'Leary heard over the radio, "The Mondeo is at the rear of the Railway Inn in Watling Street, Radlett … Champion and the two Shinkwins are into the Volvo … All six in the Volvo … They're off up Shenley Hill."

For nearly an hour, the vehicle drove on a circuitous, three-mile route that took in several plush housing developments. Convinced that a raid was about to take place, O'Leary contacted Morse at the Peel Centre. A firearms team would be on hand to help make arrests when the gang returned to their Mondeo.

Mersey menace: Paul Clarke.

Parked close to Shenley Hill, O'Leary heard over the radio that the Volvo now had just two passengers in it. Four of the suspects must have been dropped off. But where?

Minutes later, at 7.16pm, another officer reported that the Volvo had just pulled into the car park of the Porters Park Golf Club on Shenley Hill. O'Leary directed Detective Constable Richard Briers to take up covert watch in the car park.

At 7.30pm DC Briers reported that the Volvo, parked facing a six-foot-high fence, had just flashed its lights in signal. "One of them is out of the car … He's up to the fence …There's a bag gone across the fence …He's back to the car."

O'Leary knew the bag was likely to contain house-breaking equipment and maybe weapons. Should they move in now to make arrests? But the gang could have picked any one of a hundred houses. And the raid might already have started. *If we move too soon, the gang may panic, shoot someone or take hostages.*

As Coronation Street ended at 7.57pm, Deborah Burke got up from beside her husband Stephen in the living room of their home just off Shenley Hill. "Come on, Georgina. Time for bed." She scooped up her three-year-old. Then she reeled back. "Oh, my God!" she exclaimed.

Four men, all in black, were in the room. The two largest made straight for Stephen, 38, a fit six-footer who had once hurdled for Britain. He'd spent five years in the army before setting up a successful City recruitment agency with his wife. Within seconds, his hands were manacled behind his back.

"Where's the safe?" bawled one of the raiders, brandishing a claw hammer. "Look down. Don't look at us." Deborah was manhandled to the floor. A raider saw her watch. "I'll have that." Then her rings. "I'll have those too." As he began yanking at them, she took them off herself.

Little Georgina began screaming in terror. "Shut up!" yelled one of the robbers. Another carried her over to Deborah. "Sit with your mummy."

Next to Burke, a raider continued to yell, "Where's the safe?" Burke said they didn't have one. "Where do you keep your money?"

"In my back pocket. You've already got it."

He was hauled upstairs and made to sit on the floor, handcuffed to the banisters. Downstairs, he heard the volume on the television being turned up loud. But he knew that his neighbours were too far away to hear the din. Someone yelled, "If you don't tell us where the safe is, we'll kill him first. We'll take the child."

"There is no safe," Deborah was crying. "I'll show you where my jewels are." Burke was aware of his wife being led upstairs. Georgina was put in his lap—no longer crying, but shaking with fright.

In the main bedroom, Deborah rummaged in a wardrobe for her wooden jewellery box. The raiders smashed it on the floor, then scooped the contents into a pillowcase from the bed. "Now where's the safe?" one of the men screamed.

"There is no safe. There's a car in the drive. We've got a television, stereo. Take them. You've got the jewels. There isn't anything else."

The short raider was searching the spare bedroom, emptying and slamming drawers. The others led Deborah and Georgina downstairs to handcuff them to the banisters. As Georgina's hand was too small, they grabbed an ankle and manacled that. With her free arm, Deborah comforted Georgina. "Don't cry. You've been such a brave girl." At last the robbers made for the door, with £30,000 worth of valuables.

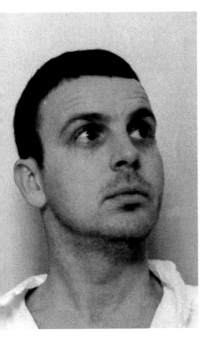

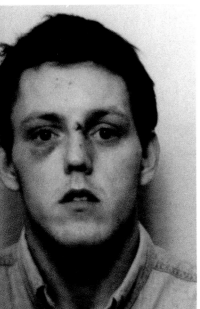

Just desserts: Stephen Lewtas (top) and Graham Barker.

At 8.12pm, O'Leary heard a whispered radio report from DC Briers. The gang had returned to the golf club car park. "They're over the fence … the small one is carrying something … they're at speed out of the car park."

Crouched behind fencing at the Railway Inn with his firearms team, DCI John Morse listened intently to the radio as two unmarked police cars set off behind the Volvo. "We are following them down the hill … towards the Railway pub."

As the Volvo pulled up behind the Mondeo, Morse gave the radio command, "Strike … Strike." A dozen police moved from their hiding places. "Armed police," they shouted. "Get down."

In the confusion, the diminutive Champion escaped but he was arrested later in his room at the New Victoria, where he was pretending to be asleep. The five others were quickly handcuffed. In the Volvo, police found the cash and jewellery taken from the Burkes, as well as masks, gloves, screwdrivers, three two-way radios, six sets of handcuffs, 13 keys. The Burkes were released in minutes.

With the arrest of the six robbers, the raids stopped. After a two-and-a-half-week trial at Woolwich Crown Court in October and November 1997, Judge Brian Pryor sentenced Shaun Shinkwin and Peter Champion to 18 years' imprisonment. Ronald Shinkwin and Paul Clarke received 15 years. Stephen Lewtas, a 37-year-old Merseyside career criminal who acted as look-out in the golf club car park, was given 12 years, and the Volvo driver, Merseysider Graham Barker, 22, got nine years.

The judge commended the "excellent" work of the police. But they had already received one other, unlikely, accolade. As Shaun Shinkwin, ashen with shock, was being handcuffed in the Railway Inn car park, he had blurted out to his arresting officer, "Nice one, mate."

IN THE
FOOTSTEPS
OF
SHERLOCK
HOLMES

BY RUDOLPH CHELMINSKI

HE HAD KILLED HIS WIFE ACCIDENTALLY AND
THEN, IN PANIC, HAD BURNED HER BODY PARTS IN
A BASEMENT FIREPLACE. BUT HOW "ACCIDENTAL"
HAD HER DEATH BEEN?

n mid-June 1991, neighbours of Alphonse Lutringer, a respected retired businessman in the eastern French town of Marlenheim, began commenting that they hadn't seen his wife, Françoise, lately. "She just departed," the 70-year-old replied curtly, and that was that. Françoise's family got the same response. Nearly two years later, a cousin persuaded the authorities that something was wrong. Investigating magistrate Jean-Baptiste Poli's gendarmes made several suspicious findings: Madame Lutringer's clothes and jewellery were still in place, a mattress showed bloodstains, and her scribblings on a calendar ended abruptly on June 9, 1991. Under interrogation, Lutringer broke down, saying he had killed his wife accidentally and then, in panic, had burned her body parts in a basement fireplace. But how "accidental" had her death been?

Poli got in touch with Jean-Marie Grafeille, a French forensic scientist and micro-analyst.

When Grafeille, a lanky 50-year-old chain-smoker with brown eyes and a slight stammer, inspected the Lutringer's house, the glass top to a bedroom night table caught his eye; so did a heavy plastic sheet of the sort commonly used for covering wood piles. He took them both to his laboratory in Bordeaux.

With a stainless steel scalpel, Grafeille lifted one of three tiny marks, no bigger than fly specks, off the table top. Placing it on a glass receptacle, he added a drop of an immuno-biological reactive serum and slid the receptacle under an optical microscope. Alphonse Lutringer's crime began unfolding before his eyes.

The sample was human blood—the same type as Madame Lutringer's. And the microscope also revealed the characteristic debris of gunshot residue.

Grafeille isolated the residue with a high-speed centrifuge and transferred it into the vacuum chamber of a high-resolution electron microscope. The analyzer read out the structure of antimony, barium and lead—unmistakable leavings of a spent cartridge.

Then, on a hunch, Grafeille slid the remainder of the tiny sample into a mass spectrometer. It showed a chemical formula of a sedative, marketed in France under the brand name of Théralène.

The plastic sheet, Grafeille had noticed, was scored by several deep cuts. He folded the sheet over several times onto itself, until the cuts lined up in perfect vertical symmetry, one under the other. Then he removed a small sample of the sheet from the edge of a cut. Using the optical microscope, he discovered a number of particles.

In the lab: forensic genius Grafeille.

Under an electron microscope, the particles emitted the X-ray spectrum of vanadium, a metallic substance commonly used as a hardener for high-grade steel—for instance, in the manufacture of axes.

Grafeille surmised that Lutringer had drugged his wife with Théralène, then shot her as she lay in bed and moved the body to the plastic sheet. Probably with an axe he chopped the corpse into pieces for easier disposal. Armed with such a stunningly accurate scenario, the police charged Lutringer with first-degree murder. Seven months later, before he could be tried, he hanged himself in his cell. Case closed.

"Grafeille's decision to attempt to analyze the sedative after it had been metabolized by passing through the liver was quite extraordinary," said an admiring Judge Poli afterwards.

Grafeille has worked on numerous interesting cases since he became a forensic investigator. The son of an architect, and a true polymath, Grafeille leapt from physics, archaeology and history to biology, chemistry, human ecology and crystallography in his college days at the University of Bordeaux. Meanwhile he worked as a lab technician to make ends meet. The combination of wide-ranging knowledge and technical expertise gave him a unique preparation for assisting police and insurance investigators.

His most famous case began one spring day a dozen years ago in Montpellier, when the charred remains of what was believed to be former insurance salesman, Yves Dandonneau, were found in a burnt-out car. Dandonneau, investigators discovered, was insured with eight triple-indemnity contracts totalling more than 11 million francs. Five months into their investigation, police hired Grafeille.

He approached the job as if he were at an archaeological dig, scraping away the accumulated mud, rust and dirt from the car's floorboards and passing the sludge

On the road: Grafeille and Arthur, seekers after truth.

in a stream of water through a series of sieves until he found a fragment that he recognized as part of a human jawbone. It wasn't Dandonneau's. Dental records later proved that it belonged to a tramp lured into the car, killed and burned beyond recognition for the big payoff. Dandonneau, who had undergone plastic surgery to alter his appearance, was located through a girlfriend. He was convicted of murder.

In Grafeille's cluttered lab computers chatter away while microscopes and photo-enlarging gear lie cheek by jowl with canisters of liquid nitrogen, vats of chemicals and a small library of books and technical reference sheets. And there's also a human skeleton named Arthur. For an on-site comparison and demonstration, Grafeille once sat him on the right side of his Peugeot and drove through Bordeaux, amusing and petrifying fellow motorists.

Like Sherlock Holmes, who published a monograph on 140 different types of cigar, pipe and cigarette ashes, Grafeille is all too familiar with ashes. He frequently works with insurance companies, tramping through the smoking ruins of burned buildings. Fraudulent claims cost French insurers an estimated 10 billion francs a year, and Grafeille has attempted to save them some of this money by detecting arson.

"You've got to be curious about everything," Grafeille insists. Take sand. With his microscopes, he can spot the difference between a single grain from a mountainous site, a riverbed, the ocean floor, a beach, a dune, or inland behind the dune.

Grafeille found himself absolutely overwhelmed with sand in the case of *La Jonque*, a French trawler that sank off the Breton coast in 1987 with the loss of all hands, in fine weather and a calm sea. The captain's family believed the trawler was accidentally rammed by a submarine or perhaps hit by a stray missile. Four years later, *La Jonque* was raised and French judicial authorities hired Grafeille to inspect and analyze the wreck in dry dock. The unlucky boat was filled with sand and mud from the sea bed, but the hull showed no sign of a missile strike. A deep dent in the stern, however, seemed possible evidence of collision.

It *was* a collision, Grafeille determined—but not with another vessel. The microscopic bits of coral polyp tissue (polypary) that he found embedded there showed that the fast-sinking boat had hit the bottom stern-first, smashing coral tissue into the paint. But there was no evidence of paint being transferred from another vessel, as there would have been in a collision. Experts finally concluded that *La Jonque* had taken in a sudden rush of water through her open stern while maneuvering to free a snagged net. Case closed.

It is often the job of the forensic specialist to make the dead speak: how did the crime happen, and who is to blame?

The strangled body of Nazmiye Illikpinar, a 15-year-old girl, was discovered in August, 1993, lying in a roadside ditch near the eastern city of Colmar. Nazmiye's parents, Kurdish migrant workers from eastern Turkey, had alerted police that she had gone missing, and lamented loud and long when informed that their daughter was dead.

But behind the lamentations, national gendarmes discovered, lay a grievous cultural clash. Strict Moslems, the parents had grown increasingly concerned with the influence of western ways upon their daughter, such as jeans, lipstick and friendship with a non-Moslem girl. After repeated beatings, Nazmiye fled the family apartment and entered a state children's home in nearby Strasbourg.

Then she was found dead. Called in by the investigating judge, Grafeille inspected the girl's clothing and the floor mat of the Illikpinar's old station wagon.

Grain of truth: a few specks of ash can point Grafeille towards the culprit.

Helping hand: taking Arthur home.

Armed with several dozen sticky carbon discs, Grafeille painstakingly lifted samples from the car and Nazmiye's shirt and jeans. The micro-particles of dust, dirt, hair and miscellaneous debris did not match. But the girl's father also had access to a van of the company where he worked—and under the microscope the van spoke.

On the back of Nazmiye's clothing the micro-particles matched exactly those in the back of the van. Grafeille was able to demonstrate not only that the girl had been transported in the van lying down, but also her position when being strangled: face up.

The family admitted that to save their "honour" they had condemned Nazmiye to death. Abdullah, her 21-year-old brother, strangled her while a cousin held her down and the parents turned their backs. They put her body in the van and dumped it by the road where they knew she would be discovered. After that, they were able to give her a proper Moslem burial. Abdullah was sentenced to life, the parents and the cousin to 20 years apiece.

The secret of Grafeille's success? "When you're puzzled by a phenomenon, you've always got to try to find the reason for it," he says. "*Il reste toujours quelque chose*—there's always a trace left behind."

SOLVED:

THE PILTDOWN

MAN

BY IAN CUNNINGHAM

IT WAS OUR CENTURY'S GREATEST SCIENTIFIC HOAX
—BUT WHO WAS BEHIND IT? NOW, AFTER MORE THAN
80 YEARS, ONE SLEUTH THINKS HE HAS THE ANSWER.

Robert Knowles, a young zoologist, was beginning to regret volunteering for one of the messiest jobs in the Natural History Museum in London. The massive south-western towers were due for re-roofing and someone had to clear out the cavernous attics, where almost a century's junk had amassed since the museum opened in 1881.

As Knowles groped among the piles of discarded papers and long-forgotten exhibits, his torch picked out a large wooden trunk, covered in red buckram, faded and peeling. Just legible were the initials M.A.C.H. They meant nothing to Knowles. He lifted the heavy lid—and recoiled in shock. Inside were hundreds of glass vials containing dissected rodents. Some vials had broken; the stench of decomposing remains was sickening.

With the help of Andy Currant, a museum researcher, Knowles hauled the trunk downstairs, where the two men examined the contents in daylight. Under the glass vials were bundles of notes and, at the bottom, a crumbling cardboard box holding what appeared to be the fossilized bones of prehistoric animals, all stained a deep chocolate brown.

Without realizing it, the pair had stumbled across a clue to unmasking one of the greatest fraudsters of the twentieth century.

One May morning 86 years ago, Arthur Smith Woodward, Keeper of Geology at the Natural History Museum, received a visitor. Then 48, Woodward was approaching the pinnacle of a glittering career. (His *Catalogue of Fossil Fishes in the British Museum*, completed in 1901, is still used by palaeontologists today.)

His visitor was Charles Dawson, a familiar sight at the museum. A solicitor by profession, this stout, affable man was also an accomplished archaeologist.

He entered Woodward's office holding a small parcel. "How's that for Heidelberg!" he said. Woodward's pulse began to race. Three months earlier Dawson had sent him a letter describing a gravel pit he had come across in an area called Piltdown in East Sussex. "I [have found] a portion of a human (?) skull," he had hurriedly scrawled, "which will rival *Homo Heidelbergensis*." This was the name given to fossil remains found in Germany four years before and hailed as evidence of the "missing link" between primitive apes and early man.

Unwrapping the package, Dawson laid out three fragments of what looked to be a cranium on Woodward's desk. In thickness they were like an ape's, yet the size of the skull would be more like a man's. Dawson explained that the pieces

New sleuth: Brian Gardiner recognized the initials on the trunk.

First, in 1903, he ousted the Sussex Archaeological Society—of which he was a member—from its headquarters by buying the premises for himself, using the society's note paper to give the impression that he was acting on their behalf. Then in 1910, when a local reviewer pointed out that his *History of Hastings Castle* had been largely plagiarized from existing books, Dawson responded by secretly trying to sabotage the man's application to join the prestigious Society of Antiquaries.

One local amateur palaeontologist, who'd obtained a Piltdown flint, had long suspected the find was faked. Although the man was now dead, Weiner tracked down his collection. Attached to the stone was a card reading: *Stained by C. Dawson with intent to defraud all.*

Kenneth Oakley, meanwhile, was keen to question Teilhard de Chardin. Now in his mid-seventies, the French Jesuit was the sole survivor of those who actually made the discovery. But Teilhard was strangely unwilling to discuss the affair. Invited by Oakley to the Natural History Museum to view an exhibition on the fraud in 1954, the old man hurried past the exhibits, his eyes averted. Questioned directly, he murmured, "I was a mere youth at the time, little more than a boy." But in 1912 he was 31.

Faulty memory or guilty conscience? Oakley never found out. On Easter Sunday 1955 Teilhard de Chardin died of a heart attack.

In 1953, a student at London's Imperial College, Brian Gardiner, took a summer job at the Natural History Museum. He gleefully read Weiner and Oakley's damning report at the back of the university lecture theatre. A few years later, Gardiner got to know Oakley and took a keen interest in the hoax. Despite the evidence implicating Dawson, there was still nothing conclusive.

Gardiner went on to become a professor at King's College. It wasn't until 1986 that a chance remark by his friend Andy Currant over one of their regular pints in the pub—about the trunk in the tower and its strange collection of stained bones—revived his interest in Piltdown Man. For Gardiner recognized the initials on the lid: Martin Alister Campbell Hinton.

Hinton had been the Keeper of Zoology at the Natural History Museum from 1936 to 1945. Gardiner had begun to suspect him when, chatting to Oakley, he learned of a strange incident in 1949, four years before the hoax was exposed. Oakley had been about to give a lecture on his fluorine tests when he was approached by Dina Hinton, Martin's wife. "Leave well alone," she said firmly, before taking her seat.

Could Hinton be the hoaxer? His very first publication had been about manganese staining of gravel deposits. In his *Who's Who* entry, he even mentioned an interest in hoaxes.

The discovery of the trunk gave Gardiner the chance to investigate. To the naked eye, the bones in the trunk and those in the Piltdown collection were identical, all stained a deep brown. If the Piltdown bones were stained artificially, what about the bones in the trunk?

The ten teeth and pieces of bone in the trunk, Gardiner established, were from a prehistoric hippopotamus and elephant. Many of the specimens had been carved and abraded with sharp metal tools. Using a technique called mass spectronomy, that can analyse the constituents of matter, Gardiner discovered that the Piltdown bones and the bones in the trunk were both artificially stained using the same mixture of iron and manganese.

The specimens from the trunk, he concluded, must have been either test runs or leftovers from the Piltdown hoax.

But are some initials on a trunk enough evidence? he wondered. He remembered that Bob Savage, an acquaintance of his and a retired professor of geology at the University of Bristol, had been a friend of Hinton's. On Hinton's death in 1961 the family had asked Savage to search through his effects for specimens that might be of interest to the Natural History Museum.

Hinton had been a hoarder on a massive scale. His possessions had included some 10,000 tobacco tins and more than a ton of papers, dating back 60 years. Some of the tins held only buttons or old coins, but some contained fossils that had found a home in the museum.

But Gardiner could find nothing in the museum's catalogues or exhibits that shed any light on the hoax. So he wrote to Savage, asking if he remembered coming across anything that might resemble Piltdown. Savage did. Among Hinton's possessions were eight small test-tubes, each containing a brown-stained tooth. Since they were unidentified, Savage had not sent them to the museum. For three decades they'd occupied a cupboard in his laboratory.

Scientist or hoaxer?: Martin Alister Campbell Hinton.

Two days later the test-tubes were with Gardiner. Peering through the old, discoloured glass, he saw that the teeth were similarly stained to those found at Piltdown and in the trunk. Tests revealed they were modern and human—and had been coloured using chemicals including iron and manganese.

But what possible motive could Hinton have had? As Gardiner scoured the records in the museum, a picture began to emerge.

Born in London, the son of a law clerk, Hinton was 12 when his father died, forcing him to leave school and earn a living as a barrister's clerk. Already a gifted palaeontologist and archaeologist, he'd spend his weekends digging for fossils. His frequent visits to the Natural History Museum got him noticed and he was taken on as a voluntary worker.

Unpaid workers like Hinton occupied the bottom rung of the museum hierarchy, all hoping their efforts would earn them a permanent position. Yet for years, despite his obvious talents and hard work, a staff appointment eluded Hinton.

Two years before Piltdown, Arthur Smith Woodward asked him to catalogue the museum's fossil rodents. Hinton enthusiastically agreed, but, keen to escape his day job, he pleaded for a regular salary. Woodward refused; Hinton would be paid a lump sum after the cataloguing was completed.

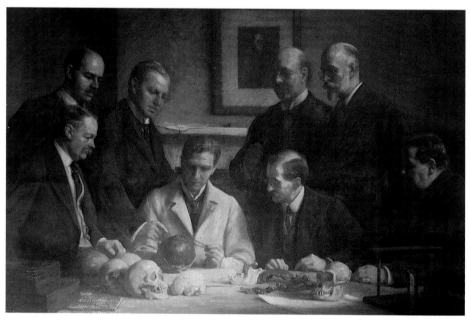

Cranial conspirators: a 1915 painting celebrates the "Piltdown Gang", including Charles Dawson and Arthur Woodward.

Woodward's unbending attitude must have rankled with Hinton, who did not receive a permanent position until 1921. Could this lack of recognition have prompted him to take revenge by perpetrating the hoax?

In May 1996, Gardiner, now white-haired, with a genial, distracted air, announced his findings at Burlington House. His conclusions drew both converts and sceptics. Henry Gee, editor of the science journal *Nature*, felt the Piltdown fraud "could finally be laid to rest". Botanist Professor William Stearn has no doubt Hinton was responsible. "I doubt Charles Dawson could have had access to all those fossils," he says. "But Hinton certainly did."

Many are still convinced Dawson was involved. John Evangelist Walsh, author of a book on the subject, insists the staining of the trunk bones represents Hinton's experiments *after* the exposure of the fraud in 1953. But, counters Gardiner, by the time the hoax had been uncovered Hinton had long since left the Natural History Museum and was living in retirement in Bristol.

"I'm not disputing that Dawson was a shyster of the first order," says Gardiner. "But I'm convinced he was just the fall guy."

There is one last piece of evidence. For there is still someone living who knew Hinton well. Bob Savage, now 70, recalls how, even in retirement, Hinton displayed an extraordinary mind. A talented watercolourist and photographer, he was also a champion chess player, conducting three or four matches at a time by post. He would discourse with eloquence on his favourite writers and musicians and was a voracious reader in French and German.

On the subject of Piltdown, however, Hinton was uncharacteristically unforthcoming. He did once claim to have visited Dawson around the time of the finds and to have glimpsed, in Teilhard de Chardin's open bag, the elephant tooth later uncovered at the pit. Yet another time, he suggested the perpetrator had been employed at the museum at the time of the hoax, though he could not reveal the name as the person was still alive—which could almost be read as a confession.

Savage admits Hinton probably was guilty, though he thinks others were involved too. "It was intended to teach a lesson to the snobs at the top. The remains would be found and the great man Woodward would announce them to the world. They'd then turn out to be fakes and Woodward would look a fool.

"But it was too successful—everyone wanted to believe in Piltdown Man. In the meantime, Martin got his post at the museum and built a reputation. Now he could never admit the truth."

Perhaps for Martin Hinton a lifetime knowing he had perverted the course of science was punishment enough. "Be kind to him," says Savage. "He was a great scientist. I hate to think of him going down in history as a hoaxer."

A
COP'S LIFE

BY BRIAN McDONALD

FRANKIE McDONALD WAS THE BLACK SHEEP OF THE FAMILY.

NO ONE EXPECTED HE WOULD FOLLOW HIS FATHER AND

GRANDFATHER AND BECOME A NEW YORK CITY COP.

When my brother Frankie McDonald was assigned to the 52nd Precinct, in the northern Bronx, his partner on the detective squad told him that the five-two "had good crime." He meant that the precinct did not have to deal with depraved, drug-addled offenses, as did the South Bronx or parts of Brooklyn where crack-heads killed their mothers for taking their dope pipes. "Good crime" meant a lot of different crimes that were hard to solve.

Early on, Frankie's team was assigned a robbery case that was typical. A nun from St Nicholas of Tolentine, which was in the middle of the precinct, was mugged by a man as she entered her building. She was shaken and bruised, but not badly hurt.

Four detectives on the team were assigned to the robbery. Usually only a pair were put on a case, but Frankie's chief was a daily communicant and personal friends with the cardinal. Any crime against the church got his complete attention.

Arriving at the scene, the detectives learned that the nun had been knocked to the floor in her vestibule, and the thief made off with her bag. But, the uniform cops added, the mugger had left something behind—his dog. Apparently he had been walking his German shepherd when he saw the opportunity for a robbery. In his haste he let go of the leash, leaving his dog trapped in the convent's entryway.

Frankie's team conferred and came up with an idea: release the dog and follow a "Lassie, Come Home" strategy. Because they were in the best shape, Frankie and fellow detective Tony Martin were picked as runners.

Storytellers all: brothers Brian (left) and Frankie with their father.

288

With bemused cops looking on, one of the detectives led the dog to the sidewalk. Frankie and Martin took a runner's stance, and they unhooked the German shepherd from his leash. The dog shot down the street and crossed busy Fordham Road, cars whizzing by on all sides, with Frankie and Martin in close pursuit. Before long the dog ran into the open door of a building.

In the vestibule, over his loud gasps for breath, Frankie could hear the animal scratching on a door a couple of floors above. Up the two detectives went. The door was opened by a woman.

"Do you live alone?" they asked.

No. With her husband, she said.

"Is he home?" they wanted to know. She shook her head.

"Mind if we come in?"

She shrugged. Just inside the apartment Frankie noticed a closet with the door ajar. On the floor was the nun's bag.

Over the next few days, the woman kept insisting she did not know where her husband was. The team pressed for more information and managed to find out that the man had relatives in the East Bronx.

Each day Frankie and Martin took trips there, but learned nothing. And each day the chief checked on the progress of the case.

Weeks passed, and Frankie and the other detectives kept the pressure on the man's relatives and on his wife, even as they worked other cases. One day as Frankie was leading a robbery suspect to the interrogation room in the station house, a short man with heavy-lidded eyes and a few days' growth of beard came up to him. Politely, he asked Frankie if they could talk.

Busy with his arrest, Frankie turned to the man and explained he had no time to talk then, but if he would take a seat he would get to him when he had a chance.

After an hour and a half of questioning his robbery suspect, Frankie took a break and walked out of the interrogation room. Again he was approached by the man.

"Please, I have to talk to you," the man pleaded as he followed Frankie to the Coke machine.

"What?" Frankie said. "What the hell is so important?"

"I'm the guy who lost the dog," the man said. After days on the run the suspect was exhausted. The relentless police work had driven him in.

Frank loved telling stories like this about his work in the New York Police Department—tales of quirky arrests, adrenaline-charged chases, moments of stark terror. "War stories" he called them.

"Being a policeman," he once said to me, "was the only thing I ever wanted to do."

FORT APACHE

We come from a cop family. It started with my maternal grandfather, Tom Skelly. Born on the Upper East Side of Manhattan in 1868, he joined the New York City police department, then called the Municipal Police, at the age of 25, and worked as a patrolman for 26 years.

In 1941 his daughter, Eleanor, met young Frank McDonald at a YMCA dance in Manhattan. My father was attending the police academy and tried to impress her by saying, "I'm a police officer."

She looked at this man who, at six feet three inches and 158 pounds, was about as wide as a mop handle. "So what?" she said. "So were my father and my uncle." Smitten, my father persisted, and they married in the summer of 1942.

When my mother met my father she was 30 and scandalously single, given the place and the time. Once I asked her about her late-in-life marriage. She looked across the room at my father sitting in his chair, wrinkled her nose and said in a giggling whisper, "Maybe I should have waited a little longer."

Unlike my grandfather, Frank McDonald wasn't about to be a patrolman his whole career. When he was promoted to sergeant in 1950, he had his first taste of being a boss and found not only that he liked it, but that he was good at it too. In less than a year's time, he was made a squad commander in the 41st Precinct in the Bronx, later known as Fort Apache. Only 33, he was easily one of the youngest commanders in the city.

During my father's first few years in the four-one, homicides were few and most were crimes of passion: drunken escalations of neighborhood grudges or domestic quarrels. But by the mid-1950s, coinciding with the infusion of heroin and teenage gangs, murders not only came with alarming frequency, they became horribly arbitrary.

One day my father found himself at his desk looking at the crime-scene photographs of a woman he knew, Mary Roznicoff,* a street vendor who sold fruits and vegetables. He had passed her almost every morning as he drove to work.

The report told what was becoming an all-too-familiar story. The killer, a heroin addict, had popped the window of Roznicoff's ground-floor apartment as she slept and smothered her with her pillow. From the crime report, my father learned she had a son who was a doctor. He imagined her saving each dime to send her son through medical school.

From 1950 to 1960 homicide arrests in the Bronx grew by 66 per cent. By 1965 that number had more than tripled.

By then my father had moved our family from the Bronx to the town of Pearl River, a suburb north of New York, seeking more room and a safe haven. My three

---

*An asterisk denotes names that have been changed to protect privacy

brothers and I knew little of his job. When he was at home, he usually erected a kind of wall between himself and his family. With each year his face became more stoic, until it looked as though it was chipped from pale rock.

After he walked in the door each evening, I remember hearing the slap his belt made as he whipped it off, his left hand holding the holster of his snub-nosed gun. I watched while he snapped open the cylinder, let the bullets drop into his hand and then locked them in a metal box. He wrapped his belt, gun and holster together and placed them deep on the top shelf of the closet. Finally, he would fix himself a Scotch and sit silently in his chair in the living room.

Often during those years I was awakened at two or three in the morning by the sound of his pipe tapping against an ashtray. I would creep to the door and see him sitting in his wing chair, smoke rising from his pipe, metallic-blue in the shaft of light from the lamp. Next to him was a half-empty glass of buttermilk, which he drank to ease the stabbing pain in his stomach.

"Damned Scotch," I'd hear him mumble, a self-admonishment for the few drinks he allowed himself. But the Scotch was not the only culprit. The stabbing pain was from witnessing every kind of wound a human can suffer. And each killing ripped open his stomach a little wider.

I got my first clear sense of what his life was like years later when I was given permission to search back-case files in the basement of the 41st Precinct station house.

I was led down a staircase to a cinder-block hallway with thick metal doors painted red. My guide unlocked one. Inside, the walls were lined with metal shelves; every inch was taken up with cardboard file boxes emblazoned with "Murder," "Rape," "Robbery" in red marker.

My eyes searched for the era when my father ran the detective squad. Finally, on a shelf in the far recesses of the room, I saw a box. "Murders 1950" was written on it.

My hands shook as I opened it. Inside were a dozen legal file folders—murders that had gone unsolved. My father's signature was on each DD 5, detective case reports.

The files also contained personal items from the victims and other evidence: a small leather-bound address book, keys to a home, a crime tip written on toilet paper that crumbled in my hand. There were crime-scene photographs, each a graphic glimpse into my father's job:

1954—Samuel Tannenbaum, * *77, owner of a toy store on Freeman Street stabbed 40 times during a robbery.*

1958—26-year-old Rosa Hernandez * and her two-year-old daughter murdered in their apartment at 660 Dawson Street. Both were beaten with the steel end of a mop* handle. *The mother was strangled and her child was drowned in a bathtub filled with scalding water.*

1959—Nicholas Serico, 69, pistol-whipped to death as he pleaded for his life in the vestibule of his apartment house. The murderer made off with seven dollars taken from the man's wife, who tried unsuccessfully to fend off the attacker.*

The box also contained the folder on Mary Roznicoff, the street vendor murdered in her bed. Her face in the crime-scene photo stared back at me just as it had at my father many years earlier.

I tried to imagine him in this world, so different than anything my brothers and I had known growing up in the suburbs.

Several times over the years he asked for a transfer. His requests were turned down repeatedly.

His tenure in the four-one would last 14 years, probably the longest any person had held that position. On December 31, 1965, my father retired.

Less than one year later he was rushed to hospital. An emergency operation removed three-quarters of his ulcerated stomach and part of his ruptured esophagus.

When he returned home, he was skinny, gaunt and looked very old. He was 48.

REBEL

While my brother Frankie was growing up, it seemed the last thing he would do was follow our father's path and become a cop. While Frankie was a teenager, the relationship between him and Dad ranged from antagonistic to hostile. Much of it stemmed from the fact that my brother loathed the classroom.

He spent much of his time in elementary school infuriating the nuns. In high school he attended classes reluctantly and did homework rarely.

Eager rookie: Frankie McDonald joined the navy and traveled the world before becoming a cop.

Frankie's behavior constantly irritated my father, who in turn deflected his feelings onto our mother. "You're breaking your mother's heart," he would say when my brother got in trouble.

These were utter falsehoods. My mother's heart could never be broken by Frankie; he was so much more her son than my father's. They were kindred spirits. That anger, that independence—these were all things Frankie inherited from her.

What made the rift between father and son even more pronounced was the comparison Dad made between Frankie and our older brother, Eugene. Like my father, Eugene was a natural student, contemplative and analytical, destined to be a successful engineer. Innately self-disciplined, he would wake before dawn on exam days to study his algebra, history and Latin textbooks. By contrast, Frankie might not even have bothered to go to school if it weren't for the pretty girls. Though not handsome in the classic sense, he had rough good looks: a single dimple in his chin, and the same intense eyes—and temper—as our mother.

His anger could be volcanic in its eruptions. I remember one summer evening my parents had gone out, and he had a party at our house. I heard shouting and found my brother facing another teenager—an argument over their girlfriends. The boy was screaming in Frankie's face.

My brother glared. When he became angry, his demeanor seemed calm, almost serene. Plenty were fooled. But I knew what was about to happen.

The punch was a lightning-quick left that lifted his opponent off the ground. There was a gasp among the others in the room. Even Frankie seemed taken aback by the suddenness of the blow.

Just as quickly, he turned and walked out of the house. I joined him in the back yard. His face now was soft, his eyes repentant. He didn't ask for the anger, and it was clear to me that each time it arose, it took an emotional toll.

That same summer of 1963 Frankie couldn't seem to stay out of trouble. The night of his graduation he totaled our mother's car, and later on he had a brush with the law. He had decided to take a trip to the New Jersey shore one night with a local gang he had joined in high school called The Brothers. When their caravan of cars arrived in the beach town of Wildwood, they divided up to look for motel rooms.

Frankie and his friends saw two girls hitchhiking and asked if they knew of any place with vacancies. Guided by the young women, they pulled into a motel parking lot a few minutes later.

Out front was a group of local guys drinking beer. As soon as the girls stepped out of his car, Frankie knew picking them up had been a mistake.

One of the locals charged him and a fistfight began. Two Wildwood police cars showed up, and everyone was held overnight in jail. The next morning Frankie pleaded with the judge, "We didn't want any trouble," he said, adding, "I'm going to be a policeman."

The magistrate glared at him: "Son, I'd be willing to bet you will never become a cop."

That was probably the first time my brother told anyone his dream.

FIRST ARREST

Frankie's antics, his run-ins with the police, and his volcanic temper caused too much disharmony for my father. When my brother joined the Navy, Dad seemed happy to see him go.

As he traveled, my brother sent me postcards from places like Madrid, Rome and Hamburg. He also wrote to my father. It was in one of his letters that Frankie first told him that he wanted to become a cop.

When Dad read the letter he shook his head, folded the paper back into the envelope, and tucked it deep on the top shelf of his closet, behind his gun.

Frankie had, in fact, begun to change. He wrote to a high school English teacher, whose class he had rarely attended, for a list of books to read. Lying in his bunk in a destroyer, my brother for the first time discovered treasures like *Crime and Punishment* and *Our Town*.

After he was honorably discharged from the Navy in 1966, he got a job working construction and began classes in Manhattan at the Delahanty Institute, a prep school for the police test. Twenty-five years earlier my father had sat in the same classrooms on 13th Street and Fourth Avenue—on the same corner where our grandfather had once been a traffic cop.

For weeks my brother studied almost every night and early in the morning before he left for his construction job. The day of the exam, his face was tight with worry when he returned to the house. He had little faith in himself as a student.

He needn't have worried. His score was 94, and with the five-point bonus given to veterans, his final mark was 99.

Once Frankie joined the police academy, his relationship with Dad began to change. Frankie would often stop by our house on the way home. Dad would put down the book or paper he was reading as soon as he heard the car, and wait expectantly for the door to open. The two men would then sit in the living room, Frankie drinking a beer, my father sucking on hard candy in lieu of a cigar, as my brother relayed the day's events.

Several times during my brother's term in the academy, recruits were pulled out of school to bolster the manpower of the Department. It was on one of those assignments that he made his first arrest.

The next day, still looking haggard, he told my father the story in our living room. With no experience as a traffic cop, he found himself in the middle of Herald Square in front of Macy's department store at Christmastime, besieged by traffic and tourists asking directions.

About 4pm he noticed that the traffic on a side street had stopped dead. Walking over to investigate, he saw a large woman spread-eagled on the hood of a cab.

At first he thought she was an accident victim, but as he drew closer he realized she was drunk. As he went to help her off the cab, she hit him in the head with a whiskey bottle, knocking his hat halfway across the street.

Frankie was more stunned than hurt, but as he again tried to pull the woman out of the street, she removed one of her shoes and began beating him in the face with it. Blood streamed from Frankie's nose.

For all of his explosive anger, underneath Frankie was something of a Boy Scout. It was certainly not his custom to go around slugging women. But as she readied for another charge, he decided he had had enough. My brother balled his left hand into a fist and when the drunken woman was nearly on him, he punched her as hard as he could.

She slammed into a building with such an impact that it knocked off her wig and exposed a bald head. In a moment she was coming at him again.

Finally, another cop called in a 10-13—cop needs assistance. It took half a dozen officers to subdue the woman and get her in cuffs.

The next day in court, she was sober and incredibly none the worse for wear. She pleaded guilty to an assault charge and, having had a record of attacking policemen, was sentenced to six months in jail. On the way out of court, she winked at Frankie.

"GET NOTICED"

After my brother got his first permanent assignment—the 34th Precinct in Manhattan—he started coming by my parents' house even more often. I noticed that he and Dad had a way of talking to one another now that seemed to exclude everyone else in the room. They both belonged to the brotherhood. They were cops.

My father was proud of his son, but I never truly knew how my mother felt about Frankie becoming a police officer. She was also proud, of course, but would have been proud no matter what his career choice was. There had always been a deep connection between Frankie and her.

I remember my mother sometimes seemed melancholy during my brother's visits. As she listened to his cop talk she would put down her crossword and close her eyes like someone listening to a sad aria. I realize now that for her—the daughter and wife of a cop—that song had played her whole life and it was painful to listen to.

During one of their chats, Frankie asked my father the best way to get off a walking beat and assigned to car patrol. Frankie, like our father, had greater aspirations than being a patrolman.

"Get noticed," Dad said. "Build a batting average. Make a lot of arrests."

In his early days as a patrol officer my brother began collaring purse snatchers who preyed on elderly women, and shop-lifters who loitered near the stores on Broadway and 181st Street. One day Frankie noticed dozens of handbags with broken straps near a place where dope addicts shot up on 165th Street. That address became a gold mine of arrests, as he would wait for junkies to return with a just-snatched purse.

POLICE DEPARTMENT • CITY OF NEW YORK

IDENTIFICATION CARD

This is the ONLY type of identification card issued to members of the N. Y. City Police Force.

It shall serve to identify the bearer as an accredited member of the force, when and only when presented with an official shield of this department.

Postmaster—Return to:
POLICE HEADQUARTERS
240 Centre St., N. Y. 13

RANK   Ptl.

NAME   Frank P. McDonald

SHIELD NO.   26732

EXPIRES DECEMBER, 1968

TAX REGISTRY NO.   856984

(IF FOUND, DROP IN NEAREST U. S. MAIL BOX)

(RETURN POSTAGE GUARANTEED)

A career begins: Frankie continues the legacy begun by his father and grandfather.

It wasn't long before he got assigned to radio patrol. His partner was an experienced policeman named Paul Gibbons. Lanky, with a wild head of red hair, Gibbons had the reputation of being an arrest machine. He taught Frankie the nuances of car patrol. "Keep turning corners" was his catch phrase.

Though simple, the tactic was brilliant. With Gibbons at the wheel, the green-and-white Dodge radio car took on the characteristics of a panther, prowling the darkness of the side streets. Each corner they turned gave them the element of surprise. That first year together, according to Frankie's tally, Gibbons and he led the precinct in arrests, and each arrest paid a dividend.

"Collars for dollars" was a favorite saying of cops in those days. An arrest meant going to court. That meant overtime pay and realizing a dream my brother and his wife had: a down payment on a house.

Just before he was accepted into the academy, Frankie had married Pam Lawler, whom he had known since high school. They had a lot in common. Like Frankie, Pam was a transplanted city kid. She even had cops in her family. Most important, Pam had a calming effect on him.

They spent their honeymoon moving into a tiny one-bedroom apartment behind a gas station in Pearl River. By the time of his first assignment he and Pam already had one child, a daughter, and wanted more. They needed a bigger place.

Those were good years. For Frankie the job was fun. He liked the way he looked in uniform. He liked the authority it gave him. But most of all he liked that he was good at it. And each arrest brought him closer to his career goal—the gold shield of the Detective Division.

Frankie and Gibbons were more than just an effective team. As often happens between partners, they became good friends and learned a lot about each other. One trait of his partner's Frankie completely admired was his absolute fearlessness.

On a warm fall day, while in plain clothes, the two were stuck in traffic. Gibbons, tugging on his red summer shirt, was offering his theories on how to solve New York's traffic problems when a call came in about a robbery two blocks away. Too impatient to wait, Gibbons jumped from the car.

In the meantime Frankie snaked the car through the traffic. When he arrived at the building, there was no sign of his partner. Suddenly a woman screamed and pointed to an alley. Lying face down was the motionless figure of a man wearing a bright red shirt.

For a split second, my brother thought his partner was dead. Then he heard Gibbons's shout for help from inside the building. Frankie drew his gun and raced up five flights of stairs.

A door to an apartment was flung wide open. Inside, Gibbons and one of the robbers were on the floor wrestling for Gibbons's gun. With a surge of adrenaline, Frankie flew into the room and kicked the attacker in the face. The man slammed into the wall and slumped unconscious.

Gibbons had gone after both men by himself. One robber, the man in the red shirt, had tried to escape the same way he came in, by jumping to a nearby window ledge. He missed and only narrowly survived the five-story fall.

A compulsive talker and a bit of a hypochondriac, Gibbons always seemed to be complaining about some ailment or another. But one malady he really did have, Frankie learned, was asthma.

He found out when the two were responding to a medical emergency call in the projects involving a baby in distress. When they arrived at the building, they learned that the child was on the 12th floor and the elevator was out of service. They charged up the stairs.

Frankie was nearly at the 12th floor when he realized his partner was no longer right behind him. But there was no time to wait. The mother stood in the doorway of her apartment screaming hysterically.

Inside, a baby lay in a plastic bathtub. She was so small and so motionless that to Frankie she looked like a doll. A blue doll. She had inhaled water and couldn't breathe.

Arresting actors: Frankie (far right) and other members of the undercover Citywide Anti-Crime Section in the early 1970s.

In a flash he recalled how in the Bronx a neighbor banged on our family's door screaming her baby had drowned in the bathtub. Frankie remembered our mother picking the baby up by its feet and slapping him hard on the back. Emulating her, Frankie took the infant and did the same. Water gushed from the baby's mouth and she began to cry.

By the time ambulance attendants arrived, the baby had recovered and Frankie headed back down the stairs. On the way he saw Gibbons sitting on a landing, an oxygen mask on his face.

"You OK, Paul?" he asked.

More embarrassed than anything, Gibbons nodded. With a voice muffled by the mask, he said: "Keep this to yourself."

Frankie did, but for months afterward he kidded his partner on his missed shot at being a hero.

PICK THE PERP

By the late '60s Washington Heights in upper Manhattan was becoming a drug dealer's bazaar. Gibbons and Frankie were assigned there as plainclothes cops. As a disguise Frankie donned jeans and a Jets football jersey and wore his hair long, nearly shoulder-length.

Becoming this new type of policeman brought with it a split personality. In New York Frankie was a guerrilla, fighting a battle on darkened city streets.

In Pearl River he was a father who put his whole heart into trying to build a home for his family.

In 1970 Frankie became a dad again when Pam gave birth to their second daughter. With two babies in diapers she had little time to worry about her husband, but whenever the phone rang late at night, a shiver ran through her.

One night the local TV news had a story of an undercover cop killed in Washington Heights. Pam sat in front of the TV watching the live report showing police cars with "34"—her husband's precinct—emblazoned on their sides. She felt her heart race. The reporter did not give the name of the officer.

Lying awake in bed, she answered the phone on the first ring. It was Frankie calling to say he was all right, but because of the shooting he would have to work through the night. During the short conversation, she pretended she hadn't watched the news.

It seemed like almost every day her husband was on duty, Pam lived in a kind of suspended terror. And with good reason. During one year Frankie went to at least a half-dozen cop funerals. Each time, he stood among the sea of navy blue, saluting as a bagpiper played "Amazing Grace." Each time, he would try not to look at the widow and family.

He thought of Pam, watching late-night TV, waiting for him to come home. He thought of his two little girls, snuggled in their Little Red Riding Hood comforters. Still, he could not let go of his dream of getting the gold detective's shield.

His big break came when he was assigned to an experimental undercover group called the Citywide Anti-Crime Section. Its squads were made up of three-person teams, often working together as a decoy and two backup cops. The decoy, pretending to be a lost tourist, a hopeless drunk or a homeless person, would attract muggers or drug dealers. When a crime was committed, backup rushed in for the arrest.

Because of his size, six feet, 200 pounds, and his unmistakable cop looks, Frankie always worked as backup with other cops rotating as decoys. He mostly patrolled Times Square, which in the early '70s was a veritable supermarket of criminal activity. As the squads drove the streets in taxis, the undercover vehicles of choice, they tried to guess which street character would commit the next crime. They called this game "pick the perp," and it was one at which Frankie excelled.

The assignment seemed perfectly suited to my brother. Never the conformist, he liked that sergeants and lieutenants worked alongside their men in tightknit teams. It was an environment in which his skills thrived and his career progressed.

When the next list for promotion to detective was posted, his name was on it. He had his gold shield. He had been a cop a little more than six years.

FATEFUL ENCOUNTER

In the early winter of 1972, Frankie dropped by a tavern where I worked. Sitting at the bar, my brother seemed out of sorts, sullen and preoccupied. Perhaps it was the house, or the kids. Or money. I knew the bills were strangling him.

Maybe it was the job or the rash of cop killings. In a 12-month period, 15 officers had been killed in the line of duty. Whatever it was, he didn't say.

We talked about having a bachelor party for our other brother, Tommy, who was to be married the following month. We began discussing where we might hold it. I suggested we check out a nightspot I knew not far from us near the town of Spring Valley.

As we drove along the back roads, I saw flashing lights in the darkness ahead. A local police car was stopped at an odd angle to the road. In front of it was a large white sedan.

As we passed slowly, Frankie's eyes were riveted on the scene: a lone cop surrounded by six black men, the occupants of the sedan. He told me to stop, then jumped out and ran across to where the men stood in a circle around the officer. I stayed in the car.

It turned out the cop was a classmate of Frankie's from high school. I watched as my brother said something to him, and then saw one of the men grab Frankie's arm.

Suddenly there were shouts and heated words exchanged, but I couldn't make them out. They were muffled by the distance, the fog. Then I saw Frankie take out his gold shield and hang it around his neck, as if to say, "That's who I am."

Chin-to-chin with one of the men, Frankie screamed like a baseball manager fighting with an umpire over a bad call. For a moment I sat frozen in dread. I feared that already seething from the combined pressures of work and home, his volatile temper would only exacerbate the racially charged situation. I prayed that he would walk away. Finally he did, but not without another torrent of angry words.

Later on, my brother sat in remorseful silence. I could tell that he knew that he had messed up.

That same night the Spring Valley officer wrote a report about what happened and left it on his captain's desk. The next day the captain sent a letter to the New York City Police Commissioner's office. The commissioner's office filed an interdepartmental charge of conduct unbecoming an officer against Frankie and scheduled a hearing.

Frankie pleaded not guilty, but it didn't matter. He could still not erase the fact that he let his anger get the better of him. Although a year later he would be officially exonerated of the charge, as far as the police department was concerned his fate had been decided. He was demoted to patrol officer and transferred to a low-crime precinct.

As a final humiliation, my brother had to drive to police headquarters and turn in his gold badge. When he pulled into the parking lot, he sat in his car and stared at the badge in his hand. He remembered when he had shown it to Dad for the first time. It had linked them even more than the uniform.

At headquarters, the keeper of the shield room, a civilian, reached over his desk, took Frankie's badge and indifferently tossed it into a box—a cardboard coffin for dead careers.

"YOU GET LUCKY"

My brother's new assignment was the 50th Precinct in the Bronx. For Frankie, it was like being exiled. Not only was he back in a radio car, the biggest excitement on a tour might be what's called a cat call, a pet stuck in a tree. The 50th was then, and remains, among the quietest in the city.

Soon after he started at the five-oh he met the precinct's new commanding officer, Captain Aaron Rosenthal. He was considered a rising star in the department and as a commander wasn't about to put up with any insubordination among his troops. After about a week, Frankie was called into his office. My brother didn't know what to expect, but he didn't think it would be good.

As Rosenthal held up his file, Frankie felt a twinge of apprehension. "I just wanted you to know," the captain announced, "as far as I'm concerned, your career starts here and now."

It was the last thing my brother expected to hear and most likely the best thing his commander could have said. He quickly learned Rosenthal wasn't spouting empty words. He matched Frankie as a sort of mentor to rookies who showed promise. Among these was a young cop named Slattery. One day the two officers sat in a radio car, taking their lunch break. As they wolfed down their hero sandwiches, Frankie looked in the rearview mirror and noticed a man walking toward them.

The way he moved set off every one of my brother's alarms: the forced casual gait, the way he held his hands in his pockets. Frankie's instincts, from his days when he was the undisputed champion of "pick the perp," kicked in.

He rewrapped his sandwich and carefully placed it on the seat next to him. The young cop looked at his partner quizzically. In a voice just louder than a whisper, my brother announced, "We're taking this guy."

Frankie leapt from the car and was on his suspect before Slattery realized what was happening.

Amid a barrage of denials—"What're you doing, man? I didn't do nothing"—my brother began questioning him. At that moment, as if by script, the radio blared to life with a description of the man he had just stopped. He was wanted for a burglary.

As the two cops drove to the station house, the suspect cuffed in the back seat, Slattery sat slack-jawed. Finally the rookie spoke. "How did you know?"

"You get lucky," my brother answered.

If Frankie had any doubts about how he was doing, they were dispelled when Rosenthal paired him with another cop, newly assigned to the precinct. As the captain introduced the two, he said to the officer, "This guy I'm putting you with is one of the best cops I have. Don't bring him down."

BAG OF TRICKS

After his transfer, just about the only time I saw Frankie was when he was running along the tree-shaded streets of Pearl River, a solitary figure, head down, legs pumping. Sometimes, when I passed him, driving in my car, I'd beep the horn and he'd raise his hand in the air in acknowledgment.

I rarely talked to Frankie, and he hardly ever stopped over at the house for one of his once-cherished cop-to-cop talks with my father. There was nothing for either of them to say.

This self-imposed solitude helped him find a new clarity of purpose. His priorities shifted. Yes, being a good cop was still on his list, but it was no longer the most important thing in his life.

A couple of years earlier, he had decided to go back to school and enrolled in Rockland Community College. To his astonishment, Frankie discovered that he liked college. There, he found a new, broader world in which he could not only survive, but thrive.

After receiving an associate's degree, he promptly enrolled in St Thomas Aquinas College in Sparkill, N.Y., finishing in 1975 with a B.S. in social science.

During this period Frankie's prowess as a street cop eventually won him a shot at his precinct's Anti-Crime Unit. It was tame compared to the Street Crime Unit in the 34th, but it was better than the "cat calls." And going to work became fun again.

My brother's partner was the star of the unit, Artie Schwartz. The two hit it off right away. An engaging and energetic insomniac, Schwartz went full-bore 24 hours a day.

Together, they compiled an impressive record of quality arrests. Schwartz kept a careful, meticulous tally in a personal ledger, and by his count, they averaged 60 to 70 collars a year—notable numbers considering that the 50th probably was the quietest in the Bronx.

One element in their success was a small leather bag that Schwartz carried with him. He called it his bag of tricks. Although Frankie knew that it held his partner's logbook of arrests and an extra pair of handcuffs, he was never entirely sure of what else was in it.

He found out one night when some kids broke into a gas station and tried to escape by running into a nearby patch of woods.

When uniform cops were unable to flush them out, Schwartz became impatient. Standing at the edge of the woods he shouted, "Get the shotgun, Frankie." Then he removed an M-80 firecracker from his bag, lit the fuse and tossed it into the thicket.

When it exploded, the kids appeared like grouse from the brush and began running down a hill. Frankie and Schwartz took off after them. In terrific physical condition, Schwartz prided himself on his foot speed. My brother, also in top shape from his daily runs, was right behind, high-stepping over fallen trees and stumps.

For some reason, about 100 yards into the race, Schwartz began to let out war whoops, and Frankie imitated him. A few hundred yards more and they caught their suspects. Tackled and cowering on the ground, the thieves looked up in astonishment at the two men dancing and whooping around them.

In the fall of 1981, a few weeks after the chase, the precinct commander stopped Frankie in the station house. Headquarters had asked each precinct to recommend one or two cops for the Detective Division. "If you want the Division," the commander said, "it's yours."

For a moment my brother stood there dumb. He wasn't sure he was hearing correctly. Getting his gold shield back was something he had stopped thinking about. With more than 12 years on the job, he had become resigned to the notion that his police career would go no higher.

Not that it was so bad. He liked working with Schwartz, and he liked that with his studies he was building a future outside the police department.

His mind was a rush of memories: the sight of his badge being thrown into the cardboard box, the look of disappointment on Dad's face. Then his thoughts went to his partner.

"What about Schwartz?" he asked.

"If he wants it, he goes too," came the answer.

My brother got his gold shield back.

ATONEMENT

Life took another surprising turn the following summer when a fellow detective asked Frankie if he would like—temporarily—to teach his class at Rockland Community College for one semester. The course was in Criminalistics, more commonly known as forensics, the scientific side of investigation. Frankie jumped at the chance.

He took the textbook with him on vacation and read it from cover to cover. For three days before the first class, he wrote and rewrote his opening lecture in the same black-and-white marbled composition books in which he kept his case notes. He memorized it, practicing in front of a mirror.

The first day of school he wore his best blazer and khaki pants, trying to look less like a cop and more like a college professor. He was so nervous he kept his hands in his pockets because they were sweating. He forgot everything. His lecture lasted all of ten minutes. Flustered, he dismissed the class so they could go buy books.

As the semester went on, he found he didn't have to spend time memorizing lessons. Much of what he taught he already knew. When he didn't know something, he brought in guest lecturers—detectives, anti-crime cops and forensic experts— and learned along with his students. He even brought in an old squad commander to speak to his class—my father—who was in top form with his stories.

Frankie took a good-natured ribbing from the detectives in his squad who called him "professor," but he didn't mind. He liked teaching. It was a job that he often found more fulfilling than running after bad guys.

But generally it was always only a matter of time before my brother would pull an assignment that would again make being a cop the important thing in his life.

One such case came in the form of a missing child. On a summer night in 1985, eight-year-old Equilla Hodrick ran down her block in the Bronx, turned the corner and then disappeared.

The police brought in bloodhounds. One dog picked up her trail, which led to a hole in the fence near commuter train tracks. Frankie personally supervised an urgent three-hour search of a busy railroad tunnel with trains coming so close he could feel the suction as they went by.

"The Professor": what he learned on the streets of New York, Frankie now presents in a university classroom.

As the days passed, my brother and his partner conducted hundreds of interviews with neighbors, shop owners, family members, anyone who might offer the smallest clue about the girl's disappearance.

With the aid of a couple of Emergency Service cops, he searched nearly 50 abandoned buildings, storefronts and apartments. Equilla's mother, Terona Hodrick, insisted on coming along. Frankie sat next to her in the squad car promising her he would find her daughter.

For Frankie it was people like Terona who made being a detective so different from any other kind of police work. As a uniform and later as an undercover cop, he thought of victims as mere crime statistics. As a detective he saw them as individuals with lives and families.

He learned that in spite of the daily grind of simply surviving in such rough surroundings, Terona Hodrick was a loving, devoted mother who had put all her energy into creating a safe home for her daughter. A religious woman, she often prayed with her daughter at night, then gently stroked her back and sang her a lullaby until she dropped off to sleep.

My brother began stopping by her house at least once a day to give her updates, even though he could usually offer no more than support and optimistic words. Several weeks after Equilla's disappearance, on one of these visits, Frankie was struggling to offer words of comfort to the bereft mother when Terona draped her arms around him and hugged him. At first, he held her woodenly, but as she laid her head on his shoulder and he felt her moist sobs against his neck, tears filled his own eyes.

My brother became obsessed with the case. In every quiet moment, during every drive home, every time he sat at his desk at work, even in his dreams, Frankie saw Equilla's face. Her bright, engaging smile, her disarming hazel eyes, her delicately smooth brown skin haunted him. For Frankie it was more than a missing-child case; in some ways the search had become an act of atonement for that angry outburst one fateful night in Spring Valley.

Months passed. Interest in Equilla's case was kept alive by missing-children organizations; leads were still coming in. Frankie followed up every clue. None led anywhere.

In spite of this, he couldn't allow himself to believe the inevitable, that Equilla was dead. So he kept on searching. He talked to Terona four or five times a week.

Finally in 1986, approaching the 20-year mark as a policeman, Frankie realized he needed to get his life in balance, to spend more of it as a husband and father. He knew he had to leave the force.

In mid-January 1987, a week before his official retirement day, Frankie once again took out the 25-pound folder containing Equilla's case and placed it on his desk. He looked through it one last time, as if, magically, he would find the answer.

That afternoon, my brother went to see Terona Hodrick. He told her he was leaving the force and another detective would be assigned to the case. When she heard my brother's news, Terona shook her head back and forth. "Well, that's the end of it," she said simply. For a few moments they stood silently on her porch. Then my brother slowly walked down the steps.

It was one of the most painful moments of his career. Of all the assignments he had, he wanted to solve this one most. He wanted to find that little girl alive.

Fourteen years later, Equilla is still officially listed as missing. My brother has never forgotten her.

LAST ACT

On the evening of January 25, 1987, Frankie sat at a desk in the 48th Precinct house and gazed out the window at the traffic crawling across the Cross Bronx Expressway. Fat, swirling snowflakes bumped against the window.

Frankie and his partner, Detective Edward Blake, had been assigned to the Major Case Squad, a kind of detective all-star team. They were among several detectives who had been working for two solid days on the killing of a rookie patrolman, Michael Reidy. While off duty Reidy was robbed and murdered in the vestibule of his apartment building. Thus far, though, the police had no witnesses and few leads.

The evening of the second day a patrolman brought his girlfriend into the station. She said her brother had overheard someone bragging about murdering a cop.

Frankie and Blake were leery, but interested. They knew many murder investigations were solved on such seemingly vague information, and after three days of nothing they were ready to grab onto anything.

The brother confirmed her story, but could tell them little more except for the man's street name, Ski, and the fact that Ski had a half-brother in prison somewhere upstate.

The two detectives went back to their office and, beginning at ten that evening, methodically began phoning each upstate prison. For hours they called without success. Most offices had only a skeleton crew manning the phone and could tell them nothing.

A break came when a warden in one prison thought he might have something. He promised to get back after he checked his files.

He called at six the next morning. Frankie remembers the exact time because he had an 8am appointment at One Police Plaza to turn in his badge. Now, with the fresh lead, he wondered if he would be able to keep the appointment. And if he really wanted to.

The warden's prison file on the half-brother gave Ski's full name—Angel Maldonado—and his last known address. Minutes later the two detectives were at the front door of the building. The superintendent there wiped sleep from his eyes as he looked at Frankie's shield through the glass. Unimpressed, he didn't even bother opening the door.

Maldonado didn't live in the building anymore, he declared through the glass. "He moved out."

As the man began to walk away, my brother, furious, slammed his shield against the glass. "To where?"

For a moment, the man hesitated. Then the door opened and he gave Frankie his answer. Quickly a stakeout was mounted at the address the super gave. That day Angel Maldonado was arrested. (He was later convicted and sentenced to 25 years to life for Reidy's murder.)

At the precinct, the captain called my brother and his partner into his office to congratulate them. A press conference was planned, and he wanted them both there.

Frankie glanced at his watch. It was 9am. "I'm going to have to miss it," he said. "I'm already an hour late for my appointment."

As he drove his ten-year-old Nissan downtown through the heavy snow, my brother thought back over the past 20 years of his life. Memories came to him revised, edited like a eulogy. In them there was no frustration, no bureaucracy, no demotions or heart-wrenching unsolved cases, just the pure contentment he had always felt as a cop.

He turned off the East Side Drive, short of the exit for police headquarters and went to a phone booth. I'll call them, he said to himself, and tell them I've changed my mind.

But as he sat there his thoughts went to his wife, Pam. For so much of the past 20 years they had struggled together just to get by. His new job offer, working with security for an airline, would mean the struggle was over.

More than that, he realized that for all his married life his priorities had been too divided between being a good father and husband and being a good cop. Frankie knew he had no choice.

That day, about the time that Angel Maldonado was being booked for the murder of Michael Reidy, my brother was handing in his gold shield, bulletproof vest and service revolver.

And so ended nearly 100 years of police service in my family.

We are still a family defined by the badge and gun of the NYPD. Every Christmas Eve, Frankie hosts a family party. Everyone comes, but, sadly, last year there was one chair left empty. My mother had passed away.

Inevitably there comes a point in the day, after the plates of lasagna and roasted turkey are cleared, when Frankie and my father regale us with their war stories. Even though we've heard them many times, everyone in my family still leans forward in their chairs to listen. I'm sure somewhere my mother is rolling her eyes.

My brother's career as a cop continues to shape his life. Since his retirement he has continued working in academia part-time, teaching criminal justice, and now also serves as security director for a university. Every year in his classes, young scrubbed faces of every hue look toward him for guidance in the hope of fulfilling their own dreams of careers in law enforcement.

Every year Frankie begins each class of the semester with the same words: "A cop's life is not for everybody." Then he always adds, "But it was for me."

SPY
ON THE RUN →

BY DAVID WISE

FOR TEN YEARS HE RISKED
EXECUTION TO HELP AMERICA.
NOW THE CIA HAD TO GET HIM OUT.

I n a third-floor office of the Soviet embassy in Athens, Greece, military intelligence chief Georgi Maslovsky, 49, ran the morning staff meeting with brisk efficiency. After the others left on this Tuesday, May 21, 1985, Colonel Sergei Bokhan stayed behind to confer.

The powerfully built 43-year-old Bokhan was a model officer in the GRU, the Soviet military intelligence arm. Trained at the GRU academy in Moscow, he had years of experience in the field. Now, as a full colonel, he was Maslovsky's deputy, privy to all the GRU's operationsin Athens—a vital hub in Moscow's espionage network.

The two men chatted for a moment; then Maslovsky said casually, "By the way, Sergei, this cable came in." He tossed it to Bokhan, who read, "Please inform BYSTROV [Bokhan's code name] that his son has a problem in the military academy in Kiev." The cable suggested Bokhan take his vacation early and return to ·Moscow to straighten out the problem.

Bokhan froze. Only three days earlier his brother-in-law in Kiev had assured him that his 18-year-old son, Alex, was fine. Something's wrong, he told himself. *They know.*

Athens: the heart of the Soviet network.

THE SIGNAL

For ten years Bokhan had lived a dangerous double life as a spy for the CIA. A secret foe of the Soviet system, which he regarded as corrupt and repressive, he had provided the United States with information of enormous value. Yet he could tell no one—not even his wife, Alla. Sharing his secret would place her, their son and their ten-year-old daughter, Maria, in jeopardy. In the Soviet Union, spies were usually executed. A sudden recall to Moscow was a danger signal.

Maslovsky pressed Bokhan to leave as soon as possible. "How about Friday?" he asked.

"Georgi, I need time to prepare," Bokhan countered. "Let's do it Monday, and I'll have the weekend to get ready."

But Maslovsky would not be put off. "Call Aeroflot about a ticket for Friday," he insisted. "Alla and Maria can come later."

What happened next was ominous. When Bokhan called Aeroflot, the reservations clerk told him, "We are holding a ticket for Friday—Maslovsky called us yesterday."

The cable had come during the night. How had Maslovsky made the reservation before it arrived? Bokhan no longer doubted that the cable was a trap: Maslovsky had been ordered to send him back.

From home Bokhan telephoned a number the CIA had provided for an emergency. It rang inside the American embassy in Athens. As instructed, he asked for a fictitious employee—actually the owner of a nearby grocery store.

"You have the wrong number," a voice responded. Bokhan hung up. The CIA had been alerted.

THE MEET

At 53, Dick Reiser, Bokhan's case officer, might not have been taken for a spy— which suited him fine. A big, taciturn man, the Illinois native had served in Leningrad in the early 1970s and was fluent in Russian. His next overseas assignment was in Beirut; when civil war broke out there, Reiser and his wife were rolled up in rugs in a basement and hidden by friendly Arab neighbors until they could escape. Reiser's risky assignments and his espionage skills had earned him the respect of his CIA colleagues.

Now, preparing to meet Bokhan at a pre-arranged rendezvous, Reiser was worried. Bokhan had never used the emergency signal before.

Reiser kept an old brown Simca with Greek plates in a downtown garage. The car was "sterile," untraceable to the CIA. On the way to the meeting, Reiser drove a circuitous route, frequently checking his rearview mirror for Soviet or Greek security-service agents.

Bokhan, waiting in the shadows, jumped into the Simca. "I'm in trouble," he told Reiser. Quickly he filled his case officer in. Maybe, Bokhan speculated, the Soviets had a source inside the CIA who had given him away. Reiser said he would report to CIA headquarters in Langley, Virginia, and the two agreed to meet later in the week.

Reiser's message—a "restricted handling" cable—was received by Burton Lee Gerber, chief of the Soviet division, on Wednesday. But copies also went to the counter-intelligence group—where Aldrich Ames worked. The mole was now in a position to tip off the Russians.

THE PLAN

On Wednesday and Thursday, while Bokhan went to his office as usual, a debate took place at Langley. Some CIA officers thought Bokhan might be exaggerating the danger. He's too valuable, they argued. Let's keep him in place.

To Gerber, however, Bokhan's sudden recall was disturbing. An "exfiltration" was always tricky, but Gerber's instinct was to pull him out.

Reiser met with Bokhan late Thursday night. "If you want to come to the United States, we will help you," he said. "You decide."

Bokhan decided to escape.

Friday morning Bokhan purposely missed his flight. Back at the embassy, Maslovsky was upset. "It's OK—I'll go Monday," Bokhan said.

That night Bokhan met Reiser again and went over the escape plan. It would be at 4pm the next day. Bokhan was to drive to a shopping center and walk to a nearby pedestrian tunnel. The CIA would take over from there.

THE DAY

Saturday dawned hot in Athens. Bokhan attended a ceremony at Maria's school, marking the last day of classes. Then he drove his family to the seaside.

Bokhan had not told Alla about his escape plan. If she chose not to go and the KGB discovered she had known about it, he reasoned, his wife would be a criminal in Soviet eyes. But now, walking on the beach, he told Alla he was at a crucial point in his career. "Let's go to the West."

Shocked, Alla asked, "What country?"

"It doesn't matter," he replied. "'If you love somebody, you will have heaven even in a tent.'" It was an old Russian expression, but Alla was not buying it. Bokhan dropped the dangerous subject.

For lunch he ordered lobster and wine, knowing it might be the last meal they had together. Afterward, although time was running out, he stopped and bought Alla two gold bracelets and Maria a stuffed animal. Then they drove home.

At their apartment Bokhan removed a picture of Alex from the family photo album. Already in his sports bag was the camera that he had used that morning to take photos of his wife and Maria. At 3pm he picked up the bag and told Alla and Maria that he was going out to exercise. Kissing them both, he left. It was perhaps the most excruciating moment of his life.

THE JUMP

There was no time for regrets. Bokhan, the colonel, felt it was like a war. He had to do it. He drove around for about 40 minutes to be sure he was "clean," then dropped his car off and walked toward the 100-foot-long tunnel. At the other end Dick Reiser was waiting in the Simca. The streets leading to both ends of the tunnel sloped sharply downward. From his carefully chosen vantage point, Reiser had a clear view in all directions. Things were quiet. It was siesta time and almost nobody was around.

Reiser watched Bokhan walk into the tunnel. He got out of his car and waited. As soon as Bokhan emerged again, Reiser hustled him into the Simca and roared off.

A jacket, hat and sunglasses were in the back seat. Bokhan put them on as they drove to a safe house. After dark they went to a small airport where the CIA had a plane waiting. In moments Bokhan was airborne, leaving Greece, the GRU and the KGB behind.

In West Germany Bokhan boarded a military transport plane to Washington. As it touched down at Andrews Air Force Base, he peered out the window at a line of black cars. "Are they waiting for a big diplomat?" he asked.

"No, they're here for you."

Within hours Bokhan was being interviewed by CIA officers. He later had reason to remember one of them: Aldrich Ames.

Why hadn't the Soviet mole betrayed the exfiltration plan? "Ames knew," says Colin R. Thompson, a former Soviet-division officer. "It was discussed in a meeting that Ames was at. I sat there."

Thompson thinks there is a simple explanation: "Ames had no emergency means of communicating with the Soviets."

When Bokhan's disappearance was discovered, Alla and Maria were flown to Moscow. After months of interrogation the KGB decided Alla was innocent, but friends shunned her, and Alex was drummed out of the military academy.

Bokhan never lost hope that his family would be allowed to join him. Finally, after six years, in August 1991, the Soviet government agreed to let his wife and daughter go.

A few days later Alla and Maria were on a flight to New York. Maria, then 16, carried the stuffed animal her father had given her on their last day together. From the airport FBI agents drove them to the motel where Bokhan was waiting. He opened the door and said, "Welcome to America."

The tough ex-Soviet colonel had tears in his eyes.

Outed: Aldrich Ames had led a double life until his arrest exposed him as a spy.

Aldrich Ames was arrested for espionage on February 21, 1994, and is serving a life sentence. Alex was allowed to join his family in 1995. The Bokhans live under new names in a suburb of New York City.

TERRIFIED, THE YOUNG AMERICAN FOUGHT THROUGH
THE DENSE JUNGLE GROWTH. THE MEN WHO'D KILLED
HIS FRIEND WERE NOW STALKING HIM.

BY BOB TREBILCOCK

HUNTED
LIKE AN
ANIMAL

Josh Silver and Patchen Miller could smell the heat as the afternoon sun broiled the lush expanse of tropical rain forest. Their muscles still ached from fighting the swift, rain-swollen current of the quarter-mile-wide Marañón River in north-western Peru. Earlier that day the two young Americans had tied up their raft on a long, narrow island thick with towering grasses. Here they could rest and study the crude map they had been given by a trader, illustrating the Marañón's course north, then east, past the small Peruvian military checkpoints and Aguaruna Indian villages that dotted the shore.

This leg of their journey had begun two days earlier on January 16, 1995, when they launched the ten-by-15-foot raft they'd built themselves at Imazita, a Peruvian settlement just below the equator. Their goal was Iquitos, a port city on the Amazon—four to six weeks and 300 miles to the north-east.

Before departing, the two men heard disturbing rumors about an Indian attack on a French rafting expedition several years before. But they were assured that river travel was safe as long as they stayed on their raft.

A tall, athletic 26-year-old from Shelburne, Massachusetts, Josh Silver began boiling water for coffee. His companion, Patchen Miller, a budding writer in his mid-20s from East Thetford, Vermont, sat listening to the jungle's restive clamor. "Can you believe we're actually here?" Miller exclaimed.

Silver smiled. While most people their age were launching careers, neither he nor his friend was in a rush to finish college. There was so much of the world to explore. Both men took odd jobs to pay for their trips, which had included visits to remote parts of Ecuador and Nicaragua.

By 6pm the sun was setting as Silver served up pasta and sardines. The two men were cleaning their plates when Silver saw an Aguaruna Indian paddling his dug-out canoe in their direction. His legs stuck out of a dirty pair of blue shorts; a worn soccer jersey covered his ribs. Sharp-featured with high cheekbones and straight black hair, he appeared to be in his early 20s.

"Shall I try to talk to him?" Silver asked. On his travels into remote areas, good-will and honest curiosity had served him well. "Yes," Miller said. "Definitely."

"Would you like to come aboard?" Silver called in Spanish, not knowing the native language. The Indian smiled, then came alongside and climbed on to the raft.

While Miller poured the young man coffee, Silver asked him about his family. "We live along the bank, there," he said, gesturing upriver. He said he raised chickens and grew bananas.

The terrain began to rise, making each step harder still. As he labored for breath, he ran smack into another mass of vines. In frustration and anger, he pushed them aside and charged ahead into a clearing.

Silver froze. Not more than 40 feet away, a flashlight beam swept through the dense growth. An Aguaruna, his back to Silver, was staring at the commotion on the island. He held a shotgun under his arm. At any moment the Indian might turn and see him. Silver had to take a chance. He bolted back into the jungle, listening intently for pursuit.

Running parallel to the river, Silver noticed a hollow in the vegetation. He smeared his body with mud, burrowed in and waited, utterly still. A few minutes later he heard rustling. Something large—a man or an animal—was coming slowly through the brush. After what seemed a lifetime, the sound diminished and moved in the opposite direction.

Now Silver went higher into the jungle, until he came upon a well-worn footpath. *Finally,* he thought, *I can get out of this damned jungle!*

But after taking a few steps, he realized he'd blundered. If it's easy walking for me, it will be easy for them. He ran about 50 feet off the path, lay down and pulled ferns around him.

Soon a flashlight swept the path where he had stood earlier. He heard footsteps along the path and held his breath until they faded away.

Silver remained in his hiding place for nearly an hour. Thinking of Patchen, he felt himself giving way to tears. He fought to suppress them. If he was to escape, his thoughts had to be positive. He had to keep alert. This much was clear: he'd never make it upstream tonight, and it would be too dangerous in broad daylight.

Then he remembered the map. There was another military checkpoint downstream at Oracuza. Silver had no idea how far he was from the tiny post, but he thought it might be quicker to float downstream than to fight through the jungle upstream. It might also throw off his pursuers.

Cautiously he crept back to the river and began to swim sidestroke with the current. At first, the exertion warmed him. But within minutes the cold water exhausted him. If he didn't stop soon, his muscles would cramp, and he might drown.

A mile downstream, he saw a clearing in the jungle. Shivering, he dragged himself ashore and crawled under a five-foot-tall palm to wait until morning. His leg wound was raw, but the bleeding was now slight. However, he was concerned about dehydration. Although he'd had nothing to drink for several hours, he didn't dare sip from the muddy river. His options, then, were limited, but he had to get liquid somehow. Urinating into his cupped hands, he forced himself to drink the warm liquid. Ants swarmed over him, biting his back and legs.

For the first time since the shooting, the horror of what had happened sank in. *Patchen's probably dead, and I'm being hunted like an animal*, he thought. He was overcome by an intense sense of doom and a loss of innocence, as if the world had suddenly turned into a terrible place. *What were we thinking when we came here to this different world?* He had never felt more alone in his life.

At daybreak Silver slipped back into the water. A mile or so downstream, he saw an Indian on shore. *Should I ask for help?* Silver's first instinct was no. Then he reconsidered. Weak from loss of blood, he couldn't stay afloat much longer. *I'll have to take a chance that he's a friend*, he decided, swimming toward shore.

The Indian looked surprised to see a nearly naked white man wash up beside him. "Mister, I need help," Silver said in Spanish.

Since Silver's shorts covered his wound, the Aguaruna didn't realize Silver had been shot. Grinning, he started toward his thatched hut. "Come. You must meet my family."

"You don't understand," Silver pleaded. "My friend is dead. I've been shot. I need your help to get to the military post."

"I will take you downriver."

Before they left, the Aguaruna gave Silver a clean, dry shirt—an extravagant gesture in one of the poorest areas of the world—then solemnly ferried him downstream to the military base.

At Oracuza, two Peruvian soldiers helped Silver out of the canoe. An officer joined them. "What happened?" he asked in Spanish.

"My friend and I were shot," Silver blurted, tears surging from his eyes.

"Take him to the infirmary," the officer ordered the two soldiers.

Silver continued to cry, releasing all the emotion he had stored up during the previous night. *I'm safe*, he thought. *Safe at last.*

After recuperating from his wounds in a local hospital, Silver was debriefed at the US embassy in Lima. On January 26 he arrived on crutches in Hartford, Connecticut, where he was greeted by his family.

Patchen Miller's body was never found. Only days after the incident, a border war broke out between Ecuador and Peru, sidetracking an investigation for almost six months. Peruvian police have now jailed three Aguarunas in connection with Miller's murder.

JUSTICE IN MARENGO COUNTY

BY HENRY HURT

A CRUSADING EDITOR AND HIS WIFE PAID THE PRICE
FOR INVESTIGATING THE POWERFUL AND POPULAR
LOCAL SHERIFF. THE DAY OF RECKONING WOULD
SURELY COME, BUT WOULD THEY BE ALIVE TO SEE IT?

Anger and confusion rippled through Jean Sutton as she looked into the eyes of the brawny young man in the police uniform. He stood six feet, four inches, and the smirk on his face now was the faintest shadow of the smile she remembered when she knew him as a little boy. Something in his blue eyes was different today.

"You know something, Jean," she recalls Sonny Breckenridge saying in a slow, easygoing voice, "if y'all don't quit writing that stuff about the sheriff, you're gonna wake up one morning at two o'clock and find your house surrounded."

Then, still smiling, he added: "And I believe you know what we'll find. And we can do the same thing in your office." His smirk faded to a somber cast.

She had sensed it before, and now Breckenridge's words confirmed what Jean Sutton and her husband, Goodloe, had hoped was not so.

There's no doubt, she thought. *This is a threat to plant drugs in our house and in our office.* And she knew that where drugs were seized, the property could also be confiscated.

Jean was certain Breckenridge was not joking. As the chief drug enforcement officer in the sheriff's department, he had complete access to an evidence room full of confiscated drugs.

And there was something else she felt sure about. The threat was a clear message from Breckenridge's boss, Sheriff Roger Davis.

At that moment, she and Breckenridge were standing in the front lobby of the stately, high-columned Marengo County Courthouse in the rural west Alabama town of Linden. Although a small town—two traffic lights and a population of 2,700—it is the county seat.

It was around noon. Breckenridge had called out to Jean as she was hurrying out of the courthouse to write up the morning's events for *The Democrat-Reporter*, the aggressive weekly paper she and her husband, Goodloe, published.

Infuriated at his arrogance, Jean Sutton, an even-tempered woman with slate-blue eyes said, "The only way you'll find drugs on our property is if you bring them. And if you try that, you'll be looking down the barrel of a 12-gauge shotgun."

As she walked away, Breckenridge broke out in what sounded to her like nervous laughter.

Still angry, she crossed the street to the small, glass-fronted *Democrat-Reporter* building. When she saw her husband, she announced, "You won't believe what Sonny Breckenridge just said to me." Then she repeated the threat.

"I wasn't really surprised," Goodloe says. "I knew we were headed in that direction from the day we ran that first story exposing Davis."

SHERIFF VS. EDITOR

A big man who stood six feet, three inches and weighed 230 pounds, Roger Davis had been an Alabama state trooper for more than 26 years. Most of that time he was assigned to the state driver's license bureau, located in Marengo County, where he dealt with people who had lost their licenses due to either revocation or to expiration.

Davis had overcome substantial obstacles to become a respected police officer, family man, member of the church choir and Mason. He was proud of the fact that he had scrambled up out of a dirt-poor farming background in rural Wilcox County.

He was also a haunted man. Friends said Roger Davis was terrified of being poor again. Money, and having it, held a special significance for him. Perhaps that was one reason he was always looking for a way to get more. There were rumors that, while a state trooper, he even sold jewelry out of the trunk of his patrol car to make a little extra cash.

At the end of his long career as a trooper, Davis had decided to run for sheriff of Marengo County. Presenting himself as a reform candidate, he had promised to bring a fresh professionalism to the sheriff's department.

Breaking story: the Suttons unleash a whirlwind of controversy.

A lot of people liked Davis. He had a way of talking that made the listener feel that he was taking a special interest in him.

The Suttons treated Davis like any other candidate running for sheriff— writing impartial articles, citing his long experience in law enforcement as well as his established role in the community.

It was not surprising, then, that he was elected sheriff with strong support throughout the jurisdiction. He beat the incumbent with 56 per cent of the vote— a success due in part to Davis's shrewd political alliance with a promising young black lawyer, Barrown Lankster, soon to become district attorney.

After he took office in 1991, Sheriff Davis quickly placed his stamp on his new regime. He had his name emblazoned on the side of each patrol car and began replacing the old-line deputies with his own men. Davis also gave all deputies a paper to sign. It was a statement saying they agreed they would not speak to the press on any matter.

A few days later, according to Goodloe Sutton, the newly elected sheriff walked across the street to the office of *The Democrat-Reporter* and announced to Sutton: "From now on you don't need to use any names from the sheriff's office in your paper but mine." Feeling more beholden to his readers than to the sheriff, Sutton decided he would honor that request as he and his wife pleased.

Despite the gag order on his employees, Davis never objected to one deputy talking to the press: Wilmer Keith Breckenridge. Known all of his life as Sonny, he had been a popular football player in high school and was a lifelong friend of the Suttons'. Before going to work for Davis at the age of 23, the young man had been a police officer in Demopolis, the largest town in

Power of the press: Goodloe Sutton delivers local good tidings, and attacks hypocrisy, in *The Democrat-Reporter*.

324

Marengo County. He had married a smart and pretty girl who became a well-regarded schoolteacher.

The sheriff put Breckenridge in charge of drug enforcement, working with another newly appointed officer, Robert Pickens. The two launched an aggressive campaign to rid Marengo County of drugs and dealers.

Breckenridge even went into local schools and lectured to children about the dangers of drugs. He took along confiscated drugs and drug paraphernalia, using them as props in his talks.

The Suttons conscientiously reported the triumphs of the sheriff and his men, trumpeting their crime fighting—especially their stepped-up campaign against drugs.

But Goodloe and Jean heard other more disturbing stories, ones they were less eager to report. Tips came to them ever so quietly, mixed in with courthouse gossip—disturbing stories about Sheriff Davis.

The Suttons at first dismissed them. Considering his long and solid record of public service, some of the stories were difficult to believe. "What we cared about most was what he was doing to make things better in Marengo County," says Goodloe. "We were happy to see Roger Davis aggressively going after drugs and crime."

But the reports persisted. The couple began to check into them, and a darker side of the lawman gradually began to emerge.

STAINS OF CORRUPTION

In his first year in office, Davis bought an expensive Christmas present for his 16-year-old daughter: a 3,000 dollar four-wheeler, a lawn-mower-size, all-terrain vehicle used to race around fields and woods. What made it noteworthy to the Suttons was they learned he paid for it with county funds.

Before the Suttons could piece together enough of the story to run it, Davis went back to the dealer and replaced the county's money with a personal check.

While the Suttons had the four-wheeler story cold, they did not print it immediately for two reasons. Sheriff Davis was brand-new in the job and may have made a mistake and then corrected it. Second, and more important, one of the Suttons' sources for the story was concerned about being fired by Sheriff Davis.

Davis's defenders dismissed the matter, claiming he was only trying to avoid paying the state sales tax, since the sheriff's office was exempt. The Suttons weren't so sure.

Over the ensuing months and years, Goodloe and Jean heard about other questionable situations.

In one case, the Suttons got a tip that one of the sheriff's paid auxiliary deputies was a convicted felon. As such, he was prohibited by law from having a gun. When asked about it, Sheriff Davis told *The Democrat-Reporter* that they were wrong—that no felony convictions showed up when he checked the man's records.

So the Suttons found the records showing he was a felon on their own and detailed them in an article—which also showed a photo of the pistol-packing felon performing his duties in uniform, his gun in plain sight. Davis fired the deputy.

Then there were tips that Sheriff Davis was abusing his access to the county's drug enforcement fund, used by the sheriff's department to make undercover drug buys. When Jean Sutton got access to the Marengo County Sheriff's Department ledgers, she saw that they contained some interesting entries: reimbursements made from Roger Davis personally to the sheriff's department "as per audit." Jean had known that the state of Alabama was auditing Davis's office, and these entries confirmed what was being whispered and hinted at around the courthouse: Davis had been ordered by the state to repay the drug fund nearly 5,000 dollars.

The Democrat-Reporter ran a front-page story that included a copy of the sheriff's department ledger showing Davis's repayments. In a published interview, Jean Sutton asked Davis what had happened to the money the county had entrusted to him. Davis never gave a straight answer.

Later, Jean said, "That was the crux of it all: what had happened to the taxpayers' money?" To the Suttons it seemed clear that Davis had made the county's money his own.

In a particularly embarrassing case, *The Democrat-Reporter* reproduced a letter signed by Sheriff Davis requesting that the West Alabama Mental Health Center make out "donation" checks to him personally whenever his deputies transported their "insanes." When the scam was exposed, Davis quickly repaid the 700 dollars he had pocketed. What made the matter outrageous was that the checks, rather than being deposited into sheriff's department accounts, had been cashed at various local businesses, including a grocery store called Papa's Foods. As the state auditor ordered Davis to straighten out his books and repay the money, the Suttons forcefully reported these improprieties.

After Davis had reimbursed the county, he went back about his business. During the exposés by the Suttons, he assumed the pose of a long-suffering public servant set upon by jackals of the press. He made almost no public statements about any of the articles—preferring instead to let his deputies whisper around the county that the reports were lies fabricated by Goodloe and Jean Sutton.

The Suttons were disgusted by Davis's claims of innocence each time he was exposed. Goodloe said that it was "like a thief, caught leaving the scene of the robbery, who runs back and returns what he stole, claiming he never did anything wrong. The thief usually doesn't get off—but Roger Davis did."

One reason the sheriff was not brought to account was that District Attorney Barrown Lankster, Davis's ally, didn't believe there was sufficient evidence to prosecute. Knowing it was unlikely that Lankster would ever prosecute, Goodloe Sutton began taking his stories and the supporting evidence directly to state authorities.

He and Jean even made personal visits to the Alabama attorney general and the Alabama Ethics Commission, each time presenting a meticulously assembled package of evidence.

In spite of all their efforts, nothing significant seemed to happen. "It was unbelievable that no one cared," says Goodloe Sutton. "But that's where we were at the end of the sheriff's first term."

Yet after years of battling, it never occurred to either of the Suttons to give up. "I believed that in the end good had to prevail," says Jean. "There was no way Roger Davis could keep on fooling so many people." She and Goodloe were in it for the long haul.

For Goodloe it was just a matter of time. From boyhood, his favorite hunting quarry had been the wild turkey—one of the craftiest birds there is. Sutton had long ago learned the secret of a successful hunt: be perfectly patient and wait for the bird to make the wrong move.

When it came to Sheriff Davis, Goodloe Sutton, the wily turkey hunter, was willing to watch and wait as long as it took.

TRADITION OF OUTRAGE

Taking on an unpopular cause was nothing new to the Sutton family. In 1963 Goodloe watched his father stand tall on a tough issue while the civil-rights movement was exploding across the Deep South. Marengo County is intersected by US Highway 80—an east-west strip of asphalt that, during the '60s, sang with the chants of marching civil-rights workers.

To the east of Marengo County lie Selma and the infamous Pettus Bridge, which, to some, was the flash point of the civil-rights movement. To the west on US 80 were the Mississippi towns of Meridian and Philadelphia—violent strongholds of the Ku Klux Klan during those years.

The trouble in Goodloe's hometown started when someone asked Joe Patterson, the pastor in the Suttons' church, what he would do if a black family wanted to worship with the congregation.

Patterson said that he would welcome them. He would never turn down an opportunity to spread the word—regardless of skin color. The Board of Deacons of the Linden Baptist Church felt otherwise and set a policy to limit the presence of black people.

Patterson disagreed and wrote in the church bulletin that he could not with good conscience turn anyone away. "To do otherwise," he wrote, "would be to reduce Christ to little more than a Southern gentleman and the church to nothing more than a social club." Shortly afterward, a cross was burned in his yard.

Among those who supported Patterson was Robert Sutton, Goodloe's father, who taught Sunday school. When the pastor eventually resigned and departed for a church in Juneau, Alaska, Goodloe's father went out of his way to praise Patterson on the front page of his paper.

"My father made a lot of people mad and the newspaper lost business, but he stood by Joe Patterson," Goodloe says. "It was a good lesson to me in how you have to stick by your guns."

Both high principles and newspapering had been part of Goodloe Sutton's life from the day he was born. His father had bought *The Democrat-Reporter* in 1917. Goodloe grew up almost in the shadow of the Marengo County Courthouse. The family's house stood only about 100 feet to the east of where the newspaper office is today.

Unstoppable: chief reporter Jean Sutton, a formidable force who fills the front page.

Running a small-town paper was such a family tradition that by the time he was six, Goodloe began working at *The Democrat-Reporter*'s office. Today, sitting in his tiny office, the thin wall trembling as the presses roar in the big room just behind him, he recalls, "When I was real little, I swept the floors in the press room and stacked papers." When he was older, he went out on the streets and hawked the paper at a nickel a copy.

After Goodloe went off to college, he met Jean Rodgers, a blond, blue-eyed girl who worked on the student newspaper at the University of Southern Mississippi. He married her in 1964, and the two settled easily into small-town life in Linden.

In the early years, Jean taught at the high school and worked with her husband at the paper. After the first of their two sons was born, the paper and her family became her life.

Now the managing editor of *The Democrat-Reporter*, Jean Sutton is also the chief reporter, and her work usually fills much of the front page. It never bears a byline, but that's how she prefers it. And, like their father, the couple's two sons became involved in the newspaper at an early age—sweeping floors, stacking papers, filling newsstand racks at first, and later taking pictures and writing stories.

Many people in the town of Linden like to say that "Miss Jean" does most of the work while "Ole Goodloe" sits back and stirs up trouble.

Jean denies the first charge, saying that her husband plays an enormous role setting the policy of the paper and selecting stories. As for stirring up trouble, Goodloe concedes his capacity for general orneriness, but explains: "What we do is report the news. If it stirs up trouble, so be it. The newspaper business is not a popularity contest."

No one stays mad for too long at Goodloe, however. Because of his basic, down-to-earth style, people keep talking to him. A deadpan look, a twinkle in his eye and the easy Southern cadence of his voice help him ask hard questions and venture his own ideas.

As the weekly newspaper's deadline approaches on Tuesday, however, his easy-going façade falls away when he sits at his computer keyboard. In a journalistic style harking back to the late 19th century, Goodloe Sutton as editor and publisher comes out swinging in his weekly editorial—lambasting injustices, lampooning fools and scorning official incompetence.

As always, he is guided by what he sees as the best course for Marengo County—including honest and professional law enforcement.

This philosophy has served *The Democrat-Reporter* well. Since Jean and Goodloe took over the paper in the mid-'60s, its circulation has increased from 1200 to a high of 7500.

In the intervening years, life was generally good for the Suttons. Their newspaper business was successful. Their two sons were healthy and happy. Goodloe, Jr., finished college and went to work in Montgomery, and William was doing well in school.

But by the spring of 1991, the Suttons' investigations of corruption had triggered a series of events that began to darken their lives.

PARIAH

"When are you going to leave our sheriff alone?" Goodloe stared at the man, a longtime friend, a member of the Presbyterian church where Goodloe had taught adult Sunday school for years. In a friendly way the man explained how wrong Goodloe was about Sheriff Davis—and how important it was for him to drop his series of stories chronicling the sheriff's misdeeds.

"I heard this over and over," Sutton says. In spite of all the responsible, carefully documented reporting he and his wife had done, people still trusted and liked Roger Davis. As the Suttons soon learned, the support for the popular sheriff could be ferocious.

One scathing letter blasted the Suttons for the "negative, biased and slanted" reporting in *The Democrat-Reporter*. The writer went on: "Sheriff Davis is a good, honest, and most important of all, Christian man. This is the type person we want, and intend to keep, as our sheriff."

Keeping pace with the stories about Davis were hate-filled anonymous telephone calls and letters threatening violence against the Suttons and their sons.

One of the anonymous letters stated: "You are brave people with your pens in your pocket, but I wonder how brave you will be when someone catches you in a place where there are no witnesses. ... Remember, your day will come soon."

The price the Suttons were paying was getting steeper by the day. Friends began to ostracize them. Even those closest to the Suttons thought they were a little too obsessed with the sheriff and stories of corruption. "We figured Goodloe was butting his head against the wall," one said. "But that's the way he is sometimes."

For the first time since Jean and Goodloe took over the paper, circulation of *The Democrat-Reporter* was declining. Local businesses started pulling their ads. Advertising revenues fell about 1,000 dollars each week—a significant drop for a small publication like theirs.

By 1994 they had been reporting on the sheriff's activities for so long they believed the statute of limitations on some of the early incidents they had covered had expired. Yet as far as they could tell, no legal authority beyond the state auditor had done anything to follow up on their accusations.

The Suttons felt there was no place to turn for help. "Who would we go to? The sheriff?" Jean asked. "To the D.A.? To the attorney general we'd already visited three times?"

Increasingly it came down to a basic question: did people believe what they were reading in *The Democrat-Reporter*, or did they believe the sheriff's men who said it was all lies?

An answer, perhaps, would come with the election of 1994. The Suttons wondered: could Sheriff Davis keep his office as he faced two strong challengers?

As election day drew near, the sheriff rolled out his most popular issue: his war against drugs. And thanks to the Suttons' fair-minded coverage, the names of Davis and Sonny Breckenridge were continually burned in the public's mind as the first line of defense against illegal drugs.

Sonny's reputation as a crime fighter had taken on heroic proportions among family and friends. His parents, Julia and Wilmer Breckenridge, spent hours every evening listening to their police scanner tracking the exploits of their son as he cruised the county busting crime.

"We followed it just the way we used to follow his football games in high school," explains his mother. "Sonny was cleaning up Marengo County. Anyone will tell you that."

Helped by his deputy's work, Roger Davis won the three-way race for sheriff and almost immediately promoted Sonny Breckenridge to sergeant.

His re-election was a bitter disappointment to Jean and Goodloe Sutton. It looked as though they had hardly made a dent in public opinion.

By this time, anyone else might have given up. But, savvy turkey hunter that he was, Goodloe had spent too many hours to be deterred. "We just kept watching them, and they just kept watching us," says Sutton.

However, Goodloe thought, if justice was going to be served, help had to come from somewhere other than Marengo County. And, unbeknown to him and to his wife, Jean, that is exactly what was happening.

THE NIGHT HAS EYES

Around midnight late one fall evening, a lone car drove slowly down a long dead-end road to an isolated airfield that was situated in a remote part of Marengo County. Waiting for it was one man, Marengo County Deputy Jesse Langley. He squinted to make out the car, and to be sure there were no others following it.

In Sheriff Davis's department, Langley was unique. After Davis's re-election, one of his first moves was to fire all the remaining deputies from the last administration—with the exception of Jesse Langley.

A quiet, serious man, he had worked for the sheriff's office in Marengo County for over 20 years. He was not only widely respected for doing his job fairly and for staying out of politics, he was a local hero. His courage had met the ultimate test— and he had the wounds to prove it.

Jesse had lost an eye when he took a shotgun blast to the face while protecting a woman from an enraged man. Losing blood fast and still in the line of fire, Langley backed his patrol car up to protect the woman, whose own vehicle had been shot and was now in flames. He shouted for her to get in his car. Then, slumped over and bleeding on the passenger's side, he told her to drive.

As she sped to the hospital, Langley, blinded in one eye and nearly unconscious from the loss of blood, managed to radio a warning about the berserk shooter to fellow police officers rushing to the scene.

From that day on, his bravery was unquestioned. For his part, Davis was shrewd enough to know that to fire someone as respected as Langley could provoke a firestorm of public outrage. But he also may have suspected, correctly, that Langley had been the source of some of the material that the Suttons had developed into stories for their paper.

Within a year of his injury, Langley was assigned to oversee the county jail. He couldn't help wondering if Davis had given him the new assignment so he would have limited contact with the other officers and thus could glean little.

It didn't matter. Jesse hunkered down, listening and looking. He was still able to uncover information even in his new assignment.

On this particular night, as he had on so many others, Langley was there to meet George Barrows, a special agent with the Alabama attorney general's office who had been assigned to figure out what was going on in Roger Davis's sheriff's department. The assignment came from Jeff Sessions, Alabama's new attorney general, who was acting behind the scenes in response to one of the Suttons' appeals for help. While the statute of limitations may have run out on some old incidents, Barrows was convinced that the pattern was continuing.

An honest man: Deputy Jesse Langley dared to expose his corrupt sheriff.

A slim, elegant man who had served many years as an agent for the US Treasury Department before retiring to his native Alabama, Barrows had already spent hundreds of hours trying to piece together evidence about Davis's activities, starting with the stories that were published in the Suttons' newspaper.

Barrows learned that Deputy Jesse Langley was an honest man who might be willing to help. One night Barrows called him at home and asked for a meeting at an out-of-town motel. There, Barrows outlined his suspicions about the sheriff.

"Langley said I was on the right track, but he didn't want to help if nothing was going to happen,"

Barrows recalled. "I promised Jesse that the attorney general and I were going to see this through to a conviction."

With that reassurance, Langley agreed to pass on what he learned. For months he met regularly with Barrows at the old airfield.

It was a high-risk undertaking. No one doubted that if Langley's meetings were uncovered, Davis might exact revenge. "We felt they were capable of anything," says Barrows. "Jesse was the man on a tightrope, yet he never flinched."

Also at risk were the Suttons. In spite of continued anonymous threats, they sought no formal protection from the state of Alabama. Says Goodloe: "William was just starting high school, and we weren't going to have him grow up with all the fear and hate that was around us. Our faith was strong that we were doing the right thing, and we lived by it."

Because of constraints of confidentiality, Barrows could not let the Suttons know what he was working on. Still, late at night he would drive by their house, just to be sure things were okay.

And he was not the only one in law enforcement who was interested in the Marengo County Sheriff's Department.

Down in Mobile, a long, lean lawyer named E.T. Rolison had become an avid reader of the stories in *The Democrat-Reporter* while visiting his mother at his boyhood home in Choctaw County, which was west of Marengo.

As a veteran criminal prosecutor in the US Attorney's office he began to take a professional interest in them. "Those stories had red flags all over them," he says.

His office felt that the Suttons were onto something that was more than just small-time corruption. "They smelled a skunk and had the nerve to print what they knew," recalls Rolison. "It was up to us to fill in the details."

Since his investigations were also secret, he could not tell Jean and Goodloe, or anybody else in Marengo County, what his office was doing. But he, too, was uneasy about the safety of the Sutton family.

Without their knowing it, Jean, Goodloe and their two sons had guardian angels who were looking out for them.

OUT OF CONTROL

Oblivious to all this scrutiny, Sheriff Davis felt so comfortable in his second term, he started behaving as though he were completely untouchable by the law. Some of his deputies seemed to feel the same.

In December, 1995, the sheriff's crack narcotics team of Breckenridge and Robert Pickens made a bold move, according to testimony later presented in a federal trial:

Deputy Pickens contacted a man named Cedric Jones. A local drug dealer, Jones based his operations in a run-down community called Uniontown, just over the Marengo County line.

Early one cold morning, Pickens and Breckenridge sat down with Jones at a Burger King in Selma, 30 miles east of Marengo County. After they ordered breakfast, the two lawmen then offered the dealer a proposition: protection for his drug operations in exchange for a share of his profits. For a fee of 1,000 dollars per month, Breckenridge promised to direct patrolling deputies away from wherever Cedric Jones was buying and selling dope. Not long afterward, they made similar protection arrangements with two other dealers.

To keep up the number of their arrests, says Pickens, the two deputies busted small-time operators, or sometimes just people that they marked as dealers. In one raid, Pickens testified through a DEA agent, he saw Breckenridge plant cocaine in a house where a police officer would be sure to find it. These petty raids—and there were dozens—were conscientiously reported in the Suttons' paper.

Sheriff Davis was busy also, hatching an extortion scheme. After his 1994 re-election, he approached Beverly Jo Rhodes and her husband, James, who operated a bail-bonding business in Marengo County and a fruit stand, and made them an offer.

If they would pay him a percentage of their profits, he could shut out their competition, making them the only bonding business in the county. As sheriff he would be able do this by simply refusing to allow other bonding businesses to operate.

The Rhodeses agreed, and paid Davis 25 per cent of the fee on each bond. For example, if they wrote a bond for 10,000 dollars, they received ten per cent, or 1,000 dollars. Of that, Sheriff Davis got 250 dollars. This meant that when Breckenridge and Pickens made a small-time drug bust, the suspects very likely posted bond with the Rhodeses. Part of that money would go straight into the sheriff's pocket.

On collection day, Davis sometimes made an innocent-sounding phone call. "I'll be coming for some peaches," he would say. It was a coded message to Beverly Jo Rhodes in case the telephone lines were tapped. To her it meant the sheriff was on his way to her fruit stand to pick up his extortion money.

Davis would show up, put a few items in a sack and then make his way to Beverly Jo at the cash register. There he would hold his sack open as she or her husband stuffed money into it.

Other times, the Rhodeses would pay off the sheriff during one of their visits to the jail, or Sheriff Davis would meet Beverly Jo at some isolated area.

Eventually the sheriff got greedier and increased his extortion rates. In 1996 alone, law enforcement officers estimate, he collected more than 20,000 dollars.

Midnight rendezvous: Special Agent George Barrows at the scene of his airfield meetings.

This did not escape the attention of George Barrows, who had gained legal access to the sheriff's bank records and was impressed with how much Davis had managed to sock away on a salary of 35,000 dollars.

According to Pickens's testimony, he and Breckenridge decided to up the ante as well: not satisfied with the protection money, the narcotics officers planned to become drug suppliers.

At first Breckenridge took the confiscated crack cocaine from the jail's evidence room and sold it to the dealers he was protecting. When he and Pickens discovered the demand for marijuana was increasing in Marengo County, they decided to fill that market niche.

Pickens met with a marijuana wholesaler named Wild Man—a ferocious-looking character with long hair, a beard and tattoos all over his body. He had agreed to supply the deputies.

On May 16, 1997, Sonny Breckenridge gave Pickens 4,000 dollars in cash to buy the marijuana. To it Pickens added 4,000 dollars of his own.

Later that day, Pickens drove to meet Wild Man near the Mississippi state line. He handed the dealer a roll of bills totaling 8,000 dollars. In return, Wild Man gave him a package containing ten pounds of marijuana. As Pickens got into his car and drove slowly away, Wild Man, who was in fact a state agent, drove in the opposite direction, signaling his colleagues to move in on Pickens. Cars filled with state and federal agents crowded Pickens's rearview mirror.

In a road chase at speeds reaching 100 miles per hour, Lieutenant Ed Odom of the Alabama Bureau of Investigation finally caught up with Pickens as they approached the Tombigbee River. When Pickens cut his car into Odom's cruiser, Odom countered and sent Pickens's car off the road and crashing down an embankment. Lieutenant Odom's car followed.

Seriously injured, Pickens ended up in the hospital under guard and was later transferred to jail. *The Democrat-Reporter* screamed the news.

After Pickens's capture, Breckenridge let it be known that if anyone tried to arrest him, "they'd better come shooting." Thirteen days later, on May 29, at 5am, federal and state agents, heavily armed and wearing bulletproof vests, quietly surrounded Sonny's apartment, where he and his wife lived.

When everyone was in place, an agent took out his cell phone and called Breckenridge, waking him. The message was simple: Sonny was surrounded and was to come out peacefully. Moments later, Sergeant Breckenridge almost broke the door down to get outside and surrender to the authorities. He was handcuffed and arrested on a number of federal drug counts—including possession of marijuana and crack, as well as conspiracy to distribute a controlled substance.

Just moments after Breckenridge was taken into custody, an army of state and federal agents descended on suspected drug dealers who were part of a ring centered in Uniontown. Subsequent arrests radiated as far west as Los Angeles and as far north as Detroit. Jean and Goodloe Sutton's newspaper stories helped to set off a chain of events that shattered a major drug and conspiracy operation stretching from the gulf coast all the way to Los Angeles.

In the aftermath of the raids, rumors swept Marengo County that Sheriff Roger Davis had been arrested too. But he was untouched and went about his daily routine, seemingly unfazed by the arrest of two of his star deputies for drug dealing.

To the Suttons, it was incredible that Sheriff Davis had not been brought to justice for his misdeeds.

SECRET POCKET

On August 13, 1997, while two of his men were on trial in Mobile, Sheriff Davis told Beverly Jo and James Rhodes to come to his office. He led the couple to an adjoining room, explaining in a lowered voice that he suspected that his office and car were bugged.

What Sheriff Davis did not know was that the Rhodeses themselves had been fully wired by the Alabama attorney general's office and the FBI. Everything the sheriff said, including comments confirming his extortion payments, was being taped.

A few days later, on the morning of August 22, 1997, Sheriff Davis told his secretary he was going out for an eye appointment. That very day a jury in Mobile was deliberating the fate of his deputy, Sergeant Sonny Breckenridge.

Sheriff Davis had already phoned Beverly Jo Rhodes saying he would like to "pick up some peaches." This time he told her to meet him on the outskirts of Marengo County.

As the sheriff pulled out of the parking lot, Jesse Langley picked up a phone and punched in a number. "He's on his way," he announced.

While the sheriff's black, unmarked police car headed to the rendezvous point, a surveillance plane glided overhead. State and federal agents followed in unmarked cars and vans. In one of them was investigator George Barrows.

The officers watched as Davis eased his vehicle next to Beverly Jo Rhodes's car. She handed a roll of money out of her window and told the sheriff that there was 975 dollars in it.

Davis, always courteous and meticulous, thanked her and said that he thought she only owed him 900 dollars.

Rhodes shrugged, saying the extra 75 dollars was to ensure that they could keep doing business in the future.

Smiling, Davis took the money and turned his car out of the lot. As he eased onto a ramp leading to a highway, he saw an unmarked car blocking the road. Davis stopped.

Out of the car stepped George Barrows. He walked over to the sheriff's car. "Turn off the car and put your hands on the dashboard," he commanded.

Davis said nothing, but did as he was told.

Barrows then stepped back. Two FBI agents came forward, took the sheriff from the car and clicked handcuffs on him.

It took four hours of tearing the vehicle apart, but the agents found what they were looking for: the payoff money. Barrows explains: "It was in a secret, specially made pocket between the front of the door and the windshield." Roger Davis had customized a police car to carry extortion money.

It was after lunch when the first calls came in to *The Democrat-Reporter*'s office. Friends of the Suttons' phoned to say they had heard rumors that Sheriff Davis had just been arrested. Goodloe started making calls, and confirmed that the FBI had arrested the sheriff and were taking him to Mobile to arraign him on federal extortion charges.

Hearing the news, Jean and Goodloe both felt drained. They had little to say to the dozens of people who began calling to congratulate them after all those lonely years.

"There was no sense of jubilation that we were right," recalls Goodloe. "We both just felt an overwhelming relief."

JUSTICE AT LAST

Without a whimper Roger Davis pleaded guilty to a federal extortion charge, as well as state tax-evasion and bribery charges. In church some time after, Davis stood up and announced to the congregation that although he had done nothing wrong, he was pleading guilty for the good of his family and Marengo County. He was sentenced to 27 months in prison and ordered to pay 43,671 dollars in fines, back taxes and restitution.

As for Sonny Breckenridge, he was offered a 12-year sentence if he'd plead guilty to lesser charges. He refused.

Sharp-eyed: Prosecutor E.T. Rolison sensed a bigger story.

In his trial, Breckenridge spent hours on the witness stand, seemingly at ease and often smiling at friends and family in the courtroom—at practically everyone but the Suttons. He denied every charge.

In the end it didn't matter. Cedric Jones, Sonny's former partner Deputy Pickens and others appeared as chief witnesses against him. The jury found Breckenridge guilty of two counts of conspiracy to distribute illegal drugs, and one count of possession. (He was acquitted of seven other counts.)

Many people still could not believe their local hero and drug enforcer was capable of such crimes. On the day of sentencing several months later, the federal courtroom in Mobile was packed with around 100 of Sonny's friends and family members. With great compassion, Judge Charles Butler said he respected the feelings of those who had written him and spoken on behalf of Breckenridge. But, the judge added, "I am convinced that Sonny Breckenridge is guilty of every one of the charges the jury found him guilty of."

Sonny's lawyer, Thomas Tompkins, made a point echoed hundreds of times by Breckenridge's friends and family: this young man was convicted on the word of drug dealers and a crooked cop, all looking for deals.

Judge Butler was not only unswayed, he was scathing as he ticked off the lies he felt Breckenridge had told.

338

Attorney Tompkins countered, "Regrettably, if the court chooses to believe the testimony of these convicted felons …"

"I am only the 13th person to [believe their testimony]," Judge Butler reminded the lawyer. "Twelve people did it several months ago."

Butler then sentenced Breckenridge to spend the rest of his life in federal prison with no possibility of parole.

Many were in tears. Breckenridge himself was weeping; his head hung low, as he was led away from the courtroom in shackles.

BACK TO BUSINESS

The *Democrat-Reporter* covered everything—the arrests, the multitude of hearings and, of course, the trials in far-off Mobile. "The greatest satisfaction," says Goodloe, "is that as a newspaper we did all we could, and the authorities took it the rest of the way."

The irony, notes Jean Sutton, was that it all began because Roger Davis refused to answer a simple question: "What had happened to the taxpayers' money that had been entrusted to the sheriff? That's all we ever wanted to know."

Many thought the stark difference between Breckenridge's sentence and the sheriff's was grossly unfair. "Roger Davis was an evil, selfish man," says Jean Sutton. "He didn't care what happened to anyone but himself."

Jesse Langley agrees there is something to that. While believing that Breckenridge's sentence is appropriate, he adds:"Sonny was too young, had too much power and had nobody to answer to. If the sheriff had done his job, Sonny would not be where he is now."

A few days after Davis's arrest, the governor appointed Jesse Langley to replace him as sheriff for the rest of the term. In the fall of 1998 Langley was elected to a full term as sheriff of Marengo County. Davis's old ally, Barrown Lankster, was defeated in his re-election bid for district attorney. In late 1998 Sonny Breckenridge's motion for a new trial was decisively rejected by the federal district court. An appeal of that decision is planned.

Meanwhile, business has rebounded for *The Democrat-Reporter*. Circulation has increased, and most advertisers have returned.

On February 9, 1999, state agents and local officers, following a tip, went digging in Roger Davis's back yard in Marengo County. They found 114,200 dollars in cash; another 54,150 dollars turned up inside his house. Davis was released from prison in December 1999 and is once again living in Marengo County.

THE CASE OF THE MISSING KEYS

KEYS

BY DAVID MOLLER

WITH JUST ONE VITAL PIECE OF EVIDENCE TO
GO ON, THE MANCHESTER POLICE COULD CATCH
THE KILLER. BUT THE CLUE HAD VANISHED.

She lay face down in a 12-foot pool of blood—a young woman in nurse's uniform, her arms above her head as if in surrender. Julie Green, 24, had just come off night duty at Wigan's Royal Albert Edward Infirmary when she met her end, some time before 10am on that Thursday, October 31, 1991. An empty pill canister lay by her right hand, a rolled-up scrap of paper by her left. Nearby on the storeroom's concrete floor was a two-pound lump hammer, heavily bloodstained.

Detective Superintendent Norman Collinson of Greater Manchester Police paused in the storeroom doorway. A stocky, white-haired 47-year-old veteran of some 50 murder enquiries, he methodically scanned the room: a wide workbench along one side, piles of building materials on the other. There was no sign of forced entry or struggle.

He and his colleague Detective Superintendent Frank Smout, 51, went cautiously inside. They found the door to the kitchen locked, a key lying at its foot. Then they retraced their steps through the storeroom's outer door into the cobbled alleyway the back of 179 Gidlow Lane, and hurried round to the front of the two storey terraced house.

The victim's handbag, knitting bag, nurse's cap and coat lay in the hall. Upstairs in the main bedroom, Collinson saw an alarm clock very like his own—a good timekeeper, but woefully inaccurate alarm.

Julie Green, an attractive, dark-haired woman with an appealing, rather toothy smile, was a popular figure in Wigan's close-knit community. Cheerful and outgoing, she was always happy to help others. Even before taking up nursing, she had worked at the hospital as a volunteer. A gifted pianist, she gave up a lot of her time to teaching others to play. She was very close to her widowed mother; even in her late teens, she often chose to holiday with her and her aunt rather than with her own friends.

In June 1989 she had married Warren Green, her childhood sweetheart from their days at Wigan's Deanery High School where Warren, quieter and more academic than Julie, had passed eleven O levels and four A levels. Later he had studied law at Lancaster University and Chester College of Law, and qualified as a solicitor in September 1990. The following month he had started work with the Crown Prosecution Service (CPS) in Salford, preparing criminal cases for trial.

The murder victim: Julie Green.

Warren and Julie had won respect in the community for their work as leaders with the Scout and Guide packs attached to nearby St Michael's Church. People were struck by their closeness. He bought her an eternity ring for their first wedding anniversary; she always baked him a cake on his birthday.

Though Julie's decision to give up her local government job and go into nursing meant a drop in their income, he was supportive. A friend says, "Julie always seemed to be laughing when Warren was around."

Now 26-year-old Warren, slim and dark-haired with a round, almost boyish face, sat in a CID office at Wigan police station, describing how their seemingly golden life had suddenly lurched into nightmare.

He had taken three days off to work on converting the storeroom into a garage, he explained. On the previous evening he had been out with his friends Stuwart Skett and Andrew Foster, visiting local pubs. Next morning, his alarm had woken him at 10.02am. Julie should have been back, since her shift finished at 7.45. But only the cat, Goliath, lay on her side of the bed. Pulling on some clothes, he went downstairs to look for her. No Julie.

Searching the house more thoroughly, he was puzzled to find he couldn't get into the storeroom from the kitchen. He peered through the keyhole and saw the key was, unusually, on the other side. Remembering a trick he had once seen on television, he slid a newspaper under the door and managed with a screwdriver to jab the key out of the lock. He heard it drop, and carefully pulled the newspaper back. But no key lay on it.

The only other way into the storeroom was through its rear outer door. He kept the key to that door with others on a keyring that had a dark leather fob bearing an E-type Jaguar medallion. He was sure he had left the keys on the kitchen worktop the night before, but they had gone.

He knew there was a spare key next door at 177 Gidlow Lane, which he owned but rented out to Joe McGuire, a funeral director. So he went round and got the spare from Mrs McGuire.

Seconds later, Green found his wife. "I ran into the storeroom," he told the police. "I knelt down in front of her head. I wanted to pick her up and hold her. There was blood all over the floor … A big lumpy pool of blood next to her head."

In the mortuary of the Royal Albert Edward Infirmary, Norman Collinson looked down at Julie's face, with a deep laceration over her left eye. "Could that have been caused by her falling to the floor?" he asked. The pathologist, Dr Edmund Tapp, shook his head. "More likely a punch or kick from her assailant at the start of the attack."

One massive blow to the side of her head had almost severed Julie's left ear. The position of the other 15 blows indicated that the killer had stood astride her as he methodically smashed her skull. This was no heat-of-the-moment attack, mused Collinson. It was a cold-blooded execution.

He was still at the mortuary when Detective Inspector Jack Booth called from Wigan police station. "Green says he woke at 10am," he said. "If you're returning to the scene of the crime, boss, would you check what time the alarm went off?"

Back at 179 Gidlow Lane with his colleague Frank Smout, Collinson turned the alarm clock's hands. Although the alarm was set for just before ten o'clock, it rang at 9.40—20 minutes early. The two officers exchanged glances. It was something, or nothing.

By 8pm, a darker, more complex picture of the couple had emerged. Detectives discovered from letters they found in the bedside table that for the past three months Julie had been having an affair with 22-year-old Stuwart Skett. They knew it was wrong, Skett acknowledged, but couldn't bring themselves to stop.

"Could Warren have killed her in a frenzy of jealousy?" asked Collinson. His colleagues thought it unlikely. In interviews, Green's friends had painted a picture of a very controlled character—a cold fish. "In any case," added Booth, "he's hardly been the model husband himself."

Warren Green, they discovered, had become infatuated with Julie Warburton, a 20-year-old law student who was spending the summer doing work experience at

Where she worked: Royal Albert Edward Infirmary.

Salford CPS. Warren had given her small presents and invited her out to dinner. When he and his wife were on holiday in Corfu, he had written her love letters.

"Could he have wanted his wife out of the way because of Julie Warburton?" Collinson speculated. Booth shrugged.

"What about Skett?" asked Smout. "Could he be involved?" Booth shook his head. "He's already been alibied out." At the engineering plant where Skett worked, his clocking-on card showed he had come in at 8am, and his workmates vouched for his presence there all morning.

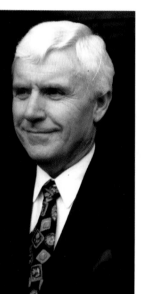

The DS: Norman Collinson

Collinson turned his attention back to Green. He said he had woken at 10am, yet the alarm had clearly gone off at 9.40am. Why was he so keen to lose those 20 minutes?

At 10pm, Green was arrested. He seemed unfazed.

As a lawyer, he knew that a spouse was often an early suspect in a inquiry. Again he gave Booth his story.

By next morning, a major incident room had been set up in the CID wing. From Green's home, detectives had retrieved some documents revealing that the couple's finances were tight. Green had bought his home at the height of the market, and taken out loans to pay for renovations as well as an £80,000 mortgage. If his marriage *had* failed, Julie would have been entitled to half the equity in the house and the adjoining property, but both were only half-renovated and difficult to sell in a dead market.

However, the couple were remarkably well insured. Their three separate policies meant that if one of them died, the mortgage would be paid off and the surviving partner would get £70,000 in cash. An additional policy on Julie's life would give Warren another £50,000.

Clearly Warren Green stood to gain financially from his wife's death. But motive is not enough to sustain a charge of murder. Collinson and his colleagues settled down to review the bare facts: Julie had been murdered in a storeroom locked, ostensibly, from the inside; the murderer must have left by the rear outer door, which could only be closed by locking it; the key, on its ring with a Jaguar fob motif, was missing.

Alternatively, Warren himself had murdered his wife and hidden the keys to make it look like an outside job. He wouldn't have risked going out to get rid of them, in case someone recognized him in the street, so they must still be in the house. If he were the culprit, he would have left the storeroom by its inner door, locking it from the kitchen side. He would then have pushed the key back under the door, to fit his claim that he had knocked it on to the storeroom floor with a screwdriver.

"At the moment, we don't have a scrap of evidence either way," Collinson concluded. "Our only real hope is to find those keys."

Detectives scoured Green's house, local gardens, bins, the patrol car that brought him to the station. No keys.

Other lines of enquiry also proved unproductive. Forensic examination of Warren's clothing failed to reveal even one speck of Julie's blood. And when police told Julie's mother, Mrs Dillys Sillitoe, that Warren had been held for questioning, she was incredulous: "You've got the wrong man. Warren would never do that."

But if Warren Green hadn't killed his wife, who had?

Booth began questioning Green again. "Was there anyone who could conceivably have wished Julie harm?" he asked. Green shook his head helplessly. Everyone loved his tender-hearted wife.

Suddenly, Green recalled that soon after the discovery of Julie's body, a policeman had told him that there was a pill canister marked Temazepam (commonly used as a tranquillizer) near her right hand. At the time, said Green, he had merely assumed that Julie had put an empty container into her pocket at the hospital. But now he wondered whether Julie had been selling drugs she brought back from the hospital, and had locked the storeroom door to avoid being disturbed. Had some transaction gone horribly wrong?

Never forget the dangers of making assumptions too early in a case, Collinson told himself sternly. The murder investigation would now have to become a drugs inquiry. Fresh teams of detectives set to work.

After more than ten hours of interviewing, Green remained calm, courteous and precise. Booth could detect no deviation in his story. On Sunday evening he was released, on condition he did not return home.

Next morning, the police began another search of Green's house, listing the entire contents of every room. They scoured the rafters and chimney, scanned nearby roofs and guttering, searched the sewers, and inspected every street drain within a half-mile radius. Still no keys.

Meanwhile, examination of the scrap of paper found near Julie's left hand revealed fresh evidence to suggest she might have been killed by an outsider in a drugs deal: it was the bloodstained bottom left-hand corner of a £10 note. Could Julie have had a row over a drugs deal, then been bludgeoned to death?

Interviews with Julie's relatives and friends offered another clue. Several people mentioned that she had been troubled by mystery telephone calls. When Julie picked up the phone, no one answered. The caller waited, then hung up. The calls came only when Warren was not at home; it was as if someone were watching the house and knew when Julie was alone. Could some sick person be stalking her?

Then Collinson's team received a call from a Mrs Sheila Sillitoe from Wrightington, just outside Wigan. The night before the murder, she told them, a man had rung her, asking, "Is Julie there?" Told not, he said, "I'm trying to get in touch with a Julie Sillitoe [Julie's maiden name]."

Told that she did not live there, the caller rang off. Could he, Collinson wondered, be the same person who had been ringing Julie at home? Perhaps even the murderer?

At a press conference on Wednesday, November 6, Warren Green, blinking into the television lights, appealed for help in his soft Lancashire accent. "If anyone, anywhere, can give any information about even the most trivial thing, please contact the police. Please do." Choking back tears, he talked about Julie: "She was full of life and extremely lovely. I loved her. I still love her." Then, against the clicking of dozens of press cameras, he held up a duplicate set of keys Collinson had had made, complete with Jaguar-emblazoned fob.

As the second week after Julie's murder wore on, the trail went cold. All enquiries indicated that she had no involvement in the drug scene. Forensic examination revealed no fingerprints on the hammer, and nothing in the Greens' home gave any clue to the killer's identity. The rest of the £10 note could not be found.

Inevitably, suspicion once more focused on Warren Green. As a CPS solicitor, he routinely sifted through evidence to go before a court, looking for flaws in a police case or in a defendant's story. He was well equipped to lay a false trail. "But how could he have killed his wife without getting blood on a single bit of clothing?" Collinson mused.

"Perhaps he took his clothes off after he had stunned her with the first blow," suggested Booth. "He delivered another 15 blows, then went upstairs to wash himself thoroughly."

Forensic investigators had found small bloodstains on the bathroom basin and on the tiles above, but not enough to pinpoint a particular blood group. Green could simply have cut himself shaving.

"What about the mystery calls?" asked Collinson.

"Green could have made them all," Smout suggested. "The caller never rang when he was there."

And the call to Mrs Sheila Sillitoe? "Green could have made that, too," said Booth. "The next Sillitoe in the directory is Julie's mother. Yet he didn't try her.

Why? Because she would certainly have recognized Green's voice.

One more cause for suspicion was the 999 call Green had made from the McGuires' funeral parlour after finding his wife dead. Instead of immediately requesting an ambulance, he had asked for the police, then begun a rambling account of what he had done that morning. And when traffic patrolman Andrew Cunliffe arrived minutes later, Green again went through his lengthy account.

Were Green's actions those of a man in shock? wondered Collinson. *Or was he, with his lawyer's training, carefully recording all the details necessary for a watertight alibi?*

The second search of Green's house had revealed a pair of shoes with traces of something that might have been blood on the soles. They were sent for analysis. But the keys were

The husband: Warren Green.

still missing. "The place has been picked clean," Smout reported. Collinson stared gloomily out of his office window. Every instinct told him Warren Green must be the killer. Yet without the keys, they still had no firm evidence.

He turned back to face Smout. "We're going to have to search the house again, Frank," he announced. "We'll bring in a new search team—perhaps we need fresh eyes."

On Monday, November 11, police began the most thorough search yet. Next morning, they lifted the hall carpet and unscrewed six short floorboards. Torch in hand, PC Ian McAuley began inching along on his stomach in the 18-inch space between the ground and the floor joists. After half an hour peering into the dust-filled gloom, his torch suddenly lit up a pipe recessed almost invisibly under the front door sill, and blocked with half-bricks and rubble, which he started to clear. He flashed his torch down the pipe—and something glinted.

Booth stopped Collinson on the station stairs. "You're not going to believe this, boss," he said, beaming. "We've found the keys. And they've got blood on them."

Early on Thursday morning, Booth and Collinson began interviewing Green once more. Eventually, Collinson began describing how McAuley had found the pipe in the wall. Slowly the colour drained from Green's face, "like a blood bank

Case solved: Jack Smout (left) and Norman Collinson.

emptying," Collinson recalls. "Guess what we found, Mr Green?" From a bag hidden on his lap, Collinson placed the keys on the table.

White-faced, Green closed his eyes and rocked back in his chair. Eventually he spoke. "It's not me."

Collinson bombarded him with more questions. But Green, in contrast to his earlier lengthy replies, just repeated, "It's not me ... it's not me."

Finally Collinson suggested that Green had either planned the murder, or killed his wife in a moment of anger following a dispute. By now Green had recovered his composure. "This is ridiculous," he responded. "I'll quite plainly say, I've not killed Julie and I couldn't do it."

As Green was taken down to the cells, Booth shook his head wearily:

"A cool customer."

On February 23, 1993, Warren Green stood in the dock at Liverpool's Crown Court No.5. Dapper in a dark suit, he maintained an air of perplexed innocence.

His mind easily a match for the other lawyers in court, he dismissed most of the evidence as circumstantial. But he was in difficulty over the keys—and the shoes, now shown to carry traces of his wife's blood. Someone must have put them where they were found. But not him. He looked across at the jury, as if appealing to them to exercise their imagination. The police, perhaps? It was his last hope.

At the end of the 14-day trial, the jury's verdict was unanimous: guilty. Green slumped in his seat, head in his hands. Sentencing him to life imprisonment, Mr Justice Ognall declared: "You killed your wife in a fashion marked by a chilling degree of control and concentration. You then took determined and sophisticated steps in an effort to mislead the police, and these steps included maligning your dead wife as a criminal and a drugs dealer. It should be recorded that whatever her failings ... she deserves to be remembered as a vivacious, caring and decent young woman ..."

Detective Superintendent Collinson and his colleagues had finally succeeded in bringing to justice one of the most calculated, cold-blooded murderers in British criminal history. "Most people plotting murder think it will be the perfect crime," says Collinson. "But Warren Green came very close to pulling it off."

JACOBS HOPE

229422

THE BOY WHO

NEVER CAME
HOME

BY HENRY HURT

THE ABDUCTION OF JACOB WETTERLING

TOOK PLACE OVER TEN YEARS AGO. DESPITE

A MASSIVE SEARCH AND INVESTIGATION,

JACOB HAS NEVER SURFACED.

Face familiar: is this what Jacob looks like today?

And Patty mentioned that she had woken up at 3.11 in the morning."

After lunch, the two went to the foundation office and were greeted by Alma Hansen, who is on the staff. "We had an unusual call on the answering machine last night," Alma said. She then played the message, in which a voice whispered: "This is Jacob Wetterling. I just want you to know I'm still alive."

The call, traced to New York, had come in at 3.11am.

TEN YEARS LATER

For the first year after the kidnapping, Trevor Wetterling slept on the floor in his parents' bedroom, terrified to be alone at night, waking up to horrific nightmares. Today he has made great strides and is living on his own while going to college.

"I think Jacob's out there somewhere," he says quietly, his direct gaze much like that of his mother. "He's probably brainwashed. I don't know whether I could even recognize him."

The odds of finding Jacob are not good. According to Neil Neddermeyer, a retired Minnesota sex-crimes expert who worked on the Wetterling case, "Fewer than a quarter of missing children abducted by strangers are found alive after the first three days, and about half are never found."

But Patty Wetterling is not swayed from her quest to find out what happened to her son: "We have one boy who is missing, and he's not a statistic."

The terrible night's most important legacy is the Jacob Wetterling Foundation, dedicated to helping families across America who have lost children to abductions. The staff provides emotional support and serves as a resource for information about missing children.

Once a shy housewife, Patty has become the graceful, eloquent force behind the Wetterling Foundation. She travels the country speaking to law enforcement groups about how to seize "the early, precious moments" when a child disappears.

"You will never look foolish if you pull out all the stops and find the child," she tells them. She also speaks to schoolchildren, telling them not to fear the world or to fear people—only to be wary of any unfamiliar adult who approaches them or anyone they know who makes them feel uncomfortable.

A MOTHER'S HOPE

The Wetterlings today live in the same house and have the same phone number— a place and number Jacob would remember and where he could contact them. Each Christmas, Patty hangs Jacob's stocking on the fireplace mantel. The lights are burning at this house, and the hope for a miracle will not be extinguished.

Patty will never stop looking for her son—searching the faces of young men on the streets, in airports, on the Metro in Washington, D.C. When driving, she looks at the faces of the men working at construction sites. She is looking for a 21-year-old man who is about six feet tall with brown hair and blue eyes.

No matter what changes have come over Jacob, his mother will know his eyes when she sees them. And no matter what has happened to him—even if his glorious, sunny smile has been extinguished—she is sure that with time she will find it and bring it back.

One of the most painful questions Patty hears is, if Jacob is alive and on his own, why doesn't he just call home?

The answer goes to the heart of the horror of what he may have had to do to survive. He could well think that he is so changed— that his life over the last ten years has been so awful—that his friends and family would no longer want him.

Patty and Jerry Wetterling say that nothing could have happened that could alter their love for their son. The words Patty wishes he could hear are these:

"We love you, Jacob, now as much as ever. Wherever you are, whatever has happened, whatever you've had to do, never doubt how much we love you. Call us, or come home, so we can begin to build the new memories."

Always hoping: Jerry and Patty Wetterling, near the spot where Jacob was abducted.

355

THE MURDER OF
JUSTICE

BY JEFFREY ROBINSON

THE FLORIDA COP AND THE 19-YEAR-OLD

STREET KID SHOULD NEVER HAVE MET. BUT

LATE ONE SUMMER NIGHT THEIR PATHS

CROSSED BRIEFLY, WITH DISASTROUS RESULTS.

Correy Major was a 19-year-old street kid from Fort Myers, Florida. Robert Clark was a 36-year-old Civil War buff from Cleveland, Ohio. Their paths crossed briefly, and only once.

Clark never knew that Major's first misdemeanor arrests came at age eight. Or that felonies followed at age 11. Or that as a juvenile he'd been charged with nearly 150 crimes. Major never knew that Clark had always wanted to be a policeman, just like his great-grandfather, a Pittsburgh cop who was gunned down by a criminal in a hallway. Or that when Clark graduated from the police academy, he received permission to wear his great-grandfather's badge number—545.

The cop and the street kid should never have met. But late one night in the summer of 1998, the lives of two perfect strangers became forever entangled.

Correy Major never had a father figure and despised the men who streamed through his mother's life. As a child he often came home to find his mother high on drugs. But he stayed with her, even after all five of his sisters and brothers drifted away.

Mother and son moved to Cleveland, then back to Fort Myers. Correy quit school after ninth grade. He started using drugs himself and was regularly getting arrested for stealing cars, robbing people and breaking into houses. He stood six feet tall, weighed 160 pounds and had six gold teeth in the front of his mouth.

When Robert Clark was 20, he met a girl named Catherine Cooper. She was 17 and worked at Arby's. He kept showing up for french fries. She had eye problems and worried that he'd walk away when she explained how serious they were. He not only stuck around, but after her eye surgery he called her in the hospital. Groggy with medication, she fell asleep on the phone. He waited on the other end until she woke up. They married and had three children. On that night in July 1998, Melissa was seven, Alaina was five and Robby was two.

About eight weeks after his 18th birthday and at the end of a sleepless, five-day drug spree, Correy Major grabbed the purse of an 88-year-old woman. When she wouldn't let go, he knocked her down and stepped on her face.

Pursued by Fort Myers police, he fled in a stolen car, crashed into a pole and started running. Two officers chased him into a ditch. Major waded through the mud toward the other side. Sergeant Andy Rudolph was waiting for him, gun drawn. "Freeze! Get down on your belly now!"

Hands raised in surrender, Major slowly lowered himself into a crouch. Suddenly he lunged forward, knocking Rudolph onto his back.

Rudolph caught Major by the throat. They wrestled, tumbling over and over, until Major was on top. He elbowed Rudolph in the chest and grabbed the barrel of the officer's gun.

Rudolph managed to snap out the magazine and toss it away so the gun couldn't fire. Then he took his baton and slammed it into Major's forehead. The blow opened a huge gash. Blood shot out. But Major never blinked. He kneed Rudolph in the chest and raced for the squad car.

Struggling to breathe, Rudolph threw himself into the passenger's side and, half hanging out the door, fought for the ignition key. Major put him in a choke hold and got the car into gear.

Rudolph ripped the key out of the ignition. That's when two civilians pulled Major out of the car and two other officers arrived at the scene.

The old woman had been rushed to the hospital. When she arrived, doctors thought she was dead.

Major was charged with nine felonies, including grand theft auto, strong-armed robbery, resisting arrest with violence, battery on a police officer and depriving an officer of his firearm. A judge ordered him held without bail, but ultimately it was set at 55,500 dollars.

Major's lawyer advised him not to post bail, hoping to keep him out of further trouble. However, on November 15, Major's grandmother signed her home over to a bondsman. And Correy Major walked free.

When he wasn't drawing cartoons, caricaturing everyone at the downtown station house, Rob Clark broke the tension of policing the streets with practical jokes on his fellow officers. One of his favorite stunts was to pull Bill Van Verth aside and tell him Jerry Zarlenga just said something awful about him. Next, he'd tell Zarlenga, "I can't believe what Bill said about you." Then he'd sit back and take in the chaos he'd created.

Off duty, Clark's favorite place was at home, where he made the most out of every holiday or special family event. On his kids' birthdays he'd decorate the house, bake a cake and go out of his way to get them what they wanted. At Thanksgiving, he baked pumpkin pies for just about everyone he knew. On Christmas Eve, no matter how late he worked, he'd wake Cathy up, slip into his red costume, and have her videotape him piling presents under the tree so the children could see Santa.

Despite the 62 charges lodged against him since December 1995, Correy Major realized that this time he was in real trouble. Now charged as an adult, he was given a take-it-or-leave-it deal. If he pleaded not guilty and lost—which would be likely—he'd be looking at 24 years in jail. If he signed the agreement, he'd go away for 14 years and could be out in 12.

Family ties: Robert Clark had requested badge number 545.

"These people are trying to get me again," he told his mother. "Before I go to prison for something I didn't do, I'd rather die."

On the morning of May 6, 1998, the clerk of the circuit court in Lee County, Florida, called out the name Correy Major. No one answered.

Later that afternoon, a warrant for Major's arrest was sent to the county sheriff's department for processing. Instead of listing all nine of Major's felony charges, the woman keying the information into the computer followed the department's customary—but incorrect—practice: she simply typed in "failure to appear."

To reduce the administrative burden on law enforcement, many states, including Florida, cast a relatively small net for fugitives wanted on lesser offenses. The clerk's error limited the extradition range in Major's case to "Southeast US only"—Florida and its bordering states.

Should Major be caught outside that area, Lee County didn't want him back.

With bounty hunters scouring Fort Myers to find him, Major moved from place to place, hiding at friends' houses. On May 12, in a panic, he slipped out of town on a Greyhound bus bound for Cleveland.

On the streets, Rob Clark was all business. To the kids he dealt with, there was nothing funny about the powerfully built police officer they called RoboCop and Power Ranger. Once, after the gang murder of a 17-year-old, Clark and Zarlenga spotted the suspects in a van. Using their squad car, the officers pinned the van against the side of a bridge, then captured all four thugs—a sawed-off shotgun and a pistol still in their laps—without a single shot being fired.

At 2.18 am on July 1, 1998, a call came into the Brook Park police station in suburban Cleveland. A young male had broken into a truck in the parking lot of a strip joint. Witnesses said the man had gone 500 yards down the block to another bar.

Six officers were dispatched. It took all of them—and more pepper spray than any of them had ever used before—to subdue and capture him. Because the suspect wouldn't give his real name, he was booked as John Doe and held overnight.

It was clear that the kid was street savvy, so the police sent his fingerprints to the FBI. By dawn they were able to identify him as Correy Major. They also determined that he had an extensive adult criminal record and was wanted in Florida.

Brook Park police informed Lee County officials that their fugitive was in custody. A sheriff's clerk in Fort Myers checked her database and saw "Southeast US only." At 11.57 am she responded: "Will not extradite from your state. Thank you."

An astonished chief of police, Tom Dease, told a dispatcher to phone Lee County again to make sure. But the clerk in Florida merely confirmed what was on her computer: "Southeast US only."

Correy Major made his one phone call to arrange for bail. Then the fines for each of his four misdemeanors—criminal damaging, resisting arrest, petty theft and giving a false name—were read from a chart. The total came to 900 dollars. A bondsman posted ten per cent.

For 90 dollars, Correy Major was back on the street.

It was 3.35 in the afternoon.

At that moment, Rob Clark was at home taking care of his three kids while his wife was out. The children helped him make dinner later that afternoon. And by the time Cathy returned, supper was on the table. At about 6.30, Rob kissed his kids good night, said goodbye to Cathy and left for work.

Correy Major spent the rest of the day in a panic. He called his girlfriend in Florida. Crying, he asked, "Why did they let me go? Are they trying to kill me?"

He was convinced the police were setting him up.

At about 10.30pm, Clark and two other plainclothes detectives—Keith Haven and Ray Diaz—were on their way to do surveillance on a bar. Driving along, they saw three people huddled suspiciously on the corner of Madison Avenue and West Boulevard. Clark thought it looked like a drug deal. "Let's bust it up," he said.

Major spotted three men, obviously cops, coming after him, and he ran to the doorway of a two-story building at 10010 Madison Avenue.

"Wait outside," Clark shouted to Haven as he and Diaz raced up the narrow, unlit stairway. Major was wild to get through a door at the top landing. Clark pinned him against the wall while Diaz, one step below, began to pat him down. Major was screaming.

Diaz pulled rock cocaine out of Major's pocket. Just as he did, Major shoved him backward. Diaz began to fall. Clark lunged to help him. They tumbled down the stairs, first Diaz, then Clark.

Major swung around. From under his belt he pulled out a 9mm pistol and started firing.

Haven rushed in. Clark was sprawled on the steps. Diaz, stunned and injured from the fall, was lying at the foot of the stairs. Major was pounding frantically on the door, shrieking to be let in.

Haven opened fire.

Detectives who later investigated the scene found Clark's leather wallet lying on the stairwell in a pool of his blood. Inside were drawings from his kids, tucked behind badge number 545.

Correy Major's funeral was held at the Apostolic Revival Center in Fort Myers. About 150 people attended.

Robert Clark's funeral was held at the Our Lady of Angels Catholic Church in Cleveland. As the first cars were arriving at the cemetery, the last were only just leaving the church 12 miles away. All along the route, tens of thousands of

Surviving the loss: Cathy Clark and her three children keep Robert's memory alive in everything the family does.

people—holding signs and banners and American flags—lined the streets, standing in silence, saluting, weeping, saying goodbye to a man they'd never met.

Since those two paths crossed …

Rob Clark's mother goes to the cemetery twice a day. Around her neck she wears a chain with a replica of badge 545.

The Lee County sheriff's office has acknowledged errors but insists the department has since improved its procedures for handling warrants and extradition.

Brook Park Police Chief Tom Dease continues to fume about Lee County's decision not to extradite Correy Major. He wonders if someone in Florida was thinking, *Hey, this is an opportunity. This guy is gone. Let's leave him gone.*

At the Clark household, Daddy still comes into everything the family does. When Cathy puts the kids to bed, they want two hugs—one for Mom, one for Daddy. Melissa falls asleep with her arms around Daddy's canvas jacket. Alaina cuddles Daddy's shirt. Little Robby just wants to know where his Daddy is.

On Robert Clark's first birthday after his murder, Cathy took the children and 20 helium balloons to the cemetery. The four of them stood next to his grave and wished Daddy a happy birthday as they watched his balloons float all the way up to heaven.

IF I CAN'T HAVE

YOU,

NOBODY

WILL

BY ANITA BARTHOLOMEW

HE'D BEEN STALKING HER FOR MONTHS.

NOW SHE WAS AT HIS MERCY.

The breeze streaming through the open car windows made Laura Kucera's long blond hair dance as she pulled up at her friend Sara Tello's house. October 1, 1994, was a picture-perfect Saturday in the north-eastern Nebraska town of Wakefield. While Sara's baby brother and sister played in the front yard, the two young women sat in the sun, engrossed in small talk. Then Laura noticed a white pick-up coming down the street.

As the truck stopped, she saw the scowling, muscled man with the Fu Manchu mustache. "Oh, God, it's him," she gasped, recognizing Brian Anderson, the six-foot-four, 240-pound ex-boyfriend who had been stalking and terrorizing her for three months.

"Come and talk to me a minute," he pleaded. Panicked, Laura dashed into the house, grabbed the phone and dialed 911. Seconds later, she realized with horror that Anderson had followed her in.

As she slowly placed the phone back in its cradle, the two toddlers, drawn inside by the commotion, saw Anderson and started crying. Laura allowed him to lead her back outside.

"All I'm asking is for you to talk to me," Anderson cajoled. Then, quick as a striking snake, his hand shot out and grabbed her arm. "Sara, get the police!" Laura screamed.

As Sara stood paralyzed with fear, her mother and 19-year-old brother, Mike, came racing out of the house. Holding Laura with one arm, Anderson backed to his truck and pulled out a pistol. "This is none of your business," he said coldly. "Get back in the house!"

Frightened, Mike and Sara retreated. Anderson tucked the gun in his belt and shoved Laura into the truck.

When 18-year-old Laura first met Brian Anderson in April 1994, she was captivated by his charm. Brian, 22, opened doors for her and bought her flowers. He conversed with her biologist-turned-farmer dad.

But Anderson's adoration quickly turned to obsession and a desire to control Laura. He'd "bump into" her friends and warn them against keeping dates with her. He'd wait for Laura until she got off work at a nearby chicken farm and insist she come with him. Uncomfortable with his demands, Laura tried to taper off their time together. But the more she tried to pull away, the more hostile Anderson became.

The night in July when she told him she no longer wanted to see him, Anderson became enraged. Putting a shotgun to her head, he said, "If I can't have you, nobody will." After the longest minute of Laura's life, he lowered the gun. Trembling with fear and anger, she fled.

Anderson began stalking her. He repeatedly called her late at night, threatening to torch her family's farmhouse unless she agreed to meet him. Hoping to scare him off, Laura filed an order of protection against him.

Yet a month later, when Laura again rebuffed his pleas to renew their relationship, Anderson grabbed her by the throat and put a pistol to her head. She watched his finger slowly tighten on the trigger; then she shut her eyes—only to hear the impotent click of an unloaded gun. "See how easy it would be?" he whispered in her ear.

When a police officer witnessed the two together—a violation of the protection order—Anderson was given 30 days in jail. But two days after his release, he ran Laura's car off the road and held her prisoner for several hours. It was two days later when he dragged her into his truck at Sara Tello's home.

Gunning his engine, Anderson zigzagged through a maze of winding, deserted roads deep into the country. Well-tended fields of corn and beans gave way to stretches of grassland and forest. Laura had no idea where they were, but she was acutely aware of Anderson's gun. *Out here, no one would hear a shot*, she thought. A chill traveled through her, but she commanded herself to stay calm. Eventually, he would have to stop. Then she would run for it.

As they crossed a paved highway, she saw a sign in the distance: Macy—6 miles. Now she knew where they were—on the Omaha Indian reservation, about 50 miles south-east of Wakefield. They bounced along a rutted back road through trees and tall grass. Finally, at the crest of a wooded bluff overlooking the Missouri River, Anderson pulled over and yanked Laura out of the truck.

"Look," Anderson said, "I just want to talk." She had provoked him, he said, but he was willing to forget and start fresh. Things would be different, he promised.

Laura pretended to pay attention, but barely heard him. Then she saw it: the truck! He'd left the driver's door open. She knew he often left the keys in the ignition.

When Anderson turned slightly to look out over the forest, Laura decided this was her chance. Sprinting to the pickup, she slammed the door behind her and banged down the door locks. Her heart hammered in her throat as she felt for the key. It wasn't in the ignition!

Through the window, she saw Anderson saunter over. Coolly he pulled the keys out of his jeans pocket, unlocked the driver's door, shoved Laura to the other seat and started up. He drove about half a mile before stopping at a meadow.

"I can see you're not going to change your mind," he said, sighing. "But can't we still be friends?"

Seething, frightened and exhausted, Laura could no longer hide her feelings. "Brian," she blurted, "I'd rather die than be friends with you."

He stared at her coldly. "Then I guess," he said, "you'd better start running."

For a split second she froze. Then the instinct for survival took over, and she vaulted out of the truck. Running into the field, she heard Anderson get out behind her and slam the door.

For a moment she heard nothing more. *He isn't following*, she thought with relief. Then she heard a blast, and a bullet ripped through her shoulder. *Keep running*, she told herself. *He can't get you if you keep going.* She heard another shot and felt it pierce the back of her neck.

He was coming after her now. *Faster … faster!* she commanded her rubbery legs. *You won't get away with this*, she swore to herself. *I won't let you beat me!*

He was gaining on her. Suddenly, he was so close she could hear him panting. "You had this coming," he rasped. A third shot rang out, hitting her in the back of the head. Laura Kucera fell face first into the hard-packed earth, two bullets in her head.

Anderson had a police scanner in his pickup. As he drove back toward Wakefield, he learned that the Dixon County sheriff's department had begun a manhunt for him. He devised a plan. Stopping at a phone, he called the sheriff's office and told them he had heard they were looking for him, and that he wanted to cooperate. He had dropped Laura off in South Sioux City, and now he had no idea where she was.

Later that night, preparing to question Anderson, county deputy sheriff Donnie Taylor recalled hearing stories of Anderson's earlier threats, abductions and assaults. *How had this monster been allowed to terrorize the poor girl unchallenged?* he wondered. The father of four, he was overcome with foreboding for Laura.

After advising Anderson of his rights, the soft-spoken deputy got straight to the point. "What did you do to Laura, Brian?"

The young man smiled amiably. "I didn't do anything to her, I swear. We drove around for a while, and then Laura asked me if I would drop her at Hardee's in South Sioux City. That was about 8.15."

Taylor smiled back. "Brian, I don't want to say you're a liar, but that Hardee's is where state police hang out on their breaks. No one saw her. Now, you want to tell me where you really took her?"

Rage flared briefly behind Anderson's smile. "I think I'd better talk to a lawyer first," he said. "That's my right, isn't it?"

———

Monday morning, state police investigator Doug Johnson was getting ready for work when his wife called to him. "Doug, did you hear? Someone has been abducted at gunpoint in Wakefield."

As soon as he got to state police headquarters in South Sioux City, he phoned Donnie Taylor. The two men had worked together several times over the years, and respected and liked each other.

Johnson agreed to help, and Taylor filled him in. Laura, carried off at gunpoint, had been missing for three days. There was no real question in either officer's mind: Anderson had killed her. Their first obligation, they agreed, was to find Laura's body and put an end to her family's horrible wait.

Taylor and Johnson met with Anderson's attorney, Douglas Luebe. With hunting and harvest seasons coming soon, they reminded him, it would be only a matter of time before someone found Laura Kucera. It would be better for Anderson if he agreed to lead police to her now.

Meanwhile, witnesses had told police that after the kidnapping Anderson's truck had headed north. In that direction, they deduced, the most likely place he would have taken her was a remote wood near the Anderson family farm.

An eight-man search team began its grim chore on Tuesday morning. Walking side by side, they made ever-widening circles—and kept watch for vultures. They were also alert for tracks of coyotes and foxes that might lead to the body. It was hard, discouraging work, but the men refused to rest. As darkness fell, however, there was still no sign of Laura.

When the search team arrived back at the county sheriff's office in Ponca, they were met by a police forensic expert. "He's ready to confess," the man said.

Anderson's lawyer and the Dixon County Attorney reached a tentative deal. In exchange for leading searchers to Laura's body, Anderson would plead guilty to second-degree murder. That carried a lighter sentence—ten years to life—than the mandatory life-without-parole he would receive if convicted of kidnapping.

Laura's parents, Mary and David Kucera, arrived soon after the investigators. Ashen-faced, they leaned on each other for strength while the district attorney told them about the possible plea bargain. Under the agreement, he cautioned,

Anderson could be back on the street after serving just five years—half the minimum term. If Anderson was going to pay fully for his crimes, the D.A. had to refuse the deal.

David choked back tears. "Take the deal," he said. "I just want my little girl back." Mary agreed.

The lawyers quickly finalized the plea agreement, and Anderson confessed that he had shot Laura Kucera. Her body was in a meadow near Macy. Johnson and Taylor looked at each other in surprise. Macy was south-east, at least 50 miles from the area they had been searching.

Within minutes, more than a dozen law-enforcement officers were driving into the night toward the crime scene. On directions from Anderson, handcuffed in the back of Taylor's red four-wheel drive, they pulled up to the meadow at about 11.15pm. Johnson and the others fanned out and formed a line. Their heavy flashlights swept over the ground, casting eerie shadows that made the brush appear to sway.

There she was!

Johnson's heart leapt into his throat as he caught sight of Laura's body, 20 feet from the road in a hollow depression under two tall elms. She was lying on her back, her right leg cocked up. Her red windbreaker and long blond hair were shining like bright flags in the darkness.

The officers moved methodically toward the body, making sure they did not disturb the crime scene. Out of the corner of his eye, Johnson thought he saw Laura's leg shift position. Startled, he tripped, then caught himself. Just shadows caused by the flashlights, he guessed.

Then he saw movement again. "My God!" he screamed. "She's alive!"

Stunned to a halt, the men stared wide-eyed at one another. Then they heard a faint moan. Quickly recovering, they raced to her in a wave, whooping and hollering. "She's alive!"

Johnson and Taylor knelt beside her. Johnson stroked her hair and the girl groaned, seemingly in acknowledgment. "It's OK, Laura," Taylor said softly.

While they called for a medical emergency helicopter, Johnson walked back to the four-wheel drive where Anderson and his lawyer sat waiting.

"Luebe," he said cheerfully, "I hate to tell you, but your plea agreement is in the toilet. Laura is alive!"

The young woman was airlifted to the Marian Health Center in nearby Sioux City, Iowa. With two bullets lodged in her head, doctors weren't certain Laura would ever regain consciousness. But her body temperature, for some unknown reason, had dropped only to 95 degrees. She wasn't nearly as dehydrated as she ought to have been after being exposed to cold and rain through four nights, nor did she seem to have lost much blood. Doctors were astonished.

Whether it was all the prayers that had been offered up for her or her own strength and courage, Laura continued to surprise doctors as she recovered her ability to speak and then to walk. She was released from the hospital on November 19, 1994, a month earlier than predicted.

Still, doctors doubted she would ever be the same as before. And that was what Brian Anderson was counting on. After his plea bargain for second-degree murder was foiled by Laura's miraculous survival, he pleaded not guilty to kidnapping and attempted murder charges, hoping that Laura, the only eyewitness to the shooting, would be too badly brain-damaged to testify—or too intimidated to try.

But Laura Kucera surprised him too. On March 3, 1995, she entered a lawyer's office and sat across the table from Anderson. Coldly, he tried to stare her down, but she would not be bullied. Facing him, she recounted the details of his terror campaign in slow, sometimes broken words, but with unbroken spirit.

Realizing that she had defeated him, Anderson changed his plea to guilty on four felony counts, including attempted murder. In May 1995 he was sentenced to not less than 85 years in prison.

Laura Kucera had made good her vow not to let him get away with his crimes.

WHO WANTED AARON DEAD?

BY FRANK ROSEN

DETECTIVE JIM MICHAUD INVESTIGATED THE
SLAYING OF A TEENAGER IN HIS BEDROOM.
CLUES LED HIM TO A SHOCKING SUSPECT.

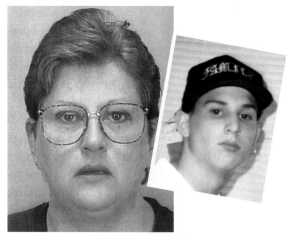

Gangland gallery: Jim Elstad, "anti-gang activist" Mary Thompson; her son, Beau Flynn, and "Crazy Joe" Brown (bottom).

To Michaud, these conversations were proof of a startling truth: Mary Thompson was not just an anti-gang activist who had crossed the line once to rescue her son. She was neck-deep in gang crime herself. The entire town had been deceived.

Thompson, it turned out, was the gang's *leader*. The wiretaps revealed her direct involvement in gang activity. Incredibly, her public stance against gangs was merely a façade to cover her recruitment of members.

Michaud realized it was time to move on Thompson.

On June 4, 1996, Thompson was put on trial for the murder of Aaron Iturra. One associate confessed that the night Aaron was shot, she called his house to make sure he was home, then notified Thompson, who gave the go-ahead for the killing.

The jury found Thompson guilty of aggravated murder. At the sentencing, the judge let Janyce Iturra make a statement. She stood before the court, angrily describing the defendant's "web of deceit." Then she turned directly to Thompson. "Aaron was your friend. You might as well have pulled the trigger."

The judge sentenced Thompson to life in prison without parole, plus 10½ years. With her incarceration, the power of the 74 Hoover Crips in Eugene was finally broken.

TERRORIZED
BY A
STALKER

BY MICHAEL WELZENBACH

IT COULD BE YOUR FRIEND, DAUGHTER OR WORKMATE

BEING SUBJECTED TO UNWANTED ATTENTIONS.

BE ALERT: SHE MAY BE IN DANGER.

Tammy Fee awoke suddenly in her otherwise empty house in an isolated subdivision of Terrace, British Columbia. It was 2am, June 22, 1995. Through the bay window overlooking the lawn, she saw that the motion light outside had come on.

The 31-year-old mother of two had fallen asleep on the couch while watching a video. The children were away for a few days with her husband, from whom she was separated, and she had looked forward to some peace and quiet—especially since having broken off relations with a boyfriend, 44-year-old Ric White, three months previously. He had refused to take no for an answer, phoning, following and threatening Tammy.

Just ten days earlier he had tried to run her and two friends off the road. Later, he had slashed her tires and those on her friend's vehicle. Tammy went to the police and requested a peace bond to keep him away, but after 11 days, her request still hadn't been processed.

Emotionally exhausted, Tammy had for weeks been staying with friends and family. This was her first night at home alone.

Her heart pounding, she heard sounds coming from down the hallway, towards the master bedroom. Brushing the long brown hair from her sleepy eyes, Tammy stepped cautiously to look down the darkened corridor. She froze with terror.

A man was sneaking round her bedroom door, a wicked-looking Buck knife clenched in his teeth. Two strips of duct tape were attached to his black T-shirt, and over one wrist were draped three sets of handcuffs. He looked up and spotted her.

"Ric!" Tammy screamed, as he barrelled up the hallway towards her.

Tammy raced for the kitchen door, but the burly man caught her in front of the fireplace. "You're dead!" he bellowed and punched her so hard that she spun and dropped facedown on the carpet.

Tammy fought for her life and screamed in terror. But there was no one to hear. And, unbeknown to her, White had cut the phone lines.

The relationship had begun idyllically. Ric White was a real estate "salesman of the month" and founder of the local Promise Keepers movement; he professed to be a devout Christian. Tammy had met him as her marriage was breaking up, and he had initially offered her support and affection.

White brought her flowers and gifts constantly, once producing a lovely bunch of roses, saying, "Count them." She did. "Oh, Ric," she'd said, "there are only 11." He grinned. "That's because you're my 12th rose."

But within months White's attentions had become cloying. His was the first voice she heard on the phone in the morning, and the last she heard at night.

What Tammy didn't know was that White, an ex-US Marine, was a stalker, using his military training and fanatical insecurity to track her every move. When she finally called the relationship off, he would try to possess her in the most irrevocable way possible.

The assault that night was brutal. White terrorized Tammy for four hours then took her to the bedroom and raped her.

Not until he had fallen asleep was she able to creep out of bed and make her way to the kitchen door. Hysterical, bleeding, she stumbled through the undergrowth and pleaded for help from her nearest neighbour. It was 6.20am. After dialing 9-1-1, Tammy locked herself in her neighbor's bathroom and sobbed until the police arrived.

The cops had to wake White up to arrest him. Beside him were two knives he'd left on the bedside table. Outside, police discovered a trailer, a duffle bag full of gear, powerful binoculars and plastic rain gear.

Tammy has been lucky ... so far. After serving 16 months of a two-year sentence, White was released in May 1997 to begin three years probation. In January 2001 his probation will be over. He now lives in Surrey, British Columbia. He can drive to Terrace in 16 hours.

"I'm terrified," says Tammy. "Even the authorities who examined him testified that he was a perfect candidate to reoffend. I live with a loaded gun and guard dogs."

Terrified Tammy Fee: "I live with a loaded gun."

Stalking is not a rare occurrence in Canada. Tammy's case was one of more than 4,000 reported in 1995. In 1999, in the Toronto area alone, there were 1,181 reported incidents of stalking behavior, loosely defined as persistent unwanted attentions of any sort. In 1993 such harassment was recognized by authorities as a serious threat, primarily to women, and made a criminal offence. Too often, victims do not even recognize that they are in danger.

When police kicked in the locked door to the Sears manager's office in Chatham, Ontario, at 1.45 the morning of June 3, 1996, the scene that confronted them was appalling. Russell Davis, 57, sat slumped in his desk chair, his head disfigured by two self-inflicted bullet wounds. In the chair opposite him, with her head thrown back, was the lifeless form of 56-year-old training administrator Theresa Vince. She had been shot once in the chest and twice in the head.

Theresa, who had planned to retire at the end of June, had complained to a Sears Canada head office official a year previously about Davis's unwanted attentions towards her. But it seems even she was unaware of the extent of her boss's infatuation. Beyond confronting Davis verbally once on the issue, she didn't pursue the matter.

Tragically, Davis's evident fixation on Theresa Vince became the source of jokes. "He'd call her in [to his office] it seemed about every 20 minutes," one employee testified at the inquest, "for basically trivial stuff." It was plain that Theresa was often irritated with her boss, but few suspected it was anything more than their manager relying too heavily on an efficient employee. Most regarded Davis as "a gentleman," if increasingly moody.

It now appears likely that severe depression, infatuation and lack of any intervention led to the death of Theresa Vince.

Even when charges of criminal harassment are laid, the law may be ineffectual. A study of 601 cases handled by police, the Crown and the courts between 1993 and 1996 in major cities showed that more than half were dropped before they reached trial, usually after the accused agreed to a peace bond. Of the 27 per cent who were convicted, most were put on probation. Only a quarter went to jail, usually for four months or less. (The maximum sentence is five years.)

"We should assume that a good proportion of these stalkers will re-offend," warns Vancouver-based forensic psychologist Randy Kropp. Once they leave prison, monitoring of stalkers like Ric White is patently ineffective. The same applies to offenders out on bail, probation or peace bonds.

The consequences can be deadly. Evidence suggests that each week two to three Canadian women are killed by current or past lovers.

To identify potentially dangerous stalking behaviour, police departments across Canada have begun to establish their own threat-assessment units, with specially trained officers and consulting forensic psychiatrists. Explains Sergeant Ed Chafe of the Ontario Provincial Police Threat Assessment Unit: "We educate police officers to understand the risks. We also devise strategies to ensure the victim is safe."

But the harm associated with stalking needn't be physical to ruin lives. A hallmark of the behaviour is that it can go on for years. When a 31-year-old office clerk from Toronto left her common-law husband after three years of increasingly obsessive behaviour, he phoned her up to 30 times a day.

"He started off saying 'You're the only person in my life.' But then it turned into 'I'll kill myself' and 'If I ever see you again, I'll kill you!'"

For eight years the threats continued, tapering off only when he met and married another woman.

Victims agree there are telltale signs women should look out for. "Where the line is crossed is the invasion of your privacy," Tammy Fee explains.

Randy Kropp concurs: "The key thing is when he gets a little too curious about your day-to-day activities."

For the concerned third-party observer, these are some things to watch for: Is your friend, child, partner or workmate being subjected to constant unwanted attentions such as phone calls, letters or gifts? Does she seem to run into a particular person everywhere she goes?

These cues should arouse suspicion, even without threatening or violent behaviour. As Kropp puts it: "You have to trust your gut instinct. Does this [behaviour] look a little weird to you?"

If you suspect that someone close to you might be the victim of a stalker, this is what you should do:

1. Express your concerns to the victim—tactfully. Halifax Regional Police Sergeant Stan McClellan warns, "It's a delicate situation, especially where there's been a prior relationship." Be supportive, and make sure the victim knows where to turn for help.

2. Do not confront the stalker. Experts agree that confrontation may place you at risk and, more important, increase the risk of violence to the victim.

If you are still concerned, contact the police. Notes the OPP's Sergeant Chafe: "The key for us is unwanted behaviour. We can recommend a police investigation even if the complaint is made by concerned parents. And we can counsel the victim."

More important is vigilance. Warns Lieutenant John Lane, formerly of the Los Angeles Police Department and widely credited as the guru of stalking identification: "To be inattentive to inappropriate behaviour is a prescription for harm."

I THINK I CAUGHT A
KILLER

BY RALPH KINNEY BENNETT

READER JENNY SCHUENEMAN LED POLICE TO THE
DRAMATIC CAPTURE OF ONE OF THE "WORLD'S
MOST WANTED" FUGITIVES.

When police found the body of 31-year-old Aileen O'Brien-Beaucage slumped on the front floor of a car in a Burlington, Ontario shopping mall, they were struck by the bloody ferocity of her murder. The divorced mother of two had been slashed on the face and neck, and there were at least 20 stab wounds through her back. Police eventually charged Aileen's ex-husband, Grant Warren Beaucage, with the murder.

But on January 22, 1997, shortly before his trial, the 42-year-old Canadian dropped from sight. More than two years passed and the trail ran cold … until September 1999 when *Reader's Digest* ran his photo and description in editions around the world. Here's the story behind the dramatic capture of one of the "World's Most Wanted" fugitives.

It was Jenny Schueneman's day off from her waitressing job at the Stardust Resort and Casino in Las Vegas, and she wasn't enthused about spending most of it at the Midas Muffler shop on Nellis Avenue. But she picked up the October issue of *Reader's Digest* and was soon oblivious to the noise of the garage. Glancing at the article "World's Most Wanted," she scanned the thumbnail sketches of criminals being sought all over the globe. On page 69, Jenny froze.

I know that man! she thought to herself. *He doesn't have that mustache anymore, but I'd know those eyes anywhere.*

The description of Grant Warren Beaucage as "a slick, gregarious talker" who "spent most of his time gambling" matched a regular in the horse race and sports betting room of the Stardust.

Born in Durban, South Africa, and transplanted to Las Vegas, Schueneman, 36, had seen so many faces in the flood of humanity passing through the Stardust during the six years she had worked there. Could she be wrong? she wondered. *No. I know it's him.*

That night Schueneman had intended to study for her American citizenship test, but felt too tired. By the time her husband got home, she was already in bed. "Honey, how was your day?" he asked. "I had to get the brakes fixed on my car for 355 dollars," she mumbled, half-asleep. "And I think I caught a killer."

"What?"

"I'll tell you tomorrow," she said pushing her head deeper into her pillow.

The next morning, Schueneman tore Beaucage's picture from the magazine and brought it to work. Hailing one of the Stardust's uniformed security guards, she showed him the photo and said, "This guy comes in here almost every day." Guard Dave Thompson was skeptical. "Well, if he shows up, you call me."

Around 11.30am a thickset man walked in wearing a white T-shirt and dark shorts. "Hi, Jen!" he called out cheerily. Most of the regulars knew her by name although she didn't know theirs. She waved back from behind the snack bar counter. Her heart was pumping. The man bantered with a couple of other regulars before he settled into a seat and began browsing a newspaper.

Schueneman waited almost a half hour, then punched in the number for casino security. Within minutes Thompson and guard sergeant Don Carlton arrived and she pointed to the third row. "That's him," she said.

Sizing up the man in the T-shirt, their initial skepticism began to disappear. They telephoned William Cage, a former California policeman who is chief investigator for Stardust security.

Caught on camera: the authorities close in on fugitive Grant Warren Beaucage.

Someone read a story about an ax murderer and they're having nightmares, Cage thought. But his practice was to follow up on everything. Surveillance cameras zoomed in for close-ups and clicked off hard copy images for Cage to compare with the Digest picture. He called the number of the Halton Regional Police Major Crime Bureau in Ontario listed in the article.

Two thousand three hundred miles away at the regional headquarters, detective sergeant Al Frost answered. He had inherited the Beaucage murder case and, after so many dead-end leads, it felt like an open wound that wouldn't heal.

"We might have your guy down here" Cage said. Stunned, Frost alerted him to the regional police website on the Internet, where there was a larger photo of Beaucage and a thumbprint. Printing out the website page, Cage compared it with the casino camera shots. He concentrated on the distance between the eyes and the bridge of the nose, the characteristic most used by police to make an identification. It was a match. A mole on Beaucage's chin and a small scar on his forehead also seemed to match. It was time for a closer look.

Sergeant Carlton had assembled an unobtrusive fence of armed guards around the area. Now Cage, who was dressed as usual in a sport shirt and slacks, sat down next to the suspect at a 25-cent slot machine. When the man got up and started to walk away Cage followed, tapped him on the shoulder and showed his badge. "You look like someone who's wanted. Can

No doubt about it: Jenny recognized the suspected killer featured in our article—he was one of her regular customers.

I see some ID?" The suspect said his name was Philip Hansen but didn't have any identification. He started, however, to reach in his pocket. "Don't do that," Cage said quietly. Then he clapped handcuffs onto the man's wrists. The digital clock an the casino surveillance television monitors read 1.59pm, September 15, 1999, as the camera captured a look of stunned resignation in the eyes of the man called Philip Hansen.

In a small interrogation room nearby, the suspect maintained he was a US citizen born in Duluth, Minnesota. When pressed for identification, he quickly rattled off a Social Security number. But he gave it in a sequence of three threes—the Canadian numbering system rather than the three-two-four sequence of American numbers.

Cage checked out the number. It belonged to a 75-year-old woman in St Louis. When he told "Hansen" this, the man hung his head and grimly joked, "Maybe I shoulda' been in drag." Cage telephoned the Las Vegas Criminal Apprehension Team (CAT) a fugitive task force made up of federal and local law enforcement.

Las Vegas Metro detective George Headley and FBI Special Agent James Patrick arrived 25 minutes later. Patrick had noticed a small scar in Grant Beaucage's right thumbprint. He asked the man in the T-shirt to hold up his thumb. There was the same diagonal scar. "Sir, we are placing you under arrest," Patrick said. They placed the man in the front seat of an unmarked Toyota Camry outside the casino. Headley was at the wheel as they drove toward the CAT office at FBI headquarters. Agent Patrick sat directly behind the prisoner.

Patrick told the man, "I'm a federal agent and if you lie to a federal agent you get five years in federal prison." Trying to break the tension, Headley added, "If you lie to a Metro officer it's a misdemeanor and you get a traffic ticket." All three men chuckled and then Grant Warren Beaucage sighed. "OK," he said. "I'm the man you're looking for."

Grant Warren Beaucage is scheduled to stand trial for the murder of Aileen O'Brien-Beaucage in Ontario, Canada. As his extradition procedure was being completed in Las Vegas, Jenny Schueneman passed her American citizenship test. The next day she was back at work at the Stardust.

COPYRIGHT AND ACKNOWLEDGMENTS

All the stories in the READER'S DIGEST CRIME CASEBOOK have been published in global editions of Reader's Digest Magazine. Those that have appeared first in the British edition retain British spelling. Those that have appeared in other editions first retain US spelling. We would like to thank the following contributors and publishers for permission to reprint material:

The Case of the Rolex Murder by Bill Schiller, condensed from *A HAND IN THE WATER: THE MANY LIES OF ALBERT WALKER* copyright ©1998 by Bill Schiller. Published by HarperCollins Publishers Ltd., Suite 2900, 55 Avenue Rd., Hazelton Lanes, Toronto, ON M5R 3L2, Canada.

Dirty Diamonds by David Kaplan and Christian Caryl. U.S. News & World Report (August 3, 1998), ©1998 by U.S. News & World Report, Inc., 2400 N St., N.W., Washington, DC. 20037, USA.

A Cop's Life by Brian McDonald, condensed from *MY FATHER'S GUN* copyright ©1999 by Brian McDonald. Used by permission of Dutton, a division of Penguin Putnam Inc., 375 Hudson St., New York, N.Y. 10014, USA.

Spy on the Run by David Wise. ©1998 by David Wise. GQ Magazine (July 1998), 4 Times Sq., New York, N.Y. 10036, USA.

Cover and pages 1, 2 and 7: large image of gun: Sussex Constabulary; cover strip (left to right): house: Don Lamont; man in scrap yard: PA News; skull: Natural History Museum; inspection badge: Metropolitan Police Service; boat: photograph: Steve Proahl, © EntrepôtLink Pte Ltd; Kimono Logo © EntrepôtLink Pte Ltd; newspaper: *New York Post*; gun: Image Bank/Co Rentmeester Inc.; police and boat: APEX; G. Brusca: Popperfoto; police sweep: Julian Zakaras; policeman: Don Lamont; cocaine: Metropolitan Police Service; CCTV image: Stardust Casino. Pages 4–5: (top) Sussex Constabulary; (middle) APEX; (bottom) Frank McDonald; page 6: (left) Frank McDonald; (centre) Humberside Police.

AP/CanaPress: 21, 26; AP/Wide World Photos/Luiz C. Ribeiro: 237; APEX: 10–12, 15, 18, 24; Arruza, Tony: 193 both, 198; *Baltimore Sun/Sun Source*: 112; Bradshaw, Ian: 61, 362, 368; Cava, Greg: 383; *Caswell Messenger*: 246; Ciccone, Stan: 215; Clark, Cathy: 359; Cornish, Graham: 171 left, 192; Davis, Richard: 251; Decout, Benoit: 272; *Democrat Reporter*: 320–1, 323; DW Stock Picture Library/Mario Fenech: 257; *Edmonton Journal Library*: 30, 32; © Entrepôtlink Pte Ltd: 126; 123, 129 (Passed Inspection Logo), 133 (Kimono Logo), 138 (Halcyon Ocean Kingfisher Logo); © Entrepôtlink Pte Ltd/Steve Proahl: 133 (photograph); © Entrepôtlink Pte Ltd/Mike Taylor: 142; Eugene Dept. of Public Safety, Oregon: 369, 374; Fairfax Photos: 208 *The Australian Financial*/Jessica Hromas); 221 (*The Sydney Morning Herald*/Nick Moir; 225 (*The Sydney Morning Herald*/Andrew Meares); 229 (*The Sun Herald*/Ken James); Freeman, Sydney: 231; Frysinger, Galen R.: 317; GETTYONE STONE: 366; Guiler, Kevin: 232–3; Hamilton, James: 286, 288, 304; Hampshire Constabulary: 41; Hollyman, Clare: 147, 171 top right, 182; Horner, Colin: 230; Humberside Police: 46; Imagination: 113, 115, 119; Immendorf/Jo Fielder: 73; Jackson family: 238, 240–1, 256; KATZ Pictures: 308, 313 all; Laffal, Ken: 320–1, 324, 328, 332, 335, 338; Lamont, Don: 369, 372; Littlehayes, Breton: 107; *Lincolnshire Echo*: 82 all, 84, 90 both, 96, 102; Mastorianni, Roger: 356, 361; Matrix Photos/Jeremy Nicholl: 71; McDonald, Frank: 287, 292, 296, 298; Metropolitan Police Service: 130, 134; Natural History Museum: 278, 280–4; Network Aspen/Jeffrey Aaronson: 122–3; Network Photographers/SABA/Nikolai Ignatiev: 68; *New York Post*: 235; Norfolk, Simon: 36–8, 264; NYPD: 236; PA News: 201, 274–7 both; PA Photos Ltd: 266–9, 271 both; Petersen, Chip and Rosa Maria de la Cueva: 314; Photo News Service: 64, 67, (Old Bailey) 81 all; Pierre, Richard: 375; Popperfoto/Reuters: 54, 57, 60; Rex Features: 153, 156–7, 167 all, 168; Parry, Ross: 44, 48, 53; Runion, Britt: 195; Solness, Peter: 206–7; Stardust Casino: 380 both, 382 both; Stock Market/William Whitehourst: 72; Stock Market/Nigel Francis: 310; Sussex Constabulary: 75–6, 79; *Torbay News*: 28; *Vancouver Sun and Province*: 377; Wetterling family: 349, 351, 354-5; *West Australian Newspaper*: 260–1, 263; *Wigan Evening Post*: 340 both, 342–4, 347–8; Zakaras, Julian: 211.

Originations by Studio One Origination Ltd, London. Printing paper and binding: Milanostampa SpA, Italy.